Thomas Adès Studies

Thomas Adès is a dominant force in contemporary music, whose work attracts significant attention and acclaim, and has been performed by many renowned ensembles. This volume – the first to present a range of scholarly essays on every aspect of Adès's music – offers authoritative accounts of Adès's major compositions from a variety of analytical, critical, cultural and historical perspectives. The opening chapters focus on Adès's earlier music, offering close readings of key works. Further essays focus on his engagement with forms and instrumental genres. The final chapters turn to Adès's texted music and highlight how themes introduced in earlier chapters cut across Adès's entire output. Richly illustrated with musical examples and supported by further online material, this book provides a multi-faceted portrait of Adès's work that opens up new ways of thinking about, and engaging with, his music.

EDWARD VENN is Professor of Music at the University of Leeds. He is author of *Thomas Adès: Asyla* (2017) and *The Music of Hugh Wood* (2008) and has published many book chapters and journal articles on the analysis and interpretation of twentieth-century and contemporary music. He is editor of the journal *Music Analysis*.

PHILIP STOECKER is Professor of Music at Hofstra University. His research focuses on post-tonal theory and analysis and the music of Thomas Adès, George Perle and the Second Viennese School. He has published numerous journal articles on the music of the twentieth century.

Thomas Adès Studies

Edited by EDWARD VENN

University of Leeds

and

PHILIP STOECKER

Hofstra University

CAMBRIDGE
UNIVERSITY PRESS

CAMBRIDGE
UNIVERSITY PRESS

Shaftesbury Road, Cambridge CB2 8EA, United Kingdom

One Liberty Plaza, 20th Floor, New York, NY 10006, USA

477 Williamstown Road, Port Melbourne, VIC 3207, Australia

314–321, 3rd Floor, Plot 3, Splendor Forum, Jasola District Centre, New Delhi – 110025, India

103 Penang Road, #05–06/07, Visioncrest Commercial, Singapore 238467

Cambridge University Press is part of Cambridge University Press & Assessment, a department of the University of Cambridge.

We share the University's mission to contribute to society through the pursuit of education, learning and research at the highest international levels of excellence.

www.cambridge.org
Information on this title: www.cambridge.org/9781108708135

DOI: 10.1017/9781108761451

First published 2022
First paperback edition 2024

A catalogue record for this publication is available from the British Library

Library of Congress Cataloging-in-Publication data
Names: Venn, Edward, 1974– editor. | Stoecker, Philip, 1972– editor.
Title: Thomas Adès studies / edited by Edward Venn, Philip Stoecker.
Description: [1.] | Cambridge, United Kingdom ; New York, NY : Cambridge University Press, 2021. | Series: Cambridge composer studies | Includes bibliographical references and index.
Identifiers: LCCN 2021025064 (print) | LCCN 2021025065 (ebook) | ISBN 9781108486651 (hardback) | ISBN 9781108708135 (paperback) | ISBN 9781108761451 (epub)
Subjects: LCSH: Adès, Thomas–Criticism and interpretation. | BISAC: MUSIC/ History & Criticism
Classification: LCC ML410.A2337 T56 2021 (print) | LCC ML410.A2337 (ebook) | DDC 780.92–dc23
LC record available at https://lccn.loc.gov/2021025064
LC ebook record available at https://lccn.loc.gov/2021025065

ISBN   978-1-108-48665-1   Hardback
ISBN   978-1-108-70813-5   Paperback

To Betty

To the Arnold Schönberg Center

Contents

Figures

Tables

Music Examples

Online Materials

These materials can be found at www.cambridge.org/9781108486651.

Contributors

Editors

EDWARD VENN
University of Leeds, UK

PHILIP STOECKER
Hofstra University, USA

Other Contributors

AMY BAUER
University of California, Irvine, USA

YAYOI UNO EVERETT
University of Illinois at Chicago, USA

JANE FORNER
University of Aberdeen, UK

EMMA GALLON
Independent, UK

SCOTT LEE
University of Florida, USA

BRIAN MOSELEY
SUNY Buffalo, USA

RICHARD POWELL
University of York, UK

JOHN ROEDER
University of British Columbia, Canada

PHILIP RUPPRECHT
Duke University, USA

NICHOLAS DAVID STEVENS
Naxos of America, Inc., USA

HENRY WEEKES
Independent, UK

Preface

Even a partial roll-call of the awards and recognition for the British composer Thomas Adès (b. 1971) demonstrates the global appeal of his music. His rise to prominence was swift: his 1997 orchestral work *Asyla* was awarded the Royal Philharmonic Society large-scale composition award (London, 1997), his Op. 12 string quartet *Arcadiana* (1994) received the Elise L. Stoeger Prize (New York, 1998), and he was awarded in 1999 the Ernst von Siemens Prize for young composers (Munich). In 1998 he was composer-in-residence at the Minnesota Orchestra's Sommerfest, and the following year his music was celebrated at the Musica Nova festival in Helsinki. The year 1999 also witnessed the premiere of his first international commission, *America: A Prophecy*, by the New York Philharmonic, and in November that year it was announced that he was to receive the 2000 Grawemeyer Award, the largest prize available to a classical composer; Adès remains the youngest composer to have received this prestigious award.

Plaudits continued into his fourth and fifth decades. Adès received the Hindemith Prize in 2001 and was celebrated at the 2004 Salzburg Easter Festival. His second opera, *The Tempest* (2003–4), won for Adès his second Royal Philharmonic Society prize (2005); *Tevot* (2007) earned him his third. There were three international retrospectives of his music in 2007: the Présences Festival in Paris, the Ultima Festival in Oslo and Traced Overheard in London, and in 2007–8 Adès held the Richard and Barbara Debs Composer's Chair at Carnegie Hall. In 2010 he was appointed foreign member of the Royal Swedish Academy of Music, having been a featured composer the previous year in the Stockholm Concert Hall's annual Composer Festival. Adès's third opera, *The Exterminating Angel* (2015–16), was co-commissioned by the Salzburg Festival, the Royal Opera House, the New York Metropolitan Opera and the Royal Danish Opera; 2015 saw him receive the Léonie Sonning Music Prize, Denmark's most prestigious musical honour. In 2018 he was appointed CBE in the Queen's Birthday honours.

Given the prominence and unarguable success of Adès's music, it is not surprising that he has been subject to far greater musicological attention than many of his peers. A positive review in the *New York Times* by Richard Taruskin of Adès's music became an early reference point as well as a marker of Adès's growing global standing;[1] writings by Arnold Whittall and Christopher Fox followed shortly afterwards.[2] In the last fifteen years, there has been a growing body of articles, book chapters and postgraduate theses dedicated to or featuring Adès's music. The first book on Adès's music, again testifying to his international stature, appeared in French in 2007;[3] a collection of interviews with the writer and music journalist Tom Service followed in 2012;[4] a monograph on Adès's *Asyla* was published in 2017;[5] and a further monograph followed in 2021.[6]

Why, then, another volume of writings on Adès's music? First, it is timely. The commission, writing and publication of this collection encompassed a period that began shortly before the twentieth anniversary of the appearance of Taruskin's review and concluded with Adès's fiftieth birthday in 2021. These two anniversaries offered the contributors – who combined represent a wide cross-section of Adès scholars in the United Kingdom and North America (locations that to date have accounted for the vast majority of publications on Adès's music) – the opportunity not only to take stock of the evolving body of work dedicated to Adès over the last two decades, but also to consider future directions that the growing field of Adès studies might take. In common with other entries in the Cambridge University Press Composer Studies series, while one might tease out from the various chapters certain biographical and cultural details on the one hand, and Adès's (critical) relationship with his peers (both national and international) on the other, the emphasis remains primarily on his musical output. The volume is correspondingly organised in a loosely chronological order, beginning with Adès's early music and working through to *The*

[1] Richard Taruskin, 'A Surrealist Composer Comes to the Rescue of Modernism', *New York Times*, 5 December 1999. Reprinted with a postscript in *The Danger of Music and Other Anti-utopian Essays* (Berkeley and Los Angeles: University of California Press, 2009), pp. 144–52 (p. 145).

[2] Arnold Whittall, 'James Dillon, Thomas Adès, and the Pleasures of Allusion', in *Aspects of British Music of the 1990s*, ed. by Peter O' Hagan (Aldershot: Ashgate, 2003), pp. 3–27; Christopher Fox, 'Tempestuous Times: The Recent Music of Thomas Adès', *Musical Times*, 145/1888 (2004), 41–56.

[3] Hélène Cao, *Thomas Adès le voyageur: devenir compositeur, être musicien* (Paris: MF Éditions, 2007).

[4] Thomas Adès and Tom Service, *Thomas Adès: Full of Noises – Conversations with Tom Service*, paperback ed. (London: Faber and Faber, 2018).

[5] Edward Venn, *Thomas Adès*: Asyla (Abingdon: Routledge, 2017).

[6] Drew Massey, *Thomas Adès in Five Essays* (New York: Oxford University Press, 2021).

Exterminating Angel. Nearly all of Adès's major works are discussed at some point in what follows, and some (particularly the operas) are given close readings from multiple perspectives.[7] All contributors expand their arguments with reference to a range of examples drawn from a variety of works by Adès, thus critiquing and rethinking patterns of development and innovation in Adès's career.

Second, an edited volume offers space for multiple voices, and a methodological and theoretical plurality, that distinguish it from single-authored monographs. Yet the diversity of approach is counterbalanced by a genuine sense of shared scholarly purpose, fostered through opportunities to disseminate and critique one another's work-in-progress in conference sessions (a 2017 event dedicated to Adès's operas, and a 2019 Special Session at the Annual Meeting of the Society for Music Theory) and, most significantly, in a series of online virtual workshops during the summer of 2020. Such encounters emphasised the continued value the contributors placed on prior writing on Adès's music – much of which might be understood, methodologically, as music-analytical and/or hermeneutic in its ambition[8] – against which newer perspectives and approaches are positioned not in conflict, but as means of enrichening and broadening of the field. The generosity and communality that informed the discussions, formal and informal, in the writing of this volume led not only to a deepening of the arguments that are contained within it, but also to the illumination of themes and concepts that cut across, in sometimes surprising and unexpected ways, work that ostensibly faces in different directions.

Chapters 1–4 focus on Adès's earlier music (up to *The Tempest*), offering not only close readings of key works but also new or revised ways of thinking about Adès's music in general. Philip Rupprecht's opening chapter on gesture (Chapter 1) draws together many of the characteristic features of Adès's music (more often treated discretely in earlier writings

---

[7] We have taken the decision not to publish a comprehensive catalogue of Adès's published works. This information, and much more besides, is provided on the composer's own website, www.thomasades.com, and the similar information, along with reviews, commissioning information, programming notes and copies of scores, can be found via the relevant section of Faber Music's website, www.fabermusic.com/composers/thomas-ades. As the information on these pages is updated regularly, we would seek to direct interested readers to them.

[8] An early juxtaposition of these contrasting (though not mutually exclusive) approaches can be found in a 2006 issue of the journal *Music Analysis*, with articles by John Roeder ('Co-operating Continuities in the Music of Thomas Adès', *Music Analysis*, 25/i–ii (2006), 121–54) and Edward Venn ('Asylum Gained? Aspects of Meaning in Thomas Adès's *Asyla*', *Music Analysis*, 25/i–ii (2006), 89–120).

on the composer) to explore a dramatically charged patterning of musical shapes and sounding identities forged on the micro- and macro-levels in the *Chamber Symphony* (1990), *Living Toys* (1993) and *America: A Prophecy* (1999). While analytically modelled gesture provides one way of rethinking structure in Adès's music, Edward Venn and Henry Weekes demonstrate in Chapter 2 how pianists, including the composer himself, offer alternative and complementary interpretations of Adès's musical designs, navigating tensions between continuity and discontinuity, and between foreground and background, in their realisations of *Darknesse Visible* (1992) and the Mazurkas (2009). Chapters 3 and 4 turn to Adès's first two operas, hermeneutic interpretation, the socio-political implications of Adès's music and matters of cultural memory. In Chapter 3, Nicholas David Stevens employs *Powder Her Face* (1995) as a lens to (re-)examine Adès's aesthetic sensibilities, teasing out the interpretative ramifications of metaphors of surface and depth, not least his use of camp as a device for social commentary. This is followed in Chapter 4 by Jane Forner's placement of *The Tempest* in the context of contemporary debates around colonial legacies, a move that allows her to model critically the ways in which Adès's reworkings (with his librettist, Meredith Oakes) of Shakespeare's play open up new interpretative vistas for the opera.

Chapters 5–8 offer close analytically informed readings of Adès's engagement with forms and instrumental genres to explore Adès's compositional rhetoric and play with (musical) history. Philip Stoecker (Chapter 5) turns to the chaconne and demonstrates how existing approaches to pitch in Adès's employment of the form in *Arcadiana* (1994), *Concerto Conciso* (1997–8) and the Violin Concerto (2005) might be enriched through an appreciation of his handling of rhythm and texture to generate larger-scale musical and dramatic structures. In Chapter 6 Richard Powell turns to *Tevot* and its dialogue with symphonic thought. Drawing on Sibelius's Seventh Symphony as a lens through which to understand better *Tevot*'s play with concepts of musical resolution, Powell points to the new aesthetic possibilities opened up by Adès's renewal of the symphonic genre. Amy Bauer's discussion in Chapter 7 of *In Seven Days* (2008) situates her detailed examination of the work's theme-and-variations structure in the context of an allegorical journey that parallels the story of creation found in Genesis, thereby demonstrating the inseparability of Adès's musical and extramusical thought. Adès's sometimes incongruous and disjunct reworkings of the potentialities bound up in generic and tonal norms form the focus of Brian Moseley's reading of Adès's Mazurkas and *Thrift (a Cliff-Flower): Mazurka-Cortège* (2011), which revisits and recontextualises the relationship between Adès's musical designs and surrealist practice.

Chapters 9–12 return to Adès's texted music, in particular the operas, and highlight how themes introduced in earlier chapters cut across Adès's entire output. Scott Lee's examination (Chapter 9) of Adès's response in *Totentanz* (2013) to a fifteenth-century frieze representing the Dance of Death demonstrates how the composer's musical narration of the dance offers, in the form of allegory, a pointed social critique. In her discussion of voice, vocality and narrative in Adès's three operas (Chapter 10), Emma Gallon gives prominence to the materiality of Adès's music and the importance of recognising its physical, embodied qualities in interpretative practice. Approaching *The Tempest* and *The Exterminating Angel* from a complementary perspective, John Roeder (Chapter 11) offers a detailed and compelling account not only of the intervallic logic that underpins Adès's compositional language, but also of the ways in which such structures respond to, and shape, the onstage drama. Finally, in her reading of *The Exterminating Angel*, Yayoi Uno Everett (Chapter 12) proposes that the opera's play of topical references, intervallic cycles and multiple temporalities presents the audience with a sonic allegory of an existential void.

EDWARD VENN
PHILIP STOECKER

Acknowledgements

We would like to express our thanks to Kate Brett and the editorial and production team at Cambridge University Press – especially Hal Churcham and Eilidh Burrett, whose generous help and assistance has been invaluable. The germinal idea for *Thomas Adès Studies* can be traced to a conference on Adès's operas organised by Edward Venn, Catherine Davies and Paul Archbold as part of the Arts and Humanities Research Council-funded Open World Research Initiative research project 'Cross-Language Dynamics: Reshaping Community', held in collaboration with the Institute for Modern Languages Research at the School of Advanced Study, University of London, and supported by grants from the *Music & Letters* Trust and the Society for Music Analysis. In addition to thanking Catherine, Paul and the funding bodies for their contributions to the above, we would also like to acknowledge with gratitude the administrative assistance from Jo Bradley and Cathy Collins, David Lefeber for filming the proceedings, and the conference participation of Thomas Adès, Philip Hensher, Meredith Oakes, Peter Evans and Mark Millington.

The volume eventually transformed from its original idea into something far more expansive. We are extremely grateful for the receipt of funding from the Arts and Humanities Research Council and a subvention from the Society of Music Theory to cover the costs of copyright permissions and production costs of music examples, and to Sally Cavender, Sam Wigglesworth and Bruce MacRae at Faber Music for their support. We also thank Drew Massey for the generous sharing of his research with the contributors of the volume.

Living Toys **Op. 9**
Music by Thomas Adès
© 1996 by Faber Music Ltd
Reproduced by permission of the publishers
All rights reserved

Powder Her Face **Op. 14**
Music by Thomas Adès
© 1996 by Faber Music Ltd
Libretto by Philip Hensher
© 1995 by Philip Hensher
Reproduced by permission of Faber Music Ltd
All rights reserved

Concerto Conciso
Music by Thomas Adès
© 1997 by Faber Music Ltd
Reproduced by permission of the publishers
All rights reserved

Darknesse Visible **(after John Dowland)**
Music by Thomas Adès
© 1998 by Faber Music Ltd
Reproduced by permission of the publishers
All rights reserved

America: A Prophecy **Op. 19**
Music by Thomas Adès
© 2002 by Faber Music Ltd
Original texts from the books of *Chilam Balam* (Mayan) and *La guerra* (Matteo Flexa)
English text from *The Destruction of the Jaguar* © 1987 by Christopher Sawyer-Lauçanno (by permission of City Lights Books)
Reproduced by permission of Faber Music Ltd
All rights reserved

The Tempest
Music by Thomas Adès
© 2004 by Faber Music Ltd
Libretto by Meredith Oakes (after William Shakespeare)
© 2004 by Meredith Oakes

Piano Quintet Op. 20
Music by Thomas Adès
© 2007 by Faber Music Ltd

In Seven Days
Music by Thomas Adès
© 2008 by Faber Music Ltd

Mazurkas **Op. 27**
Music by Thomas Adès
© 2010 by Faber Music Ltd

Violin Concerto: *Concentric Paths* **Op. 23**
Music by Thomas Adès
© 2010 by Faber Music Ltd

Thrift
Music by Thomas Adès
© 2011 by Faber Music Ltd (subsequently withdrawn from publication)

Totentanz
Music by Thomas Adès
German text adapted by Thomas Adès
English translated by Timothy Adès
© 2013 by Faber Music Ltd

Tevot **Op. 24**
Music by Thomas Adès
© 2014 by Faber Music Ltd
Reproduced by permission of the publishers
All rights reserved

The Exterminating Angel
Music by Thomas Adès
© 2016 by Faber Music Ltd
Libretto by Tom Cairns in collaboration with Thomas Adès
© 2016 by Tom Cairns
Based on the original screenplay 'The Exterminating Angel' © 1969 by Luis
    Buñuel and Luis Alcoriza
Reproduced by permission of Faber Music Ltd

Notes on the Text

In addition to the numerous examples, figures and tables reproduced in this volume, supplementary material can be found at www.cambridge.org/9781108486651. Reference to this material is prefixed by 'Online' in the text (e.g. 'Online Table 2.1').

All references to bar numbers correspond to the versions found on the Faber website at the time of writing. In the case of scores that use rehearsal numbers, the rehearsal number is represented in a square box. Where rehearsal numbers are followed by a superscript number, the latter indicates the number of bars before (for negative numbers) or after (for positive numbers) the rehearsal number. Thus $\boxed{90}^{-8}$–$\boxed{90}^{+1}$ refers to the passage beginning eight bars before rehearsal number 90 and concluding one bar after.

All musical examples are reproduced in C. Where specific registers are indicated in the text, C_4 is used to represent middle C, C_3 the octave below, C_5 the octave above and so on.

The notations and symbols used to describe various pitch collections and rhythmic motives are given below. These terms are defined, where necessary, in the main text of relevant chapters.

C-E-G	Chord, simultaneous pitches
C–E–G	Melody, motive, succession of pitches or pitch classes
C_4	Pitches with registral designation
[2468]	Pitch-class collection in normal form
(0135)	Pitch-class collection in prime form
⟨3⟩	A repeating interval, Interval Cycle
⟨4,3,2⟩	Aligned Interval Cycles
{C, D, E, G♯}	An unordered collection of elements, usually pitch classes
«4,2,2»	Durations
<+5,+2,-7,+8,+5>	Ordered list of intervals; intervals are specified with integers that denote the number of chromatic steps they span; plus signs represent ascent and minus signs descent

1 | 'Chronically volatile'

Gesture in Adès's Living Toys *and* America: A Prophecy

PHILIP RUPPRECHT

A single note pierces the air, offered up jointly by bassoon and trombone; others augment the sonority a split second later; then a higher note, and another, nervously crescendoing; brighter winds (an oboe, a clarinet) appear, the melody rising before quickly evaporating, piccolo and piano trailing off overhead. A string-harmonic cloud lingers as an after-image, the memory of a single, composite gesture. Then a gong strikes: a new gesture. For all the detail of the preceding three sentences, the sounding effect of the opening of Thomas Adès's *Living Toys* (1993), as notated in the score (Ex. 1.1), escapes the medium of words. Prose description hardly seems adequate to music's gestural fluency: a tracery of continuously arcing lines, intricate woven textures and delicately fluctuating timbres and weightings. Even so, a notion of gesture as perceptible musical shape – emergent, or recalled – remains intuitive for musicians, whether performing or listening. And while notations for pitch, duration, volume or articulation apparently exceed prose in precision of reference, a verbal language of gestural connotations creeps back in to the score itself. Adès writes instructions ('felt hats', 'pedal'), for example, to control muting and resonance details. Other expression marks are more overtly metaphorical: the percussionist is told to strike the gong 'nobly' (*nobilmente*), as if to convey ceremonial purpose, and there is the movement's title, 'Angels'. Already the musical gestures – whether traced in notation or words – trigger associations, connotations of physical, social or cultural worlds.

No amount of verbal or notational refinement will banish the metaphorical quality of musical gesture. My prose description above is itself metaphor-bound; sounds do not literally 'evaporate', the piccolo is not spatially 'overhead'. But ordinary language is saturated with figurative translations between musical and non-musical domains. If metaphor is the bedrock of verbal evocations of music's passage, the task of defining specific gestures – far from eschewing figurative language in a quest for the 'structural' – will actively engage metaphor as a precise instrument of analytic enquiry. Listeners often acknowledge the element of interpretation in perception – a metaphorical 'hearing as'.[1] The distinctive melodic-registral profile of a given gestural unit, though, might signal many things – some untexted pictorialism, an

1

Ex. 1.1 *Living Toys*, 'Angels', bars 1–5, opening gesture

intertextual allusion or a nod to Baroque and Classical traditions of conventionalised gestures (so-called *topics*). Openings 'ex nihilo', from a weightless, high-treble entrance, are for Adès something of a signature.[2] Does the racing opening ascent of *Living Toys* resemble the kind of arpeggiated 'rocket' theme familiar in late eighteenth-century symphonic openings?[3] Adès's gesture climbs faster than a Classical theme, its flashing woodwind and

---

[1] Among recent theoretic perspectives, see, respectively, Daniel Leech-Wilkinson and Helen M. Prior, eds., *Music and Shape* (New York: Oxford University Press, 2017); and the colloquy by Joseph Dubiel, Marion A. Guck and Bryan Parkhurst, 'Hearing as Hearing-as', *Music Theory and Analysis*, 4/ii (2017), 229–70.

[2] See for example Adès's Violin Concerto (2005) or the upper-treble register emphasis of the early piano works.

[3] On the Mannheim 'rocket' as beginning gesture, see William Caplin, 'Topics and Formal Functions: The Case of the Lament', in *The Oxford Handbook of Topic Theory*, ed. by Danuta Mirka (New York: Oxford University Press, 2014), pp. 415–52 (p. 415).

trumpet colours delineating a single arc. But the gesture is also fluent and subtly modulated, less conventional than sui generis. Rapidly cutting between distinct moments, without obvious pattern, Adès here pursues aesthetic proclivities he himself describes evocatively – a lava-like flow, a search for the 'chronically volatile': 'my music is naturally always transitioning, always slipping'.[4]

Before considering this central notion of volatility more closely, let me briefly outline some axiomatic features of a gestural approach to Adès's early music. We may recall, to begin with, the composer's rejection of a tidy distinction between abstract and programmatic writing – 'to me all music is metaphorical, always' – and his emphatic embrace of music's potential for semiotic correlation: 'Musical and non-musical things are inextricably connected.'[5] The specificity of music's 'non-musical' meanings, *chez* Adès, often evolves according to a range of metaphorical signals – including titles, programme notes and other paratexts. 'Angels', opening *Living Toys*, invites listeners to varied proximate associations – the playthings of the title, a child's imagination of their animated adventures or brightly ethereal realms. Adès's own programme notes, in this vein, speak of the horn's solo in 'Angels' as 'haloed with gongs and little trumpets'.[6] The programmatic view of musical gestures will often centre on a proto-dramatic event sequence, and within it, interpretation will soon discern the activity of defined musical agents.

Definitions of gesture, in the present essay, will interweave structural and semantic traces – not only tonal and metric features, but also a bevy of micro-expressive detail inflecting the passage of even brief musical units. In Robert Hatten's evocative phrase, gesture encompasses all that pertains to the 'energetic shaping of sound through time'.[7] The Adèsian gesture, as already seen, transcends definition solely in rhythmic or pitch domains, demanding attention to the less codifiable realms of timbre and texture. The notion of 'energetic shaping' applies both to brief single events and to much larger continuities including extended 'movements'. The characteristic gesture in Adès's music, moreover, is fleeting and mobile – its

---

[4] Thomas Adès and Tom Service, *Thomas Adès: Full of Noises – Conversations with Tom Service*, paperback ed. (London: Faber and Faber, 2018), pp. 4, 75.

[5] Ibid., p. 5; Joseph Finlay, 'A Jewish Quarterly Interview with Thomas Adès', *Jewish Quarterly*, 60/iii–iv (2013), 126–7 (p. 127).

[6] Thomas Adès, programme notes on *Living Toys*, 1993, www.fabermusic.com/music/living-toys-2373.

[7] Robert S. Hatten, *Interpreting Musical Gestures, Topics, and Tropes: Mozart, Beethoven, Schubert* (Bloomington: Indiana University Press, 2004), p. 95.

interplay of parameters producing what Hatten terms 'perceptually *synthetic* gestalts with *emergent* meaning, not simply "rhythmic shapes"'.[8] As for semantics, Adès's cyclical pitch patterns in particular have attracted analytic attention for the expressive effects of transmuted 'lament' figures, intersecting 'orbits' or continuous 'spiral' transformations.[9] To play classical integration off against modernist 'disorientation', Arnold Whittall observes, is a basic Adèsian strategy of some dramatic force: 'idyllic sublimity tilts towards nightmarish horror'.[10]

With images of unending gestural transformation, we return to the cardinal idea of a volatile music in perpetual flux. An early exemplar, Adès's *Chamber Symphony* Op. 2 (1990), shows the degree to which 'returning' materials lack stable identity. The first movement's forthright Beethovenian horn-call (*maestoso*, C major, bar 46) soon deteriorates chromatically, losing pulse definition behind the topically alien jazz of the solo clarinet. Later reworkings of the opening murmuring theme (alto flute and viola, bars 6–14) – a semitone lower (trombone, bar 131), then a fourth lower (basset-clarinet, bar 282) – exhibit characterological shifts to the point of erasure. While all musical 'repetition' spans a dialectic of identity and difference, Adès's variation procedures invite awareness of textural and timbral signatures (as well as intervallic or rhythmic profiles) as integral to hermeneutic understandings of their sounding evanescence.

This chapter concentrates on 'early' Adès, in particular on two major works from his first professional decade: *Living Toys* and *America: A Prophecy*, for mezzo-soprano and orchestra with (optional) chorus (1999). With gesture as guiding concern, I shall explore two facets of a conceptual spectrum. At one end are the directly mimetic gestures and 'actions' (bullfight, battle, funeral, etc.) defined in the literary programme accompanying *Living Toys*; in *America*, meanwhile, the composer charts a more metaphoric network of gestures grounded in historical circumstances – the sixteenth-century conquest of Mayan peoples in Mexico by arriving Spanish *conquistadores*. With the singer as lonely prophetic witness, Adès creates temporally shaped gestures of apocalypse, in a language whose volatility is rooted in the denial of pulsation and the fracturing of time's flow.

---

[8] Ibid., p. 94 (emphasis original).

[9] On 'lament' as expressive topic, see Edward Venn, *Thomas Adès: Asyla* (Abingdon: Routledge, 2017), pp. 31–4; for 'spiral' motions, see Chapter 5.

[10] Arnold Whittall, 'The Adès Effect', in *British Music after Britten* (Woodbridge: Boydell, 2020), pp. 255–69 (pp. 261, 264).

Living Toys: **Gesture and Programme**

Beyond the arresting opening of 'Angels', *Living Toys* describes a continuous seventeen-minute sequence of discrete, titled movements whose main gestures correspond to – or even enact – the imaginary hero's life mentioned in the score's prefatory epigraph. As Adès's invented text ('from the Spanish') begins, 'When the men asked him what he wanted to be, the child did not name any of their own occupations, as they had all hoped he would, but replied: "I am going to be a hero, and dance with angels and bulls."'[11] The literary scheme is supplemented by a visual dimension in the score-cover reproduction of Goya's etching *The Agility and Daring of Juanito Apiñani in the Bullring of Madrid*. For concert listeners, then, the gestural life of Adès's work corresponds to the elaborate metaphor of a literary-cum-pictorial paratext. Where Goya's matador is frozen in a single instant, musical gesture restores him to life. The interpretive challenge, amid the temporal unscrolling of gestures, will be to sort out the degree to which changes of gestural state – Adès's characteristic 'slipping' – support coherent musical agents – dramatic actors, individual or collective – or the distanced perspective of a narrator.

Before discussing specific gestures, we may ponder the narrative precision of Adès's epigraph and programme notes. These 'dream-adventures' range from excited combat ('into the ring charges an **Aurochs** ... He is whipped and goaded by the brutal, elegant matador-kid') to a ritualistic 'three-gun salute' in the closing scene.[12] Adès's programme is as anthropomorphic as anything in Schumann or Strauss and equally bound by the essentially arbitrary quality of its real-world denotations.[13] The unfolding plot sequence, as in Berlioz's *Symphonie fantastique*, conveys dream-experiences bound by a logic of uncanny doubles or strange repetitions. Gestural transformations, in this realm, may transcend 'realistic' narrative. We may also consider the verbal tokens of Adès's programme as a supplementary or dialogical response to the score's internal musical logic. The formal scheme in *Living Toys* comprises eight titled segments, five of which bear numbers; interspersing them are three interludes whose anagrammatical titles promise a disguised continuity. A prominent melody – which Adès calls the 'hero' theme – is first announced in 'Aurochs' (Ex. 1.2).

[11] Adès, programme notes on *Living Toys*. 'I invented this story ... after I'd written the piece' (Adès and Service, *Full of Noises*, p. 72).
[12] Adès, programme notes on *Living Toys* (bold emphasis original).
[13] For closely hermeneutic readings, see Jacqueline Susan Greenwood, 'Selected Vocal and Chamber Works of Thomas Adès: Stylistic and Contextual issues' (unpublished PhD dissertation, Kingston University, 2013), pp. 277–339.

Ex. 1.2 *Living Toys*, 'Aurochs', bars 223–30, the 'hero' theme announced

It returns to preface the later anagram segments, so enacting an underlying three-stage progression:

I Angels **II** Aurochs ['hero' theme, E] BALETT

III Miliatiamen **IV** H.A.L.'s Death ['hero' theme, F♯] BATTLE

V Playing Funerals ['hero' theme, G♯, E] TABLET

Since the 'hero' theme enters on an E tonic, moving later to F♯ and finally to G♯, its returns trace an emergent tonal progression. Such a pattern offers long-range formal coherence, even as the shifting tonal level, locally, embodies change. With more fragmented flashes of materials within the anagram interludes – and a constantly evolving instrumental palette between and within each segment – *Living Toys* can sound almost kaleidoscopic in its moment-to-moment agility. Before revisiting the distinctive role of the 'hero' theme itself, there is room to consider more closely the pattern of brief, apparently ephemeral gestures contributing to such an impression.

Adès's score signals 'childish' detachment from the adult world by the use of timbral coding: the emphasis on high-range percussion (very small cymbals, piccolo snare drum) or markedly 'high' solo sonorities – piccolo trumpet, sopranino recorder – defines a palette of pronounced brightness, set in relief by deep bass touches (contrabassoon). Such timbral choices bear cultural-semiotic affinities with the magical realm of fairy tales (where large and small are subject to strange inversions). Timbre itself – particularly where 'unusual' instruments are heard – defines or inflects gestural meanings in conjunction with a host of stylistic or topical references. For example, in 'Aurochs', the solo piccolo trumpet hardly signals any specific national origin, but Adès's choice of accompaniment – prominent clicking castanets and handclaps (by pianist and conductor) – clearly indexes the Spanish locale of a bullfight. Apart from the folk-traditional allusions, the Iberian setting is further delineated in Flamenco-tinged harmonies. The trumpet deepens the reference through characteristic *jota* triplets, and by imitation (in staccato repeating notes) of *rasgueado* guitar strumming. With this multiplicity of references, Adès constructs a Spanish topical field by a fusion of signs.

The piccolo trumpet solo in 'Militiamen' – a 'mad bugler', according to Adès's programme – 'talks' with a plunger-muted, *parlato* stream of snarls and growls. The stylistic borrowing here is from jazz, framed as a historical topic (a style relocated to a new context),[14] and more specifically from the 1920s playing of Bubber Miley. With fusion or collision of 'otherwise incompatible style types', as Hatten observes, expressive meaning arises by a *troping* of musical gesture.[15] Adès's jazz trumpet is further marked as a topic by audible paradox – a sounding incompatibility of materials. Directing the player to feel his/her 'own meter' (3/4 against the ensemble's 9/8) and meticulously notating cross-rhythms and 'speech' syllables, Adès maintains palpable performative tension throughout 'Militiamen'. The plunger-muted idiom is a stylistic about-face in relation to the earlier *brillante* role in 'Aurochs' – as if the player, switching between trumpets, has suddenly donned a disguise. Nor is this the only stylistic topic on display in 'Militiamen'. Adès's opening direction – *in modo populare* – gives a verbal hint, but most listeners will immediately catch, at the end (bar 336), the jolting arrival of a famous James Brown phrase (from the 1965 hit song 'I Feel Good'). The acrobatic arpeggio figure is not actually

---

[14] See Danuta Mirka, 'Introduction', in *The Oxford Handbook of Topic Theory*, ed. by Danuta Mirka (New York: Oxford University Press, 2014), pp. 1–57 (p. 2).

[15] Hatten, *Interpreting Musical Gestures*, p. 68.

new: the trumpet calls it out three times, moments earlier (bars 325–9). Only with heavy percussion – bass, field and snare drums – does the ensemble's punching syncopated response suddenly speak intertextually as Brown's funk horn section. Perennially volatile, the stylistic-topical reference vanishes almost instantly. Adès continues the rising F♯^{9} arpeggio string – F♯–A♯–C♯–E–G♯ – with seven further pitches – G–D–A–E♭–F–B– C – an answering descent that completes a twelve-note aggregate (stylistically remote from the quoted funk lick).

Within a programmatic frame, *Living Toys* coaxes semiotic precision from individual gestures by a timbral-textural dialogism founded on the meaningful interplay of solo instruments and larger groupings. Possible concertante situations (as in the *Chamber Symphony*) reflect the basically soloistic scoring. Adès's street-band vernacularisms, along with the prominent percussion and virtuoso trumpet soloist, recall Stravinsky and Walton as precursors.[16] With the rhetorical and dramatic force of virtuoso soloists – the 'Militiamen' trumpet, the horn in 'Angels' and 'BATTLE' – *Living Toys* also continues an 'instrumental-drama' genre whose hallmark is the assignment of instruments to character-like roles.[17] An account of musical gesture, as Hatten has shown, will entail a rigorous delineation of *agency* within music's 'virtual-fictive world'.[18] To understand the agentive function of individual gestures, we revisit Adès's 'hero' theme, attending closely to its first entrance, and later transformations.

Arriving suddenly, the 'hero' theme (Ex. 1.2, above) quells the frenetic bullring combat of 'Aurochs' in a salient 'rhetorical gesture'.[19] In melodic terms, the tune's rising third (E–F♯–G♯) reverses the falling motion of the nursery-rhyme tune ('Three Blind Mice', E–D–C) that dominates the earlier hectoring brass phrases.[20] The bullfight's taut machismo display is countered now by a relaxed loping motion at a slower tempo (bars 224–52), a kind of dream-march by a triumphant hero (as in 'O Albion'

---

[16] As a seventeen-year-old, Adès listened 'obsessively' to *L'histoire du soldat* and *Façade* (Adès and Service, *Full of Noises*, p. 118).

[17] On British genre contributions, see Philip Rupprecht, 'Images in Sound: Movement, Harmony and Colour in the Early Music', in *The Music of Simon Holt*, ed. by David Charlton (Woodbridge, Suffolk: Boydell & Brewer, 2017), pp. 56–79 (pp. 59–61).

[18] Robert S. Hatten, *A Theory of Virtual Agency for Western Art Music* (Bloomington: Indiana University Press, 2018), p. 37.

[19] I use the term in Hatten's strict sense, to denote 'sudden change in energy, force, direction, and character' of some musical discourse. Hatten, *Interpreting Musical Gestures*, p. 165.

[20] On interactions between 'hero' and 'mice' themes within a network, see James Donaldson, 'Living Toys in Adès's *Living Toys*', presentation at the Annual Meeting of the Society for Music Theory, Columbus, OH, 8 November 2019.

from *Arcadiana*, the elegant swoons recall Elgar). The instantaneous shifts of mood, perspective and tonality are further marked, as gesture, in the timbral domain. With two-string unisons on muted violins and viola and lazy sliding portamentos, tuning is meaningfully fuzzy. Previously raucous brass timbres are now reduced to soft doubling lines (*espressivo* and *cantabile*). Behind the hero's song-like march, the gentle accompaniment reveals a new instrumental colour (talking drum).

The 'hero' theme, after defining a public triumph at the end of 'Aurochs', reappears in two later movements – 'H.A.L.'s Death' (at bar 369) and 'Playing Funerals' (bars 512, 520) – in each case in gestures quite distant in character, bearing and dramatic effect from the original theme's presentation. Tonally, I have noted, this 'hero' theme accumulates a long-range coherence as *Living Toys* unfolds, rising by step from E to G♯ before loosely revisiting E (a possible 'home' tonic cruelly swept away in the F minor cadence of 'Playing Funerals', bars 549–53). With an ear to timbre, again, it is volatility of gesture that tells in performance. For the two funereal dream-scenes, Adès finds fresh instrumental colours: the sopranino recorder's bird-like piping (*lugubre*) announces the tune as H.A.L. expires; for the hero himself, finally, the tune is borne with great solemnity in a respectful collective blending of instrumental voices (each new timbre entering softly 'inside' those already sounding). This tune gradually loses definition, as perceptible pitch is lost to hearing: in a cloud of ghostly percussion strokes ('slacken drums', bar 530), prolonged trombone glissandos and string shivering effects (*pizzicato tremolo*), gestural coherence fades, along with any outline of musical figure, into the distance.

Gesture and Myth: *America: A Prophecy*

History as Gesture

Where gestures in *Living Toys* cast solo instrumental agents as proto-dramatic enactors of a literary programme, in *America: A Prophecy* the modalities of music's temporally unfolding shapes spring from the very different textural situation of a lone voice pitted against the collective. The solo mezzo-soprano in *America* issues her prophetic visions of destruction as a challenge to the massed sonority of a full orchestra and chorus. Like William Blake (from whom he took his title), Adès seeks to illuminate within documented historical events an underlying layer of deeper archetypes. This historical 'America' refers to the home of Mayan and Mexica

(Aztec) peoples in the Yucatán peninsula, invaded in 1519 by Spanish *conquistadores*. Adès's vocalist is a seer, her 'Prophecy' delivered in words sacred to the vanquished, from books of their 'jaguar priests' (*Chilam Balam*).[21] 'O my nation / Prepare … They will come from the east', she warns in the first of the two panels of Adès's fifteen-minute diptych form; in the second she foretells inevitable destruction: 'we shall burn, we shall turn to ash'. The music's fierce progression is from a briefly glimpsed antediluvian calm, through states of disturbance, to a climax of mounting excitement, moving on finally to an awful emptiness, the aftermath of destruction. *America*'s Panel I falls into six sections, while the shorter Panel II comprises three.[22] Like a mural, the score treats actual historical events, yet seems to avoid diachronic 'history' in its local arrangement. The piece, instead, works in gestures with more abstract referents: fear of the future, a fateful moment of encounter, apocalypse as calendrical certainty. *America* does not create a musicalised drama so much as give sounding form to the broader cultural representations of myth.[23]

The grand gestures in Adès's scheme cannot be reduced to some schematic 'before–after' sequence. The whole piece is taken up with the 'priestess'-singer's prophetic visions. At the end of Panel I Adès writes only a comma, directing that Panel II follow *attacca*: the absence of transition or real pause marks a filmic gap in representation (a black screen between visual scenes). 'Prepare', she warns (but there is no time to do so). When she returns, just a few seconds later ('Weep'), she sings in a prophet's future-tense vision of that which is to come. The Mayan texts, Adès observes, 'are both prophecies and histories',[24] and it is from this double-temporal perspective that we may listen for the telling musico-gestural signals of *America*. The sumptuous brass fanfares, for example, midway through Panel I (bars 124–93), in context, announce a self-evidently 'Spanish' music, yet the musical battle, as Paul Griffiths suggests, sounds ambiguous in tone, mingling graphic destruction with flamboyant

---

[21] Hélène Cao calls the soloist a 'Mayan priestess' ('la prêtresse maya'). Cao, *Thomas Adès le voyageur: devenir compositeur, être musicien* (Paris: MF Éditions, 2007), p. 97. Adès's literary source for Mayan texts is Christopher Sawyer-Lauçanno, trans., *The Destruction of the Jaguar: Poems from the Books of Chilam Balam* (San Francisco: City Lights Publisher, 1987).

[22] On the temporal proportions, see Christopher Fox, 'Tempestuous Times: The Recent Music of Thomas Adès', *Musical Times*, 145/1888 (2004), 41–56 (pp. 44–5).

[23] Valuable historiographic contexts include Matthew Restall, *Seven Myths of the Spanish Conquest* (New York: Oxford University Press, 2003); and Inga Clendinnen, *Ambivalent Conquests: Maya and Spaniard in Yucatan, 1517–1570* (Cambridge: Cambridge University Press, 1987).

[24] Quoted in Tom Service, 'Altered States', *Guardian*, 29 August 2002, section G2, p. 17.

excitement.[25] Listening for gesture at a mythic level, we may discern the crusading certitude of European Christianity, and also the strangeness of encounter, of 'contact' – for both sides – with the unknown.[26] Stories of Hernán Cortés in March 1519, greeted by the Mexica ruler Moctezuma as a returning lord, the god Quetzalcoatl foretold by astrologers, constitute a widely circulated apotheosis trope which was inscribed by the 1570s in Franciscan conquest narratives.[27] Cortés's establishment of 'New Spain' on the ruins of the cities of indigenous peoples – and Europe's rapacious imperialism – sprang from a collision of mutually strange selves and others, channelled through voices speaking for opposing faiths and cosmologies.

Preparing *America* as a literary scheme, Adès foregrounded a rhetoric of interruption at the level of the chosen texts. The centre of consciousness here is the priestess's voice: her English words, in Panel I, predict the future: 'They *will* burn all the land … it is foretold.' The Spanish arrival interrupts, but does not ultimately displace, the sibyl's visions, which remain in the future tense in Panel II's premonitions ('On earth we *shall* burn'). While she sings in English, the words of the European invaders are 'foreign' and present tense: the chorus's arrival quotes Spanish words from a sixteenth-century source, Matteo Flecha's 'La guerra', rowdily praising 'good soldiers' ('Todos los buenos soldados'). The New Testament Latin words they sing to end Panel II – 'Haec est victoria …' ('This is the victory by which our faith conquers the world', I John 5:4) – are also from Flecha. The contradictory perspectives of Adès's libretto are all too starkly opposed: for Spanish invaders, present-day victory and 'eternal glory'; for Meso-American people, a coming slaughter.

Access to the metaphoric levels in Adès's music will entail recognition of the density of its gestural discourse. One reconciles the forward flux of musical time – a syntagmatic concatenation of events and shapes – with music's paradigmatic axis of accruing change ('variation'). Adès's focus in *America* on a rhetoric of interruptive 'encounter' – the shock of contact – beyond its literary definition registers forceful disruption of recognised patterns. Hearing gesture in *America*, the density of 'hearing as', in Michael Spitzer's terms, assimilates experience to schema while affirming

---

[25] Paul Griffiths, 'Thomas Adès: *America: A Prophecy*', note to recording (EMI 5 57610-2, 2004), p. 5.

[26] See James Lockhart, 'Introduction', in *We People Here: Nahuatl Accounts of the Spanish Conquest of Mexico*, ed. by James Lockhart (Berkeley and Los Angeles: University of California Press, 1993), pp. 1–46 (p. 4).

[27] See *Florentine Codex*, book 12, chapters 3 and 16, trans. in Lockhart, ed., *We People Here*, pp. 60–2, 114–19; and Restall, *Seven Myths*, pp. 112–16.

the 'replete', infinitely rich semantic potential of specific gestures as living 'figures'.[28] Identifying musical gestures, further, as the sounding animation of mythic tropes, we dwell on a Mayan world of prophecy bounded, in Inga Clendinnen's phrase, by patterns of 'recurrence behind occurrence'.[29]

Adès's gestural imagination, I have noted, transcends the directly mimetic – the piece is neither opera nor imaginary cinema – while sounding its own accents of apocalypse. In a semiotic layering, the first-order 'language' of *America* – the history of 'Conquest' narratives – becomes the conceptual referent for a second discursive layering, that of musical gesture.[30] *America* re-envisions a thematics of ending in music eschewing most conventional signs of cadence or easy consolation. Adès's exploration of the dynamically open and inchoate, using his favoured vocabulary of strictly turning melodic and rhythmic cycles, speaks of the eternal 'transition' of apocalypse. If end-times are a double gyre, between past and future, history and prophecy, *America* reverberates with impending crisis.[31] The following analysis will highlight facets of a sounding gestural continuum: beyond the shock of interruption, discussion explores tensions in rhythmic-temporal patterning, between static 'floating' movement and the more periodic, embodied rhythms of dance and lullaby. Registering the violence of conquest, meanwhile, Adès fashions moments of contrapuntal build-up – crowding out individuated line in full-orchestral 'eclipse' gestures of overwhelming weight.

Calendars and Rhythms

America constructs musical images of intrusion – gestures by which some existing state of being is challenged or undercut – at multiple levels. The rhetoric of interruption is evident from the very opening, where each detail carries metaphorical significance. A hypnotic opening flute figure (labelled *M* in Ex. 1.3) is quickly disrupted by a shocking challenge (in piano, clarinets, strings). Within *America*'s historical frame, the revolving flute figure is Mayan, a sign of meso-American identity; the unmistakable tutti

---

[28] Michael Spitzer, *Metaphor and Musical Thought* (Chicago: University of Chicago Press, 2004), pp. 110–11.

[29] Clendinnen, *Ambivalent Conquests*, p. 135.

[30] Interpreting *America* as a semiotically layered discourse, I have in mind the model of Roland Barthes, 'Myth Today', in *Mythologies*, trans. by Annette Lavers (New York: Hill and Wang, 1972), pp. 109–59.

[31] Frank Kermode, *The Sense of an Ending: Studies in the Theory of Fiction* (New York: Oxford University Press, 1967), p. 101.

a)

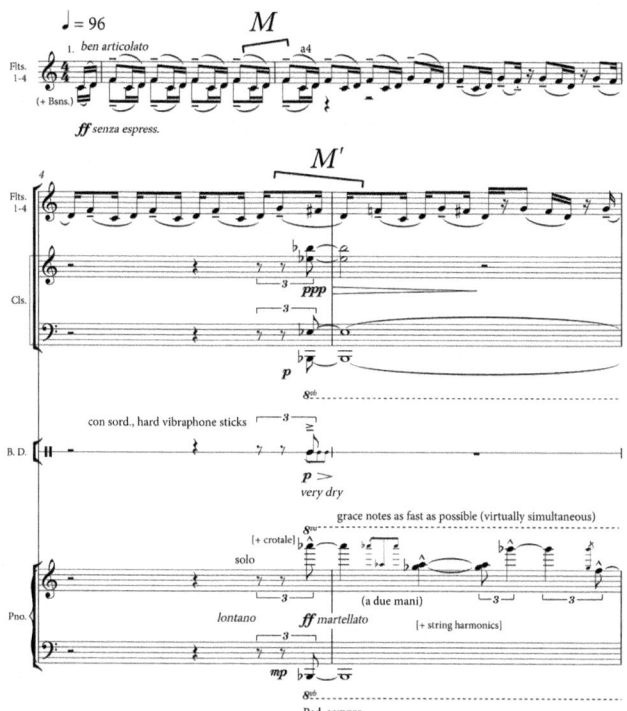

(b)

(c)

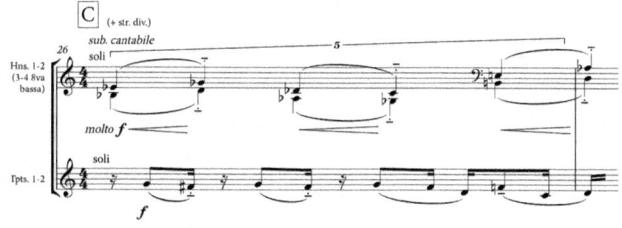

Ex. 1.3 *America: A Prophecy*, opening orchestral layers. (a) Bars 1–5, flutes at MM 96, interrupted; (b) bars 10–11, tuba and wind entrance; (c) bar 26, horns at MM 120

response to the singer's 'my nation' call (at bar 45) confirms as much. Four flutes in unison, low in register, produce a markedly breathy timbre, as if to echo 'folk' sonorities (pan pipes or ocarina).[32] Their fluent, ostinato-like undulations (hinting at a hocket) are also pentatonic. The shocking piano entrance (with crotales as metallic 'edge', bar 4), by contrast, is much higher in register and treads slowly downwards in doleful 'lament' (familiar material for Adès).

The collision of the two opening gestures is confirmed in the temporal-rhythmic dimension. Where the flutes project a mid-tempo tactus (crotchet = MM 96) with metrical depth (by quaver and semiquaver sub-pulsation), the striding piano arrives a third slower, moving at MM 72 (notated in sharply audible tactus beats of four triplet quavers). Avoiding a smooth 2:3 polyphony of layers, Adès maximises the jolting effect by means of metric displacements. The piano enters one triplet ahead of the bar line; the flutes, too, drift from the 4/4 metric grid (by one semiquaver, bar 6). The double displacement conveys radical lack of coordination. Each orchestral layer has its own flux, but the polyphonic result – as in Stravinsky, Nancarrow or Birtwistle – is dissociation of metrically independent layers.[33] Only with the entrance of a third layer (tuba and wind triplet quavers, bar 10) are flute and piano layers manoeuvred into uneasy metric coexistence in relation to the opening MM 96 tactus. One more new layer at bar 26 (Ex. 1.3c) – horns in quintuplet crotchets, projecting MM 120, in 5:4 ratio with the opening MM 96 – further intensifies the polyrhythmic build-up.

Fracturing of music's time-flow – of pulse, metre and tempo, out of joint – defines the gestural universe of *America* and wider metaphoric resonances. The independence of musical layers is also tonal (the flutes affirm an F tonic, the piano 'lament' ends on E♭ – but the hypnotic rhythms, in particular, mark out the ostinato as something culturally specific. These low flutes, in context, circle enigmatically as tokens of a Mayan world view bounded by seasonal-cyclic repetitions. The original *Chilam Balam* texts are calendrical, rife with recurring cycles of twenty named days, with thirteen-fold repetitions completing a 260-day ritual cycle. Wider historical 'wheels of time' count off *katún* cycles (twenty years), turning towards a prophesied end: each time division in the Mayan calendar was named as a deity.[34] The extant codices are peopled

---

[32] Initially (bars 1–3), the four-flute unison timbre is prepared by flute/bassoon doubling.

[33] For analyses of fluctuating intensity of rhythmic dissociation in Adès's music, see Chapter 5.

[34] Clendinnen, *Ambivalent Conquests*, p. 145; Sawyer-Lauçanno, *Destruction*, pp. ii–iii.

with gods on earth and in the underworld.[35] In Adès's flute ostinato, accumulating repetitions meet capricious interruption. The initial *M* fourth-shape (see Ex. 1.3) from middle C rises seven times in a row, an expected eighth iteration disrupted by the new pitch G (bar 2), from which a complementary *M'* shape falls. Do the next four *M* statements pursue hidden calendrical purpose, or do we simply hear a play of flutes, less strictly cyclic in melody and rhythm than the piano and crotales layer? With the arriving brass layers (at bars 10 and 26) the 'Mayan' flutes are increasingly occluded, overtaken by metrically independent ideas of greater sonic force.

A Prophet's Voice, Signs of Warning

The opening tumult is silenced by the priestess's voice: a Prospero-like entrance establishing her power and authority. Her single-syllable cry ('O', bar 17) is metrically 'early', cutting off the crowd-like polyphony; she follows with a first plea ('O my nation / Prepare', bars 41–8). Placing the singer in a balcony above the orchestra (as at the premiere) heightens the dialogic *mise en scène*. Except for two quite brief appearances of the chorus, the gestural sequence of *America* is controlled by the priestess's keening voice. I have noted that gestures here function less as mimetic acts within a *scena* than as temporally bound metaphors, tokens of an underlying mythic-historical complex. A hearing of the opening gestures reveals already Adès's metaphoric precision in wordless instrumental textures. But gesture, more typically in *America*, involves the interplay of voice(s) and full orchestra, as close readings of specific passages in Panel I and the shorter Panel II will reveal. Approaching sonic details, one recognises equally in Adès's libretto an originary, verbal layer of gesture, comprising significant speech acts for the solo singer and chorus – a backdrop to the piece's larger formal sweep.

We may assume that Adès created his libretto for *America* before finalising many (or even most) details of melodic shape, rhythmic layering or orchestral shadings. The composer's 'adaptation' from English-language poetic renditions of the *Chilam Balam* books includes much reshaping and

---

[35] In the cover image reproduced in *America*'s score (Faber Music, 2002) twenty day signs surround a skull in a calendar-square further framed by four 'deceased and bundled' gods and four human figures. Gisele Díaz and Alan Rodgers, *The Codex Borgia: A Full-Color Restoration of the Ancient Mexican Manuscript*, ed. by Bruce E. Byland (Mineola, NY: Dover, 1993), pp. xxii, 52.

1 MM 96 (bar 1) introduction (orch); *Mezzo:* 'O my nation'

    2 (bar 55) 'The people move as if in dreams'

        3 MM 96 (bar 84) 'End of all our ways'

            4 MM 162 (bar 124) *Chorus:* 'Todos los buenos ... eterna gloria'

        5a MM c. 90 (bar 194) *Mezzo:* 'Your gods'

      5b (bar 221) *Orchestra* 'scaffold'/eclipse (bars 229–30) *rit. molto*

    6a MM 32, 46 (bar 231) 'They will rule from the backs'

6b *a tempo* [MM 90] (bars 236–50) 'Prepare'

Fig. 1.1 *America*, Panel I, synoptic overview

reordering of the source texts.[36] Where Mayan seers address specific regional groups ('O Itzá make ready! / Your villages will be turned / into piles of rubble'), Adès's priestess speaks, from the start, to an unnamed 'nation'.[37] The next section ('The people move as if in dreams') conflates several *Chilam* passages.[38] Later in Panel I, Adès treats the opening call ('O my nation / Prepare') as a simple refrain, in a couplet and separate lines. The fire images of Panel II ('ash feels no pain') derive from one complete *Chilam* poem, but diction is pared to stark monosyllables.[39] Defining the priestess's voice timbrally as non-operatic (*senza vibrato*), Adès universalises her unflinching speech by excising proper names and direct references to 'foreign lords' or 'conquerors'; the Spanish invaders figure verbally as a shadowy other ('*They* will come from the east'). The interpolated Spanish and (in Panel II) Latin words are direct linguistic images of a 'foreign' conquest represented as anything but heroic. The Europeans in *America*, with their crude, collective chanting, are a rudimentary musical crowd.[40]

From a text of terse fragments, how does a composer assemble a continuous musical form in two contiguous parts? Panel I, in synoptic overview (Fig. 1.1), comprises an arch-like progression of six blocks. With minimal

[36] The poet Sawyer-Lauçanno, in turn, credits prior sources, including Ralph L. Roys, *The Chilam Balam of Chumayel* (Washington, DC: Carnegie Institution, 1933); Sawyer-Lauçanno, *Destruction*, p. v.

[37] Sawyer-Lauçanno, *Destruction*, p. 18.   [38] Ibid., pp. 26, 21–2, 6.

[39] Sawyer-Lauçanno's line is 'Ash does not suffer'; *Destruction*, p. 10.

[40] Though the score lists 'large chorus' as optional, performances without massed voices surely deprive *America* of a vivid embodiment of foreign invaders.

Ex. 1.4 *America*, Panel I, section 2, bars 59–68, 74–8, tempo canon,
orchestral and vocal entries

transition or instant shifts between musics of contrasting speed, the argument
elaborates the splintered, interruptive energies of the layered opening.[41] The
entire progression is witnessed by the prophet's increasingly urgent warnings
(sections 1–3) leading to the central moment of Spanish 'arrival' (section 4),
during which she falls silent. Her return, with further predictions of catas-
trophe (sections 5–6, the latter subdividing by tempo), concludes a scheme of
elemental temporal fracturing. *America* maps a gestural universe defined by
opposing forces of musical motion. Where the juxtaposition in section
1 reflects an interplay of pulse-streams of evident regularity, the full metaphorical force of this cyclic-'calendrical' music comes into starkest relief in
relation to its dynamic opposite – a music of near-stasis, virtually devoid of
coherent motion. In section 2 of Panel I – 'The people move as if in dreams' –
the Mayan blindness to fate finds its most intricate sounding realisation.

As a musical image of pre-invasion obliviousness to impending catas-
trophe – a failure to heed astrological omens – the 'dream' motions of
section 2 unfold in a weave of canonic imitation (see Ex. 1.4). Melodic

---

[41] The shorter three-part Panel II (considered below) lacks abrupt tempo shifts.

phrases hover eerily for some two minutes in performance. The sounding images of destruction are rhythmic-metric – an apocalypse felt by a nation adrift from the basic calendrical-spiritual parsing of existence. Mayan flutes play on in section 2 as a remnant of the past, but their sonority is now divided and 'weak' (*ppp*) – 'from fuck and drink', the priestess sings – and increasingly obscured by creeping contrapuntal chaos. The flutes still move at MM 96, yet their time-flow is undermined by the circling vocal-orchestral tapestry. The priestess's utterances are stable (their alternating long and short beats are fixed in duration), yet her song floats amid rhythmic incoherence. On the eve of the 'jaguar's misery' at the hands of the 'foreign fox', time has lost all measurable pattern.[42]

The musical image of suspended time-flow is constructed by rigorous melodic imitation. Twelve canonic entries in the orchestra (bars 55–84) crowd around the priestess's four phrases, but since each instrumental voice follows its own languorous path – turning at a unique rhythmic rate – one hears endless wandering.[43] Temporal elasticity denies listeners any stable counting unit or regular pulsation. The first and third of the singer's entries (see Ex. 1.4) are *comes* phrases, following an orchestral *dux*. Her eight syllables alternate long and short beats (dotted minim, dotted crotchet), the resulting «long, short» motive in phrase 1 ('The peo-ple') echoing the slower violin line at an 'irrational' tempo ratio (10:3, in crotchets).[44] In a second pair of entries ('The pro-phets'), Adès further subverts pattern by melodic inversion, and by reversing the clarinet and cello *dux* – now «short, long», from C♯ – while the singer maintains her «long, short» entrance (creating new ratios – 7:12 and 5:2, respectively – between C♯s and Bs). As the flutes pursue their forlorn counting-out of history, the priestess confirms wider temporal vagrancy ('It is the end of all our ways'). Without measurable time, one hears the Mayan apocalypse.

After the violent temporal layerings of *America*'s opening, the rhythmically static 'dream' music floats on a hazy scrim of strings (*sul tasto*), a delicate prelude to the raucous woodwind-brass colours of the more histrionic section 3. Convinced of imminent disaster, the prophet's voice climbs ominously from its early high F♯ ('the end', bar 86) to an ululating

---

[42] Sawyer-Lauçanno, *Destruction*, pp. 17, 16.

[43] For an overview of the canon, see Shin Young Aum, 'Analysis of *America: A Prophecy* by Thomas Adès' (unpublished DMA dissertation, University of Illinois at Urbana-Champaign, 2012), pp. 21–5.

[44] The imitation is not quite strict: the violin's six-pitch subject falls a fifth (A–D), while the voice rises a fourth, before circling back to opening pitches.

G ('pre-*pare*', bars 98–9). Her final, desperate plea – 'O my nation' (bars 122–3) pushing on to G♯ – is silenced, abruptly, by the sounds of arrival.

'Todos los buenos soldados': Battle Sounds

For a musical representation of 'contact', Adès gives the invading Spanish forces historically marked materials. The blaring brass fanfares, running scales and garish reiterations of a B major tonic triad in the arrival of section 4 mimic, in modern orchestral colours, some sixteenth-century European keyboard *batalla*, overpowering everything heard to this point. Even the jingoistic chorus – yelling words from Flecha about 'good soldiers' dying for glory – is almost drowned out in the shrill paranoid style of this military parade.[45] The encounter foretold by prophecy races forward with accelerating speed and deafening sonority, in just over a minute, from preliminary fanfares to its closing *tutta forza* shriek ('eternal glory'), a hectic montage with the kaleidoscopic feel of a cinematic newsreel.

Spanish and Mayan conquest chronicles abound in descriptions of war as sound – cannons, trumpets, drums, the throbbing of hoof-pounding cavalry;[46] Adès stages the military presence in equivalent sonic close-ups. We feel the army's rumbling in the drum tattoo (bars 121–3), drowning out the priestess seconds before the brass burst in. The entrance itself is immediately much faster (MM 162) and rhythmically anarchic, with pseudo-Renaissance hemiola groups disturbed by internal lurches (Ex. 1.5). A virtuosic piccolo trumpet (as in *Living Toys*) is the brash musical standard-bearer for the full ensemble. The pace quickens again as the chorus enters (at MM 171, bar 142), its boorish chant competing with a swaggering *gallarda* in the brass (Ex. 1.6).[47] A pair of B and E triads, matching the chorus tune, asserts a crude major-mode tonality, with an overlay of complicating chromatic detail (trombones, after bar 180). One could hear the tuba's F♮ calls as a Mayan challenge to the 'European' B major; on the orchestrational level of the metaphor, shrieking piccolos supplant Mayan flutes.

This arrival *batalla* is a forceful gesture of interruption writ large, but the heavy triple-metre *Totentanz* subsides almost as quickly as it appeared. The priestess's visions of an aftermath (sections 5 and 6) reinstate the slower

---

[45] Adès mentions the presence in *America* of one distinctly recent historical trope, 'the invasion paranoia that gripped the States in the 1950s'. Service, 'Altered States'.

[46] For passages from the *Florentine Codex* see Lockhart, *We People Here*, pp. 186, 110.

[47] The dance phrase is subtly prefigured in the layered texture of the previous section (bars 102–3).

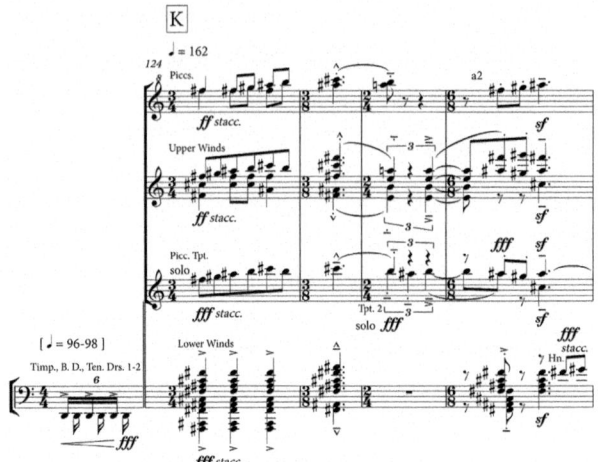

Ex. 1.5 *America*, Panel I, bars 123–7, sounds of European arrival

Ex. 1.6 *America*, Panel I, bars 175–8, Spanish soldiers, with brass *gallarda*

time-flow and jagged faultlines of the pre-invasion cosmos. 'Your cities will fall', she sings with dogged rhythmic fixity.[48] Her subsequent vision of 'scaffolds' is engulfed by dense orchestral polyphony (bars 221–30), an 'eclipse' of the previous 'dream' subject of section 2 ending with an extreme slowing (*rit. molto*) of musical time (a second 'eclipse' gesture will arrive in Panel II). One final Mayan response concludes Panel I (at bars 241–50) as jittering tam-tam pulses (five semiquavers) run microscopic interference with the unison flutes (four semiquavers), pitched an octave higher than

---

[48] Each syllable (at bars 208, 217), with minor variation, lasts eight triplet quavers.

usual. With such metric-temporal shards, the closing cycles of calendrical time reach an end.

'On earth we shall burn': Dense Gesture in Panel II

Addressing her nation, the mezzo-soprano 'priestess' of Panel I delivers a prophet's warnings. In the more compact and continuously flowing sequence of Panel II, however, her role shifts. 'They will come' gives way to 'we shall burn': the singer is no longer a witness, but herself a victim. Adès creates a macabre incongruity between her words and their musical form. 'Burn, burn, burn', she begins, with strange composure, in a euphonious D major, without orchestral preface ('line 1', Ex. 1.7a). As in Panel I, a weightless initial proposition is quickly undermined by something more lugubrious: the unyielding challenge of an E♭-B♭-rooted attack (in piano, with contrabass clarinet to the fore). The singer's terse repeating monosyllables, one begins to realise, are a form of hieratic utterance, a funereal incantation possibly. It is with her second line – 'On earth we shall burn' – that the priestess slips into the first-person plural, speaking in numbed and mechanical accents, of trauma.

At its 1999 premiere, as a 'Message to the Millennium', *America* already performed cultural memory in the public sphere. Animating a scene of Mayan–Spanish 'contact', the music provides imagined documents of a historical conquest whose witnesses were mostly annihilated. The memorial process, psychologically, is a working-through. We who listen are displaced, historically and affectively. While we feel their suffering (the suffering of the other), identification is qualified by distance.[49] To acknowledge the public memorial work of Adès's *America* (however briefly) is to align its mythic viewpoint with the bracing energies of vocal, choral and orchestral utterance. Of pre-Columbian societies destroyed by European invaders we learn what we may through listening to gesture.

Framing gesture as a working category, the preceding analysis gives particular emphasis to the shifting rhythmic-temporal dimensions of *America*. At the same time, I have treated certain features of the broader theoretic construct as touchstones: gesture's emergent synthesis (of rhythm, theme, timbre) into meaningful gestalt; and its sheer density, both

---

[49] On affect and narrative in cultural memory, see Mieke Bal, Jonathan Crewe and Leo Spitzer, eds., *Acts of Memory: Cultural Recall in the Present* (Hanover, NH: University Press of New England, 1999). On the score's significance for North American audiences post-9/11, see Service, 'Altered States'.

(a)

(b)

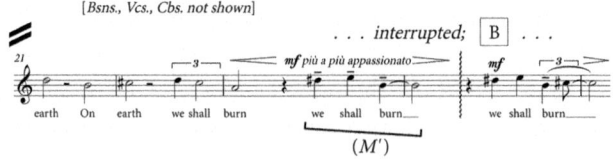

Ex. 1.7 *America*, Panel II, opening. (a) Bars 1–4, D major, undermined; (b) bars 16–24, B minor lullaby phrases

in the replete individuation of each local figure and in the cumulative, 'ever-increasing' hermeneutic density of returns concatenated over musical time.[50] To conclude this hearing, attention turns to the patent density of the priestess-victim's few closing words, and to the wordless orchestral moments with which *America*'s 'prophecy' reaches an ending.

With the solo singer centre stage, Panel II unfolds lucidly as an animation of her words. Its smoother continuities are managed by gradual slowings of pulse, a large-scale calming of Panel I's interruptive discourse. Dense with accrued history, these closing gestures surround texted utterance with lavish orchestral accompaniment, or punctuate speech with wordless continuations of the evolving argument. Despite the sinister challenge to the opening D major, the priestess continues her prophecy undeterred.

'On earth, on earth, we shall burn, we shall burn': each word in line 2 repeats as part of a lullaby-like rocking. Balancing four-bar phrases unfold a period (bars 8–12, 12–16) that repeats with restrained orchestral backdrop (bars 16–24; Ex. 1.7b). Tonally, the simple melodic descent affirms a steady B minor, unsettled by a 'de-tonicising' swerve, pushing the line away from B (D♯, enharmonically, transmutes the previous E♭ challenge). The lullaby enfolds two forms of the original M' trichord, a signature of the Mayan peoples whose incineration is impassively recounted now. The priestess's melody is slowly enveloped by delicate *divisi* polyphony, multiplying and diffusing – but not obscuring – the contours of her voice. Ringing high above, soft pedal notes – violin and piccolo Cs, Ex. 1.7b – limn a celestial ceiling below which happenings 'on earth' unfold.

'We shall turn to ash': reaching this extraordinary vision, the soloist abandons the lullaby's gentle rocking. As the ash drifts over mountains and out to sea, she regains her penetrating high F♯ (stretching the word 'sea', bars 47–51) to unlock the movement's climax. This second orchestral 'eclipse' – counterpart to Panel I's section 5b – is a brief, fierce crescendo of less than thirty seconds in performance (bars 47–62). The effect, as before, is of frightening erasure of melodic presence. Amid the sonic force of massed brass (bells up) and roaring percussion, figural gesture is lost: line becomes surface. The notion of 'eclipse', my interpretive intervention, seeks both descriptive precision – a label adequate to the specificity of score events – and metaphoric resonances. Each eclipse overwhelms the priest-ess's singing, as if to move beyond human linguistic presence into wordless

---

[50] See, respectively, Hatten, *Interpreting Musical Gestures*, p. 94; and Spitzer, *Metaphor and Musical Thought*, p. 111.

(instrumental) 'divination'. We listen to the orchestra on the priestess's terms. We hear what she sees, so to speak. As her voice falls silent, its echoing melodic shapes are magnified and pulled, contrapuntally, into a swirling mass. Where Adès's percussion choices for the Panel I eclipse correlate in performance to a sung image (murderous 'scaffolds'), the deeper rumbling in Panel II mimics 'thunder', a natural omen for a *Chilam* seer.[51] Just how precisely do listeners interpret the impossibly dense orchestral emanations – as enactments of monstrous slaughter, or glimpses into the obsidian surface of a seer's black mirror?[52] The evolving volatility of musical gesture exceeds the reassuring fixity of verbal or visual denotation. And yet the orchestral climaxes in *America*, for many listeners, will assume metaphorical-semantic potentialities within the larger diptych, as the vortex-like nexus of complex interference patterns spanning this prophecy-cum-history – between Mayan and Spanish, between American and European visions, between past history and present memory.

With what gesture does a musical myth of apocalypse conclude? In the verbal realm of the libretto, the priestess's valediction ('Know this, the ash feels no pain') defiantly undercuts the chorus's mumbled 'victory' (Ex. 1.8a). The pitch-structural basis of her defiance is a repeated E♭, frozen in unyielding chromatic resistance to the chorus. As the chorus adopts the lullaby's fragile B minor, the priestess voices the 'challenge' that has haunted *America* since the very opening. (Typically for Adès, enharmonic doubling, D♯/E♭, acquires mythic-semantic significance.) Tending towards stasis, registral depths and, ultimately, silence, *America*'s final gravitation towards a B minor tonic has many ghostly precursors.

'No pain': coming to rest on the flutes' low 'Mayan' F–C fourth, the priestess herself falls silent. The final gesture in *America* will be an orchestral coda (bars 78–86; Ex. 1.8b and c) – wordless, extremely slow, but not quite motionless. Over the sepulchral B tonic, the archetypal opposition of major and minor third – D♯ (E♭) and D♮ – prolongs the struggle for focus, stability, ascendency, closure. The scumbling of the major/minor duality involves the microtonal blurrings of trombone and lower string glissandos (enhanced by flutter-tongue 'growls' in trumpets). Only in the fourth and final chord is D♯ extinguished, a 'chilling of ember to ash'.[53] The gesture is

---

[51] For 'thunder' omens, see Sawyer-Lauçanno, *Destruction*, pp. 47–9. The Panel I eclipse (bars 221–31) comprises tenor drums with metal beaters, joined by crotales; in Panel II (bars 50–62) timpani and bass drum (rolls) augment tenor drums as timbral signifiers.

[52] On the mirror as Meso-American ritual object, see Pedro Lasch, *Black Mirror/Espejo negro* (Durham, NC: Duke University Press, 2010).

[53] Griffiths, 'Thomas Adès: *America: A Prophecy*', p. 6.

(a)

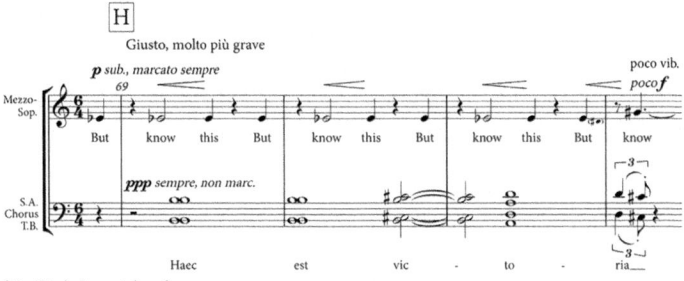

[*Str., Winds, Perc. not shown*]

(b)

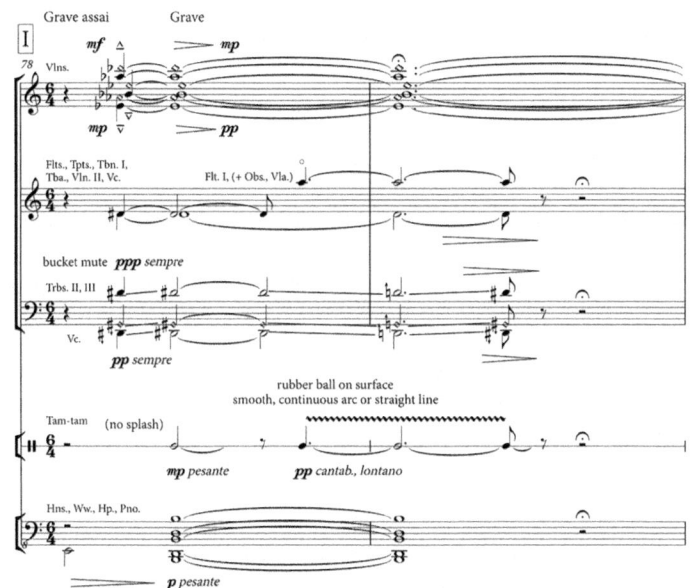

(c)

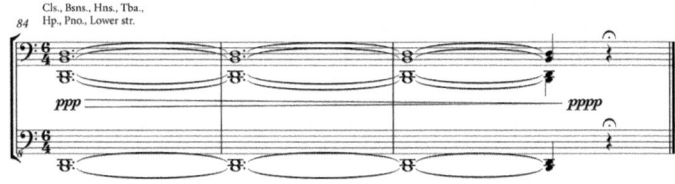

Ex. 1.8 *America*, Panel II, closing rites. (a) Bars 69–72, chromatic resistance to the chorus's mumbled 'victory'; (b) bars 78–9, closing cortège: modal scumbling; (c) bars 84–6, D♯ erased

also timbrally specific, for it is in the unison Mayan flutes that the last D♯ vanishes from hearing, leaving only the coldness of the bare third, B-D (Ex. 1.8c).

Hearings of volatile gesture, couched in verbal language, drift impercept-ibly from the structural to the metaphoric. Adès's fondness for endings that survey events 'as if from a great height'[54] continues in the registrally vast space of *America*'s orchestral coda. Contemplating the wordless utterance of this ending, we are bound, as listeners, to move beyond purely structural understandings of gesture towards a semantic frame. Could the distance between spectral harmonics and the nethermost vibrations of the bass (contrabassoon, tuba, double bass) speak, for instance, of the Mayan cosmos – of an earthly existence hanging 'between the thirteen heavens and the nine cold hells'?[55] To invoke such a culture-specific schema is to interpret more directly the registral position of those flute D♯s, expiring in a middle register evacuated of other voices.

While the episodic dream programme of *Living Toys* inhabits a very different affective realm from the mythic landscape of *America: A Prophecy*, one senses vestigial rhetorical similarities between the endings of the two scores. The military salute of the boy 'hero' in *Toys*, of course, is a child's daydream, worlds away from the collective historical trauma glimpsed in *America*; one links the scores only in schematic terms, as two versions of a recognisable gesture of closure: single-chord repetitions, punctuated by near-silence. Technically, musicians recognise 'cadence'; in a more metaphorical vein, we might call the chords ending *America* a brief cortège. Perhaps we should not be surprised to discover an understanding of the most characteristic moments in this composer's art in relation to music's most archetypal and universal forms of motion. If the concept of musical gesture hovers beguilingly at the intersection of physical sonority and metaphysical sense, it may also tell us much about how Adès's music goes.

---

[54] Thomas Adès, programme notes on *Chamber Symphony*, 1990, www.fabermusic.com/music/chamber-symphony-2009.

[55] Sawyer-Lauçanno, *Destruction*, p. 50.

2 | Performing Adès

EDWARD VENN WITH HENRY WEEKES

Thomas Adès's first musical successes were as a performer rather than composer.[1] While a student at the Guildhall School of Music, he won the 1986 Guildhall Lutine Prize for instrumentalists, and in 1988–9 he studied the piano in chamber music with György Kurtág. In 1989 he reached the semi-final of the BBC's biennial Young Musician of the Year competition. This proved pivotal in focussing Adès's attention away from performance towards composition:

It was on TV, and it gave me quite a fright. . . . I suddenly found myself at quite an advanced stage as a performer. I hadn't taken the idea very seriously. Everyone was commenting on this or that and I just didn't care – I wanted to go work on something new . . . I went home and said, 'I'm going to become a composer today, and do it properly.'[2]

But becoming a composer 'properly' did not mean that Adès neglected his performance activities; rather, he developed ways of balancing both. He came to national attention through a piano recital he gave with the Park Lane Group on 11 January 1993. The programme contained works by Nicholas Maw, Kurtág, Olivier Messiaen and Paul Ruders. However, it was the inclusion in the recital of Adès's *Still Sorrowing* (1992) which made the biggest impact on the critics, who concentrated more on Adès's arrival as a composer than as a pianist.[3] This was doubtless inevitable, given the then-recent announcement that Adès had signed a publishing contract

---

[1] The bulk of this chapter was written by Edward Venn. Henry Weekes provided *Sonic Visualiser* data for the analyses of the Mazurkas Op. 27 and *Darknesse Visible* and contributed to early drafts of the analysis of the latter.

[2] Alex Ross, 'Roll Over, Beethoven: Thomas Adès', *New Yorker*, 26 October 1998, pp. 111–41 (p. 126).

[3] Andrew Porter's description of *Still Sorrowing* concentrated entirely on the work's material and its deployment; the way in which Adès performed the piece was left unmentioned ('Pianistically Young, Gifted, and Blu-Tack'd', *Observer*, 17 January 1993, arts section, p. 46). This, perhaps, was the result of discretion: Michael White, in *The Independent*, while describing Adès as both a compositional 'enfant prodige' and a 'pianist of formidable intelligence', noted that the removal of Blu-Tack from the prepared piano in *Still Sorrowing* led to an inadvertent 'overlay of plucking noises that were certainly not in the score' ('Stars of Tomorrow Shine Today', *Independent*, 17 January 1993, arts section, p. 18).

with Faber Music. Nevertheless, it also provides an early example of audiences encountering Adès's music as performed by the composer. Indeed, Adès has been involved in (depending on how arrangements of his works are counted) around half of the premieres of his pieces and has recorded (as pianist or conductor) an even greater number.[4] Adès's activities as composer and performer are thus closely entwined.

This connection between composition and performance has a greater bearing on the reception and interpretation of Adès's music than has hitherto been acknowledged.[5] Daniel Leech-Wilkinson argues that performances shape the musical imaginations of composers, listeners and analysts, and that the valorisation of scores over performances obscures the manner in which shifts in performance styles can have a profound bearing on our responses to pieces and repertoires.[6] While he acknowledges that living composers – especially when they know the performers they are writing for (as is often the case for Adès) – have a much closer relationship between compositional input and imagined sounding output,[7] the fact remains that the types of decisions performers make, whether rehearsed during many hours of practice or emerging spontaneously in the moment in response to the peculiarities of recital halls and audiences, can mean that the same piece can differ greatly in the hands of different performers. For Leech-Wilkinson, 'it would be wise to try to get out of the habit of ascribing much of what we hear in scores either to the composer or to the inherent nature of a work. The agency is in fact the listener's or the analyst's response to the performer's responding to the notation.'[8] Such habits are hard to shake off: the responses to Adès's Park Lane recital demonstrate just how ingrained the work notion remains in the critical imagination (in the sense of the work being conceived of as existing outside performance). The same is true for Adès scholarship: for all of the significant gains which have been made in our analytical understanding of Adès's music, or what it might mean within a broader cultural sphere, the actual *sound* of it and the range of meanings a performer might tease from it have barely begun to be addressed.

---

[4] A list of performances and recordings of Adès's music is maintained at www.thomasades.com.

[5] My argument applies to any composer who performs and records their own music.

[6] Daniel Leech-Wilkinson, 'Compositions, Scores, Performances, Meanings', *Music Theory Online*, 18/i (2012), https://mtosmt.org/issues/mto.12.18.1/mto.12.18.1.leech-wilkinson.html.

[7] Ibid., §5.1.

[8] Ibid., §5.4. On musical agency, see Seth Monahan, 'Action and Agency Revisited', *Journal of Music Theory*, 57/ii (2013), 321–71.

Although Adès has been increasingly willing in recent years to discuss his musical creative processes, his preference remains to describe it in terms of metaphor rather than detailed examination of his compositional or rehearsal procedures.[9] As a result, any scholarly enquiry into Adès's performance practice is, to a greater extent, limited to inferences which can be made from actual performances or (pragmatically) from recordings of those performances.[10] This serves to narrow what can be said about the performance to those details that can be captured analytically – a restriction which shifts the focus of enquiry away from understanding the richness of what performers do in all its complexity towards representations of a performance which are, in essence, bound up with many of the same epistemological concerns as score analysis.[11] Though I remain mindful of such tensions, the close connection Adès has demonstrated between composition and performance throughout his career suggests that a methodological approach which balances data from recordings and scores is not entirely unwarranted.

At stake here are the ways in which musical structure, broadly defined, might be conceived.[12] To illustrate this, I shall provide theoretical and methodological orientation through the consideration of the different conceptual frameworks Adès has brought to bear on the music of Janáček.[13] After teasing out the commonalities, as well as important distinctions, in the way these frameworks conceptualise musical structure,

---

[9] See Thomas Adès and Tom Service, *Thomas Adès: Full of Noises – Conversations with Tom Service*, paperback ed. (London: Faber and Faber, 2018), pp. xi–xiii, 92–115.

[10] Nicholas Cook has described the limitations of treating studio recordings (and patched live recordings) as objects of performance analysis. *Beyond the Score* (New York: Oxford University Press, 2013), p. 142.

[11] See, for instance, Mine Doğantan-Dack, 'In the Beginning Was Gesture: Piano Touch and the Phenomenology of the Performing Body', in *New Perspectives on Music and Gesture*, ed. by Anthony Gritten and Elaine King (Farnham: Ashgate, 2011), pp. 243–65.

[12] My use of the term 'structure' follows Daphne Leong, who, while noting the narrower sense in which music analysts engage with structure that emerges 'from elements found in a score', offers a broader sense 'in which structure is created in the process of making music – by composers, performers, listeners, and analysts. Structure in this broader conception explicitly includes perceived, performed, and even imagined elements. It can be active, fluid, and dynamic.' More specifically, '[s]tructure is a means of making sense of music. It is a way of approaching sound and symbol, image and movement, and "hearing-as" ("understanding-as," "seeing-as," "feeling-as"). In doing so, it gives flight to imagination.' Daphne Leong, *Performing Knowledge: Twentieth-Century Music in Analysis and Performance* (New York: Oxford University Press, 2019), pp. 8, 10.

[13] Adès's interpretations of other composers' music suggest an exhaustive and much-needed study in and of itself. The recordings of other composers listed at www.thomasades.com/recordings does scarce justice to the diversity of figures Adès has performed live.

I turn to realisations of two of Adès's own works, in recordings by the composer and other pianists. First, I examine Adès's Mazurkas Op. 27 to consider the dynamic interaction between such structures, genres and performance traditions in recordings of these works. Finally, I turn to recordings of *Darknesse Visible* to consider the role performance can play in rethinking the relationship of expression and structure in Adès's music. Underpinning both accounts is a sense of how performances can access the temporal experience of how time passes in Adès's music.

Structuring Janáček

Of all of the figures in Adès's musical pantheon, Janáček is the only one to have been approached by Adès in the overlapping roles of composer, performer and analyst. The ways in which Adès responds to, and structures,[14] Janáček's music from these complementary but distinct subject positions reflect their differing epistemological concerns.[15] For instance, Adès has described how Janáček will

take one moment, and show you the inner instability in that moment ... And the ramifications of several of those moments placed next to one another are then only revealed on the last page. In that piece, *In the Mists*, nothing changes, but you're aware that every time the silence comes back, and he tries another doorway, it transforms from being a phenomenon that opens a new possibility to something that closes the structure. Yet the material doesn't change.[16]

For all that Adès frames such comments in terms of his analytical interest in Janáček's piano music,[17] the impression is at least as much of Adès engaging in a transhistorical shop talk with a fellow composer, considering ways in which one might conceive of organising material, embracing its potential for musical continuity and discontinuity, to 'close the structure'.

In his contribution to Cambridge University Press's *Janáček Studies*,[18] however, the emphasis skews towards modes of knowledge – and

---

[14] Central here is the notion that structure arises from engagement with music, rather than existing separately from such engagement.

[15] Reflecting on such concerns, Leong describes how scores 'mediate between the musical worlds of composition, performance, and scholarship. They fulfill different functions within each of these domains, yet are recognizable and accepted across all of them.' *Performing Knowledge*, p. 25.

[16] Adès and Service, *Full of Noises*, p. 21.   [17] Ibid., p. 19.

[18] Thomas Adès, '"Nothing but pranks and puns": Janáček's Solo Piano Music', in *Janáček Studies*, ed. by Paul Wingfield (Cambridge: Cambridge University Press, 1999), pp. 18–35.

representations of that knowledge – derived explicitly from analytical discourse. For Adès, the 'apparent **ABA** tonal structure' of Janáček's 'In memoriam' ('Na památku'; composed around 1886–7) arises through deft enharmonic shifts. He describes the cadential resolution of B major to A flat major in bars 15–16, and with it the enharmonic transformation of D♯ to E♭, as the 'defining event of the piece'.[19] Adès argues that the central section (bars 9–16; see the score in Ex. 2.1b) prepares for this transformation in specific ways, highlighting how all parameters contribute to the compositional effect (Table 2.1 maps these 'events', marked with letters from A to P, onto the annotations below Ex. 2.1b).[20] In this way, salient enharmonic events are made to integrate with, and arise from, all aspects of the piece's architectural structure.

Differing modes of knowledge can be inferred from Adès's performance of the work. He recorded 'In memoriam' the year after *Janáček Studies* was published;[21] aspects of this performance are presented in Ex. 2.1. The graph in Ex. 2.1c plots the duration in seconds of each event in bars 9–16: alternate events correspond to the double-dotted crotchets at the start of each bar (A, C, E etc.) and the semiquavers at the end of each bar (B, D, F, etc.). Although this replicates the bias in empirical performance studies towards more measurable parameters such as tempo and duration (along with dynamics),[22] tempo, as a synthetic 'summarising [of] multiple musical processes',[23] offers a convenient means by which one might approach musical expression. Given that there are numerous musical reasons why a performer might shape musical time, the data only offer a guide to how one might interpret what is heard; they are prompts for close listening, reflection and interpretation, rather than ends in themselves.[24] In the case of the events of bars 9–16, one might be encouraged by the data to attend to the pitches which Adès lingers on in performance, and to observe that these pitches are those identified as enharmonically significant in Table 2.1 (events A, F and H, and to a lesser extent their resolution, events N and P).

---

[19] Ibid., pp. 18, 20. Adès's focus here on specific pitches prefigures his later discussion of 'fetish notes', which 'will often become an enharmonic point in the piece'. Adès and Service, *Full of Noises*, p. 49.

[20] The quotations from Table 2.1 are taken from Adès, 'Nothing but pranks and puns', p. 20.

[21] *Janáček: The Diary of One Who Disappeared/Piano Works* (EMI Classics 5572192, 2001).

[22] See John Rink, 'The State of Play in Performance Studies', in *The Music Practitioner: Research for the Music Performer, Teacher and Listener*, ed. by Jane W. Davidson (Aldershot: Ashgate, 2004), pp. 37–51 (p. 38).

[23] Cook, *Beyond the Score*, p. 143.   [24] Ibid., p. 149.

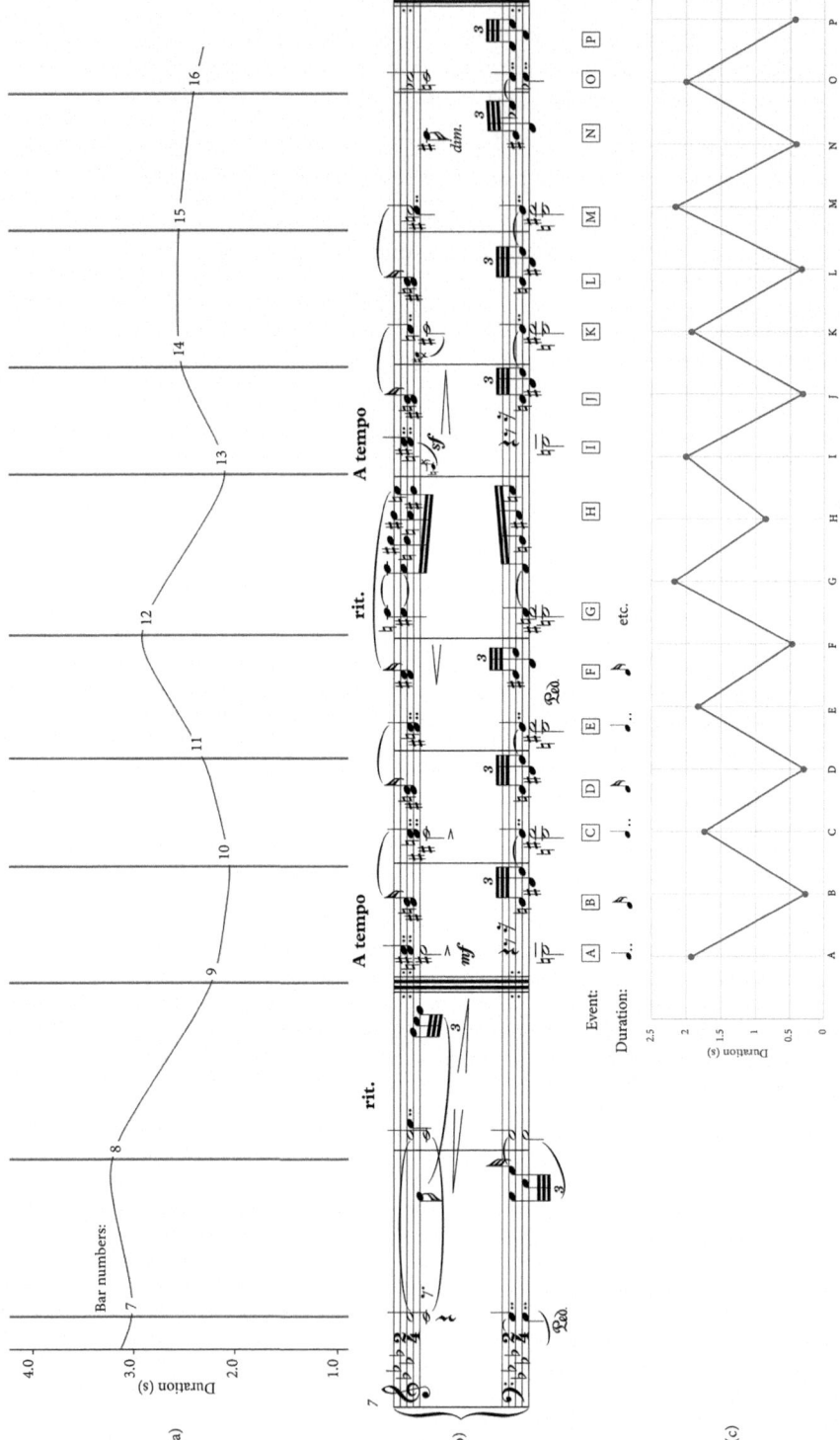

Ex. 2.1 Janáček, 'In memoriam', bars 9–16. (a) Duration curve of Adès's performance; (b) score; (c) durations of specific pitch events

Table 2.1. Details from Adès's analysis of Janáček, 'In memoriam',
bars 9–16

Bar	Event	Description
9	A	'significant *subito* dynamic increase'
9	A	'an accent distinguishing the central d#^{1} from the melodic eb_2/eb_1 of bars 1–8'
10	C	'This coloration [i.e. an accent] is sustained in bar 10, raising the db_1 of bars 1–8 into the new context as a c#$_1$,'
11	F	'rich d# of bar 11 … evident from its textural and rhythmic position as a coinage from the eb of the first seven bars'
12	G	'stretched spacing …'
12	H	'… in which the otherwise consistent triplet figure at the end of every bar is slowed down threefold, placing an answering e♮ on the final semiquaver of bar 12, which is in turn resolved, on the final semiquaver of bar 15'
13	I	'contrast between the voice-specific accent of bar 8 and the bare *sfzorzando* of bar 13'
14	K	'resumption [of inner voice] in bar 14 is gently, though still unequivocally, pointed by an unconventionally spread chord'
15	N	[Resolution of e♮ from bar 12]
16	O–P	'the control of this enharmonic shift over the cadence into bar 16 is sealed by it assuming the rhythmic personality of the principal melodic voice'

Adès's performance gives time, too, to the 'stretched spacing' of bar 12
(event G) but not so much to that of bar 14 (event K). In this interpretation, close listening would draw out the correspondences between written
and performed accounts of 'In memoriam'.

Nevertheless, one must not assume that Adès's performance is determined entirely by what we might term his composer-analyst's response to
structural elements within the musical design. As the duration curve in
Ex. 2.1a demonstrates,[25] Adès's performance of bars 9–16 might also suggest
a different set of interpretative imperatives (and hence emergent structures).

---

[25] As the curve rises, the performance slows down; as it drops, the performance speeds up. As each
point on the curve represents a *duration* rather than a continuous change, all we can say for
certain is that, for instance, bar 8 of Adès's performance is quantitively longer than bar 9: it does
not tell us how this change is perceived musically.

Adès marks the tonal shift and dynamic change in bar 9 by ignoring Janáček's marking of 'a tempo', pressing forward at a noticeably faster pace (his average speed in section A is crotchet = MM c. 44; in section B, crotchet = MM c. 51). But Adès also maintains the four-bar phrasing which he employed in section A, lingering every fourth bar (regardless of whether Janáček indicates a ritardando). Within these groups, the tendency is to slow down subtly as the melody ascends (e.g. bars 10–12) and accelerate as it descends (bars 14–17).[26] Although one must be wary to ensure that performance data *contribute* to, rather than substitute for, close listening, I would argue that these details are readily audible. If anything, the resulting shapes (and with it, Adès's careful control of pedalling, dynamics, articulation and colour) throw the musical emphasis onto the repeated A♮ and C♯s of the melody, so that the final slide down to A♭ and C♮ in bar 16, rather than the enharmonic transformation, emerges as the 'defining event'. In this second reading, therefore, the isolated pitch events of Ex. 2.1c (and in Adès's prose) are accommodated within the broader gestural shapes of Ex. 2.1a, the latter of which articulates a particular formal interpretation and gives emphasis to its underlying continuity.

'In memoriam' is the only example to date of Adès offering detailed analytical comments in prose about a work as well as a recorded performance. For Adès, 'the score is just a map of intentions. The score isn't the thing. The music came before the score.'[27] And yet his differing realisation of these intentions – the diversity of structures that emerge from the affordances of the score – demonstrates how analysis and performance offer different ways of conceiving and experiencing a work. Of particular relevance for this chapter is the way in which close listening to performances might suggest alternative approaches to structure, or a rethinking of established hierarchies, which complement or even challenge existing analytical approaches to Adès's music.

Performing Tradition(s)

Adès's Mazurkas Op. 27 were written for Emanuel Ax to perform at the Chopin bicentennial celebrations in 2010.[28] The choice of the mazurka is

---

[26] What is not shown in Ex. 2.1a is the way in which Adès's dynamic plan also establishes an *eight*-bar shape, rising cumulatively to bar 12 before receding to bar 16.

[27] Adès and Service, *Full of Noises*, p. 100.

[28] Paul Griffiths, programme notes on Thomas Adès, Mazurkas Op. 27, 2009, www.fabermusic .com/repertoire/mazurkas-5475. Here, and throughout, I distinguish between the mazurka as a genre (lower case m) and Adès's Mazurkas (upper case).

telling, for it 'represents a highly constructed genre more or less identified with Chopin'.[29] Building upon this identification, Samuel Wilson has noted the relationship between Adès's metrical structures and reports of Chopin's (possibly idiosyncratic) use of rubato in performance.[30] Elsewhere, Jennifer A. Maxwell has traced a compositional lineage from Chopin's transformation of folk dances, via Szymanowksi, through to Adès.[31] In these accounts, Adès's relationship with Chopin is presented as a response to both performance (embodied) and compositional (stylistic) traditions. Yet Adès's insistence that 'the music is the thing behind the surface', and that '[i]t doesn't seem real to me, the style of a piece', would appear to question the significance of these inherited practices.[32] There is as a result a tension in analytical accounts of the work, in which examination of the topical surface floats on top of more expansive discussion of the musical procedures (primarily its intervallic properties) beneath.[33] In the analytical imagination, Adès's Mazurkas have been constructed more in the image of Adès than of Chopin, focussing on idea rather than style.

Performances of Adès's Mazurkas reveal (and require) alternative ways of negotiating the relationship between surface and depth, and between past and present. Here, the issue of 'generally accepted interpretative practices' around the mazurka tradition looms large,[34] not least when Adès's topical foregrounds appear to recede.[35] These practices are well documented within empirical performance studies, especially in the domains of tempo and duration, ranging from the ways in which pianists realise larger-scale structures;[36] via smaller-scale formal articulation of phrase groupings through *phrase arching* (an acceleration and subsequent

---

[29] Cook, *Beyond the Score*, p. 158.

[30] Samuel Wilson, 'An Aesthetics of Past–Present Relations in the Experience of Late 20th- and Early 21st-Century Art Music' (unpublished PhD dissertation, Royal Holloway, 2013), pp. 251–63.

[31] Jennifer A. Maxwell, 'Tracing a Lineage of the Mazurka Genre: Influences of Chopin and Szymanowski on Thomas Adès' *Mazurkas* for Piano, Op. 27' (unpublished DMA dissertation, University of Boston, 2014).

[32] Adès and Service, *Full of Noises*, pp. 100, 78.

[33] See Maxwell, 'Tracing a Lineage', pp. 113–41; Wilson, 'An Aesthetics of Past–Present Relations', pp. 251–63; and Chapter 8.

[34] Leong, *Performing Knowledge*, p. 68. Here, Leong was talking about the affordances of scores within particular performance traditions, rather than mazurkas specifically.

[35] Maxwell charts a shift from the strong topical resonances of the First Mazurka through to the more topically neutral Third, which is the 'most personal of the set'. 'Tracing a Lineage', p. 138.

[36] Neta Spiro, Nicholas Gold and John Rink, 'The Form of Performance: Analyzing Pattern Distribution in Select Recordings of Chopin's Mazurka Op. 24 No. 2', *Musicae Scientiae*, 14/ii (2010), 23–55.

deceleration through a phrase) or *group-final lengthening* (GFL – 'a means of conveying grouping structure by decelerating at the ends of groups'),[37] down to the execution of characteristic mazurka rubato at the level of the individual beat.[38] Other parameters that might contribute to the mazurka tradition, such as dynamics, articulation, pedalling and timbre, are much less well modelled.[39] Accordingly, my analysis of recordings of Adès's Mazurkas focusses primarily on quantitative data on tempo and timing, supplemented secondarily by qualitative interpretations of their sound. The recordings in question are by Thomas Adès, Winston Choi and Richard Uttley; references in the text will consist of the performer's initials followed by M1, M2 or M3 (for First, Second or Third Mazurka) and track timings (e.g. TAM1 00:00–00:08 refers to the first eight seconds of Adès's recording of his First Mazurka).[40]

Figure 2.1 presents annotated duration curves for recordings of the First Mazurka. Section labels along the x-axis refers to the thematic material of each movement; the strong contrasts between these sections in motivic shape, texture, dynamics and intervallic content means that they are readily audible. The high-level overview offered by Fig. 2.1 allows generalisations of the aural perceptions of formal shapes to be made, and with them the ways in which performers balance the potential for thematic contrasts to suggest formal discontinuities with larger-scale continuities that arise through temporal shaping. Specifically, greater differentiation between the tempos of sections can be observed (in keeping with the notated tempo markings), but the ways in which section boundaries are negotiated by individual performers reveals differing responses to the demands of the sectional construction inherited from the mazurka and a sense of continuous line implied by Adès's material.

There are notable commonalities between the three recordings of the First Mazurka. All three pianists employ GFL at the end of section A1 (bar 8), and

---

[37] Mitch Ohriner, 'Grouping Hierarchy and Trajectories of Pacing in Performances of Chopin's Mazurkas', *Music Theory Online*, 18/i (2012), https://mtosmt.org/issues/mto.12.18.1/mto.12.18 .1.ohriner.php, §3. See also Cook, *Beyond the Score*, pp. 176–223; and Spiro, Gold and Rink, 'The Form of Performance'.

[38] Cook, *Beyond the Score*, pp. 157–75.

[39] For a discussion of dynamics in the performance of mazurkas, see John Rink, Neta Spiro and Nicholas Gold, 'Motive, Gesture and the Analysis of Performance', in *New Perspectives on Music and Gesture*, ed. by Anthony Gritten and Elaine King (Farnham: Ashgate, 2011), pp. 267–92.

[40] Thomas Adès (Warner Classics 0885602, 2011), Winston Choi (La Buissonne YAN005, 2015) and Richard Uttley (Artist Recording Co. ARC01002, 2015). As this chapter was being completed, two further recordings were released, by Han Chen (Naxos 8574109, 2020) and Kirill Gerstein (Myrios MYR027, 2020).

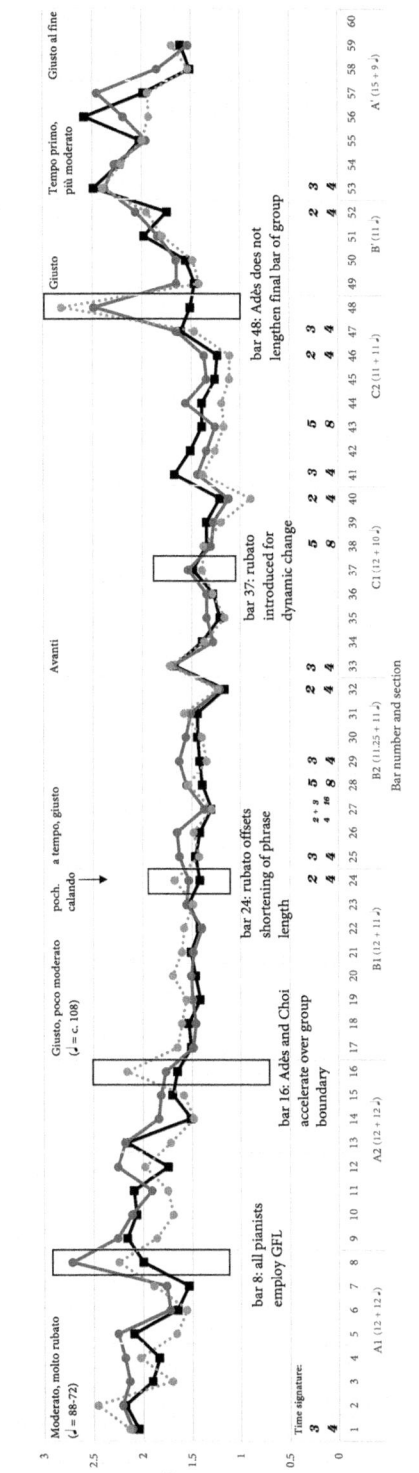

Fig. 2.1 Duration curves of performances of Adès's First Mazurka

perform A2 at a subtle, but aurally perceptible, faster tempo than A1. Uttley alone introduces a second GFL at the end of A2 (RUM1 00:18–00:33), reinforcing the periodicity of the opening sixteen bars; Adès and Choi push forward into section B (TAM1 00:16–00:30; WCM1 00:19–00:35). From here, there is a remarkable consistency of approach in all three recordings to both tempo and phrasing throughout sections B and C, prior to an extended GFL at the end of section C2 in two of the recordings (WCM1 01:11–01:24; RUM1 01:06–01:18). Both sections B′ and A′ are taken at a slower tempo than sections A and B (doubtless reflecting the more subdued indicated dynamic) as part of a broader strategy to slow down during the final sections (save for the accelerated final few bars). Uttley, therefore, is the most consistent in applying GFL at the end of sections, while Adès is the least likely to do so. The former approach foregrounds the sectional construction of the Mazurka; the latter welds the sections together to create a large-scale, and continuous, energetic shape. This is something rather different from what might be implied by the tempo markings at the start of each section in the score and shifts emphasis away from the sectional divisions of theme and intervals towards identifying the continuities between them.[41]

In the case of the Third Mazurka, larger-scale continuity is achieved through relative consistency of pulse throughout.[42] Online Fig. 2.1 presents duration curves of performances of the work, in which the notated bars of section B (bars 20–47) are grouped in fours to highlight the tempo correspondence between this and the outer sections (Adès's and Uttley's performances demonstrate this continuity most clearly; Choi takes section B at a faster tempo). Given that section B is characterised by the superimposition of non-aligned rhythmic cycles, the tempo relationship between sections may not be audible; nevertheless, it clearly informs the interpretative choices of the performers.

The main large-scale difference of interpretation in performance concerns the function of phrases Aa and A′a. These phrases are characterised

---

[41] One might also note that, melodically, the B♭ that concludes section A2 becomes the focal pitch of the entirety of the B section; in this light, Adès and Choi bring to the fore the linear connections between sections. (Similar linking of intervallic patterns characterises the transition between all sections.)

[42] This is also, to a lesser extent, true of recordings of the Second Mazurka as well. Compare this with Spiro, Gold and Rink's analysis of multiple recordings of Chopin's Op. 24 No. 2, in which they observe that 'across all performers, average beat length differs in successive sections' (albeit realised in different ways). This contrasts with the alternative approach of maintaining a more consistent pulse ('through-performed'). 'The Form of Performance', p. 36.

by the unfolding of an intervallic pattern in the outer voices, between which a mazurka-like melody (with characteristic dotted rhythm) is added in the middle register in phrases Ab and A′b.[43] Uttley takes phrases Aa and A′a at a notably slower tempo than those which follow: to my ears, this serves to present the mazurka-like idea as the main thematic content of the movement, and retrospectively casts Aa and A′a as introductory. In the performances by Adès and Choi, the lack of strong tempo differentiation between the subphrases of section A suggests that it is the intervallic patterns in the outer voices – a typical Adèsian compositional fingerprint – that form the main musical subject. This is consistent with the performers' respective treatments of the transition between sections A and B in the First Mazurka, in which Uttley emphasises the topical surface and Adès and Choi the background line, and points to the extent to which performances can inflect the degree to which material is heard as thematic.

The distinction between topical foreground and background structure described in these two movements is something of an analytical artifice, however. For instance, the upper voice (and later the inner voice) at the start of the First Mazurka is based on an expanding intervallic series; each repetition of this series is confined to a two-bar unit (Ex. 2.2). Not only does the distribution of the basic pitch material reflect the regular two-, four- and eight-bar phrasing of the prototypical mazurka, but the falling and rising melodic contour lends itself to phrase arching. This is clearly heard in Uttley's performance of the opening eight bars (RUM1 00:00–00:18), in which there is an acceleration through the first bar and a deceleration through the second. Adès's performance of the same passage (TAM1 00:00–00:15) does not form quite the same consistent curve: the slightly shorter duration of the second crotchet of bar 2 with respect to the first creates a sawtooth shape to his realisation. Nevertheless, the overall contour of this two-bar figure suggests that it is likely to be perceived in a similar fashion to the phrase arching heard in Uttley's recording;[44] the same can be said for Choi's performance. Subsequent two-bar phrases in all three recordings follow the same approximate durational contour of an acceleration followed by a ritardando. To the extent that Adès's material

---

[43] Analysis of the intervallic content of the Third Mazurka can be found in Maxwell, 'Tracing a Lineage'; Wilson, 'An Aesthetics of Past–Present Relations'; and Chapter 8.

[44] Such microvariations, as Ohriner discusses, may arise from errors introduced in the data capture; others may simply be inaudible to a listener. Although he develops a sophisticated means of determining the likely salience of such changes, for the purposes of the present chapter, a more informal approach is sufficient. See 'Grouping Hierarchy and Trajectories of Pacing', §§12–20.

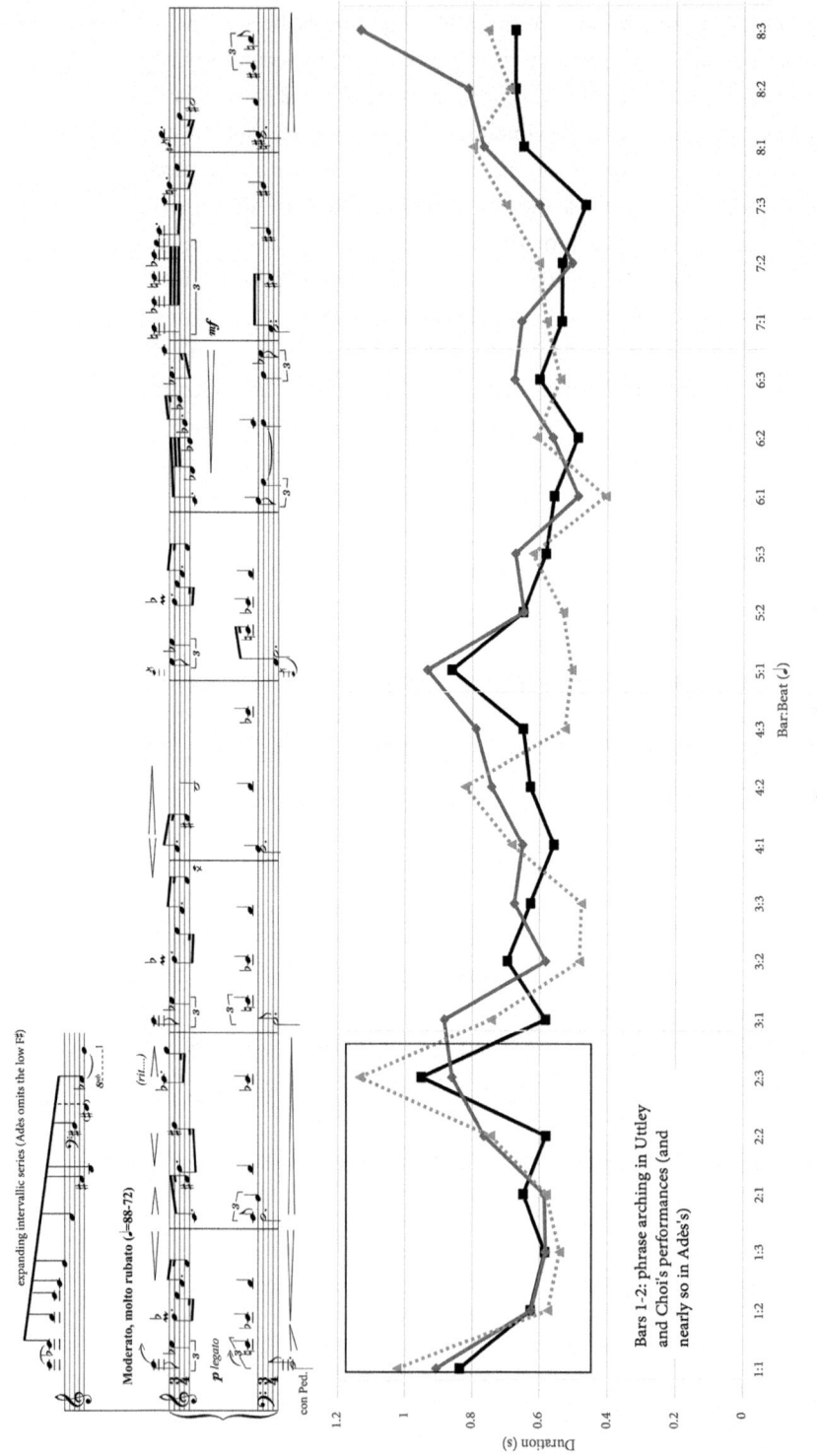

Ex. 2.2 First Mazurka, bars 1–8 and duration curves of performances

invites such a traditional performative response, we might say that expressive phrasing is *composed into* the structure.[45]

The relationship between composed structure and performance traditions is more complex in sections B and C, both of which include bars in which the prototypical mazurka four-bar, twelve-crotchet phrase is reduced progressively in length (see Fig. 2.1). Yet in performance, and especially Adès's (TAM1 00:30–01:16), such reductions are offset by rubato, whether written (bar 24; here the GFL in all performances creates a sense of expansion rather than contraction) or introduced to bring out dynamic changes (bar 37). (The acceleration into and lingering on arrival of the section boundary between bars 32 and 33 are the exception here.) Adès's modifications are such that by the end of phrase C1, the 2/4 bar has in fact roughly the same duration as the 3/4 bar in bar 35. This is not to say one necessarily *perceives* bar 40 as longer than bar 35 (I do not), but here, and in the recordings by Uttley and Choi, the performance favours a mazurka-like freedom of phrasing over strict adherence to the contractions implicit in the notation itself.[46] To put this another way, performances of the First Mazurka steer a course between fidelity to written tempo modifications and metrical changes on the one hand, and to inherited performance traditions on the other.[47]

Inflections of the underlying pulse of the Third Mazurka are most audible in bars 48–67, during which an inner voice provides a (notated) regular crotchet motion (Fig. 2.2). Even so, the performances suggest a lack of explicit mazurka rubato and local phrase arching, with GFLs restricted to the end of each phrase. The fluctuations that arise through elongation of beats, especially in Adès's and Uttley's performances, seem connected to the moment-by-moment expressive (and possibly technical) demands of the far-flung melody in the upper voice (TAM3 01:47–03:07; RUM3 01:58–03:28). In this context, the steadier tread of Choi's performance takes on a more

---

[45] The idea of tempo modifications being composed into music has been broached by Adès: 'The idea of the ritardando, the slowing down, was there in the music before [the composer] wrote the instruction.' Adès and Service, *Full of Noises*, p. 107.

[46] There are numerous accounts of Chopin's fluidity of phrasing giving the impression of a duple, rather than triple, metre in his mazurka performances.

[47] A more extended study of the performance of Adès's music than the present chapter would consider the myriad ways in which his notation implies rubato. It is there in the tempo marking (in which a deceleration is implied by placing the faster end of the tempo range first). It is also present in the parenthetical *rit.* in bar 2 of Ex. 2.2, the hairpin dynamic markings and (not shown) subsequent expression markings (*calando, rubato, cantab.*). Note, too, the curved arrows from the outer voices in bar 1 (their concluding counterparts can be found in the treble of bar 16 and bass of bar 17), encouraging the performer to consider larger-scale groupings.

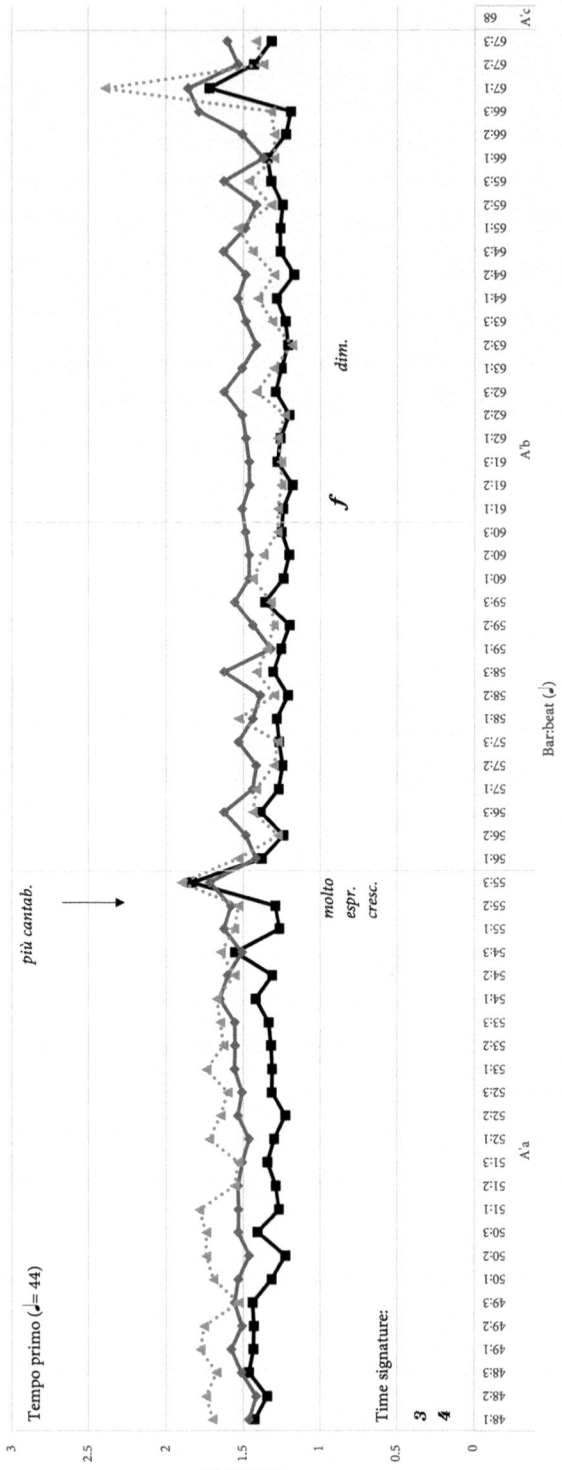

Fig. 2.2 Duration curve of performances of the Third Mazurka, bars 48–68

monumental, if not implacable, character, for he avoids marking the crescendo of bars 55–61 and diminuendo of bars 63–8 with a corresponding accelerando and decelerando (WCM3 01:52–03:23). For all that the movement borrows its air of melancholy from the mazurka genre,[48] it is the cumulative power generated from its continually spun-out intervallic cycles that Choi harnesses at the climax of his performance.[49]

On the basis of this limited sample,[50] it would appear that the closer the relationship between Adès's foreground to the mazurka topic, the greater the extent to which inherited traditions inflect performers' interpretative choices (no less in the case of Adès than other pianists). How transferable this finding is to other works with strong topical associations remains unclear: for instance, the significance of the phrase contractions found in the topical references to the tango that opens *Powder Her Face* and the electronic dance music of 'Ecstasio', the third movement of *Asyla*, lies in their audibility.[51] What the performances here suggest is that not all metric deviations in Adès's music need necessarily be heard (or understood) in the same way. It is perfectly possible to imagine a performance in which the pianist follows the notation strictly to convey the notated contraction of material.[52] Such a performance would doubtless reveal yet further interpretative potential in the tension between foreground and background that animates existing recordings.

Illuminating from Within

Darknesse Visible, like the Mazurkas, has been recorded on multiple occasions. Although the piece is a transcription of John Dowland's 'In Darknesse Let Mee Dwell' (1610), the manner of Adès's reworking largely

---

[48] Griffiths, programme notes on Thomas Adès, Mazurkas Op. 27.

[49] Here, it should also be noted that the closer placement of the microphones to the piano in Choi's recording results in a more strident character throughout his performance of the Op. 27 set than either Uttley or Adès.

[50] Space prevents a discussion of the Second Mazurka, the characteristics of which lend themselves more to an account of qualitative aspects of performance (colour, pedalling, attack) than to one of quantitative aspects (tempo fluctuations appear to be as much a consequence of negotiation of the rhythmic complexity of the A sections as they are of GFL, for instance).

[51] See John Roeder, 'Co-operating Continuities in the Music of Thomas Adès', *Music Analysis*, 25/i–ii (2006), 121–54 (pp. 133–5); and Edward Venn, *Thomas Adès: Asyla* (Abingdon: Routledge, 2017), pp. 99–109.

[52] Of the five commercially available recordings (see n. 40), Han Chen's is the closest to realising such an interpretation.

obscures its stylistic origins in the Elizabethan lute song tradition. Online Table 2.1 maps Adès's setting onto the Dowland song, demonstrating how closely Adès follows the original structure. Differences lie in the notation (Adès adopts a consistent common time throughout, in contrast to Dowland's irregular barring) and in bars 67–9, in which Adès adds four extra crotchet beats. Above all, the difference is textural: Adès describes *Darknesse Visible* as an 'explosion', in which '[p]atterns latent in the original have been isolated and regrouped, with the aim of illuminating the song from within, as if during the course of a performance'.[53]

Example 2.3 illustrates how this is achieved, moving from (a) Dowland's original; via (b) an analytical representation of Adès's isolation of voice-leading patterns (including, in small noteheads, his omissions and, in parentheses, additions – square brackets show how the additions relate to pitches in other voices); through to (c) the realisation of these patterns in the score, in which the voice and bass are distributed across many octaves.[54] The nature of the transcription thus offers two primary inter-pretative options to the performer: one, fidelity to the vocality inherent to the transcription (and hence continuity), the other, adherence to Adès's fragmented, expressionistic and discontinuous textures.

The extent to which such options are realised in performance can be discerned from Fig. 2.3, the duration chart for the performances by Adès, Choi, Andreas Haefliger and Matan Porat.[55] GFLs can be observed at the phrase boundaries at bars 18 and 54, corresponding with double bar lines in the score, and at bar 83 (the end of section C). Within these broader sections, there are local tempo fluctuations and smaller-scale GFLs through which alternative interpretations emerge. Bars 1–18 (section A) consist of three waves: an introduction (bars 1–7) with variable tempo, followed in bars 8–13 by a slightly faster and more even passage (particularly in Adès's and Choi's performances) corresponding to the first line of Dowland's text. A similarly even passage, save for the final GFL, is heard in bars 14–18

---

[53] Note to the score. One might compare this with the way in which Adès's prose analysis of 'In memoriam' seizes upon the 'latent patterns' connected to enharmony.

[54] The original score distinguished patterns by colour. Although Adès's note to the score suggests that there is no significance to the choice of colour, the original vocal line is almost exclusively represented in black.

[55] Thomas Adès (EMI Classics 5696992, 1997), Winston Choi (La Buissonne YAN005, 2015), Andreas Haefliger (Avie AV0041, 2004) and Matan Porat (Mirare MIR400, 2018). Inon Barnatan's recording (Avie AV2256, 2012) will be discussed, but has been omitted from Fig. 2.3 for reasons of clarity. Han Chen's recording (Naxos 8574109, 2020) was released too late to be incorporated into the research.

Ex. 2.3 (a) Dowland, 'In Darknesse Let Mee Dwell', bars 7–8; (b) short score showing Adès's omissions and voice leading; (c) *Darknesse Visible*, bars 14–18; (d) duration curves of performances

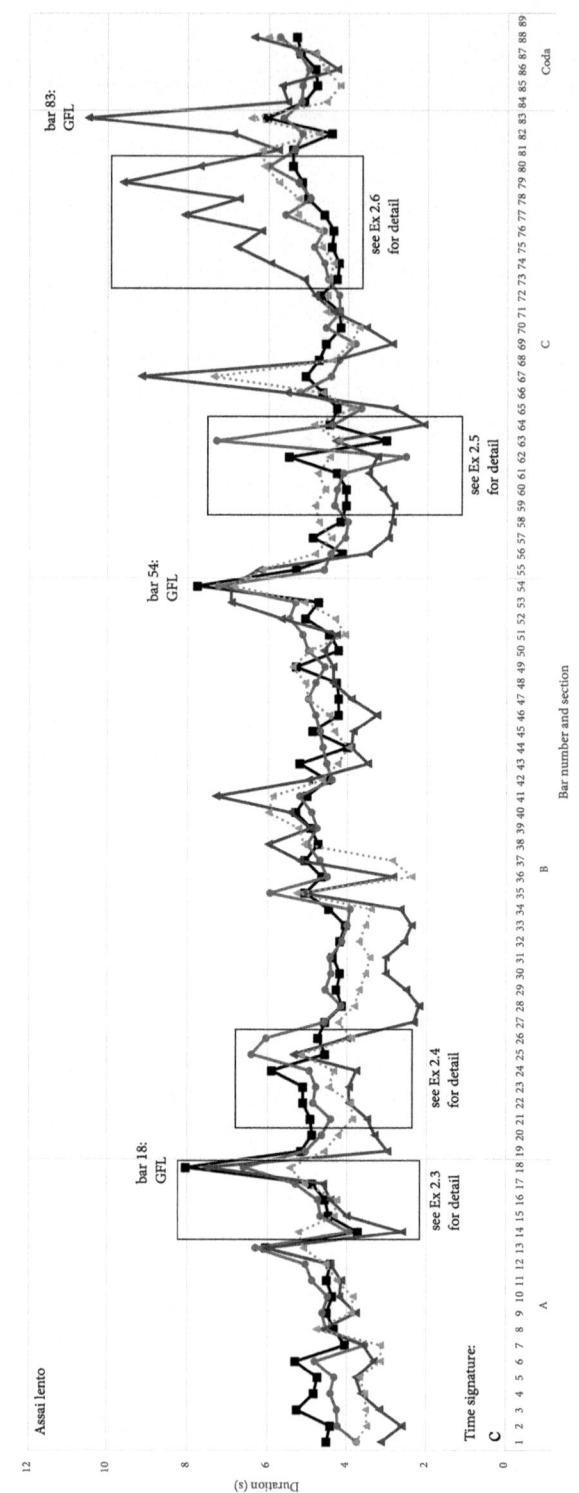

Fig. 2.3 Duration curves of performances of Adès's *Darknesse Visible*

(Ex. 2.3d).[56] If Adès's and Choi's performances in the main appear to respond to the Dowland original through their focus on the long-breathed melodic line originally given to voice, Porat and, most of all, Haefliger seem to employ tempo fluctuations within an interpretative strategy that emphasises the fractured, volatile surface.

The performance decisions apparent in section A are intensified in section B (bars 19–54): Adès and Choi maintain a comparatively steady tempo, against which the readings by Haefliger and Porat are demonstrably more unstable, emphasising surface discontinuities through extremes of tempo (as well as other features such as attack and colour). This variability is nevertheless motivated by the score, for in section B the performer is offered greater scope for how internal divisions are articulated. Bars 21–6 illustrate this clearly (Online Ex. 2.1). All of the recordings except Adès's bring out the cadence in bar 25: Inon Barnatan (IBDV 01:49–02:17), Choi (WCDV 01:36–02:02) and Haefliger (AHDV 01:21–01:42) delay the arrival of G_4 on beat 4; Porat (MPDV 01:24–01:46) delays the following downbeat (as above, each abbreviation consists of the name of the performer followed by DV for *Darknesse Visible*). But Adès does not in fact, for he lingers slightly during the previous bar (delicately placing the upper octave in the right hand) and pushes through bar 25 (TADV 01:37–02:04). As with the handling of motion between sections A and B of the First Mazurka, Adès appears to be concerned with projecting larger-scale continuities.

This is true too of Adès's realisation of sections C and A′ (bars 55–89), which in comparison to the other recordings emerge as particularly uniform in tempo. Nevertheless, all performers show some variability in the passage around bars 59–64 (Online Ex. 2.2).[57] Adès's performance (TADV 04:38–05:03) adopts a characteristically steady pulse through the first three bars, with only the slightest rubato elongating the *sforzato* accent in bar 61. He applies considerably greater rubato to the second half of the phrase (which corresponds to the vocal melody in the original), as if in response to the accentuation. At this level of the structure, Adès's tempo fluctuations appear to arise through a combination of fidelity to Dowland's vocal line and to the articulation of local textural changes. These different interpretative imperatives remain carefully balanced within the overall shape of his performance.

---

[56] Bar 14 begins with a rest, which means the placement of the bar line with *Sonic Visualiser* is open to interpretation. This may account for the perceived shorter duration of this bar in Fig. 2.3. The durations of the last minim of bar 14 and the first minim of bar 15 were divided into two to give data for Ex. 2.3d.

[57] The duration of the minims in bar 62 was determined by dividing the entire bar into two equal components.

Choi adopts a similarly measured pacing through the first three bars of Online Ex. 2.2, and he too varies the second half of the phrase for apparently expressive purpose (WCDV 04:39–05:05). But here he, of all the performers, departs most radically from Adès's precedent: where Adès presses forward, Choi lingers (and vice versa). Indeed, Choi is the only one who does not give the *sforzato* accent in the second half of bar 63 additional time. Rather, his preference appears to be to extend the 2–3 suspension on the downbeat of bar 63 and, less so, on the second minim of bar 64, suggesting that his concern is more with the projection of traditional patterns of dissonance and release than with the dramatic realisation of the expressionist overlay of *sforzato* accents that seem to be the focus of the other performers.

The closing passage (bars 73–80) in which the music dissolves into gently arcing and interlocking lines, marked *tranquillo*, offers a moving acceptance, perhaps, of Dowland's 'till death do come' (Ex. 2.4). Adès's performance of this passage is again marked by a consistent pulse (TADV

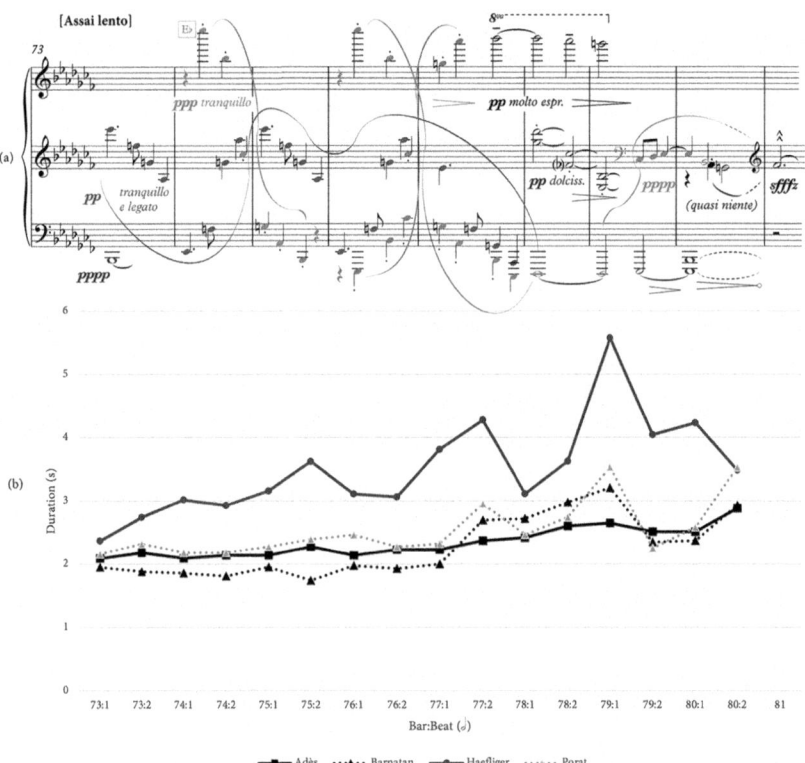

Ex. 2.4 (a) *Darknesse Visible*, bars 73–81; (b) duration curves of performances

05:39–06:17).[58] Haefliger, by contrast (AHDV 04:55–05:51), draws out bar 75 (here focussing on the pattern derived from Dowland's vocal line). A further rallentando in bar 77 (also heard in Barnatan's and Porat's performances) corresponds to the close of the varied repetition of this vocal line. Yet Haefliger introduces his largest rallentando of all, elongating the first minim of bar 79, perhaps in response to the fifths in the middle voice. This serves to fragment the continuity of the original vocal line, which in Adès's recording (and Choi's) is maintained. Taking Adès and Haefliger as the two extremes through which to hear this passage, to my ears, Adès's steady tread speaks of numbed acceptance; Haefliger's arguably more engaged response offers a more consolatory tone following the emotional turmoil of his performance.

Adès's performance, therefore, and to a greater extent Choi's, are characterised by continuity of tempo and a flexibility of phrasing that accommodates the contrasts generated by the volatile foreground. For all its textural invention, *Darknesse Visible* remains in performances such as these a transcription of a song, responding less to the detail of Adès's notation, articulation and texture than to a long-breathed sense of phrasing. This is also in line with Adès's interpretation of Janáček's 'In memoriam'. The greater variability of tempo in Haefliger's performance, as well as Porat's, corresponds to a more fragmentary approach to both phrase structure and individual events. (Barnatan's performance belongs to a middle ground between Adès and Haefliger.) There is a focus on the discontinuous rhetorical foreground of the work – one that derives from twentieth-century expressionism and heightened emotional response – rather than on the more measured, stylised emotions of the lute song in the background. In this respect, Haefliger's and Porat's recordings point to the dramatic, theatrical, almost ritualised performance practices of the twentieth century and, with it, a broadening of the expressive vistas of *Darknesse Visible*.

* * *

The performances of the Mazurkas and *Darknesse Visible* studied in this chapter, few as they are, point nevertheless to the range of interpretative possibilities that are already being brought to bear on Adès's music. A fuller account of performances of Adès's music would enrich discussions of tempo fluctuations through consideration of those parameters that are harder to capture – colour, attack, pedal and so on – as well as through study of

---

[58] Choi's performance, not included in Online Ex. 2.2, is remarkably consistent with Adès's.

performances for forces other than solo piano.[59] This chapter thus makes no attempt at comprehensiveness, but rather points to ideas and themes to be developed in Adès studies in the future. While Adès's own performances will inevitably – as here – remain a point of focus in the reception of his music, it is notable not only that there are divergences from his own readings but that these divergences are musically compelling in their own right. This indicates the interpretive richness of his music, already a common theme in analytical writings about Adès but one considerably less prevalent in writings about performances of his work. Given that Adès's music benefits from repeat performances around the world and, increasingly, multiple different recordings of individual works, critical evaluation of the interpretations brought to bear on these pieces is surely long overdue.

Perhaps the most obvious route into such an evaluation is to consider the extent to which performers negotiate the relationship between continuity and discontinuity in Adès's music. Both the First Mazurka and *Darknesse Visible* offer compelling examples of how a strongly sectional musical surface might conflict with the global demands of extended musical structures. This is not news to analysts (or many listeners, I suspect), but the solutions performers bring to the problem of reconcile these conflicting impulses are not necessarily those that analysts routinely consider. What is at stake in performances, I would argue, is the *experience* of temporality. Although it is perfectly feasible to generate momentum through the juxtaposition of contrasting materials (as in the mosaic forms of, say, Stravinsky or Tippett, or in the succession of 'frozen moments' in Janáček's *In the Mists*), it is clear that Adès is aiming for something different in his recording of the First Mazurka, in which his large-scale tempo choices results in a performance that fuse the individual sections together into a single energetic shape. In a work such as *Darknesse Visible*, the decision whether to foreground continuity or discontinuity can give rise to competing, but complementary, interpretations of its structure. Here, and in the play of topical reference in the Mazurkas, the expressive surface has a pivotal role in how structures emerge in real time. Adès frequently invokes the metaphor of a journey in descriptions of his music; performances of his music remind us that we might attend not just to the space that is traversed, but to the qualitative nature of the time passed in doing so.

---

[59] It is possible that the intricacies of Adès's rhythmic and metrical writing might constrain the degree to which performances of works for ensemble exhibit the same specialised control of rubato found in the works considered in this chapter. (This is, perhaps, true for comparisons between performances of solo and ensemble music of any composer.) I would argue nevertheless that my claims of what performances can bring to our understanding of Adès's music hold for all of his works.

Appendix

Initial research for this chapter was made possible thanks to the award of a Laidlaw Undergraduate Research and Leadership Scholarship to Henry Weekes. Performance data for this chapter were generated using *Sonic Visualiser*.[60] Original stereo recordings were reduced to monophonic files, and note onsets calculated using the '$_{Mz}$Attack' plugin developed by the CHARM Mazurka Project.[61] Results were confirmed and refined using visual analysis of the spectrograms of the recordings along with repeated listening (using the 'Time Instants Layer' and the audible clicks this provides); in the case of the recordings of the Mazurkas and *Darknesse Visible*, this involved multiple checks by both Henry Weekes and Edward Venn over a number of iterations in order to reduce error.[62] The onsets of spread chords were typically taken from the bass note unless musical context clearly projected the bass as an anticipation.

Note onsets were labelled in a variety of ways. In the case of the First Mazurka, it was possible to capture individual beats (in the case of irregular time signatures such as 5/8 the preference was to label dotted crotchets rather than crotchets). In the Third Mazurka, the lack of rhythmic information in the opening nineteen bars meant that data were captured at the level of the bar; more nuanced information at the level of the beat was additionally recorded for bars 48–67. In the case of *Darknesse Visible*, each attack was recorded as an 'event';[63] where events fell on regular beats it was possible to also generate data for bars and beats.

Dynamic information was captured using the '$_{Mz}$PowerCurve' plugin of the Mazurka Project. It was found that Adès's use of extremes of register and (particularly in *Darknesse Visible*) accentuation generated complex data in which the boundaries between constraints of the instrument and performative interpretation were hard to discern. For the purposes of the present chapter, and its focus on tempo, dynamics were thus omitted from the discussion.

---

[60] See www.sonicvisualiser.org.   [61] www.mazurka.org.uk/software/sv/plugin/.

[62] Errors of measurement by a few milliseconds each way are always likely; see Ohriner, 'Grouping Hierarchy and Trajectories of Pacing', §19; and Cook, *Beyond the Score*, pp. 145–6.

[63] See Nicholas Cook, 'Inventing Tradition: Webern's Piano Variations in Early Recordings', *Music Analysis*, 36/ii (2017), 163–215 (p. 165).

3 | 'Fountain of Youth', 'River of Meaning'

Aesthetics of the Superficial in Powder Her Face

NICHOLAS DAVID STEVENS

In a 2017 interview, Thomas Adès referred to his chamber opera *Powder Her Face* (1995) as his 'fountain of youth piece': a source of musical vitality to which he has often returned.[1] Although the label reveals much about Adès and his work, it also hints at the opera's complex reception history. Controversial for its sordid stage action,[2] it springs eternal as a font of alluring musical material among audiences, performers and presenting institutions, having yielded multiple commissioned instrumental adaptations for piano and for orchestra.[3] However, *Powder Her Face* also stands as a source of renewal for Adès in a less literal sense: as the point at which a distinct assemblage of sensibilities, compositional procedures and sociopolitical implications first surfaced in his art in a coherent form. Since then articulated in interviews and writings by the composer and evident in his subsequent works, this Adèsian aesthetic hinges on a guiding metaphor of surface and depth.

In diving for the musical and dramatic foundations of Adès's first evening-length work, I revisit established lines of enquiry into his historical (self-)consciousness and frequent reworking of pre-existing music, whether his own or that of others. Edward Venn summarises Adès's career in terms of consistent preoccupations that sink beneath perception or rise to audibility depending on the work in question: 'a continuous shuffling and reconfiguration'.[4] Drew Massey sees the tension between the retrospective, reiterative tendencies of Adès's work and his drive to create anew in a singular idiom as but one manifestation of a broader imperative to aporia, dialectical working-out of material and self-contradiction.[5] The composer's

---

[1] 'Thomas Adès in Conversation with Drew Massey', presentation at 'Be not Afeard: Language, Music and Cultural Memory in the Operas of Thomas Adès', Senate House, University of London, 25 April 2017, video available at YouTube, www.youtube.com/watch?v=Ng5jIUtiLZk.

[2] See Emma Gallon, 'Narrativities in the Music of Thomas Adès' (unpublished PhD dissertation, Lancaster University, 2011), pp. 208–9.

[3] These arrangements include a *Concert Paraphrase* for piano (2009; rearranged for two pianos in 2015) and numerous suites for orchestra (2007–18).

[4] Edward Venn, *Thomas Adès*: Asyla (Abingdon: Routledge, 2017), p. 163.

[5] Drew Massey, *Thomas Adès in Five Essays* (New York: Oxford University Press, 2021), pp. 4–5.

shuttling between the visionary and revisionist, Massey argues, corresponds with such likewise Adèsian oscillations as those between referential excess and rigorous process; modernist and postmodern treatment of musical material; and objectivity and subjectivity of perspective.

Construing Adès's 'fountain of youth' as a site of artistic origins and periodic pilgrimage, at once manifesto and microcosm, I read it as the work in which he first pursues this dialectical approach at length, setting the stage for a career in which the themes and procedures evident in *Powder Her Face* resurface time and again. Musical *surface*, Adès's own preferred term for such categories as *style*, *genre* and *topic*, operates in tension with underlying meanings, termed *depth*, the 'cellular level', or other metaphors of the hidden yet determinative.

The metaphor of surface and depth helps explain not just the opera's plot and characters, but also the nature of Adès's music. Musical allusions and jokes; chameleonic timbres and textures; and lewd onomatopoeias jostle for listener attention as harmonic, thematic-motivic and formal processes push the protagonist towards a final crisis. The surface/depth metaphor pervades Adès's descriptions of his and others' music, from apologias for Berg, Stravinsky and Janáček to the 'fountain' image itself, which implies periodic immersion in and resurfacing from this early grand-scale reservoir of ideas. An opera critiqued for *having* a quality – superficiality – in fact thematises and, in the end, exterminates it, opening the door to subsequent decades' worth of operatic variations on the same dialectic: on and off the island, trapped in and free beyond the parlour. Twenty years after his first opera's premiere, Adès mixed three metaphors in describing the process of composing his third, *The Exterminating Angel*:

It's rather like watching an embryo develop . . . you might understand the DNA of this tiny cell later on and see how it relates to everything else. Rather the larger structure eventually develops from trying to link these cells together. My image of music as a natural process, as a living, growing organism, is a fairly precise analogy of an opera and the way in which it is created.

. . . [T]he movements of this underground river [of meaning] are so complicated from line to line. . . . You need to have a strong sense of the overall architecture in order to find the specific character of the music.[6]

---

[6] Christian Arseni, "'Why do we ever do anything?" Thomas Adès and Tom Cairns Talk about *The Exterminating Angel*', in *The Exterminating Angel* programme booklet, Salzburger Festspiele, 22 July–31 August 2016, pp. 46–57 (pp. 47–8).

Architecture, organic growth via cell division, underground rivers of meaning: as in interviews with Adès before and since, gluts of evocation belie a recurring if ever-reformulated theme of underlying essence and mysterious interrelation going mostly unheard under audible and visible manifestations of musical-dramatic 'character'. Adès's dialectic animates (or flows through, or undergirds) operatic black comedies of the privileged, complicit and doomed twenty years apart, an indication of consistent aesthetic priorities just, as it were, beneath the surface.

Below, I explore Adèsian metaphors of surface and depth in four crucial passages of *Powder Her Face*. In Act I, Scene 1, the framing of stage action and music as camp parody at once establishes a mood of frivolity and sets the stage for a portrait of virtuosic self-deception: triumphs of false surface over inherent truth.[7] Styles of music historically denigrated as superficial provide character exposition from without and within the protagonist's mind. Scenes 3 and 5, the only stretches of the opera in which the main character never appears, introduce the perennial Adèsian theme of class conflict – workers' resentment of the superficial upper crust – as the composer alludes once in each scene to the same richly connotative dance topic, the waltz, in tellingly divergent ways. Scene 8 finds Adès fulfilling imperatives to musical organicism and teleological inexorability, ideals rooted in the same nineteenth-century Germanic soil as musical metaphors of depth, as Holly Watkins has argued.[8] Camp, the queer sensibility that exaggerates and parodies surface features to call attention to hidden truths, persists as a corollary of the surface/depth dialectic throughout the action. In the score, ironies, allusions, topical gestures, puns and parodies float atop an ineluctable process of decay.

In examining camp and class-consciousness through dance topoi and morbidity through musical allusion and organicism, I propose not a rigid grid of drama–music relationships so much as a pool of ideas fed by a common, distinctly queer preoccupation with the divisibility of outer from inner life. Even the opera's title plays on the metaphor of stratification. The directive 'powder her face' calls for the spread of superficies over skin, a surface-level rejuvenation of one who remains mortal – no true fountain of youth. However, the phrase, like others in Philip Hensher's libretto, also

---

[7] Scene numbers in *Powder Her Face* are continuous between Acts. Scenes 1–5 are thus in Act I, and Scenes 6–8 in Act II.

[8] See Holly Watkins, *Metaphors of Depth in German Musical Thought: From E. T. A. Hoffman to Arnold Schoenberg* (Cambridge: Cambridge University Press, 2011), pp. 44–50.

recalls Webster's *The Duchess of Malfi*.[9] Having had that play's title character murdered, her brother Ferdinand commands her assassin: 'Cover her face; mine eyes dazzle: she died young.'[10] As in *Powder Her Face*, a comic opening belies a duchess's grim fate. Planting jokes at their protagonist's expense in the title – she will *not* die young, for one – Adès and Hensher present a three-word key to their aesthetic gambit, in which parodic insouciance thinly veils existential anguish.

'Gratuitousness': Tango as Drag (as Doppelgänger)

In Polari, a cant of social marginality in early twentieth-century Britain – of entertainers, sailors and, in particular, queer communities – 'Duchess' can refer to a wealthy, or at least grand-acting, gay man.[11] Whether Hensher and Adès knew of the obscure double entendre embedded in their protagonist's monym or not, the resonance rings true: according to their vision as preserved in the score, at Scene 1, bar 114, audiences first see her furs and wig on 'a very tall black [*sic*] man – as Duchess in a *very camp* Statue of Liberty pose'. Her story first unfolds in his tenor voice. Beneath this conflation of the Duchess with a hotel Electrician runs a subtler connection to queer aesthetics: the opera's irreverence towards stable identity and musical respectability, in other words its camp approach to characters and their music. In Scene 1 and beyond, Adès blurs the lines separating people in the Duchess's life and presents both dignified and seamy sides of a cultural object – the tango – long associated with superficiality and sexuality. Tango becomes the Duchess's identity and life story in sound, hers to lose and her tormentors' to steal.

In an overture, eight scenes and a 'Ghost Epilogue', *Powder Her Face* follows the British social climber as she marries a Duke, emerges disgraced from a divorce trial that publicises her adulteries and falls into isolation and debt over subsequent decades. Hensher's libretto never identifies 'the Duchess' by name, but he and Adès acknowledge the fictionalised figure's basis in the life of Margaret, Duchess of Argyll, the twentieth-century aristocrat hauled over the coals in tabloids in the 1960s. Her death, and

---

[9] See Claire Seymour, '*Powder Her Face*, ENO', *Opera Today*, 8 April 2014, www.operatoday .com/content/2014/04/powder_her_face.php.

[10] John Webster, *The Duchess of Malfi*, ed. by Brian Gibbons, 5th ed. (London: Methuen Drama, 2014), p. 106.

[11] See Paul Baker, *Fantabulosa: Dictionary of Polari and Gay Slang* (London: Continuum, 2002), p. 26.

the publication of the obituaries and interviews that would inform Hensher's writing process, preceded their labours by mere months.[12] The opera ends in Scene 8 when and where it began in Scene 1: in the London hotel suite – 'fabulously hideous', as the stage direction at bar 114 elaborates, per camp's preoccupation with extravagance rendered tasteless amid decay – that the elderly Duchess rents as her home, at the hour in 1990 when the Hotel Manager evicts her for unpaid bills. The Maid and Electrician, present from the start and like their supervisor recast as figures from her memory in each of six flashback scenes, mock her before they sing. Behind each of the opera's distinguishing dramatic peculiarities – its refusal to assign anyone other than the Duchess a singular stable guise, its doubling of her through drag impersonation in Scene 1, its savouring of gaudiness and undertow of sombre fate – lie camp impulses. What Polari does for language and drag accomplishes in attire, camp does through (re)mediation of cultural objects: surfaces mask unspeakable depths.

As a noun, 'camp' refers to self-conscious, referential, over-the-top theatricality; as a verb it refers to behaviours of the stereotypical 'Queen', as Richard Dyer writes.[13] As an adjective, the form that – tellingly – appears in the opera's first stage direction, it can index either or both. As Christopher Moore and Philip Purvis phrase the customary hedge of writers assaying the noun's meaning, camp-as-sensibility remains 'notoriously hard-to-define and ever-evolving'.[14] Susan Sontag, whose 'Notes on "Camp"' remains an unavoidable scholarly touchstone, denied queer ownership of the concept while also, as Ann Pellegrini writes, subtly acknowledging the roots of its affective contradictions in the death-haunted humour of twentieth-century gay communities.[15]

Powder Her Face opens with laughter at the Duchess's expense and depicts characters mocking, denouncing and dismissing her for six

---

[12] Her words appear, rephrased and overlaid with interviewer commentary, in Charles Castle, *The Duchess Who Dared: The Life of Margaret, Duchess of Argyll* (London: Sidgwick & Jackson, 1994). Hensher also consulted Margaret Campbell, Duchess of Argyll, *Forget Not: The Autobiography of Margaret, Duchess of Argyll* (London: W. H. Allen, 1975).

[13] Richard Dyer, 'It's Being So Camp as Keeps Us Going', in *Camp: Queer Aesthetics and the Performing Subject: A Reader*, ed. by Fabio Cleto (Ann Arbor: University of Michigan Press, 1999), pp. 110–14 (pp. 112–13).

[14] Christopher Moore and Philip Purvis, 'Introduction', in *Music & Camp*, ed. by Christopher Moore and Philip Purvis (Middletown, CT: Wesleyan University Press, 2018), pp. ix–xvi (p. ix).

[15] Susan Sontag, 'Notes on "Camp"', in *Against Interpretation: And Other Essays* (New York: Farrar, Straus and Giroux, 1966), pp. 275–92; and Ann Pellegrini, 'After Sontag: Future Notes on Camp', in *A Companion to Lesbian, Gay, Bisexual, Transgender, and Queer Studies*, ed. by George E. Haggerty and Molly McGarry (Malden, MA: Blackwell, 2007), pp. 168–93.

intervening scenes. Does this pillory of a dead woman remain shallow or, as Richard Taruskin writes, achieve ethical depth when, in Scene 8, it 'turns around and honors her'?[16] For those attuned to camp's distortions of affect and identity, this question makes little sense: the latter and former effects are coterminous and inextricable. In Scene 1, the sound of camp's surface/ depth polarity is the sound of a single tune issuing from two different claimants of the Duchess's identity, to divergent ends.

Seldom have opera companies and directors followed Hensher's stage direction calling for the Electrician's 'very camp Statue of Liberty pose', which hints at the real Duchess of Argyll's New York upbringing.[17] Yet her operatic avatar's taste for transatlantic entertainments of the jazz age becomes clear in the overture, which paraphrases the instrumental introduction to Carlos Gardel's tango 'Cuesta abajo'. The tango's original lyrics lament 'baleful destiny', 'sliding downward', loss, shame and the pain of losing the past – in short, the Duchess's fate. Hilarity nonetheless lingers into Scene 1 as sung laughter picks up where orchestral guffaws leave off.

The Electrician-as-Duchess sings a first-person account of her bygone beauty, fame and wealth to one of the opera's quasi-pop tunes, a second tango melody grounded in B minor. The Duchess will sing the same melody later, at which point the audience learns that the burlesque was accurate: he sings *her* song, in words barely less self-centred and grandiose than her own. However, notated performance instructions, as well as vocal pitch and timbre, mark the Electrician's version as queer parody and the Duchess's as sincere. Where her rendition floats among harp arpeggios at the top of the treble stave, his veers from 'innocent' serenity to 'sudden vulgarity' (see Online Ex. 3.1a and b).

The Duchess's minor-mode tango melody turns out to be the B side to another popular song about her, set in the relative major D. After his narration of the Duchess's fame and fall to the tango tune, the Electrician moves on to a crass contrafact of this love ballad in bars 211–36, which audiences later hear in full in bars 171–304 of Scene 2, set in 1934. Both songs share traces of what Emma Gallon identifies as the opera's 'Duchess theme', a series of falling sixths, as well as melodic and harmonic contours

---

[16] Richard Taruskin, 'A Surrealist Composer Comes to the Rescue of Modernism', *New York Times*, 5 December 1999; reprinted with a postscript in *The Danger of Music and Other Anti-utopian Essays* (Berkeley and Los Angeles: University of California Press, 2009), pp. 144–52 (p. 145).

[17] See Castle, *The Duchess Who Dared*, pp. 7–10.

determined by Adès's signature aligned interval cycles.[18] Already freighted with the genre's connotations of sexuality, the B minor tango of *Powder Her Face* becomes a theme of memory, (auto)biographical recounting and an impossible future.[19] Both songs serve character exposition and act as portals to her memory, but their precise functions differ: the D major ballad resembles her treasured photo albums, the tango tune her aggrieved attempts to explain herself in old age. The Electrician corrupts both songs before the Duchess can sing either herself, thus allegorising the process by which her infamy spread.

That *Powder Her Face*'s contrasting pop songs arise from related motivic and harmonic materials while serving divergent narrative functions is unsurprising, given the composer's ideas on the relationship between sonic surface and underlying concept. In Adès's analysis, an allusion to Stravinsky's *The Rake's Progress* later in this opera emerges like 'a skin on the milk', and the former opera itself resembles a crab always shedding one shell – an outer surface – for new ones. He dismisses the notion of style as a 'mirage', counter-proposing: 'I'm ... fascinated with surface, the play of surfaces.' Comments ensue on topoi and the 'struggle between ... topos, or genre, and some logic in the [musical] material', or in other terms, musical surface and depth:

Even nakedness, 'no style', is a form of clothing, of drag, in that sense ... if the composer has properly heard beneath these surfaces, you are not really conscious of them ... what I hope to do is make what's underneath the surface clearer, by making it honestly unignorable [*sic*] that the surface is just that – transparent, evanescent ... that may actually involve some things from the dressing-up box.[20]

Before this passage and shortly after discussing the inevitability of *Powder Her Face*'s ending – a quasi-death scene followed by yet another tango sequence – Adès names tango first in a list of 'light music' with a 'dark side': 'enjoyment of those [genres] comes from the sense that you are one step ahead of a great black beast'.[21] In both the overture and Scene 1,

---

[18] Gallon, 'Narrativities', p. 222. On aligned cycles in Adès's music, see Philip Stoecker, 'Aligned Cycles in Thomas Adès's Piano Quintet', *Music Analysis*, 33/i (2014), 32–64. On their use in *Powder Her Face*, see Kyle Shaw, 'Promiscuity, Fetishes, and Irrational Functionality in Thomas Adès's *Powder Her Face*' (unpublished PhD dissertation, University of Illinois at Urbana-Champaign, 2018), pp. 42–72, 92–117.

[19] On the tango, sexuality and scandalousness, see Gallon, 'Narrativities', pp. 218–26.

[20] Thomas Adès and Tom Service, *Thomas Adès: Full of Noises – Conversations with Tom Service*, paperback ed. (London: Faber and Faber, 2018), pp. 79–80.

[21] Ibid., p. 64.

then, the sonic drag of tango dresses up the Duchess's situation without concealing its direness.

That tango would intimate dark fate behind a facade of fun was likewise not a shocking choice for Adès at this point in his career. Before *Powder Her Face*, his *Chamber Symphony* (1990) and *Arcadiana* (1994) figured in a glowing early reception. Alluding to Mozart, Elgar, Schubert and more in the latter, he makes an exception to the general rule of borrowing from the Classical and Romantic canon: the movement 'Et. . . (tango mortale)', its title half a riff on a Poussin painting featuring the epitaph *Et in Arcadia ego*, half a dance designation. A tango figure lurches through the early pages of the *Chamber Symphony* as well, yet it soon becomes one thread in a tapestry of eclectic quotations and topoi. As Alastair Williams contends, Adès's juxtaposition of diverse influences within a personal compositional system distinguishes him as neither a high modernist nor a postmodern *pasticheur*, but a reconciler and rejecter of such categories – or, as Massey has posited, a metamodernist who moves between and beyond them.[22]

In Scene 1, Adès takes the 'lightness' of tango as a musical analogue to the Electrician's costume. In both instances, the tenor 'wears' the Duchess's identity. Yet the audience will not receive the punchline of the drag performance and its tango scoring until this moment in 1990 resumes in the opera's final scene: unbeknown to viewers, the staff laughed at the Duchess knowing that their Manager was on his way to put her out. 'Are you checking out *today*, Madame' the Maid taunts (Scene 1, bars 279–87), emboldened by secret knowledge – a consistent trait across the high soprano's characters. The Electrician's parody is a penultimate indignity masquerading as a lark; he becomes her Doppelgänger, a portentous ghost ahead of its time. The tango becomes a *Totentanz* in hindsight. Twenty years later, Adès would title an entire symphony-cantata with that Teutonic moniker, once again emphasising a recurring message that no one, whatever their social status, escapes death – the same 'underground river of meaning' as in *Powder Her Face*, initially clad in the carnivalesque drag of mere fun.

The appearance of a drag Doppelgänger for the Duchess, evocative of Romantic gloom, also leads back to camp. Massey has posited the surreal, the Freudian uncanny and the queer as overlapping aesthetic influences on

---

[22] Alastair Williams, 'Between Modernism and Postmodernism: Structure and Expression in John Adams, Kaija Saariaho and Thomas Adès', in *The Routledge Research Companion to Modernism in Music*, ed. by Björn Heile and Charles Wilson (New York: Routledge, 2019), pp. 327–52; and Massey, *Thomas Adès in Five Essays*, pp. 4–5.

Powder Her Face: all help to explain its character doublings, subversions of gender and inversions of social hierarchy. When Massey writes of queer aesthetic calling cards in the opera, he includes aspects identifiable as camp. Adès himself named *Powder Her Face* when answering interview questions about a 'gay aesthetic' in his oeuvre.[23] As the opera's co-creators worked towards a queer approach to writing music theatre in the early 1990s, such slippage between labels of sexuality, aesthetics and sensibility pervaded attempts to update definitions of camp, yet the fundamental tactic of destabilising identity remained consistent. In the 1994 volume *The Politics and Poetics of Camp*, Moe Meyer defines camp simply as 'queer parody'. Rejecting Sontag's view of the sensibility as an apolitical aesthetics-without-ethics, he expands: '*Camp* embodies a specifically *queer* cultural critique. . . . What "*queer*" signals is an ontological challenge that displaces bourgeois notions of the Self as unique, abiding, and continuous while substituting instead a concept of the Self as performative, improvisational, [and] discontinuous.'[24]

Multiple instances of the identity flux that Meyer describes appear in *Powder Her Face*, beyond the doubling of the Duchess. The identities of the other singers fluctuate, each switching between occupations and relationships to her from one scene to the next. At the start of Act II, the bass who plays the Judge in the Duchess's divorce trial enters (Scene 6, bar 112) still costumed as the Duke from Act I, only then donning regalia *in front of the audience* – literally pulling an identity out of a dressing-up box. He thus reveals this new persona as a surface, even as the truth of the Judge's connection to the Duke – both are agents of patriarchal domination over the Duchess – becomes plain. Adès's elision and conflation of characters, a move noted in contemporaneous works of queer theory as camp's weapon against straight upper- and middle-class individual autonomy, begins with drag parody, an appropriation of the Duchess's tango as sonic identity. Musical style, then, is akin to identity in this opera: mirages alike, illusory surfaces concealing deeper continuities. The Duke and Judge are costumes, the patriarchy real; as I argue below, their shared harmonic tendencies likewise contradict surface differences while indexing their profound sameness as musical agents.

---

[23] Peter Culshaw, 'Don't Call Me a Messiah', *Daily Telegraph*, 1 March 2007, features section, p. 33.

[24] Emphasis mine. Moe Meyer, 'Introduction: Reclaiming the Discourse of Camp', in *The Politics and Poetics of Camp*, ed. by Moe Meyer (Abingdon: Routledge, 1994), pp. 1–22 (pp. 1–3).

In the same 1994 volume, Chuck Kleinhans speaks to another camp element evident in *Powder Her Face*: what Adès terms 'gratuitousness'. Kleinhans defines camp anew: 'an ironic and parodic appreciation of an extravagant form that is out of proportion to its content, especially when that content is banal or trivial'.[25] In works of intentional camp, authors revel in bad taste while demonstrating awareness of the material's lack of artistic or cultural import.[26] Dyer affirms Kleinhans's emphasis on form/surface over content/depth as the defining polarity of camp, the source of its power to reveal traditional values and hierarchies as Potemkin facades: 'a way of prising the form of something away from its content, of revelling in the style while dismissing the content as trivial'.[27] For comparison, Adès on the Duchess:

Her structure of denial, the lie that she has constructed, begins to fall apart during the course of the evening. The opera is a cumbersome way of conveying that, but *the extravagance is the point*. I think at that time I was fascinated by the gratuitousness of music. In that sense it's like scent, like somebody's perfume, as in the libretto at the beginning of the opera.[28]

A drag takedown of an aristocrat's self-praise allows the co-creators to deflate the innate grandeur of operatic utterance. Tango is the musical vehicle of this parody, first heard in the 'Cuesta abajo' allusion in the overture and continuing throughout much of Scene 1: the Electrician's 'vulgarity', camp exaggeration of the Duchess's real tendencies and queer appropriation of her identity unfold along its rhythmic grid and melodic contours. However, it does not retain this function. The tune returns transfigured in bars 345–401 of the scene, wrenched back into service of the Duchess's delusions. Adès explains the moment as 'my "Ode to *Joy*", here the Duchess's perfume, *Joy* by Patou'.[29] As she praises her scent ('which outlasts fashion and outlasts time, and lasts for ever') the harpist plays arpeggios behind the motivic falling sixths, visions of a future identical to the past traced overhead as the Duchess sings of herself as 'heaven'. The Duchess here initiates the transition from the 1990 of Scene 1 to Scenes 2–7's farragoes of memory and fantasy.

In restoring the tango tune to its rightful owner, Adès retains its superficiality. Yet with its camp parodic function stripped away, it instead

---

[25] Chuck Kleinhans, 'Taking Out the Trash: Camp and the Politics of Parody', in *The Politics and Poetics of Camp*, ed. by Moe Meyer (Abingdon: Routledge, 1994), pp. 182–201 (pp. 185–6).

[26] Ibid., pp. 182–3.   [27] Dyer, 'It's Being So Camp', p. 113.

[28] Adès and Service, *Full of Noises*, p. 61.

[29] Adès, programme notes on *Concert Paraphrase on* Powder Her Face, 2009, www.fabermusic .com/music/concert-paraphrase-on-powder-her-face-5420.

serves her self-deception, fantasies as illusory as the Electrician's impersonation. The audience knows how wrong time will prove her, and the passage thus calls attention to the 'great black beast' haunting her (and, according to Adès, all) tango: death. Meyer writes: 'Camp encodes the unmasking of the ideological illusion ... the lie that tells the truth. Peer beneath the surface and all you find is another surface.'[30] Adès removes the surface of camp parody only to reveal another fabrication set to the same tune. What both lies cover over, and thus paradoxically betray, is the real reason why the hotel staff despise and mock the Duchess, the same thing that sustains her belief in eternal life and luxury: her social class.

Eating (with) the Rich, Waltzing through a (Class) War

Scenes 3 and 5 do not include the Duchess. However, they lay bare the social and interpersonal dynamics that bring about her demise: a series of hierarchies pitting working-class against luxury-class characters, and everyone against powerful women. Appropriating a dance type associated with wealth, Adès plays with a topic to which, as Yayoi Uno Everett writes, he would return at length twenty years later in *The Exterminating Angel*, to similar ends: the waltz.

Powder Her Face integrates many formal schemata: the rhyming binary of the Duchess's double silencing, once by oral sex and later by death; a teleological drive towards oblivion that stretches from first to final bar; and a palindromic arch to match the Duchess's rise and fall. The overture and 'Ghost Epilogue' find the Maid and Electrician alone together in the hotel room, and Scenes 1 and 8 present halves of the Duchess's final crisis in 1990. Scenes 2 and 7 depict her as oblivious yet ever surrounded by more knowing characters played by the tenor and coloratura soprano, while Scenes 3 and 6 feature the singers of highest and lowest Fach commenting on a wedding and a divorce, respectively. Scenes 4 and 5, the only pair set in the same year, offer the closest correspondence, as each half of the Ducal couple meets someone for extramarital sex.

Throughout Scene 5, the Duke and his Mistress, played by the high soprano, repeatedly return to an E major waltz melody. Despite its clear topical referent, the tune never unfolds over the customary om-pah-pah waltz accompaniment pattern, and at points lapses into duple metre.

---

[30] Moe Meyer, 'Under the Sign of Wilde: An Archaeology of Posing', in *The Politics and Poetics of Camp*, ed. by Moe Meyer (Abingdon: Routledge, 1994), pp. 75–109 (p. 105).

A darkly post-Romantic association of the dance type arises when the Mistress launches a flight of coloratura on the word 'war'. As she speculates about how global conflicts affected the high-society party scene, the Duke – who fought in one – cuts her off at bar 77, his message set in relief by a violent Bartók pizzicato: '*I remember it*'.

The interrupted waltz renders audible the power dynamics that converge to bring down the Duchess. The Duke trusts his wife, but the Mistress teases her knowledge of the Duchess's affairs in an attempt at marital sabotage, just as the same singer hinted at her foreknowledge of the eviction as the Maid in Scene 1. The Mistress triumphs when the Duke finds incriminating photographs of his wife, but only after confronting his anger and dismissal along the way. He cuts her off, orders her to pour him champagne and barks at her to speak English after slipping into French himself, treating her as plaything and servant. Yet he is also old, drunk and oblivious. The Mistress has the upper hand when it comes to sex and secrets.

Among the affordances created by *Powder Her Face*'s multiple casting of singers for each part other than the Duchess's, the ability of Adès and Hensher to toy with narrative, social, sexual and political agencies across shifting grids of privilege and power helps give the opera's critique of aristocratic dissipation coherence and force. Much as tango's lightness indexes the dark implications of Scene 1, the waltz melody in Scene 5 drapes the Duke and Mistress's games of domination and submission – depicted as literal sexual bondage and role play in the televised and video-recorded 1999 production by David Alden – in a threadbare cover of pleasantries and romance.[31] The underlying transactional and dysfunctional aspects of their affair become more, not less, apparent through its soaring sentimentality.

If Scene 5 offers only the melody of a waltz without the bass pattern, then Scene 3 presents the latter element in grotesque inversion. Looking up and out at the excesses of the aristocracy from behind the scenes of the Duke and Duchess's wedding, a Waitress sings in groups of two and four, never matching the rhythms of wealth (Ex. 3.1a), as the orchestra loops a motive that, pitched down and in retrograde, would resemble a conventional waltz accompaniment (Ex. 3.1b). Without workers like her, Adès suggests, the foundation of the aristocracy's luxuries would fall away.

---

[31] Thomas Adès, *Powder Her Face*; directed for stage by David Alden, directed for television by Margaret Williams (Channel Four Television Corporation, 1999); released on DVD (Digital Classics DC 10002, 2005).

Ex. 3.1 (a) *Powder Her Face*, Act I, Scene 3, bars 1–3; (b) waltz figuration with hypothetical inversion and transposition

Beyond their shared musical topic, the waltz, gustatory preoccupations link Scenes 3 and 5: the champagne of the latter, coyly withheld by the Mistress, recalls the incredulous Waitress's dumping of an entire bottle over an overwhelmed glass in the former. The material abundance of the wealthy, mutually constituted by those who enjoy it and those who prepare it, assumes scenic form as champagne, banquets under aspic and casually devoured lobster, and musical form as a waltz, split across scenes and into bass and melodic superstructure. The shared message of these waltzes is that the waste and decadence of the early twentieth-century peerage were its undoing. Yet beneath the class resentments of Scenes 3 and 5 and the camp humiliation of the Duchess in Scene 1 runs a deeper, more powerful force, which is surfaced in Scene 8: death itself.

Cradle to Grave: Metaphors to Die By

After the Duchess abandons her hotel suite in Scene 8, the Maid and Electrician do another tango in her bedroom. Their dance on the grave of a necrotic aristocracy ends with a terminal gurgle of B flat minor in piano, low brass, and bass and contrabass clarinets. As the critic Alex Ross notes, this B flat minor triad functions throughout the score as the emissary of the men who torment the Duchess: 'when her bright harmony lurches down to a terrifying B♭ minor, [Adès] exposes the male cruelty that quickened her fall'.[32] The 'Ghost Epilogue' to the opera in which this sonority triumphs consists of a tango, which paraphrases both the overture and the Duchess's melody of Scene 1. Yet just as the formal structures of and social forces depicted by the opera conspire to dispose of the Duchess, the score's harmonic structure ensures her doom – this *particular* doom, on these *particular* pitches – from the start.

Gallon grounds her understanding of the opera's D- and B♭-based sonorities in Carolyn Abbate's notion of voice and/as narrative agency:

---

[32] Alex Ross, 'Roll Over, Beethoven: Thomas Adès', *New Yorker*, 26 October 1998, pp. 111–41 (p. 127).

the B flat minor triads that resound in Scenes 2, 4, 6 and 8 represent a patriarchal silencing of the Duchess's D major-centred voice.[33] Kyle Shaw reaches a similar conclusion, positing the latter tonic as the keynote of the Duchess's delusions of eternal youth: 'D then is a symbol for the lie the Duchess wants to believe and B-flat is the symbol of cold reality and her imminent doom.'[34] Shaw ties the D major and B minor tonal tendencies to the popular songs that define the Duchess and her reputation from the first: the tango tune and the love ballad.[35]

Missing, however, from accounts of *Powder Her Face* to date is a principle that seems to subsume discourses of (quasi-)tonality, musical structure and opera composition in particular for Adès, another corollary of the surface/depth dialectic: organicism. This metaphor of plant-like propagation wraps itself around discussions of his and others' music in many an interview.[36] In one instance, Adès singles out Janáček as paragon:

Janáček's music is organic – a flower that blooms, because the sap of the feeling in the music is there from the very beginning and that's what drives it. ... [His] response to what is happening in the drama is so direct in the music[.] ... [W]hen I say 'organic', I don't exclude violent dislocations. ... It's like pruning a tree. You often have to cut to preserve the life of the plant.[37]

For Adès, then, the organic metaphor describes globally consistent approaches to composition that allow for sharp contrast at local scale and, in dramatic or programmatic music, involves 'direct' response of sound to story and vice versa. Taking the B♭ sonority in *Powder Her Face* as a case study, one may see how the student becomes the master.

In Scene 2 (bars 99–101), the future Duchess sings, to a bluesy B flat minor triad with passing E: 'I could never grow bored of dukedoms.' Later (bars 319–21), D sounds on a bell, which the percussionist immerses in water as the Duke appears. The ringing bell's pitch drops to D♭, the mediant of the B flat chord, as two quavers sound on B♭ and D♭. The entering Duke sings an F to complete the triad (Ex. 3.2). Each a kind of fate motive, as Hélène Cao labels the quavers, the rhythm and the sonority

[33] Gallon, 'Narrativities', pp. 208–53.   [34] Shaw, 'Promiscuity', p. 98.

[35] Adès and Service, *Full of Noises*, pp. 47–9.

[36] See, for instance 'Thomas Adès: "Roots, Seeds & Live Cultures" – "Kirill Gerstein Invites" @ HfM Eisler Berlin', online video interview, 18 June 2020, YouTube, www.youtube.com/watch?v=I0kHP_npxJA.

[37] Adès and Service, *Full of Noises*, pp. 19–20.

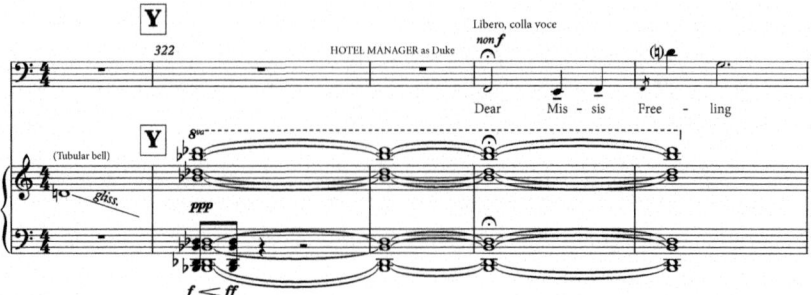

Ex. 3.2 *Powder Her Face*, Act I, Scene 2, bars 321–5, Hotel Manager's entrance as the Duke

converge here.[38] Gallon identifies these among several motives that conspire to drown out the Duchess's voice.

Gallon and Shaw find skirmishes in this harmonic clash throughout the score. The gesture that dominates the 'fellatio aria' of Scene 4, a series of onomatopoeic slides from a pitch to those a semitone and perfect fourth below it – tonic–dominant alternations – implies a tonic of B♭. After the Duke finds the Duchess's resulting polaroids during the 'Paper Chase' of Scene 5, Act I ends with a burst of B flat minor, from which a D♮ emerges and fades to silence. Pedal A♯s or B♭s persist through long stretches of the Judge's verdict aria in Scene 6, and when the Hotel Manager ejects her in Scene 8, the low winds sound the quaver motive on the B flat minor triad. The stage direction at bar 325 indicates the triumph of the sonority: 'Complete breakdown of Duchess'. The opera's last sung line in the 'Ghost Epilogue', a taunt from the Electrician, ends with a held D, followed by the final B flat minor chord.

As Shaw indicates, however, the harmonic conflict begins long before the listener hears either key area in full flower. Organicist thinking requires early planting of a generative musical particle, and Adès introduces his within the first ten seconds of the opera's overture.[39] After six bars, the snippet of Gardel's desolate 'Cuesta abajo' resounds. In Adès's adaptation of the tune, D and B♭ appear as the first melodic pitches, harmonised by E and G. Too lofty, the pitch that keeps the half-diminished seventh chord from the intervallic symmetry of the fully diminished seventh chord is the Duchess's D; it would need to bend down to D♭ to conform. At the level of a single bar, through the combination of a song allusion with a defining

---

[38] Hélène Cao, *Thomas Adès le voyageur: devenir compositeur, être musicien* (Paris: MF Éditions, 2007), p. 72. As Gallon observes, the sound is as grotesquely visceral as it is surprising; see Gallon, 'Narrativities', p. 228.

[39] Shaw, 'Promiscuity', p. 95.

harmonic clash, Adès implies that the opera will recount an idealised past ruined by a spiral to abjection; that D and B♭ will remain in conflict as musical agents; and that the D will bend into flattened-mediant compliance with B♭.

Powder Her Face introduces two potential tonal centres subtly, through the inclusion of both B♭ and D in the opening tango melody. Yet the viability of the Duchess's D-based sonorities wanes as those rooted on the Hotel Manager's B♭ accrue significance amid increasing frequency of appearance. The latter rises from but one pitch-class in a mundane G minor triad to become the tonic of its own triad and thus the 'black full stop' of the entire opera: from a seed germinated alongside the D-based sonorities to the *fleur du mal* that chokes them, and the Duchess's florid music, out.[40] It rises, over two hours' duration, from soil to surface, outcompeting all other possible tonal centres in Scene 8. Misgivings about Wagner notwithstanding, Adès integrates plot and score to an extent best described by the music dramatist's phrase 'deed of music made visible'.[41] Per his comments on Janáček, this mutual 'growth' together of score and drama fulfils the organicist impulse. So too does allusion to existing music within Adès's compositional system, in a way comparable to biological mimicry or grafting. In a telling passage that links the organicist metaphor to that of surface and depth, he lauds Stravinsky and discusses the illusion of style in terms that clarify the connection between his favourite analogies, which are one and the same on closer inspection:

[Y]ou need to recognize that the surface is almost like skin ... which is just a series of translucent layers ... that's what style is. ... What people lazily call style is only the top surface of the skin. But it's all – in something that's any good – *cellular material*. So that, in fact, there is no such thing as style. It's all idea.[42]

Adès has praised *Lulu*, a key influence on *Powder Her Face*, for its integration of 'low' material into a work 'overgrown' with manifestations of Berg's motivic-harmonic relationships and running thematic threads.[43] Later, he speaks of *Powder Her Face* in similar terms: '[the] expanding harmony that I saw in the tango ['Cuesta Abajo'], I identified the inherent

---

[40] Adès and Service, *Full of Noises*, p. 61.

[41] The original phrase, 'ersichtlich gewordene Thaten der Musik', comes from the essay 'On the Term "Music Drama"': Richard Wagner, 'Über die Benennung "Musikdrama"', in *Gesammelte Schriften und Dichtungen*, vol. 9 (Leipzig: E. W. Fritzsch, 1872), pp. 359–65.

[42] Adès and Service, *Full of Noises*, p. 82.

[43] He also refers to the music of *Lulu* as 'overgrown'. See Adès and Service, *Full of Noises*, pp. 23, 123.

tendency in it; I took that as a cell and I put it in my own petri dish and it ramified in all sorts of ways, which have absolutely nothing to do with that tango.'[44] Borrowed material, 'light' music shadowed by death's inevitability, provides the initial seed or cell that generates the harmonic structure and allegory of the opera. Adès's art of creating music and drama as an interdependent whole, of grafting pre-existing material into new music and of imposing coherence across works belongs to a genus of persistent metaphors valorising organic growth and cellular propagation. Whether or not he intends the reference to Arnold Schoenberg's *Style and Idea* in this passage, he upholds an Austro-German Romantic and modernist ideal in which musical part–whole relations resemble those of a living thing.[45]

It is towards a final yielding of D to B flat, embedded in a paraphrase of two nineteenth-century art songs at once, that the harmonic and dramatic tendrils of *Powder Her Face* grow: all take place within the Hotel Manager's aria in Scene 8, a barcarolle or *berceuse* in rhythm and the climactic victory of B♭ in pitch. The aria, in which the Manager informs the Duchess that her 'time to vacate' has come, begins in D minor, sinks to C sharp minor – the enharmonic equivalent of D flat – in the second strophe, and from there to B flat minor in the third.[46] He takes his leave of her with an augmented fifteenth from high D to low D♭ on the phrase 'Your Grace'; not content to bend her pitch into its flat Doppelgänger, the bass also drags it into a register in which only he and the other men he has played hold sway. As Gallon observes, the aria borrows melodic and structural elements from the 'Lullaby' in Mussorgsky's *Songs and Dances of Death*; the Hotel Manager stands in for the song's Death incarnate, while the Duchess, interjecting with pleas, assumes the subordinate role, melodic sinking and accompaniment textures of a mother with a dying child.[47] The orchestra introduces the aria with a quotation of Death's melody from Schubert's 'Der Tod und das Mädchen', which then overlaps with the Mussorgsky tune. Audiences may hear the Schubert tune as a facile joke about the Duchess's lack of maidenhood, as Gallon observes.[48] Yet Adès also makes a serious point about the value she places on youth, here expiring at last.

---

[44] Ibid., p. 153.

[45] See Arnold Schoenberg, 'Folkloristic Symphonies', in *Style and Idea: Selected Writings of Arnold Schoenberg*, ed. by Leonard Stein, trans. by Leo Black (Berkeley and Los Angeles: University of California Press, 2010), pp. 162–84 (p. 165).

[46] Also see Thomas Adès, '"Nothing but pranks and puns": Janáček's Solo Piano Music', in *Janáček Studies*, ed. by Paul Wingfield (Cambridge: Cambridge University Press, 1999), pp. 18–35 (p. 35).

[47] Gallon, 'Narrativities', p. 244.   [48] Ibid., p. 245.

The original music of the aria also gestures back to Liszt and Wagner: in adopting the triplets of Mussorgsky's *berceuse*, Adès also evokes the rocking rhythms of the barcarolle. As Jeremy Dibble writes, the musical topic that represented Venice for Romantic travellers outgrew its role as the folk song of the gondoliers soon after composers appropriated it as a standard form for arias and character pieces. Artists from Chopin to Offenbach and Fauré to Wagner lent operas and keyboard pieces a touch of the city's mystery and decadence through the compound metre and broad harmonic rhythm of the barcarolle.[49] Notable in Adès's output is the inspiration for the movement 'Venezia notturna', 'the ballad of some lugubrious gondolier', as he teases it in his programme note on *Arcadiana*.[50] The referent, Liszt's *La lugubre gondola I*, became a funerary piece for Wagner after its composition coincided with his death. The cabbie called to take the Duchess away – the unseen source of the honking double-quaver 'fate' motive – becomes her gondolier out of this mortal coil, hers a death in Venice. Like the Elderly Fop of Britten's opera of that name, she clings to superficial markers of youth well after it has faded. However, like the Old Gondolier and Hotel Manager of the same opera, played by the same singer as the Fop, the bass's characters in *Powder Her Face* repeat the memento mori message until it sinks in.[51] The layering of these many allusive and ironic surfaces together in Scene 8 leads to their collapse, revealing an uncanny boatman who beckons, his chthonic river (or nocturnal canal) to the hereafter revealed.

Conclusion: Dancing in the Dark

Above, I have argued that dance types such as the tango and waltz, along with allusions to particular songs and to the topoi of the *berceuse* and barcarolle, allow Adès to import social meaning into *Powder Her Face* as musical surfaces. The flip side of the contention – that his own words imply hidden depths that, upon analysis, indeed appear to operate in mutually

---

[49] Jeremy Dibble, 'Venice and Opera: Tradition, Propaganda and Transformation', in *Venice and the Cultural Imagination: 'This Strange Dream upon the Water'*, ed. by Michael O'Neill, Mark Sandy and Sarah Wootton (Abingdon: Routledge, 2016), pp. 59–78 (pp. 70–4).

[50] Thomas Adès, programme notes on *Arcadiana*, 1994, www.fabermusic.com/music/arcadiana-2365.

[51] A reviewer writing under a nom de plume first made the comparison between *Powder Her Face* and *Death in Venice*: Indiana Loiterer III, 'rrreviews: *Powder Her Face* at BAM', *Parterre Box*, 35 (December 1998), https://parterre.com/review35.html.

constitutive dialogue with the musical characteristics and referenced cultural objects of those surface features – contributes to a reckoning with the opera's enduring appeal. However, the underground river metaphor and its implications, illuminating as they may be in the context of Adès's chronic re-engagement with his own first opera, cannot quite explain why audiences' love affair with the piece have likewise continued. That producers flock to chamber operas because of the relatively low production costs is obvious, but the question of listener attention remains. The answer probably lies on, and with, the surface: *Powder Her Face* has memorable tunes in recognisable forms, rhythms and (to an extent) pitch schemata.

Given the composer's own fascination with the outermost layers of musical experience, the scholar or critic interested in *Powder Her Face* cannot afford to miss the surface for the depths. Rita Felski has lately called for a 'post-critical' posture among the hermeneut's repertoire of stances.[52] Citing most humanists' tendency to 'dig down' for cultural traces 'beneath the surface' of literary, visual and performed art, Felski – whose work on perceived affinities between femininity and consumption in the early twentieth-century imaginary sheds light on works, such as *Powder Her Face*, that evoke such connotations – asks why quests for depth so often preclude considerations of surface altogether.[53] To be sure, *Powder Her Face* offers trenchant commentary on social injustices involving war, class, gender and sexuality (while arguably perpetuating others in its silencing of women, an effect examined by Gallon).[54] However, following Felski, I offer that a central reason for the opera's continuing popularity is its ability to enchant with camp Doppelgängers of familiar musics, concealing deep messages while revealing earworm melodies.

In reworking parts of the opera's score to create new instrumental music – the original subtext of the 'fountain of youth' metaphor – Adès has taken full advantage of the surface appeal of the opera's music. He surrounds his own melodies with glittering arcs of virtuosic elaboration in the *Concert Paraphrase* for piano (2009), ironically yet affectionately revisiting the *bravura* fashion in which Liszt glossed operas by Verdi, Mozart and others – a practice of homosocial tribute obsolete for most of the twentieth century and thus awash in camp implications now, as Ivan Raykoff has argued.[55] Before

---

[52] Rita Felski, *The Limits of Critique* (Chicago: University of Chicago Press, 2015), pp. 56–60.

[53] Rita Felski, *The Gender of Modernity* (Cambridge, MA: Harvard University Press, 1995).

[54] Gallon, 'Narrativities', pp. 229–31.

[55] Ivan Raykoff, 'Transcription, Transgression, and the (Pro)creative Urge', in *Queer Episodes in Music and Modern Identity*, ed. by Sophie Fuller and Lloyd Whitesell (Urbana: University of Illinois Press, 2008), pp. 150–76.

adopting the tiered nomenclature of the *Three-Piece Suite, Hotel Suite* and *Luxury Suite from Powder Her Face* (2007, 2018 and 2017 respectively), Adès titled his first set of orchestral extracts simply (and tellingly) *Dances from Powder Her Face.* The harmonic, rhythmic, motivic-thematic and allusive depths of Adès's music, along with the rabbit holes of socio-political implications and cultural memory that pervade his work, will no doubt beguile analysts years hence. I conclude with an ode to the superficial lest we forget that sometimes, all one needs is a bit of song and dance.

Postcolonial Perspectives on Adès's The Tempest

JANE FORNER

For over four centuries, musical versions of and compositions inspired by Shakespeare's *The Tempest* have proliferated. At the same time, rewritings and critical interpretations of the play have formed their own parallel *Tempest* corpus: looming especially large in the last half-century are those that tease out the work's colonial and postcolonial themes. That operatic adaptations have generally not succeeded is well known, but more importantly, the genre has yet to be a significant vehicle for interrogating *Tempest*'s (post)colonial possibilities. Thomas Adès and Meredith Oakes's *The Tempest* (2003–4) is that rare thing, a successful contemporary opera, but it also represents a hitherto relatively unexplored meeting of these two threads of artistic interest in the play. This chapter offers a complement to existing music-analytic readings of the opera by placing the work in dialogue with colonial and postcolonial readings. In particular, I examine Adès and Oakes's complication and reimagining of the play's hierarchical power relationships between Caliban, Ariel and Prospero. Jyotsna G. Singh's recent overview of scholarly interest in and stagings of Shakespeare in the Global South argues that the plays are used in these contexts 'to tell stories of disparate lives, often in non-Western arenas or in culturally contested milieus in metropolitan centres'.[1] Adès and Oakes's opera is inescapably embedded in scholarly and performance spaces of Western privilege. It is vital, therefore, to pay attention to how the opera intersects with the long lineage of critical Shakespeares from diasporic and historically marginalised voices.

With this in mind, I first give an overview of the 'constellation of Calibans' figuring in this history.[2] Second, I focus on Oakes's transformed text and Adès's musical setting at three key moments in the opera: the first appearances of Caliban and Ariel, Caliban's Act II aria and the substantially modified ending; I touch also on the aesthetics of the opera's contrasting stagings. I argue that throughout the opera, Caliban actively and

---

[1] Jyotsna G. Singh, *Shakespeare and Postcolonial Theory* (London: Bloomsbury, 2019), p. 127.

[2] Here, I paraphrase Nadia Lie and Theo D'Haen, 'Preface', in *Constellation Caliban: Figurations of a Character*, ed. by Nadia Lie and Theo D'Haen (Amsterdam: Rodopi, 1997), pp. i–iii.

consistently articulates ideals of freedom and political agency, a freedom attained at the opera's conclusion that is at least in part catalysed by his own power. Finally, I propose that critical appraisal of the opera's cultural and political contexts is indispensable for a fuller understanding both of this adaptation and of broader themes in contemporary discourses of colonial legacies in twenty-first-century Britain.

Calibans Reimagined

Postcolonial reimaginings of *The Tempest* since the mid-twentieth century have grown so numerous that Nadia Lie and Theo D'Haen referred in 1997 to the rise of 'Calibanology'.[3] There is not space here to map out the extensive and fascinating array of theoretical, literary and theatrical invocations of Caliban.[4] Within the rich and extensive history of multidisciplinary critical attention to the play, five major modes of postcolonial engagement can be identified through which the figure of Caliban might be surveyed:

1. Literary adaptations which alter the play's drama from a (post)colonial viewpoint, by authors of colonial, formerly colonial and/or diasporic backgrounds;
2. Novels, films, etc. inspired by but not directly adapting the play;
3. (Critical) theatrical stagings;
4. Literary, psychological and philosophical analyses of *Tempest* by authors of colonial, formerly colonial and/or diasporic backgrounds;
5. Critical analyses of works in modes 1–4.

Classic techniques of postcolonial writing that are employed in all of these categories may include, among many, 'writing back' through 'subversive strategies employed by post-colonial writers ... not only through nationalist assertion, proclaiming itself central and self-determining, but even more radically by questioning the bases of European and British metaphysics, challenging the world-view that can polarize centre and periphery in the first place'.[5] Theoretical concepts including Edward

---

[3] Ibid., p. i. The term 'postcolonial' itself has attracted considerable scrutiny since at least the end of the last century. See, for instance, Sara Ahmed, *Strange Encounters: Embodied Others in Post-coloniality* (London: Routledge, 2000), p. 10.

[4] For a recent overview, see Alden T. Vaughan and Virginia Mason Vaughan, eds., The Tempest: *A Critical Reader* (London: Bloomsbury, 2014).

[5] Bill Ashcroft, Gareth Griffiths and Helen Tiffin, *The Empire Writes Back: Theory and Practice in Post-colonial Literatures*, 2nd ed. (London: Routledge, 2002), p. 32.

Said's 'contrapuntal reading'[6] have been applied to *Tempest* to reveal the text's 'reliance on, and endorsement of, the political structures and institutions of imperialism through clues that might otherwise go undetected'.[7] For *Tempest*, such 'clues' may include the context of colonial explorations of late Elizabethan England, as well as the representation and perceptions of people of colour in early modern Europe.[8]

Invoking Caliban specifically throughout these five postcolonial modes has continued to be a central pursuit for, among others, authors, literary theorists and philosophers. Octave Mannoni offered one of the earliest deployments of Prospero and Caliban as symbolic proxies for coloniser and colonised,[9] a psychological analysis which proved formative for subsequent thinkers, if subject to necessary and extensive critiques, especially by Frantz Fanon.[10] For Mannoni, Fanon and the next generation of postcolonial writing from Caribbean authors in the 1960s, their position within ongoing colonial conflicts and the eventual processes of decolonisation inevitably shaped how they approached the political and psychological potential of *Tempest*'s themes. Within this history, Paget Henry's survey of Afro-Caribbean philosophy describes Caliban as 'one of the most enduring narratives of Caribbean identity to emerge from European literature and philosophy',[11] and reframing that identity in the context of mid-century independence movements was a crucial part in reappropriating Caliban to 'write back' against empire.

George Lamming's influential *The Pleasures of Exile* (1960), for instance, interrogates 'the circumstances of my life, both as a colonial and exiled descendant of Caliban', and more broadly invokes Caliban's position in *Tempest* as a strategy to read historical and modern colonial politics through the play's narrative.[12] In the Barbadian poet Edward Kamau Braithwaite's collection *Islands* (1969), the poem 'Caliban' similarly functions, as Eric Doumerc observes, 'as a journey into the past in order to

---

[6] Edward Said, *Culture and Imperialism* (New York: Vintage Books, 1994).

[7] Bill Ashcroft and Pal Ahluwalia, *Edward Said*, 2nd ed. (London: Routledge, 2009), p. 99.

[8] Two recent excellent studies which illuminate these themes in early modern England are David Olusoga, *Black and British: A Forgotten History* (London: Pan Macmillan, 2016) and Miranda Kaufmann, *Black Tudors: The Untold Story* (New York: Simon and Schuster, 2017).

[9] Octave Mannoni, *Psychologie de la colonisation* (Paris: Éditions du Seuil, 1950).

[10] Frantz Fanon, *Peau noire, masques blancs* (Paris: Éditions du Seuil, 1952), particularly pp. 26–7, 87.

[11] Paget Henry, *Caliban's Reason: Introducing Afro-Caribbean Philosophy* (New York: Routledge, 2000), pp. 4–5.

[12] George Lamming, *The Pleasures of Exile* (London: Michael Joseph, 1960), p. 13.

make an act of possession and thus reclaim the Caribbean as home'.[13] Braithwaite extemporises on the play's parody of Caliban's speech ('Ban, ban, Caliban', II.ii.1229)[14] in a multitude of overlapping sonic and historical associations, from slave ships to Caliban as a carnival steel pan player. The sound 'Ban' becomes 'bangs' of both drum and limbo stick, but also the 'stick is the whip / and the dark deck is slavery', perhaps evoking Prospero's magic staff.[15] For the next generation of Caribbean and Latin American intellectuals, Caliban continued to be deployed both as a metaphor for (re)writing colonial histories and as a strategy to decentre the hegemony of 'Northern intellectual production'. Pioneered by the Cuban author Roberto Fernández Retamar's essays on Caliban and *Tempest* beginning in 1971,[16] this is described by César A. Rodríguez Garavito as the 'Calibanist turn' ('el giro Calibanesco') in which 'the Calibanist thinker recovers the intellectual tradition of the South'.[17] This *giro* was so extensive as to be described as a 'School of Caliban' by José David Saldívar.[18]

At the same time as philosophers and writers were drawing on the symbolic potential of Caliban (and usually Ariel and Prospero), postcolonial theatrical reimaginings of *Tempest* drew on similar techniques of what Rob Nixon calls 'repeated, reinforcing, transgressive appropriations of *The Tempest* … which in turn served as one component of the grander counterhegemonic nationalist and black internationalist endeavors of the period'.[19] Aimé Césaire's *Une tempête* (1969),[20] casting Caliban and Ariel as a black slave and a mulatto slave respectively, remains one of the most

---

[13] Eric Doumerc, 'Caliban Playing Pan: A Note on the Metamorphoses of Caliban in Edward Kamau Brathwaite's "Caliban"', *Caliban: French Journal of English Studies*, 52 (2014), 239–50 (p. 249).

[14] All quotations from Shakespeare's *Tempest* are given in the format Act, Scene, line, following the First Folio (1623). William Shakespeare, *The Tempest*, Folio I (1623), ed. by Paul Yachnin, Internet Shakespeare Editions, University of Victoria, https://internetshakespeare.uvic.ca/Library/facsimile/overview/book/F1.html. Modernised spellings are used but contractions preserved.

[15] Edward Kamau Braithwaite, *Islands* (London: Oxford University Press, 1969), p. 37.

[16] Roberto Fernández Retamar, 'Sobre cultura y revolución en la América Latina', *Casa de las Américas*, 12/lxviii (1971), 124–51.

[17] César A. Rodriguez Garavito, 'Prólogo' to Roberto Fernández Retamar, *Todo Caliban* (Bogotá: ILSA, 2005), pp. 13–24 (p. 17). All translations are my own.

[18] José David Saldívar, *The Dialectics of Our America: Genealogy, Cultural Critique, and Literary History* (Durham, NC: Duke University Press, 1991), p. 123.

[19] Rob Nixon, 'Caribbean and African Appropriations of *The Tempest*', *Critical Inquiry*, 13/iii (1987), 557–78 (p. 557).

[20] Aimé Césaire, *Une tempête: adaptation pour un théâtre nègre d'après 'La tempête' de Shakespeare* (Paris: Éditions du Seuil, 1969).

significant rewritings. Among stagings of the play, Jonathan Miller's production in 1970 for the Mermaid Theatre, London, is widely considered the first to present a (post)colonial interpretation, denoting Ariel and Caliban explicitly as black slaves.[21] In the late 1970s and 1980s, *Tempests* such as Derek Jarman's 1979 film and Philip Osment's play *This Island's Mine* (1988) subtly intertwined these themes with the contemporary political subtexts of Thatcherite England, especially homophobic legislation and burgeoning gay rights advocacy movements.[22] Trevor Griffiths's survey of stagings from the seventeenth century to the 1980s illuminates historical entanglements of changing perceptions of race in Britain with Caliban's place in *Tempest* productions,[23] and while this extensive history cannot be recounted here, many of its key elements are perceptible in Adès and Oakes's opera.

Adès and Oakes's *Tempest*

How can this rich corpus of Caliban invocations be used to contextualise this opera? Neither librettist nor composer has expressed that their *Tempest* advances a colonial- or postcolonial-inspired interpretation: Oakes has publicly dismissed that notion,[24] and Adès is generally reluctant to engage in discussions of his work's political significance. In a recent discussion with the pianist Kirill Gerstein, debating the stereotyped dearth of a strong British musical tradition in the nineteenth century led Adès to quip that Britain was 'very busy enslaving the rest of the world for a long time!' When Gerstein suggested that 'this is the price of colonialism', Adès replied, 'I'm much more comfortable if we leap back to just a mile less that way down the road, to Purcell's time.'[25] In this context, I read Adès's

---

[21] Subsequent British productions which continued this theme include Adrian Noble's (1998) and Rupert Goold's (2006), both for the Royal Shakespeare Company.

[22] On Jarman, see Jim Ellis, 'Conjuring *The Tempest*: Derek Jarman and the Spectacle of Redemption', *GLQ: A Journal of Lesbian and Gay Studies*, 7/ii (2001), 265–84. Chantal Zabus compares Jarman's and Osment's *Tempests* in 'Against the Straightgeist: Queer Artists, "Shakespeare's England", and "Today's London"', *Études anglaises*, 61/iii (2008), 279–89.

[23] Trevor Griffiths, '"This Island's Mine": Caliban and Colonialism', *Yearbook of English Studies*, 13 (1983), 159–80.

[24] Meredith Oakes, in Paul Archbold, 'Philip Hensher and Meredith Oakes in Conversation with Paul Archbold', presentation at 'Be Not Afeard: Language, Music and Cultural Memory in the Operas of Thomas Adès', Senate House: London, 25 April 2017.

[25] Thomas Adès in conversation with Kirill Gerstein. Kirill Gerstein, 'Thomas Adès: "Roots, Seeds & Live Cultures" – "Kirill Gerstein Invites" @ HfM Eisler Berlin', online video interview, 18 June 2020, YouTube, www.youtube.com/watch?v=10kHP_npxJA.

indifference to (post)coloniality as a frame for the opera as a desire to avoid 'uncomfortable' topics as well as a perception of British colonialism as a predominantly nineteenth-century phenomenon, rather than a significant historical context for Shakespeare and Purcell's work.

Adès's self-distancing from such discussions exists in tension with how the opera nevertheless participates in the critical discourses surrounding the play's political, cultural and historical significance. As will become apparent in the interrelated realms of production aesthetics, narrative and music, this *Tempest* consistently valorises ambiguity but in doing so shies away from commitments to overt critical stances in its adaptation. Adès's approach to creating the opera reflects this tendency: for instance, he is adamant that it simply captures the 'generalised atmosphere that the play produces',[26] rather than setting Shakespeare's text to music. Emphasising his ambition to avoid a modernised version that would be 'half-timbered, mock Tudor', Adès further argues that he does not 'take the famous text at all' in the opera.[27] Moulding Shakespeare's plays into feasible operatic forms has occupied composers, librettists and scholars for centuries.[28] Adès appears to sidestep traditional tensions through 'a translation that would be faithful to the spirit and atmosphere of the original'.[29] Yet the opera exists co-dependently with 'the famous text', not just in Oakes's (in)fidelity to it but because for most audiences, the opera is read *against* the play, in what it has changed and reinterpreted. My following discussions focus on these transformations rather than on the adaptation as a whole, which has been reviewed elsewhere.[30]

Transforming Ariel

Before I turn to Adès's Caliban, an account of the operatic relationship between Prospero and Ariel is useful, for it is indicative of Adès and Oakes's approach to the narrative's fundamental concepts of servitude and

---

[26] Thomas Adès and Tom Service, *Thomas Adès: Full of Noises – Conversations with Tom Service*, paperback ed. (London: Faber and Faber, 2018), p. 159.

[27] Ibid., p. 128. This comment is also part of an acerbic commentary on Benjamin Britten which should be taken with a large grain of salt.

[28] See, for example, Michael Graham, 'Shakespeare and Modern British Opera: Into *The Knot Garden*' (unpublished PhD dissertation, Royal Holloway, University of London, 2017).

[29] Adès and Service, *Full of Noises*, p. 158.

[30] See, for instance, Drew Massey, *Thomas Adès in Five Essays* (New York: Oxford University Press, 2021), pp. 66–9.

power. These are themes integral to the play's colonial contexts, and their redefinition in the opera is key to its narrative transformations. Oakes's libretto delineates Caliban's and Ariel's dramatic identities and their relationship with Prospero, the putative 'master', in ways that both align with and diverge from the long history of postcolonial *Tempest* reimaginings. If ostensibly bound, magically, to Prospero, Ariel is demonstrated throughout the opera to be consistently beyond the reach of his full power. This entails a fundamental shift in the arc of the drama as a whole; as Christopher Fox noted, 'the play turns on Prospero's powers ... in Adès and Oakes's version, it is these spirit creatures who achieve transcendence'.[31]

In the opera, Ariel and Prospero's first interaction from Shakespeare's Act I, Scene ii is split between two scenes in the opera (Act I, Scenes 3 and 5). Ariel's servant status remains in Prospero's words as he hails 'Spirit, servant', but rather than have Ariel respond 'All hail, great master!' (I.ii.300), Oakes writes a long solo passage, set by Adès as a dramatic introduction to the role's vocal acrobatics: 'Fear to the sinner / Fire to the impure' (etc.), swooping dramatically from E_5 to E_6 on 'Fear'.[32] From the outset, we are introduced to an operatic Ariel whose voice tears through the musical fabric, an Ariel far from subservient and obedient, but one whose physical and sonic existence exceeds human bounds and human bonds.[33] While the opera does not fully erase Prospero's control over Ariel, from their first interactions it is evident both sonically and textually that Ariel wields significant power.

The remainder of Shakespeare's discussion of Ariel's 'employment' establishes Ariel and Prospero's relationship as a mix of indentured servitude and slavery. Prospero refers to Ariel as his slave multiple times, but also portrays the relationship as primarily transactional, slipping between 'servant' and 'slave'. Unlike Caliban, Ariel is also given an explicit promise of freedom by Prospero, who agrees that 'after two days I will discharge thee' (I.ii.429–30). Both are enslaved through magical forces, but also through the psychological guilt of indebtedness; Prospero consistently

---

[31] Christopher Fox, 'Tempestuous Times: The Recent Music of Thomas Adès', *Musical Times*, 145/1888 (2004), 41–56 (p. 54).

[32] Ariel's textual nuances discussed here are not immediately audibly perceptible, requiring the aid of both surtitles and libretto. All text quotations from the opera are taken from the separately published libretto, Meredith Oakes, *The Tempest* (London: Faber, 2004).

[33] A note on the gendering of Ariel: it is unclear in the play, and stage productions play with this in various ways. Other recent settings of Ariel's songs such as Kaija Saariaho's *Tempest Songbook* (2000) explicitly gender Ariel's voice as female. Adès's Ariel is ambiguous, though the vocal part is female. I use the pronouns 'they', 'them' and 'their' to indicate their Ariel's existence outside an imposed gender binary.

comments that they are not performing the expected gratitude for the improvements he has made on their situations in life. He reminds Ariel: 'Dost thou forget from what a torment I did free thee?' (I.ii.375–6), referring to their time with the 'foul witch Sycorax' who confined them in a 'cloven pine, within which rift imprison'd, thou didst painfully remain a dozen years ... It was mine art, when I arrived and heard thee, that made gape the pine, and let thee out' (I.ii.404–5, 419–21).

Shakespeare's text thus projects the pervasive trope of the 'grateful slave', which George Boulukos argues is dependent on the notion 'that Africans can be induced not just to accept slavery, but to embrace it, to be over-whelmed by ecstatic gratitude toward someone who continues to claim mastery over them'.[34] Ariel and Prospero are consistently placed in this position in the play, their gratitude thematised as debt and thus depend-ency. Paula Dumas similarly assesses this trope in eighteenth-century British plays and novels, where 'the commonly used image of the grateful slave challenges the idea that slavery is necessarily cruel or evil'.[35] In Shakespeare's text, Ariel is 'freed' from Sycorax's enslavement to a pur-portedly better life with Prospero, their gratitude then driven home in their grovelling compliance at the end of this dialogue: 'I thank thee, master ... Pardon, master; I will be correspondent to command, and do my spiriting gently' (I.ii.431–2).

Oakes's text clearly challenges these tropes in Act I, Scene 5. Prospero reiterates frequently his 'gift' of freedom ('Sycorax died / Lest you forget / Left you inside / I prised you out') and insists on Ariel's gratitude ('Fickle spirit ... Is this your thanks?'). The operatic Ariel, however, persists in demanding liberty and refuses to show gratitude even though remaining bound under Prospero's magic. First, they emphasise that they are owed ('Shall I be paid? ... It's due! My release ... my fee, my ransom, my freedom'), and when Prospero counters with guilt from past debts, Ariel doubles down, demanding release: 'I have been captive with you twelve years / I must be active / In higher spheres ... I only thrive / In liberty!' Adès's setting hears Prospero and Ariel sing alone, then in a combative duet, the end of which is shown in Online Ex. 4.1. They are rhythmically and harmonically at loggerheads, their lines suggesting contrasting patterns of accentuation and coinciding only on a unison

[34] George Boulukos, *The Grateful Slave: The Emergence of Race in Eighteenth-Century British and American Culture* (Cambridge: Cambridge University Press, 2007), p. 3.

[35] Paula E. Dumas, *Proslavery Britain: Fighting for Slavery in an Era of Abolition* (Cham: Springer, 2016), p. 86. My thanks to Julia Hamilton for introducing me to Dumas's and Boulukos's work.

D at the climax – spilling into Adès's dramatic setting of Ariel's song 'Five Fathoms Deep' (Oakes's version of Shakespeare's 'Full Fathom Five'). Michael Halliwell interprets Ariel's voice in the opera as a metaphor for the 'cruel imprisonment and even "torture" of the character' by Prospero, arguing that he '"silences" language and thus strips the character of his humanity who struggles through "inhuman" vocal effort to assert himself'.[36] Yet throughout the opera, Ariel challenges rather than submits to Prospero's will, and I hear, rather, Ariel's voice as perpetually exceeding the bounds of his control.

Transforming Caliban

Oakes's libretto performs similar alterations to Caliban's first presentation in the opera. As with Ariel, it is in the nature of Caliban's response and challenge to Prospero's purported authority that the most substantial transformations to his character's dramatic role can be found. Prospero's insults remain ('Don't ask questions, slave / Know your place'), but Oakes's Caliban counters lucidly. Caliban's claim to the island is roughly identical: 'This island's mine, by Sycorax my mother, which thou tak'st from me' (I.ii.470–1) becomes 'This island's mine / I am king / Yet you treat me like nothing.' Both Calibans assert that they performed a service of care to Prospero upon his first arrival. Shakespeare's 'When thou camest first, . . . then I loved thee, and showed thee all the qualities o' th' isle' (I.ii.471, 475–6) becomes 'When I first found you, you were weak / Crouched by a rock, your child in your cloak.' In contrast, the operatic Caliban strongly emphasises that it is Prospero who owes *him*, asserting, 'I came to save you / I was your friend / . . .All I had you were given / But now you have forgotten . . . You are ungrateful.' In challenging who is really indebted to the other here, Oakes neutralises Prospero's powers of manipulation and control.

Notably, the passage on Miranda and Prospero's 'gift' of language to Caliban in the play, in which Miranda 'took pains to make thee speak, taught thee each hour one thing or another; when thou didst not, savage, know thine own meaning, but would gabble like a thing most brutish' (I.ii.495–8), is cut entirely. Most postcolonial *Tempests* interrogate this

---

[36] Michael Halliwell, 'The Sound of Silence: A Tale of Two Operatic *Tempests*', in *Silence and Absence in Literature and Music*, ed. by Werner Wolf and Walter Bernhart (Leiden: Brill, 2016), pp. 196–219 (p. 208).

moment, as it encapsulates both the notion of imperial conquest as benefi-
cial to the colonised – weaponised gratitude – and Caliban's resistance
('You taught me language: and my profit on't is, I know how to curse',
I.ii.504–5). Ngũgĩ wa Thiong'o argues that the process of 'decolonising the
mind' involves addressing the place of language in 'the domination of the
mental universe of the colonised'.[37] When Césaire's Caliban cries 'Uhuru!'
(the Kiswahili word for 'freedom' or 'independence') in response to
Prospero's summons, for example, it is a powerful symbol which, as
Steve Almquist observes, 'gives Caliban a voice, specifically an African
voice, and it contributes to Césaire's overall project in creating a diasporic
textual counter to Shakespeare'.[38] There is nothing in Oakes's text and
Adès's music, however, to suggest that Caliban's 'mental universe' has ever
been 'dominated' by Prospero, unlike Césaire's and others' focus on language in reappropriating *The Tempest*.

Excising the 'gift' of language removes, however, one of the key aspects
which Shakespeare used to establish Miranda and Caliban's relationship,
for it is in response to his and Prospero's dialogue on his attempted rape
that she responds with the crucial passage on her teaching Caliban. While
there is no suggestion in the libretto of any sexual assault, Caliban is still
described as exhibiting stalking and predatory behaviours towards
Miranda, and later demands her as his wife and queen in Act III, Scene
3 ('Give me your daughter / We'll have Calibans'). This aspect of the
narrative exemplifies the opera's unevenness in its critical stance.
Spectators are, for the most part, presented with an empowered and
respected Caliban, yet his sexual harassment of Miranda appears barely
changed. Oakes writes Prospero's disgust at Caliban's attraction to
Miranda as rife with eugenicist implications during the Act III confron-
tation ('Have you thought of my daughter's honour / Burdened with such
a husband ... Poor beast / Last in the race'). That we should be *sympathetic* to Caliban here is clear, but it is left ambiguous as to whether the
accusations against him are in fact entirely baseless. That Prospero's final
insult, 'You have no future', will be disproven in the opera's conclusion
does not detract from the fact that Caliban's own discussion of Miranda
does little to dismantle lingering stereotypes centred on his racialised
identity: the hyper-sexualised native who preys upon innocent white

[37] Ngũgĩ wa Thiong'o, *Decolonising the Mind: The Politics of Language in African Literature*
(Nairobi: East African Educational Publishers, 1981, reprinted 1986), p. 16.
[38] Steve Almquist, 'Not Quite the Gabbling of "A Thing Most Brutish": Caliban's Kiswahili in
Aimé Césaire's *A Tempest*', *Callaloo*, 29/ii (2006), 587–607 (p. 588).

women.[39] Although morally perfect characters rarely make fascinating operatic subjects, the fact that those stereotypes are left (mostly) unchallenged reflects some of the blind spots in this adaptation.

The lack of linguistic separation between Caliban and Prospero/ Miranda in Oakes's text is ambiguous in purpose, neither explicitly suggesting that their implied cultural differences have been erased nor offering a new status regarding their communication. Caliban in the opera needs neither to defend his mother tongue nor to be in his coloniser's 'debt', but it is left unclear how Oakes and Adès conceive of the intersection of language, culture and power in their interpretation. We could think of the opera's characters operating in their own 'musical language' – Miranda and Ferdinand's sweetly simple lines exemplifying their youthful naivety, Ariel's sky-scraping coloratura the voice of the superhuman. Caliban, a high tenor, rarely adopts the gloomy descending lines Adès writes for Prospero, instead singing with what Halliwell calls a 'mixture of lyricism and rhythmically harsh and jagged lines with large interval leaps'.[40]

On other occasions, however, just as their use of language is often not differentiated, Caliban and Prospero match one another musically. This is evident in their very first interaction, and also brings us to a crucial musical detail that is present throughout the opera: a short motivic fragment consisting of variations on a tone and a fifth. Emma Gallon has extensively analysed leitmotivs in the opera, naming two 'Revenge' (alternations of descending semitones and perfect fifths) and 'Freedom' (alternating ascending whole tones and perfect fifths).[41] In Prospero's music throughout Act I, we hear primarily the 'Revenge' version, while in Ariel and Miranda's music the 'Freedom' motive, a 'perfected' version of the descending motive, is already pre-empted, a sonic emblem of the operatic Ariel's resistance to the 'grateful slave' trope. Example 4.1a shows several instances of what I refer to in this chapter as the 'fifths' motive throughout Act I, marked by brackets with intervals denoted in numbers of semitones. The motive's inherent propensity for interlocking

---

[39] Extensive scholarship exists on this racist trope throughout colonial histories as well as in contemporary culture. Rebecca Kumar touches on these questions specifically in *Tempest* in '"Do You Love Me, Master?" The Erotic Politics of Servitude in *The Tempest* and Its Postcolonial Afterlife', in *Early Modern Black Diaspora Studies: A Critical Anthology*, ed. by Cassander L. Smith, Nicholas R. Jones and Miles P. Grier (Cham: Springer, 2018), pp. 175–96.

[40] Halliwell, 'The Sound of Silence', p. 210.

[41] Emma Gallon, 'Narrativities in the Music of Thomas Adès' (unpublished PhD dissertation, Lancaster University, 2011), p. 268.

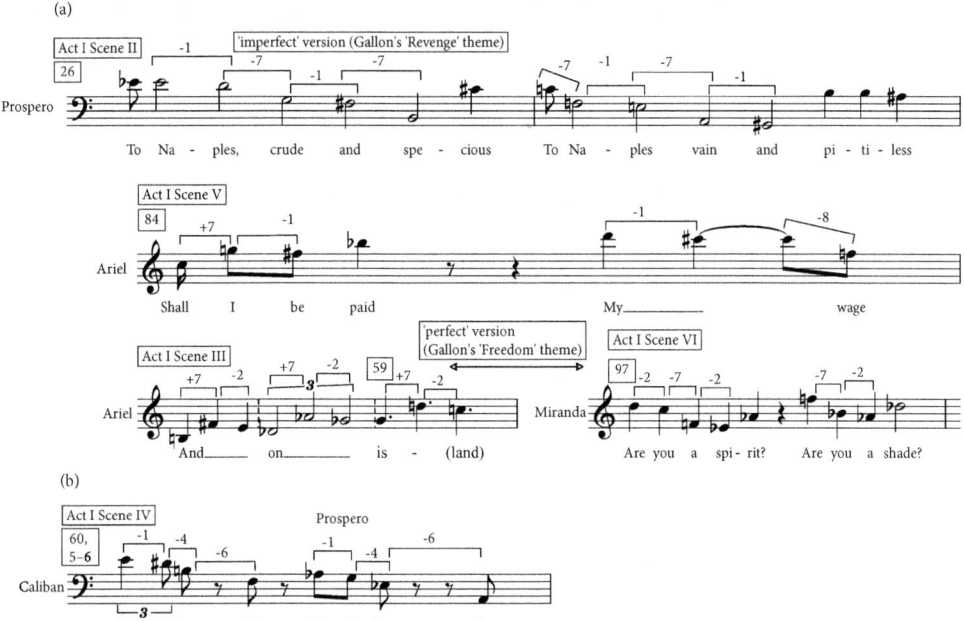

Ex. 4.1 *The Tempest.* (a) Interlocking 'fifths' motive throughout Act I in 'perfect' and 'imperfect' versions; (b) Act I, Scene 4, Caliban and Prospero's overlapping musical 'language' in modified 'fifths' motive

sequences can also be discerned.[42] In other references to this motive in the opera, especially in the ending, I consider the 'perfect' version to consist of alternating tones and perfect fifths, whether ascending or descending. In Ex. 4.1b we see that Caliban and Prospero's first dialogue presents identical intervallic content, a modified version of the 'fifths' material, thus illustrating their entanglement.

Before the ending of the opera, the passage that reflects most strongly on the status of Caliban's 'savage' language is his centrepiece Act II aria. Oakes's text follows Shakespeare closely, compressing 'Be not afear'd / This isle is full of noises / Sounds and sweet airs which give delight and hurt not' (III.ii.1492–3) to 'Friends, don't fear / the isle is full of noises / Sounds and voices / It's the spirits' (etc.). Adès's writing powerfully evokes Caliban's humanity and self-possession and is full of extraordinary lyricism. For Ian Bostridge, 'Caliban's capacity for a sort of nobility is knitted into his music and underlined in the plot', which he understood explicitly

---

[42] See also Scott Lee, 'Musical Signification in Thomas Adès's *The Tempest*' (unpublished PhD dissertation, Duke University, 2018), especially p. 150.

as expressing the postcolonial potential of the opera, something it 'seems at first sight to sidestep. In a sense, however, it pushes it to the limit.'[43] Caliban's lyrical aria is thrown into even sharper relief by its placing at the apex of frenzied ensemble passages, in which, drawing on all the power of the opera chorus's mob psychology, the orchestra and voices whip up into a wild, dissonant fever ('Higher and higher / Who's there? / It's air! / Haunted coast / It's a ghost'). Caliban enters unobtrusively into this chaos, singing 'Friends' on G_4 for twelve beats before rising to A_4 at the climactic moment when the orchestra erupts in a luxuriant A major, shown in Online Ex. 4.2 in reduction. (Caliban's vocal line is also dominated by the 'perfect' version of the 'fifths' motive, as indicated in brackets.)

In the play, Caliban's voice is associated with incoherence and inhumanity, his mother tongue demeaned to the status of brutish gabbling, a *langue barbare*. Not only is this counteracted by Oakes's removal of all these references, but so too is Caliban musically and vocally set apart in this lyrical, emotionally powerful aria. Halliwell's analysis reads in this moment that the ensemble is '"silenced" by Caliban's high A',[44] drawing attention not only to the metaphorical and literal power of Caliban's voice but implicitly also the fact that the power *to silence* is decentred from Prospero. My appraisal of the aria's effects admittedly rests on valorising standards of 'beautiful' sound in which conventional Western tonality is associated with positive qualities. If it does sound as 'a hymn to music itself, rather than the ravings of a drunk savage', as Massey describes it,[45] it is less comfortable to accept that we should not need Caliban to excel and delight in A major in order for his humanity to be rightfully acknowledged.

Caliban's ultimate failure in the play is rooted in an apparent unwillingness to transcend his station, written as simply exchanging one master for another ('I thy Caliban / For ay thy foot-licker', IV.i.1893–4). His claim for dominion ('This island's mine') is ridiculed in Shakespeare's characterisation but presented as a viable possibility in the opera – and one which will be fulfilled in the final scenes – partly by Oakes's firmer assertion of Sycorax as queen, not just mother.[46] The aria establishes Caliban's 'public' voice on the island – as distinct from his interactions

---

[43] Ian Bostridge, 'Me and My Monster', *Guardian*, 6 February 2004, Friday pages section, p. 8.

[44] Halliwell, 'The Sound of Silence', p. 212.   [45] Massey, *Thomas Adès in Five Essays*, p. 67.

[46] Oakes offers more detail about Sycorax than the play, although she is not physically present. Jarman's film provides a rare example of Sycorax being presented as an actual character. On the erasure of Sycorax in postcolonial *Tempest*s, see Irene Lara, 'Beyond Caliban's Curses: The Decolonial Feminist Literacy of Sycorax', *Journal of International Women's Studies*, 9/i (2007), 80–100.

with Prospero – as lucid, eloquent and compelling to the court (we hear Gonzalo address him as 'Sir', for example). In the opera's treatment of Stefano, Trinculo and Caliban's plot to usurp Prospero and establish Stefano as 'king', to which the narrative moves following the aria, Caliban is no dim fool; instead, as Bostridge put it, the other two 'are clearly Caliban's stooges'.[47] Oakes makes this explicit at the beginning of Act III when, although nominally supporting Stefano's bid for the throne, Caliban's aside positions him as the true puppet master: 'By my art you are deceived / Do your part, I'll be free.' The appropriation of the notion of 'art' from Prospero is a pointed reinforcement of Caliban's increased agency, as well as asserting that his freedom will come as a result of his own skill and cunning, not as a gift given from a 'benevolent' master.

In the opera's four distinct productions to date, the aesthetics of Caliban's physical appearance alternately work with and against these transformations in text and score. In Tom Cairns's Covent Garden productions (2004 and 2007), Bostridge's Caliban is not especially othered visually, wearing a distressed, shiny suit to match Simon Keenlyside's Prospero in his tattered suit jacket. In Ludger Engels's Budapest production (2016), Caliban and Prospero wore fully 'human' attire (trousers, brogues, sweaters and suits), Caliban in a flowery shirt, oversized sheepskin jacket and John Lennon sunglasses. Conversely, in both Jonathan Kent's (Santa Fe, 2006) and Robert Lepage's (Metropolitan Opera, 2012) productions, Caliban's empowerment, especially in his aria, is undercut by a reliance on 'savage' visual tropes. William Ferguson appeared barely clothed and dirtied at Santa Fe, and Alan Oke, singing at the Metropolitan Opera, as a feathered surrealist Papageno. Despite the fact that it is the Italian court who are the 'strangers' to the isle, in the opera's reconfiguration of Ariel and Caliban, most productions nonetheless have focused on the strangeness of their onstage bodies.[48] While I cannot here examine fully all the directorial choices, it is striking that none of the four productions opted to engage any form of colonial or postcolonial aesthetic. Even in the European *Regietheater*-inflected staging in Budapest, there seems to be little impetus for directors to engage with the opera's political potential.[49]

---

[47] Bostridge, 'Me and My Monster'.

[48] See Ahmed, *Strange Encounters*, passim, and her treatment of the ideas of the 'stranger' and 'alien' in colonial encounters.

[49] I am not aware of how closely Adès and Oakes were involved with the staging of each production, although Adès often served as conductor, so I do not attribute the aesthetics to their control.

'Who was here?'

The opera's final scenes form the crux of the transformed destinies of Caliban, Ariel and Prospero. Adès and Oakes replace Shakespeare's solo Epilogue for Prospero with an entirely new scene that has no counterpart in the play. The action preceding the end itself is also substantially changed, consequently altering how the various subplots in the narrative are concluded. In the play, the end of Act V centres on the resolution of Prospero's relationship with the court and on Miranda and Ferdinand's marriage preparations, Ariel's freedom and Caliban's pardon from Prospero. Oakes divests these elements from one another: rather than crumble apologetically ('How fine my master is! I am afraid he will chastise me', V.i.2255–6), Caliban is absent entirely. The Italians' narratives are wrapped up in Adès's setting of a sentimental, passacaglia-style a cappella chorus, with only Antonio's bitter riposte souring the air of reconciliation.

This tableau-style finale has the air of an ending, but while it offers a conclusion to part of the narrative, it is followed by two more endings: Prospero's exit, and Caliban's and Ariel's final scene. The chorus is also perceptibly trite as an ending moment, because the opera so far has considerably diminished the significance of the plot threads now coming to an end. Gallon characterises the opera's structure as presenting 'four narrativities [which] overlap with each other and unfold at different rates'.[50] They are also palpably hierarchised. Miranda and Ferdinand's relationship functions in the play as a compelling dramatic catalyst for Prospero's transformation and redemption as father and Duke, but the vast majority of their interactions are cut in the opera (notably the opening scene of the play's Act III and the masque in Act IV). Ferdinand does not discover Miranda's name until the end of the opera's Act II, their romance distilled into the subsequent duet, which structurally concludes the business of their relationship at the end of Act II. Diluting the dramatic power of the Italians' narrative arc is also a strategy derived directly from classic postcolonial *Tempest*s such as Aimé Césaire's, reduced, as A. James Arnold argues, 'to the status of a secondary plot', and in which Césaire deliberately 'trivialized the courtship of Ferdinand and Miranda'.[51]

Shakespeare affords Prospero the last word in every sense in his musing, stately Epilogue ('Now my charms are all o'erthrown / And what strength

---

[50] Gallon, 'Narrativities', pp. 283–4.

[51] A. James Arnold, 'Césaire and Shakespeare: Two Tempests', *Comparative Literature*, 30/iii (1978), 236–48 (pp. 242–3).

I have's mine own', Epilogue, 1–2). Excising this passage strips Prospero's final moments of magnanimous philosophical pondering; it is replaced with scattered remarks in the preceding scene ('Pride, pride, all will die') and his resignation to a bitter future ('I'll drown my book / I'll break my stave / I'll rule in Milan / Beside my grave'). For Prospero to exit here would be a show of resolute, if depressing, respectability – an impression amplified by Adès's setting of *ff* minor chords, heavy with brass, on 'stave'/ 'rule'/'Milan'. Instead, freeing Ariel with the breaking of his staff, he is suddenly bereft and unsteady, breathlessly pleading, 'Stay with me Ariel / Save me Ariel'. Prospero's dramatic arc tends to be discussed in terms of his move towards forgiveness, mercy and redemption, but these elements are barely perceptible in the concluding scenes.

Having radically altered how the themes of power and servitude guide the narrative, in its conclusion the opera focuses on affirming Caliban's and Ariel's futures, with Prospero no longer a presence on the island. Act III, Scene 5 presents Ariel's voice floating unseen, and only Caliban physically onstage, questioning what has gone before:

Who was here?
Have they disappeared?
Were there others?
Were we brothers?
. . .
They were human seeming
I was dreaming.

Caliban's questioning suggests the possibility that the preceding action was illusory, an interpretation amplified in Robert Lepage's production, where the theatre-within-a-theatre conceit nests the idea of artifice within the entire narrative.[52] (Santa Fe's alfresco theatre, on the other hand, probably worked well to capture this space of imagination and freedom that Caliban and Ariel inhabit at the end.) For Heather Wiebe, Lepage's setting productively reflected what she felt to be the opera's innate hermeticism, its 'sense of enclosure, its airless and oppressive character', an effect 'of ossification'.[53] While I agree with this impression, Caliban's downstage

---

[52] Both Halliwell and Massey also discuss the affinities between Adès and Oakes's ending and the concluding parts of W. H. Auden's epic *Tempest*-inspired poem *The Sea and the Mirror* (1942–4), particularly in the latter's extraordinarily long soliloquy for Caliban's and Ariel's postscript, which also explores similar themes of theatricality and artifice. See Halliwell, 'The Sound of Silence', and Massey, *Thomas Adès in Five Essays*, pp. 62–92.

[53] Heather Wiebe, 'Prospero's Ossified Isle: Thomas Adès's *The Tempest*', *Opera Quarterly*, 30/i, (2014), 166–8 (p. 167).

emergence in the final scene, away from the false onstage theatre, to me rends open that claustrophobia. Alan Oke delivered his lines towards the audience, the only illuminated presence amid the vastness of the Metropolitan Opera's stage, faded to black.[54] Oakes suggested that the island is potentially an external manifestation of Prospero's psyche, but his absence from the ending works against this idea.[55] Oke's performance in particular struck me as a perfect embodiment of the utopian vision of his post-Prospero existence, suggesting conversely that if anything it is in *Caliban*'s imagination that the action has occurred.

The transition from Scenes 4 to 5 of Act III is marked by pervasive harmonic indeterminacy which lends weight to the feeling of slipping out of (or into?) reality. Example 4.2 provides an annotated reduction from Prospero's exit (Oakes's change from 'Now my charms are all o'erthrown' to 'Now I've no art') to Caliban's first line in Scene 5. The harmonic progression strongly implies a resolution in C major, but deviates at the last moment from a perfect fifth (D–A) to octave D♭s in the first bar of the last scene, a semitonal expansion outward indicated by arrows on Ex. 4.2. The effect, sonically and dramatically, is of dissolution, of suddenly entering a different world. The melodic content of the final scene is entirely suffused with interlocking presentations of the 'perfect' version of the 'fifths' motive, as indicated in brackets, which constitute the majority of the orchestral accompaniment until the end. Gallon summarises the importance of the 'Freedom' leitmotiv as 'growing to encapsulate different kinds of freedom as the work unfolds, namely, freedom in nature and love, and freedom from servitude, captivity and parental control'.[56] Its over-whelming presence in the ending is a sonic encapsulation, therefore, of these intersecting freedoms, heard in Caliban's long, lyrical lines and Ariel's voice heard singing only the vowels of their name (A-i-e).

As the opera draws to a close, the dream/reality ambiguity persists. Ariel's insistence that they 'must be active in higher spheres' is fulfilled to the letter, freed from human language entirely and from humanity itself;[57]

---

[54] The passage in question can be found between 2:00:08 and 2:01:08 on the Metropolitan Opera's recording of *The Tempest*, produced by Robert Lepage and directed by Gary Halvorson, DVD (Deutsche Grammophon DVD 0040 073 4932, 2013).

[55] Oakes, in Archbold, 'Philip Hensher and Meredith Oakes in Conversation'. Jarman's film presents this interpretation with Prospero asleep in his crumbling manor. Ellis argues that 'this is only one version of England, which Prospero is attempting to dream his way out of'. 'Conjuring *The Tempest*', p. 280.

[56] Gallon, 'Narrativities', p. 266.

[57] Although it is beyond the bounds of my analysis here, there is considerable scope for investigations into how the category of 'human' is interrogated through this operatic Ariel, especially through the lens of recent work in posthumanism and on 'queering the non/human'. See e.g. Norren Giffney

Ex. 4.2 *The Tempest*, Act III, transition between Scenes 4 and 5, 327 – 328 +8, harmonic slippage from C to D♭, prevalence of interlocking perfect 'fifths' motive

they are 'the wind, an elemental force of nature'.[58] Caliban's position is equally though differently ambiguous. While Oakes's text hints at the restoration of a natural order, it is full of questions, stretching towards an unknown horizon still yet beyond; towards, in Waldo McNeir's poetic characterisation of Shakespeare's epilogues, 'a clouded but perceptible afterwards'.[59] Caliban's repeated self-naming is a vivid manifestation of

and Myra J. Hird, eds., *Queering the Non/human* (Farnham: Ashgate, 2008); and Dana Luciano and Mel Y. Chen, 'Has the Queer Ever Been Human?', *GLQ: A Journal of Lesbian and Gay Studies*, 21/ii–iii (2015), 183–207. Further exploration of how Adès and Oakes's Ariel plays into tensions between posthumanist feminism and decolonial critique would also be apt.

[58] Adès, interview with Andrew Ford on 'The Music Show', *ABC Radio National*, 9 October 2010, quoted in Dominic Wells, 'Plural Styles, Personal Styles: The Music of Thomas Adès', *Tempo*, 66/260 (2012), 2–14 (p. 7).

[59] Waldo McNeir, 'Shakespeare's Epilogues', *CEA Critic*, 47/i–ii (1984), 7–16 (p. 15).

his liberation, and the uncertainty of his future is full of hope: it is Caliban 'in the gleam of the sand / in the hiss of the spray / in the deep of the bay / in the gulf in the swell'. In Priyamvada Gopal's recent study of resistance in the British Empire, she challenges the notion that liberty flowed primarily from 'progressive' imperial agents to its subjects, wherein 'decolonization emerges *ab nihilo*, magical consequences of imperial policies developed in a vacuum immune to anticolonial pressures'.[60] In the opera, unlike Ariel, Prospero does not free Caliban. We could believe, then, that his freedom is a product of the 'anti-colonial pressures' he has applied in the form of sustained resistance to Prospero. It is his island, and he *is* the island, but the implications of both the opera's past action and the futures it barely hints at are left deliberately foggy.

Unlike the disruption and long-term scars that colonialism leaves behind, an operatic utopia is achieved in the space of a few bars. If for much of the opera Caliban's identity is still irrevocably framed through his relationship with Prospero, this ending presents us with what Gayatri Spivak's classic essay on subalternity describes as a utopian political ideal, where 'oppressed subjects speak, act, and know for themselves'.[61] Caliban's voice seems to evaporate as he repeats his name for the last time, reaching a falsetto D_5 which merges seamlessly with Ariel's entry. Example 4.3 shows Caliban's and Ariel's final moments. The unanticipated flatward shift to D flat in the earlier scene transition proves to be more than a momentary disjunction, returning in the bass register as a prominent pedal in the final passages. Brackets show the continued presence of interlocking 'fifths' motives. Beginning at 331, a bass progression repeated nine times descends from E_3 to rest on Db_1, tonal ambiguity being maintained through its enharmonically functioning also as C♯. The last iteration of the bass progression forgoes a final D♭ to rest on a (sounding) first-inversion E major chord, supported by Ariel's last notes, but the music evaporates, not resting in any one tonality.

I find it unsatisfying to believe that the fictional world of the opera is *doubly* fictional, dreamed up by Caliban (or Prospero). Instead, we as spectators, scholars, performers and directors can participate in Caliban's space of imagination as he wonders what might have been and what could still be.

---

[60] Priyamvada Gopal, *Insurgent Empire: Anticolonial Resistance and British Dissent* (London: Verso, 2019), p. 11.

[61] Gayatri Chakravorty Spivak, 'Can the Subaltern Speak?', in *Marxism and the Interpretation of Culture*, ed. by Cary Nelson and Lawrence Grossberg (Chicago: University of Illinois Press, 1988), pp. 212–314 (p. 276).

Ex. 4.3 Caliban's and Ariel's final lines, ambiguous harmonies and interlocking perfect 'fifths' motive throughout the ending of *The Tempest*

As Caliban sings and voices himself as a person in his own right, his own mind is free to wander and stretch into the 'clouded afterwards', luxuriating in the sound of Ariel's voice lingering just beyond the falling curtain.

Tempestuous Futures

At the beginning of this chapter, I suggested that greater critical attention to this *Tempest*'s intersection with the many literary, critical and philosophical afterlives of Shakespeare's play is needed. Perhaps especially in light of Adès's reluctance to engage openly in the political discourses in which many of his works inescapably participate, my analyses here have aimed to open up paths for historically and culturally informed approaches to this opera and to

Adès's music in general. Examining *The Tempest* in this manner offers a valuable example to situate operatic analysis productively within broader discourses of colonial legacies, race and politics in modern Britain and further afield. Halliwell proposes that Caliban's and Ariel's liberated ending can be interpreted as 'suggesting the ephemeral nature and ultimate failure and, indeed, final silencing of the colonial project'.[62] Yet the more I return to the opera, the more it seems that its many ambiguities – especially the open horizons of the ending – reflect not a 'final silencing' but a potentially productive, unstable space in which we might probe the symbolic, legal, psychological and physical violences that the 'colonial project' continues to exert today.[63] As Nadine El-Enany has recently demonstrated, moreover, Britain's imperial past is more than a matter for historians; she argues that through racialised legal practices the country is a 'contemporary colonial space'.[64] When Caliban was appropriated for the opening ceremony of the London 2012 Olympics, it was as part of an atemporal, imagined space of British identity that recast the 'isle full of noises' not as an exoticised location in a colonialist fantasy but as Britain itself.[65] For Lamming, Braithwaite and others, Caliban functioned in the 1960s as a vehicle to interrogate their Caribbean identity at the tail end of British colonial rule, but sixty years later his place in the director Danny Boyle's vision of universal hope contrasted uneasily with the ceremony's staged arrival of the *Empire Windrush* as a symbol of British 'inclusivity'.[66] As Caliban thus continues to be invoked symbolically in divergent contexts, and with productions of and music inspired by the play not appearing to be lessening in popularity, there is much room to consider how as teachers, scholars and listeners we might use this operatic *Tempest* to think through constructions of past and present, and the myriad possibilities for it to enrich musical, social and historical knowledge in the twenty-first century.

---

[62] Halliwell, 'The Sound of Silence', p. 215.

[63] Alex J. Gapud's recent ethnographic study in Bristol gives an excellent indication of perceptions of empire today: 'Displacing Empire: Aphasia, "Trade", and Histories of Empire in an English City', *History and Anthropology*, 31/iii (2020), 331–51.

[64] Nadine El-Enany, *(B)ordering Britain: Law, Race and Empire* (Manchester: Manchester University Press, 2020), p. 28.

[65] This segment of the ceremony was titled 'Green and Pleasant Land' and featuring Kenneth Branagh dressed as Isambard Kingdom Brunel and reciting Caliban's Act II 'Be not afear'd' speech, accompanied by Elgar's 'Nimrod'.

[66] Akala also scrutinises the 2012 Games, referring to the BBC's coverage of the men's 200 m final, before which a problematic short film was broadcast on the subject of evolutionary biology, eugenics and athletic performance; see *Natives: Race, Class, and the Ruins of Empire* (London: Two Roads, 2018). The subsequent *Windrush* scandal of 2018 also paints this part of the ceremony in a very different light.

Chaconnes in the Music of Adès

PHILIP STOECKER

It has often been noted that repetitive pitch patterns and 'continuities' are an integral part of Adès's music, and these patterned structures have received increasing attention since the pioneering essays by Aaron Travers and John Roeder.[1] Subsequent analyses by Roeder, Philip Stoecker and Edward Venn have shown the frequency with which such 'aligned cycles' and 'expanding (or contracting) intervallic series' appear in Adès's compositions ranging from his Op. 1 *Five Eliot Landscapes* (1990) to his most recent opera, *The Exterminating Angel* (2015–16).[2] These authors have demonstrated how Adès's pitch patterns and cycles often govern local, small-scale events. Venn has noted, however, that 'Adès frequently combines or extends [pitch cycles] in order to generate larger structures or even the premise behind entire movements. The use of cycles lends itself well to chaconnes and passacaglia sections and movements.'[3]

Most enquiries into Adès's chaconne movements focus on pitch and how the repeating harmonic cycle is varied. Adès himself, when describing his chaconnes, also favours pitch. In an interview with Tom Service, Adès makes a connection between the repetitive nature of a chaconne and serial compositions of the twentieth century:

---

[1] Aaron Travers, 'Interval Cycles, Their Permutations and Generative Properties in Thomas Adès's *Asyla*' (unpublished PhD dissertation, University of Rochester, 2004); John Roeder, 'Co-operating Continuities in the Music of Thomas Adès', *Music Analysis*, 25/i–ii (2006), 121–54. Roeder defines 'continuities' as 'an association between two percepts, formed when the second realises a mental projection that was made as part of the first' (p. 122).

[2] John Roeder, 'A Transformational Space Structuring the Counterpoint in Adès's "Auf dem Wasser zu singen"', *Music Theory Online*, 15/i (2009), https://mtosmt.org/issues/mto.09.15.1/mto.09.15.1.roeder_space.html; John Roeder, 'Transformation in Post-tonal Music', *Oxford Handbooks Online*, 4 August 2014, www.oxfordhandbooks.com/view/10.1093/oxfordhb/9780199935321.001.0001/oxfordhb-9780199935321-e-4; Philip Stoecker, 'Aligned Cycles in Thomas Adès's Piano Quintet', *Music Analysis*, 33/i (2014), 32–64; Philip Stoecker, 'Harmony, Voice Leading, and Cyclic Structures in "Chori"', *Music Theory and Analysis*, 2/ii (2015), 204–18; Philip Stoecker, 'Aligned-Cycle Spaces', *Journal of Music Theory*, 60/ii (2016), 181–212; Edward Venn, 'Asylum Gained? Aspects of Meaning in Thomas Adès's *Asyla*', *Music Analysis*, 25/i–ii (2006), 89–120; Edward Venn, 'Thomas Adès's Freaky Funky Rave', *Music Analysis*, 33/i (2014), 65–98; Edward Venn, *Thomas Adès: Asyla* (Abingdon: Routledge, 2017).

[3] Venn, *Thomas Adès: Asyla*, p. 23.

[Y]ou could say that any serial piece is a chaconne of a kind, in the sense that you're going through rotations of the twelve notes of the row in order. You could describe the whole serial process as a chaconne if you felt like it, but it's really just to do with the way the notes recur. And if they happen to recur in a certain recognisable way – suddenly the piece is a chaconne.[4]

The connection that Adès makes between a serial composition and a chaconne is revealing. In a twelve-note composition, the prime row is rarely repeated verbatim.[5] While the prime row provides unity throughout a movement or an entire composition, it is constantly subjected to rhythmic and registral changes and to alterations in dynamics and articulations, and it undergoes operations such as transposition, inversion and retrograde motion. Adès's chaconnes are similarly designed so that after the initial chaconne statement continuity is achieved through subsequent varied restatements of a particular harmonic progression.

In the same interview with Service, Adès uses the word 'spiral' to describe his chaconnes: '[a] chaconne is simply one kind of harmonic motion. In my music it's very often spiral rather than circular — in other words, it's transposed down with each appearance, or whatever it is.'[6] Elsewhere, Adès compares a chaconne to a spiral in reference to his opera *The Exterminating Angel*, commenting: 'Obviously, depending on how it's written, a chaconne can have the quality of constantly not going through a door … With this chaconne – as opposed to the chaconne in *The Tempest* – my idea was that it never ends; that it just goes round in a spiral, down and down.'[7] The notion of spiral form in Adès's music has been developed by Christopher LaRosa, who writes that

[a]lthough Adès set out to write the lyrical theme [of *Asyla*] as a repetitive chaconne, each subsequent presentation varies the theme to a point that he refers to the section as a 'spiral form'. The metaphor of a spiral seems apropos; once the melody circles around and begins anew, the ground has shifted slightly and the theme alters or diverts toward a slightly new destination.[8]

---

[4] Thomas Adès and Tom Service, *Thomas Adès: Full of Noises – Conversations with Tom Service*, paperback ed. (London: Faber and Faber, 2018), p. 8.

[5] A twelve-note row is an ordered set of the twelve pitch-classes of the chromatic scale. Forms of this ordered set include the original row (prime) and its inversion, retrograde and retrograde inversions. The prime form of the row is the main form to which all others are referenced.

[6] Adès and Service, *Full of Noises*, pp. 7–8.

[7] Christian Arseni, '"Why do we ever do anything?" Thomas Adès and Tom Cairns Talk about *The Exterminating Angel*', in *The Exterminating Angel* programme booklet, Salzburger Festspiele, 22 July–31 August 2016, pp. 46–57 (p. 56).

[8] Christopher LaRosa, 'Formal Synthesis in Post-tonal Music' (unpublished MM dissertation, Boston University, 2015), p. 47.

By equating the repetitive nature of a chaconne to a spiral, Adès highlights the pitch transformations that occur with each restatement of the repeating harmonic cycle. A spiral, as defined by Adès and discussed by LaRosa, is a consequence of pitch, and as a metaphor it belongs to the dominant strand of Adès scholarship that focusses on pitch.

The centrality of pitch in readings of Adès's chaconnes is exemplified by Roeder's and Mark Hutchinson's analyses of the fourth and central movement of *Arcadiana* (1994), 'Et... (tango mortale)'. Both have written detailed analyses about the movement's seven-chord chaconne cycle,[9] and a common thread in their writings is how subsequent statements of the chaconne's harmonic progression encounter conflicts.[10] But their accounts of Adès's chaconne in 'Et... (tango mortale)' leave unstated the role of rhythm, thereby offering only a partial understanding of the complex forces at play. While Adès's chaconnes undergo the usual kinds of variations we might expect – in instrumentation, register, texture and so on – his superimposition of independent layers of rhythmic cycles has not attracted a great deal of critical comment. Attention to the temporal implications of Adès's chaconnes offers new insights into the local level as well as the processes that structure his form on the larger scale.

This can be demonstrated with reference to the fifth chaconne statement in bars 35–40 of Adès's 'Et... (tango mortale)', a passage worthy of study in which Adès superimposes four distinct rhythmic layers, the greatest number of independent rhythmic patterns unfolding at the same time throughout the entire movement. Example 5.1a provides an annotated score of bars 35–7, and a summary of the rhythmic layering that takes place in the entire passage is given below the score (Ex. 5.1b) as a duration circle.[11] Reading clockwise, each numbered segment is the sum

---

[9] Its harmonic structure consists of six trichords and ends with a tetrachord that is a subset of the 'odd-numbered' whole-tone collection C♯-D♯-F-G-A-B. The 'even-numbered' whole-tone collection contains C-D-E-F♯-G♯-A♯.

[10] Mark Hutchison writes that the movement is constructed not as a chaconne but as a 'passacaglia ground-bass', and that it 'is gradually overwhelmed by disruptive forces'. *Coherence in New Music: Experience, Aesthetics, Analysis* (Abingdon: Routledge, 2016), pp. 34–36. Roeder writes that 'while such linear continuity remains sporadically evident, it is persistently beset by dissipative forces that eventually exhaust the chaconne's self-sustaining energy. Each reiteration of the cycle encounters different impediments.' 'Co-operating Continuities', p. 144.

[11] Because each layer has its own unique smallest common duration, the numbers on the circle refer to different durations. Thus, a «2» in the second violin layer (quintuplet demisemiquavers) does not have the same duration as two «1»s in the first violin layer (triplet semiquavers).

(a)

'expanding intervallic series':
G♭–F–E♭–C (intervals 1,2,3)

(b)

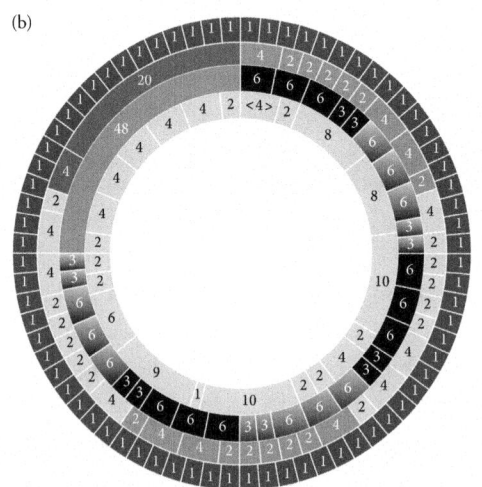

outside circle to inside circle: vln 1, vln 2, vla, vlc

Ex. 5.1 *Arcadiana*, movement IV, 'Et. . . (tango mortale)'. (a) Rhythmic layers in bars 35–7 (chaconne statement 5); (b) duration circle of bars 35–40 of all the articulations, rests and sustained notes for a single pitch or harmony.[12] Here, and elsewhere, the smallest common duration is enclosed within a box on the score, and brackets are used to show repeating durational patterns.[13] In bar 35, the C minor harmony in the viola – the first chord of the chaconne cycle – projects a duration of twenty-four hemidemisemiquavers which is partitioned into a «6,6,6,3,3» pattern. A change in pitch or harmony initiates the next duration. When the chaconne sonority of B-Db-F enters at the end of bar 35, the next duration of twenty-four hemidemisemiquavers, also partitioned into a «6,6,6,3,3» pattern, begins.

The repeating chaconne cycle is articulated by the viola, shown in the duration circle as the second ring from the centre, and organised by a consistent duration of «6,6,6,3,3». This pattern, highlighted with brackets on the score, is presented six times, once for each chaconne chord. I use different shades to show the repetition of this rhythmic motive on the duration circle. The viola's regular rhythmic pattern ends with the cha-conne's final chord, which lasts forty-eight demisemiquavers.

Superimposed over this chaconne cycle are three other distinct layers, each with its own unique rhythmic profile. The smallest common duration and the only rhythm assigned to the first violin is a tripletsemiquaver. Shown by the outermost duration circle, the first violin consistently pre-sents a durational pattern of one triplet semiquaver («1») which is repeated for the entirety of this chaconne statement.[14] The rhythm of the second violin, calculated in quintuplet demisemiquavers and given as the third circle from the centre, presents a durational pattern of «4,2,2,2,2,2,4,4,2». This rhythmic pattern occurs four times, and Adès marks the start of each with an ascending triple stop.[15]

---

[12] By using the smallest common duration to analyse rhythmic patterns, I follow the model set out by Julian Hook in 'Rhythm in the Music of Messiaen: An Algebraic Study and an Application in the *Turangalîla Symphony*', *Music Theory Spectrum*, 20/i (1998), 97–120.

[13] Following Hook, a number in <angle brackets> indicates a rest, and in this study these rests most often appear at the start of a duration circle since an independent layer may start after the bar line. A number in parentheses at the beginning of a duration circle indicates a duration before a cycle begins.

[14] Despite the first violin's consistent durational pattern, its pitch structure does not always agree with the underlying harmonies of the chaconne. Roeder discusses the rhythm and pitch continuities of this passage. See Roeder, 'Co-operating Continuities', especially pp. 137–8.

[15] Adès notates the rhythm of the «4,2,2,2,2,2,4,4,2» pattern a different way each time by using different combinations of notes and rests. The different notations can be observed by focussing on just the first two rhythms of the larger pattern, «4,2». In bar 35, Adès notates «4,2» as «4,1<1>», with the bracketed number indicating a rest. In bar 36, «4,2» is now notated as «1<3>,2» and in bar 37 as «2<2>,2».

While the violins and viola play repeating rhythmic patterns, the cello, shown by the innermost duration circle, does not have any kind of recurring, consistent rhythmic configuration. With a smallest common duration of a demisemiquaver, the cello does not participate in the consistent patterns of the other three individual layers. This inconsistent rhythmic stratum relates to Adès's comment that '[m]usic has a tendency to arrange itself either in terms of patterns or cycles. On a tiny scale, in a single bar, as well as on the huge scale of an entire opera there is always the possibility to decide *not* to be part of a pattern. This is part of my musical make-up'.[16] Although the cello presents a four-note expanding intervallic series, a highly structured *pitch* pattern, its rhythmic organisation is irregular and deviates from the highly repetitive, regularly recurring rhythms in the upper strings. For instance, as shown at six o'clock on the duration circle, Adès organises the layers so that when the upper strings all coincide at the same time the cello does not cooperate and continues its musical line. This deferred alignment in the cello drives the music forward to nine o'clock, when all four instruments are finally aligned. This synchronous moment occurs with the last whole-tone chord of the chaconne, and the consistent rhythmic cycles in the second violin and viola leading into this moment – «4,2,2,2,2,2,4,4,2» and «6,6,6,3,3» respectively – suddenly no longer unfold consistent patterns; the first violin, however, continues to unfold its steady pattern of triplet semiquavers («1»).

The four layers here are distinguished from each other through their rhythmic organisation. Adès achieves rhythmic independence through differences in the smallest common duration, and each layer presents its own distinct rhythmic profile. In addition, the length of each pattern is also different. The second violin's «4,2,2,2,2,2,4,4,2» configuration extends across the bar line, while the first violin presents numerous reiterations of «1» within each bar. Rarely do these three patterns – «4,2,2,2,2,2,4,4,2», «1» and «6,6,6,3,3» – begin at the same time except at the opening of this passage. There are connections among the varying strata in how the melodic structure of each layer relates to the harmonies of the underlying chaconne, but from a rhythmic perspective the four independent streams rarely align and cooperate in this passage. Because none of the other statements of the chaconne cycle contain as many simultaneously unfolding and independent rhythmic layers, the fifth chaconne statement is thus projected as the climax of this movement.

---

[16] Arseni, 'Why do we ever do anything?', pp. 55–6.

Adès generates different intensities of layering in 'Et... (tango mortale)', and recognising the increases and decreases of these intensities helps to reveal the large-scale shape and musical drama of an Adèsian chaconne movement.[17] Lynne Rogers uses the term 'dissociation' to describe this layering compositional technique in the music of Stravinsky. According to Rogers, '[a] layer consists of one or more lines. It is harmonically independent if it exhibits a self-sufficient pitch organization... While contrasting and self-sufficient pitch organizations are primary in effecting dissociation', other elements such as rhythm 'are necessary as well for the layers to be distinguished easily from one another'.[18] Rogers also notes that 'variations in the strength of dissociation create a shape'.[19] Complementing Rogers's tendency to consider these independent layers in terms of pitch, my focus on the layering of different rhythmic patterns in Adès's chaconnes opens up new dimensions in the study of his music. I demonstrate first how various levels of dissociation create a sense of drama in another early work, the *Concerto Conciso* (1997–8), to show how these rhythmic procedures were in Adès's music from the outset. I conclude with an analysis of the chaconne in the second movement of Adès's *Violin Concerto – Concentric Paths* (2005), a work that greatly expands the proportions of the rhythmic continuities found in his earlier chaconnes.

Concerto Conciso

As in *Arcadiana*, the chaconne in Adès's *Concerto Conciso*, which consists of six statements of a repeating harmonic cycle, appears in the very centre of the work. Observing Adès's rhythmic procedures of this movement reveal that the level of dissociation increases as the movement unfolds until the fourth chaconne statement in bars 22–8, the climax of the movement. While the thirteen-chord chaconne is subjected to typical variations in pitch, register and instrumentation, the rhythmic organisation of the movement

---

[17] Hutchinson includes a detailed chart of the chaconne statements in his study and provides a description of 'the chief characteristics of the different cycles, highlighting the points where aspects of the ground-bass are undercut by other disruptive elements'. Hutchinson, *Coherence in New Music*, p. 34. See his example 2.6 on p. 35.

[18] Lynne Rogers, 'Stravinsky's Break with Contrapuntal Tradition: A Sketch Study', *The Journal of Musicology*, 31/iv (1995), 476–507 (pp. 477–8). Also see Lynne Rogers, 'Dissociation in Stravinsky's Russian and Neoclassical Music', *International Journal of Musicology*, 1 (1992), 201–28.

[19] Rogers, 'Stravinsky's Break', p. 478.

Ex. 5.2 *Concerto Conciso*, movement II, thirteen-chord chaconne progression

transcends its local significance by combining with other parameters to shape the texture, density and form. I will show that as increasing numbers of independent rhythmic layers are added to the repeating chaconne cycle the different degrees of dissociation generate both a sense of forward momentum and the musical drama of the movement.

Concerto Conciso (1997–8) is in two movements, and according to Adès, the second movement 'has two parts: firstly, a slow *ciacconetta*, which runs through six divisions upon a seven-bar chord sequence announced by the piano'.[20] The *ciacconetta* cycle contains thirteen different harmonies (Ex. 5.2), and there are five complete statements of this chaconne progression, each seven bars in length.[21] Each statement in Table 5.1 is labelled with a roman numeral. All of the chaconne statements except for the fourth have a crotchet as the smallest common duration. Chaconne statements II, III and V have the same rhythmic profile and are forty-two crotchets in length, as shown on the far right of the table. Statement I differs only from these three statements in the duration of the seventh chord. The sixth statement is unlike the other chaconne progressions since Adès presents a complete breakdown of the previous pattern. There is no consistent rhythmic organisation, and only a few of the chaconne's harmonies appear in order, while others are sporadically articulated throughout the seven bars. An overview of the rhythmic structure and the level of dissociation for each chaconne statement is given in Table 5.1.

As shown in Table 5.1, the intensities of dissociation increase as the movement unfolds. The first statement is the unambiguous presentation

[20] Thomas Adès, programme notes on *Concerto Conciso*, 1997, www.fabermusic.com/repertoire/concerto-conciso-2822. Emma Gallon has briefly discussed the rhythmic procedures of the *Concerto Conciso* chaconne. She notes that 'temporal features [of the first movement] pave the way for an enriched interpretation of the "Ciacconetta". The conventional opening statement of a seven-bar chord sequence and its five repetitions that ground the piece forms the chaconne'. 'Narrativities in the Music of Thomas Adès' (unpublished PhD dissertation, Lancaster University, 2011), p. 107. Gallon also suggests that '*Concerto Conciso* is an example of a work that is much more complex in its use of past forms, in particular in the first part of the second movement, the "Ciacconetta"' (p. 106).

[21] The metre throughout this chaconne movement is 3/2.

Table 5.1. *Concerto Conciso*, movement II, summary of chaconne cycles

	Bars		①	②	③	④	⑤	⑥	⑦	⑧	⑨	⑩	⑪	⑫	⑬	
I	Bars 1–7	♩	6	6	4	2	4	2	2	2	4	2	2	2	2	40
	Chaconne presented by solo piano, beginning in the extreme registers of the piano and gradually moving to the central register.															
II	Bars 8–14	♩	6	6	4	2	4	2	4	2	4	2	2	2	2	42
	Entire ensemble articulates chaconne. Addition of embellishing passing notes, anticipations and suspensions. Separate layer presented by the clarinet melody. Mild level of dissociation.															
III	Bars 15–21	♩	6	6	4	2	4	2	4	2	4	2	2	2	2	42
	Chaconne cycle in strings. Consistent «1,6» semiquavers pattern in the piano. Long–short rhythmic motives in brass and low woodwinds; not aligned with chaconne. Increase in the level of dissociation.															
IV	Bars 22–8	♪	24	21	21	7	15	8	16	8	16	8	8	8	8	168
	Superimposition of five independent layers. Intense level of dissociation.															
V	Bars 29–35	♩	6	6	4	2	4	2	4	2	4	2	2	2	2	42
	Chaconne in strings (upper register). Dampened notes in the piano with inconsistent rhythmic patterns; progresses from middle to lower register.															
VI	Bars 36–43	?														
	Complete breakdown of the chaconne cycle.															

of the chaconne progression. Adès transforms the second chaconne cycle (or 'division') in bars 8–14 not only through instrumentation and register, but also by adding embellishing notes that are not members of the underlying pitch structure of the chaconne.[22] The clarinet has a prominent melodic line with a pitch structure that sometimes agrees with the chaconne and at other times is counter to it. Although the clarinet's rhythmic profile is not organised by a consistent pattern, it adds an independent layer to the chaconne to create a mild form of dissociation. With the third statement, bars 15–21, Adès superimposes two independent strata to the repeating cycle, and each layer has its own unique rhythmic profile and lowest common duration. The chaconne is given to the strings, while the piano presents a consistent, repeating «1,6» rhythmic pattern (calculated in semiquavers) that is eventually taken over by the clarinet in bar 19 for the rest of the passage. At the same time, the brass and low woodwinds play numerous long–short rhythmic motives in the lower register with a smallest common duration of triplet-quavers, but there is a lack of any kind of rhythmic consistency here. The addition of independent streams thus increases the level of dissociation.

The analysis above shows that with the fourth chaconne statement Adès superimposes several different independent rhythmic layers, each unfolding distinct durational patterns at different speeds. This layering technique is similar to what occurred in *Arcadiana*. Because Adès creates five different rhythmic strata and avoids synchronicity among these layers, this chaconne statement achieves a high level of dissociation and thus functions as the climax of the movement. Example 5.3 provides an annotated score of bars 22–4, and a summary of the superimposing of rhythmic layers that occurs in the entire statement is given below the score as a duration circle, in which the smallest common duration of the chaconne is a semiquaver.[23] The chaconne progression is played by the three violins,

---

[22] By using the term 'division' – a seventeenth-century improvisatory musical device in which the notes of a cantus firmus or a ground are divided into smaller note values – Adès seems to refer not only to the progressive shortening of note values with each chaconne statement, but also to an increase in the complexity of the texture and the rhythmic layers.

[23] Since the lowest common duration in the fourth statement of the chaconne is a semiquaver, its durations are four times greater than those of the other chaconne statements that all have a crotchet as the lowest common duration. Notice that chords 2–5 of the fourth statement have durations that are slightly altered in comparison to the other statements, and these are shown in Table 5.1 in bold italic font. The durations should be «24», «16», «8» and «16» demisemiquavers instead of «21», «21», «7» and «15», but the total duration of 168 is consistent with the total durations of the chaconne statements, i.e. «42» × «4» = «168».

(a)

(b)

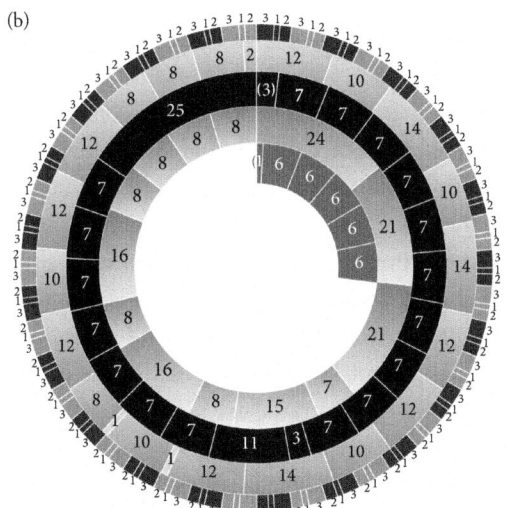

outside circle to inside circle: piano RH, piano descant,
clarinet, chaconne, piano LH

Ex. 5.3 *Concerto Conciso.* (a) Bars 22–4, chaconne statement 4, rhythmic layers;
(b) duration circle of bars 22–8

often employing harmonics, and occasionally only by the piano (chords 3, 11 12 and 13).[24] The durations of the repeating chaconne cycle are given as the second circle from the centre.

Throughout this passage the piano right hand presents a highly consistent «3,1,2» rhythmic pattern calculated in triplet semiquavers. This pattern is repeated forty-two times and is reproduced in the example as the outermost circle. The clarinet presents its own extremely regular durational pattern of «7» semiquavers that is then take over by the double bass in bar 25 and the tuba in bar 26. This seven-duration configuration occurs eighteen times, deviating temporarily from the norm in bar 20 with durations of three and eleven semiquavers.[25] The smallest common duration of the piano left hand is triplet quavers, and for the first two bars in this passage the left hand presents a repeating «6» pattern. Presented only five times, this repeating «6» pattern abruptly ends when the left hand articulates the third chord of the chaconne B♭-D♭-F as it temporarily leaves the high register in the strings to occupy the low register of the piano. The highest notes articulated by the piano descant, which Adès notates on the upper treble clef, generate yet another rhythmic stratum. Shown as the third rhythm circle from the centre, the triplet semiquaver durations of twelve, ten, fourteen and so on do not have a consistent repeating pattern. Once again, Adès includes a rhythmic stream that does not conform to the highly repetitive patternings found in the other layers.

The five independent layers in this passage are distinguished by contrasting rhythmic profiles and differences in the smallest common durations. The lack of cooperation among the distinct rhythmic strata adds tension to an already altered chaconne cycle. The conflicting, non-coordinated pulses and varied rhythmic patterns and durations thus create an especially intense level of dissociation. This passage is followed by the fifth chaconne statement, in which the texture and dynamics suddenly drop with just two independent layers of activity. None of the conflicts and discontinuities that were generated with the fourth chaconne statement are resolved in the fifth. Finally, in bars 36–43, the last chaconne statement falls completely apart. Adès makes it difficult to hear

---

[24] At the end of bar 23, when the strings finish articulating the second chaconne chord, the third chord is played by the piano left hand. Meanwhile, the strings double the clarinet line in bar 24. The fourth chaconne chord is then handed back to the strings at the end of bar 24.

[25] One could argue for a larger, hypermetrical pattern of fourteen semiquavers that is grouped as «7,7» with one instance of a «3,11» partition.

any kind of consistent durational patterns, and the repeating chaconne cycle can barely be heard. Although the conflicts and tension presented by the fourth chaconne statement remain unresolved, Adès's manipulation of his repeating harmonic progression by continually adding independent streams of activity functions as a tension-building device. This form-functional strategy creates directionality and foreward motion that acts as a large-scale upbeat to the second part of the second movement, 'a fast brawl'.[26]

Violin Concerto – Concentric Paths, Second Movement, 'Paths' (2005)

On the front cover of the published score of Adès's *Violin Concerto – Concentric Paths* (2005) is a reproduction of a map by Andreas Cellarius (c. 1596–1665) titled 'Map of the Earth and Planetary Orbits'. This map, dated 1661, is part of a larger collection titled *The Celestial Atlas*. Cellarius designed his map so that the earth is positioned in the centre, surrounded by many different orbits of various sizes. Most of these orbital paths encircle the earth, while a few smaller ones are located above the north and south poles.

I find that the layout of Cellarius's map, with the numerous orbits circling around the earth, visually captures the structural design of Adès's concerto, and especially that of 'Paths', the second movement of the concerto.[27] In a 2014 interview, Adès was asked to comment on the design of his concerto:

ADÈS : ... I noticed that what the movements had in common was a certain kind of circular thinking. ...
TOM SERVICE : Where does that circular thinking happening [*sic*]?
ADÈS : All over the place.
SERVICE : You're talking the structure, harmony, everything?
ADÈS : Yes. Yes. All of the above. Yes.[28]

---

[26] Adès notes that the second part of the second movement is 'a fast *brawl* in a tonality discovered by an unexpected resolution of the last cycle of the *ciacconetta*'. Adès, programme notes on *Concerto Conciso*.

[27] The three movements are titled 'Rings', 'Paths' and 'Rounds', respectively.

[28] BISrecordsVIDEO, 'A Chat in the Park, Part I: Thomas Adès Discusses His Music with Violinist Peter Herresthal, Conductor Andrew Manze and Music Journalist Tom Service', 12 February 2014, YouTube, www.youtube.com/watch?v=OAhcZwi3f0Q.

Such comments, along with the title of the work and the reproduction of Cellarius's map on the cover of its score, provide intriguing ways to approach the circular organisation of this work.

Although Adès implies that his 'circular thinking' takes place 'all over' the concerto, I will focus only on the second movement, 'Paths', for I believe its rhythmic structure best demonstrates the circular designs that Adès mentions in his interview. Discussions of 'Paths' by Alexi Vellianitis and Peter Van Zandt Lane focus more on its harmonic structure and the two chaconne progressions that Adès employs.[29] The repetitive pitch structures of both chaconne cycles indeed play an important role in generating the form of the movement. Adès also provides an intriguing and a more detailed description of 'Paths' that will serve as my point of departure. He writes: 'This concerto has three movements but it's really more of a triptych, as the middle one ["Paths"] is the largest. It is the "slow" movement, built from two large, and very many small, independent cycles, which overlap and clash, sometimes violently, in their motion towards resolution.'[30] I show that it is the rhythmic organisation of 'Paths' that best projects the large and small independent cycles as well as the tension and resolution that Adès mentions in his description of the second movement. Observing the varying levels of dissociation throughout 'Paths' helps to reveal the musical drama that Adès incorporates into his movement.

On the basis of Adès's claim that 'Paths' is 'built from two large ... independent cycles', I further interpret the movement in two sections (composed of rotations, or 'cycles', through minor- and major-triad chaconnes of fourteen and fifteen chords each) with a brief coda (an abbreviated chaconne). The large-scale form of 'Paths' is shown in Ex. 5.4a. Section I (bars 1–48) is the longest in the movement, and it is here that Adès not only creates tension by superimposing different rhythmic patterns that unfold at different speeds, but also generates gradual increases in the levels of dissociation to enhance rhythmic complexity. Section II (bars 48–69) is almost half the length of Section I and provides the resolution of the conflicts that were created in the first part. The coda, bars 70–9, is the shortest section of the movement and consists of only two rhythmic layers that simultaneously progress at separate speeds. Whereas each section has a

[29] See Peter Van Zandt Lane, 'Narrative and Cyclicity in Thomas Adès's Violin Concerto' (unpublished PhD dissertation, Brandeis University, 2013); and Alexi Vellianitis, 'Kuusisto's Joke: Reconstructing the Rubble of Tonality in Thomas Adès' Violin Concerto' (unpublished MA thesis, University of Oxford, 2012), pp. 42–50.

[30] Thomas Adès, programme notes on *Violin Concerto – Concentric Paths*, 2005, www.fabermusic .com/repertoire/violin-concerto-4.

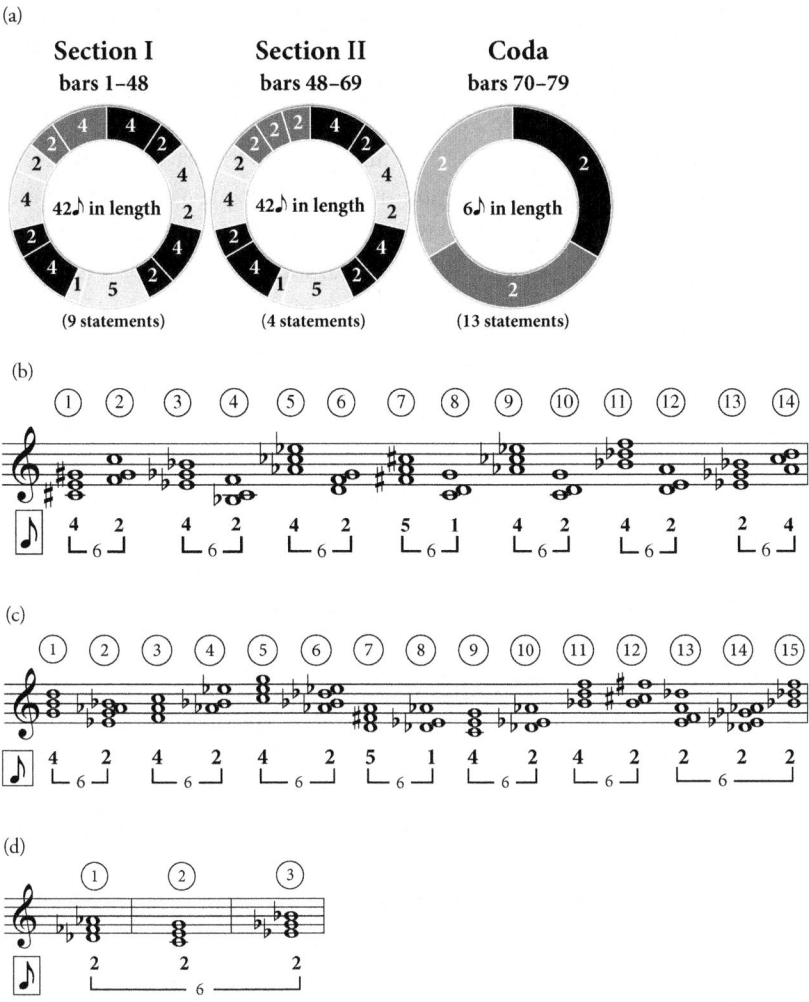

Ex. 5.4 Violin Concerto, movement II. (a) Overview of the chaconne progressions and form; (b) fourteen-chord chaconne progression in Section I, bars 1–48; (c) fifteen-chord chaconne progression in Section II, bars 48–69; (d) three-chord chaconne progression in coda, bars 70–79

different formal function in 'Paths' – to establish tension and provide resolution and dispersion – all three are generated by rhythmic and harmonic chaconne patterns that are continuously repeated.

Example 5.4b provides a reduction of the first chaconne, or 'large independent cycle', which consists of fourteen trichordal harmonies that alternate between minor triads and chords built of a major second and a perfect fourth or a minor third.[31] This chaconne cycle is presented nine times in Section I, and as Lane observes, 'the harmony itself takes a circular path, beginning on and returning to C♯ minor', the first chord of the progression.[32] The rhythmic structure of this minor-triad chaconne is given below the reduction in Ex. 5.4b and as the leftmost duration circle in Ex. 5.4a. With a smallest common duration of a quaver, the chaconne repeatedly projects a duration of six quavers, most of which are grouped into long–short «4,2» patterns.[33] The last duration of six quavers is structured as a short–long «2,4» pattern while the middle segment projects the only instance of «5,1». Because the metre of 'Paths' is 4/4, the long–short «4,2» and «5,1» patterns establish a 3/2 hypermetre, creating a triple metre that is characteristic of the early eighteenth-century dance form. The entire duration of this fourteen-chord chaconne for all nine statements is forty-two quavers.

The fifteen sonorities of the chaconne in Section II, bars 48–69, consist of alternating major triads with tetrachords and trichords built of a perfect fourth and a major second, shown in Ex. 5.4c. This harmonic progression occurs four times in Section II, and statements 2–4 are transposed down a perfect fifth from the first statement. Whereas the chaconne's pitch structure changes between statements, its rhythmic profile remains constant throughout, and as I shall show, rhythmic variety is achieved through superimposition of layers. The smallest common duration of the second chaconne is a quaver, and it repeatedly projects durations of six quavers, which are mostly partitioned into long–short «4,2» segments. In comparison to the rhythmic profile of the first chaconne (see Ex. 5.4a), the second chaconne projects the same long–short «4,2» durational patterns except for the last unit, which is partitioned into «2,2,2». All four statements of this fifteen-chord chaconne last a total of forty-two quavers.

Although Adès does not mention that 'Paths' consists of a third 'independent cycle', the movement concludes with one last repeating harmonic progression of only three chords: D flat minor, C major and E flat minor.[34] The smallest common duration of this chaconne is also a quaver, and, as shown in Ex. 5.4d, each triad projects a duration of two quavers. Its

---

[31] The minor triads, set class (037), alternate with set classes (027) and (025).

[32] Lane, 'Narrative and Cyclicity', p. 44.

[33] Adès differentiates the larger six patterns by alternating between arco and pizzicato.

[34] This three-chord progression replicates the opening of the first minor-triad chaconne with the C sharp minor chord enharmonically spelled as D flat minor and the F of the second chord moved down a semitone to E to form a C major chord. My thanks to Edward Venn for bringing this to my attention.

repeating durational pattern of «2,2,2» thus projects a triple metre within the 4/4 metre of the movement.[35] The overall time-span of this final harmonic progression is only six quavers, and it appears thirteen times.

All three of the chaconne progressions have a quaver as the smallest common duration. The rhythmic organisation of the solo violin's highly consistent rhythmic patterns cuts across the rhythmic continuities of the chaconnes, often carving its own rhythmic and melodic path. While the 'large independent cycles' repeatedly unfold, Adès gradually increases tension by superimposing layers of different rhythmic patterns and cycles that overlap with the chaconne progressions in ways that are analogous to the orbits surrounding the earth in Cellarius's map.

Example 5.5 provides the rhythmic organisation of the second chaconne statement of Section I, bars 6–11. Two different rhythmic cycles are presented in this passage. Adès assigns the chaconne to the full orchestra and alters the first, second, fifth and sixth rhythmic segments from «4,2» durations to short–long «2,4» or «1,5». Every minor chord of the chaconne is played by the entire orchestra and given a *f*, *ff* or *fff* dynamic marking, and is a quaver in length followed by a quaver rest. The solo violin, represented as the outer circle in Ex. 5.5b, presents a new melodic line (or path) with a different rhythmic profile. Its smallest common duration is a triplet quaver, and it has a repeated pattern of «3,4,2,1.5,1.5» or «7,2,1.5,1.5». This pattern appears four times, while the last statement is partitioned into a «3,4,2,2,2,2» pattern. For the most part, the violin's rhythmic structure does not veer too far off track from the chaconne, since there are multiple instances when the violin and the chaconne are rhythmically aligned and initiate a durational segment at the same time. Although two different smallest common durations are used in this passage, the level of dissociation is mild.

The third statement of the minor-triad chaconne occurs in bars 11–16, and in this passage Adès superimposes three different rhythmic layers (Ex. 5.6). Each layer projects its own durational continuities and has different rhythmic patterns. The chaconne cycle is now played by the strings, bassoons and horns, and its rhythmic profile is represented by the innermost duration circle. Once again, Adès alternates back and forth between «4,2» to «2,4» and concludes this statement with a «3,3» partition. The melodic line that the solo violin played in bars 6–11 is stated again and

---

[35] This forms what Samuel Ng calls a 'hemiolic cycle'. See Samuel Ng, 'The Hemiolic Cycle and Metric Dissonance in the First Movement of Brahms's Cello Sonata in F major, Op. 99', *Theory and Practice*, 31 (2006), 65–95.

(a)

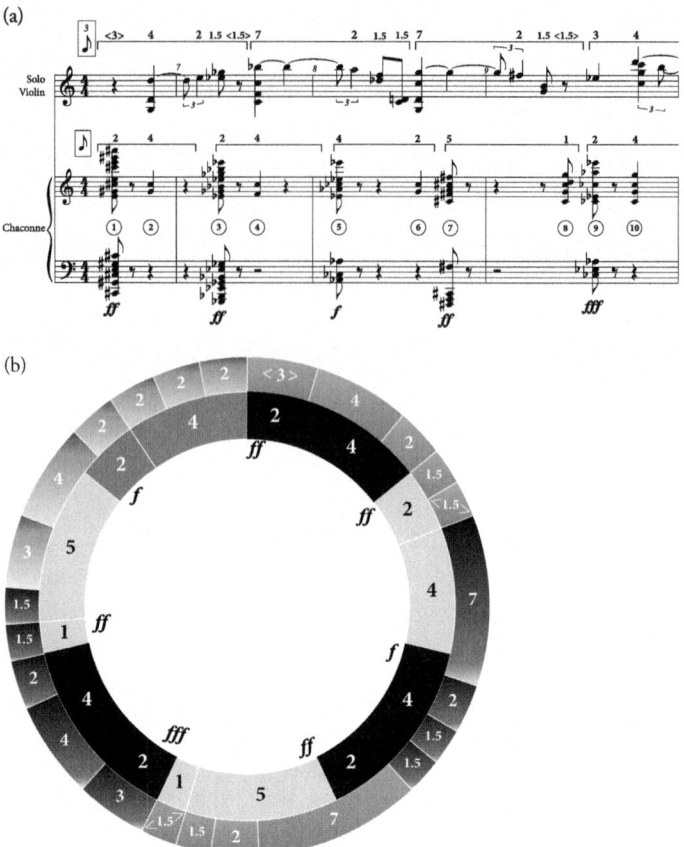

(b)

outside circle to inside circle: solo violin, chaconne

Ex. 5.5 Violin Concerto, movement II. (a) Bars 6–9 (Section I, chaconne statement 2); (b) duration circle of bars 6–11

with the same rhythmic profile of «7,2,1.5,1.5» but now given to the clarinets, horns and violas. The solo violin, shown with the outermost circle, presents a new melody – or 'path' as implied by the title of this movement – and the third independent rhythmic layer in this passage. With a smallest common duration of triplet semiquavers, the solo violin establishes a repeating pattern of «6,4,4,3,3,3». There are five statements of this pattern, and at the end Adès adds a «3,3,6» pattern that carries over into the start of the next chaconne statement. In this passage the level of dissociation has increased. Each layer has its own unique smallest common duration and its own distinctive rhythmic pattern. Rarely does the solo violin coincide with the other two patterns, which intensifies the forward momentum towards the next chaconne statement.

(a)

(b)

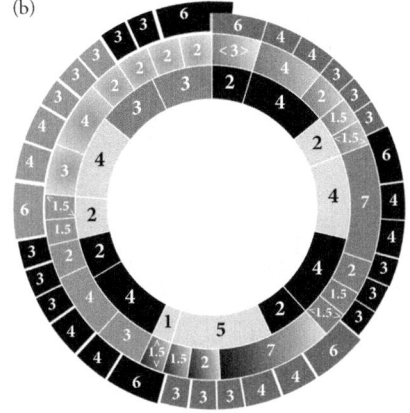

outside circle to inside circle: solo violin; clarinet,
horns, viola; chaconne

Ex. 5.6 Violin Concerto, movement II. (a) Bars 12–13 (Section I, chaconne statement 3); (b) duration circle of bars 12–16

Perhaps the most tension-filled passage in 'Paths' in terms of dynamics, texture and intense dissociation occurs in bars 22–7, the fifth statement of the minor-triad chaconne. As shown in Ex. 5.7, Adès creates a dense texture by superimposing four independent layers, thus achieving a heightened level of dissociation. Each layer presents its own unique rhythmic profile unfolding at its own pace. The rhythmic streams seldom align with one another at the same time, and this lack of concurrence not only heightens the level of dissociation, but also propels the music forward.

The chaconne, which is represented by the innermost circle (see Online Fig. 5.1), is presented by the strings, a solo trombone that sustains the chaconne rhythm throughout this passage and a tuba solo that does not enter until the ninth chord. Both of the rhythmic layers represented by the middle two circles were initially played by the solo violin but are

Ex. 5.7 Violin Concerto, movement II, bars 22–3 (Section I, chaconne statement 5)

now articulated by different instruments of the orchestra. The circle that is closest to the chaconne was originally presented by the solo violin in bars 6–11. Its smallest common duration is triplet semiquavers, and the flutes, clarinets and bassoons present a repeating pattern of «6,4,4,3,3,3» a total of five times with an added «3,3,6» at the end. The third rhythmic layer was first articulated in bars 17–22 by the solo violin, and its smallest common duration is also triplet semiquavers. This melodic line is played by the horns and oboes and occasionally supported by the trumpets and piccolo. The rhythmic profile of this line cannot be partitioned into a regularly repeating durational pattern, which is counter to the rhythmic continuities established by the other layers. After the initial pattern of «3,2,3,2,3,2,2,2,2,2», the subsequent statements are slightly altered: for example, the second partitioning of «3,2,3,2,3,2,2,2,2» is shortened by two triplet semiquavers, the third partitioning «3,2,3,2,2,2,2,2,2» eliminates the third «3,2» duration, and so on. The solo violin, shown with the outermost circle, is based on quintuplet semiquavers, the smallest common duration in the movement so far.[36] Within each quintuplet segment, Adès further partitions the rhythm into long–short dotted rhythmic motives that do not generate a consistent pattern. Not only has Adès created a high degree of dissociation here, but he also increases tension even further by incorporating several layers that have no a

[36] Adès progressively shortens the note values in the solo violin part. The intense level of dissociation and the numerous short rhythmic values at this point in the concerto take us far away from the measured crotchets of the chaconne statement that began the movement.

consistent rhythmic pattern. While these two rhythmically inconsistent streams share many points of occurrence with each other, there is a lack of collaboration with the chaconne and the «6,4,4,3,3,3» repeated figure. This delaying of coincidences among the four layers thus creates conflicts that Adès alludes to in his description of 'Paths'.

With each successive chaconne statement in Section I of 'Paths', Adès builds tension by superimposing multiple rhythmic layers. Each added layer carves its own melodic and rhythmic path, and as these independent streams of rhythmic activity unfold, they overlap with the constantly repetitive chaconne progression. As layers are added with each successive chaconne statement the moments of convergence or coordination among the layers become less frequent, and as these strata unfold their own rhythmic logic a heightened sense of complexity, a dense texture and a high level of dissociation are created.

The second 'large independent cycle' begins in bar 48 and presents the kind of resolution that Adès mentions in his description of 'Paths'. Most notably, the solo violin and the chaconne are synchronised for the first time since the opening of the movement, and in terms of pitch the minor harmonies of the first chaconne are altered to major triads. Example 5.8 provides bars 48–51, and a summary of the unfolding rhythmic layers is shown in Online Fig. 5.2. The smallest common duration for both the chaconne and the solo violin is a quaver, and the violin's repeating «2,2,4» durations often coincide with the long–short «4,2» durations of the cha-conne. The «2,2,4» pattern occurs five times with an additional duration of «2» added at the end. The outermost circle is presented by the piccolo, first violins and clarinet, and its smallest common duration is a semiquaver; these instruments continually project a «3,1» durational pattern, which appears twenty-one times in this passage. In contrast to Section I, all three

Ex. 5.8 Violin Concerto, movement II, bars 48–51 (Section II, chaconne statement 1)

layers sustain a pitch or harmony for the entire duration of every rhythmic segment in this passage. Section I, with its minor-triad chaconne, can be characterised by frequent rests and short–long rhythmic ideas, whereas in Section II, all the instruments, including the solo violin, contain no rests. And finally, all the strata here are aligned with one another to offer a sense of resolution and collaboration.

The rhythmic alignment between the solo violin and the major-triad chaconne does not last long. Although the violin often doubles the pitches of the underlying chaconne throughout the rest of Section II, it does not project its own rhythmic continuities or a consistent durational pattern, nor does it align with the consistent repetitive «4,2» patterns presented by the chaconne. Statements 2, 3 and 4 are transposed down a perfect fifth, and as the second 'large independent cycle' approaches the end of its cyclic journey the texture becomes denser with many pitch-class doublings.

After the metric dissonance and tension that was created in Section I and the resolution that occurred in Section II, the coda in bars 70–9 presents a kind of dispersion and spiralling, returning to a mild level of dissociation. Adès superimposes just two rhythmic streams throughout the entire coda and creates the impression that there is no way to get out of the cycles and patterns, thus spiralling into space forever. Both strata are notable for their extremely consistent durational patterns, in which each layer presents its own unique patterns that are constantly repeated without any rhythmic changes. Bar 70 is shown in Ex. 5.9, and a duration circle for the entire coda is included in Online Fig. 5.3. The three-chord chaconne is given as the inner circle. The total duration of the chaconne is six quavers, and it is evenly partitioned as «2,2,2». There are thirteen statements of this chaconne, and at the end, in bars 77–9, the triadic texture is stripped down to one-note utterances in the double bass and timpani (C–E♭–D♭–C).

Overlapping with the chaconne, the solo violin presents its own exceptionally consistent durational pattern of «4,3,4,3,3,3,3,3» calculated

Ex. 5.9 Violin Concerto, movement II, bar 70 (coda)

in triplet demisemiquavers. Despite the variety in its pitch structure throughout the coda, it eventually becomes stuck in the last four bars on a rocking two-note motive of G_3 and Ab_3. The rhythmic profiles for both the violin and the chaconne are repeated without any alterations, and rarely do the two streams align or coordinate. As these two rhythmic layers independently unfold, the texture gradually thins along with a dramatic drop in the dynamic level. Thanks to the consistently repeating patterns with their unchanging rhythmic structures, Adès creates a sense of infinite spiralling.

* * *

In the three instrumental movements examined in this chapter the pitch structure of Adès's chaconnes undergo the usual kinds of changes that we expect of this variation form. Previous studies of these movements have offered detailed analyses of the changes and conflicts that occur in the harmonic structure. Yet attention to only the pitch organisation does not provide a complete picture of the complexities of an Adèsian chaconne. For Adès, a chaconne is not simply a set of pitch variations on a repeating harmonic progression. Rather, the repetition of the cycle provides an opportunity to superimpose independent layers of rhythmic patterns that heighten and enrich the pitch and harmonic musical transformations. As I have demonstrated, pitch and rhythm have a much more independent existence than has been recognised. Adès's treatment of rhythm in general and, specifically, his superimposition of independent layers of rhythmic activity allow rhythm in these chaconne movements to transcend its local significance and collaborate with other parameters to shape texture, density and large-scale form. Recognising the different levels of dissociation and how the increases and decreases of intensities in a movement generate directionality allow us to better understand the form-functional strategies that Adès employs with his chaconnes.

Dissociation is thus a valuable tool to reveal the complex rhythmic processes in Adès's chaconne movements. While there are a number of other compositions in which Adès employs a chaconne – *In Seven Days*, the trial scene in *Powder Her Face* (Act II, Scene 6) and *The Exterminating Angel* – dissociation can also be used to analyse a number of his works that are not structured in this way. For instance, in 'Chori', the third and final movement from Adès's solo piano piece *Traced Overhead* (1996), each stratum has its own regularly repeating rhythmic patterns, while the pitch structures are also unique to each stratum. In *Asyla* (1997), there are numerous passages with varying levels of dissociation, and recognising when these unsynchronised stratified layers finally cooperate, if even for a brief moment, helps us better understand the shape and drama of Adès's orchestral composition. Adès's compositional technique of superimposing multiple layers that progress by their own rhythmic logic and temporalities can be also be found in his very first composition, the *Five Eliot Landscapes*. Acknowledging the many repeated rhythmic patterns, together with the superimposition of these continuities and the wide variety of dissociation, allows us to recognise the powerful and complex relationships not just in Adès's chaconnes but throughout his body of works.

6 | Closing the Circle?

Tevot *and the Question of Symphonic Resolution*

RICHARD POWELL

While some artists adopt a more cloistered approach to their work, Thomas Adès's proactive engagement with musical history continues to distinguish his compositional activities. It is in this sense that he has been able to transcend a boundary that Alastair Williams traces 'between a modernist distrust of tradition and a postmodernist reassertion of it'; for Williams, Adès in fact numbers among those composers who are able to assume the role of a musicologist 'because their activities as composers are so firmly embedded in strong discourses that the two aspects – music and discourse – are inseparable'.[1] Certainly, the discourses that both pervade and surround some of Adès's most recent projects continue to evidence this, from his immersion in *fin de siècle* salon styles in his score for Wash Westmoreland's 2018 film *Colette*[2] to his dialogue with the music of Liszt for Wayne McGregor's ballet adaptation of Dante's *Divina commedia* (2019–20).[3] The Romantic gestures that permeate his Concerto for Piano and Orchestra (2018) similarly suggest a conscious extension of the composer's engagement with the concerto tradition,[4] a relationship encompassing two further ensemble works that throw the solo piano into relief – *Concerto Conciso* (1997–8) and *In Seven Days* (2008) – as well as the Violin Concerto (2005).[5] While the unique fusion of tension, lyricism and virtuosity that the concerto genre offers has sustained its popularity across the last two centuries, Adès has also been equally candid in his embrace of an arguably thornier, more voguish form: the symphony. His orchestral pieces

---

[1] Alastair Williams, 'Between Modernism and Postmodernism: Structure and Expression in John Adams, Kaija Saariaho and Thomas Adès', in *The Routledge Research Companion to Modernism in Music*, ed. by Björn Heile and Charles Wilson (New York: Routledge, 2019), pp. 327–52 (p. 344).

[2] Adrian Edwards, 'Adès: *Colette* (Original Motion Picture Soundtrack)', *Gramophone*, 96/1173 (2019), 58.

[3] Kirill Gerstein, 'Thomas Adès: "Roots, Seeds & Live Cultures" – "Kirill Gerstein Invites" @ HfM Eisler Berlin', online video interview, 18 June 2020, YouTube, www.youtube.com/watch?v=I0kHP_npxJA.

[4] Andrew Mellor, 'Adès: Piano Concerto; *Totentanz*', *Gramophone*, 97/1187 (2020), 36.

[5] In 2016 Adès also adapted his four-movement piece *Lieux retrouvés* (2009) for cello and small orchestra.

Asyla (1997), *Tevot* (2007) and *Polaris* (2010) amount to a trilogy of such works in all but name, as he himself acknowledges, and this engagement has been extended further in 2020 with a symphony adapting material from his opera *The Exterminating Angel* (2015–16).[6]

Once perceived as 'the apex of classical music'[7] and as a 'touchstone of compositional prowess',[8] the symphony has carried, in the words of Daniel Grimley, 'perhaps the greatest ideological baggage of any large-scale musical form'.[9] The significance of this impediment is not lost on Adès, who laments the expectations of 'a certain inevitable kind of structure or decorum' that – mistakenly, he feels – accompany the label. He invokes the supposition that a symphony should be 'something which closes a circle', hinting at a symphonic philosophy that tends towards resolution.[10] Nevertheless, he cites the music of Jean Sibelius (1865–1957) on account of the way in which it grapples with closure. He highlights a tension between the inclination to conclude and an 'inner desire' – inherent in the musical material – to venture outwards into new territories:

The conflict becomes more and more powerful as the symphonies go on. In the Fifth it is a huge struggle which is achieved, in the Sixth it seems so powerful that it has to happen just offstage, and in the Seventh there is a sense that although he makes it in the end he is all but broken by the effort. It becomes an increasingly agonising process. But in the tone poems, he is released from the conflict of having to make an abstract argument that functions logically. So the end of *Tapiola* is deeply conclusive, but the end of the Seventh Symphony is painfully inconclusive.[11]

Indeed, Adès seems to suggest that it is precisely this tension with 'symphonic completeness' that may have allowed these works to attain such influence: 'I think he was the first to break, painfully, the mistaken idea that a symphonic argument had to have a sort of structural order to it.'[12]

Given the paradox of reconciliation and rupture that Adès highlights in Sibelius's Seventh Symphony Op. 105 (1924), along with the emphasis he

---

[6] London Symphony Orchestra, 'Thomas Adès: *Asyla, Tevot, Polaris*', online video interview, 28 February 2017, YouTube, www.youtube.com/watch?v=xEZe4-y720I.

[7] Alexander Goehr, 'The Reith Lectures – The Survival of the Symphony: The Old Warhorse', BBC Radio 4, 18 November 1987, www.bbc.co.uk/programmes/p00h196j.

[8] Mark Evan Bonds, 'Symphony: II. 19th Century', *Grove Music Online*, www.oxfordmusiconline.com/grovemusic.

[9] Daniel Grimley, 'Symphony/Antiphony: Formal Strategies in the Twentieth-Century Symphony', in *The Cambridge Companion to the Symphony*, ed. by Julian Horton (Cambridge: Cambridge University Press, 2013), pp. 285–310 (p. 285).

[10] Thomas Adès and Tom Service, *Thomas Adès: Full of Noises – Conversations with Tom Service*, paperback ed. (London: Faber and Faber, 2018), pp. 172–3.

[11] Ibid., p. 172.   [12] Ibid., p. 173.

places on the Finn's progressive approach to structure, it is interesting to note the surface parallels between that work and Adès's own *Tevot*: both are designated symphonies, last approximately twenty minutes in length and are cast in single-movement forms demarcated by intricate sequences of related tempo changes. Indeed, when Tom Service introduces Adès's music into their discussion of Sibelius, the composer is quick to invoke both *Tevot* and the shorter *Polaris* as apparent parallels to his musings on the Seventh Symphony and the tone poem *Tapiola*.[13]

I suggest that the connection between Sibelius's Seventh Symphony and Adès's *Tevot* extends to aural experience. Consider both openings: two gestures – one ascending, the other descending – that in spite of their relative simplicity, hold the potential for the forms that will unfold. In the Seventh Symphony, a rising scale fragmented through several instrumental parts (bars 1–2) obliquely references several potential keys before offsetting these mounting expectations by stalling at a contrasting harmonic plane (bar 3); this apparent polarity engenders an immediate friction between two sets of sonorities, a complex tonal tension that seemingly requires resolution and will accordingly come to define the unfolding of the work. At the outset of *Tevot*, meanwhile, stratospheric cascades of falling fifths (indicated by white double-ended arrows in Ex. 6.1) and semitones (lines and downward black-ended arrows) seamlessly emerge in the upper strings, their oscillations underlined by sustained woodwinds to create the impression of a chromatically descending chorale-like texture (Ex. 6.1). The effect is not so much of a direct source of harmonic conflict as of a sense of long-range tension: a tonal restlessness takes hold, a seemingly perpetual chain of modulations engendering an audible dynamism that will provide a continuing source of structural direction.

The musical tensions that both openings contain ultimately prove decisive in the way in which their broader forms play out. In this manner, the works can be seen as subscribing to long-held conceptions of symphonic as synonymous with organicism – the very 'profound logic' that Sibelius opined to Mahler in their oft-cited 1907 meeting.[14] At the same time, however, there is a sense in which both symphonies subvert this linearity; stylistically distinctive approaches to issues of continuity, repetition, direction and resolution allow listeners to experience forms that are at once stable and volatile, recurrent and changing, static and dynamic, closed and open. In these terms – and, indeed, in this chapter – Sibelius's Seventh

---

[13] Ibid., pp. 172–3.   [14] Guy Rickards, *Jean Sibelius* (London: Phaidon Press, 1997), p. 96.

Ex. 6.1 *Tevot*, reduction of bars 1–4

Symphony offers a potent lens through which *Tevot* can be viewed. It sheds light not only upon the unique strategies by which Adès navigates the issues of symphonic resolution that he perceives, but also upon the way in which he – like Sibelius before him – engages with elements of the symphonic tradition at large, in turn encouraging listeners to embrace the temporal paradoxes that unfold.

Symphonic Thought

Grimley's suggestion that the symphony is 'concerned explicitly with the musical representation of time and space' is affirmed by a preoccupation with form evident in avenues of scholarship.[15] In particular, what Arnold Whittall identifies as an often close relationship between organisation and organicism in formal thought emerges – even if only through implication – as a feature of several influential twentieth-century discourses on symphonic music.[16] Take Robert Simpson's observations in 1966:

---

[15] Daniel Grimley, 'Symphony/Antiphony', p. 285.
[16] Arnold Whittall, 'Form', *Grove Music Online*, www.oxfordmusiconline.com/grovemusic.

At the end of a great symphony there is the sense that the music has grown by the interpenetrative activity of *all* its constituent elements. Nothing is ever allowed to lapse into aimlessness, or the kind of inactivity that needs artificially reviving … The great thing to keep constantly in mind is that no single element is ever abandoned, or deliberately excluded, that the composer must master them all and subordinate them to the demands of the whole.[17]

Simpson's own compositional endeavours within the genre are lauded by Hans Keller, writing nearly a decade later, precisely on account of their navigation of what Keller asserts as 'the fundamental symphonic problem – the definition and large-scale integration of the contrast between statements and developments'.[18] Though these re-framings of the underlying issues of organicism undeniably represent a particular aesthetic outlook on the genre, they nevertheless bear notable relevance to Adès's own perspectives on such issues. Indeed, they emerge as a central tenet of his disenchantment with the work of Wagner:

I don't find Wagner's an organic, necessary art … His material doesn't grow symphonically – it doesn't grow through a musical logic – it grows parasitically … He's quite weak on articulating an actual section of music. The reason is that Wagner is not interested in releasing the inherent, organic power – what I would mean by genuinely 'symphonic' power – of his (often magnificent) cells. It's just a pose. Good symphonies are often in some ways an unfolding sequence of miniatures.[19]

Adès's veneration for such sequential designs is intriguing given the apparent evidence of multi-movement thinking that some commentators have identified in Sibelius's Seventh Symphony. To give an early example, Cecil Gray seeks to reconcile the work with convention, identifying within it four successive interconnected movements that simultaneously constitute 'a single and indissoluble organism'.[20] More recently, Edward Laufer has proposed a 'bold refashioning of the classical design' through a mapping of Sibelius's original idea for a 'Hellenic rondo' in which the typical development section is in fact separated out into episodes throughout the work to ensure 'a sense of continuous growth, cumulation, and completion

---

[17]   Robert Simpson, 'Introduction', in *The Symphony*, vol. 2: *Elgar to the Present Day*, ed. by Robert Simpson (Aylesbury: Penguin Books, 1966), pp. 9–14 (p. 10).

[18]   Hans Keller, 'The State of the Symphony: Not Only Maxwell Davies's', *Tempo*, 125 (1978), 6–11 (p. 10).

[19]   Adès and Service, *Full of Noises*, pp. 15–16.

[20]   Cecil Gray, *Sibelius: The Symphonies* (London: Oxford University Press, 1935), p. 71.

of sections'.[21] Though writers like Veijo Murtomäki argue that the Seventh Symphony represents no less than a 'new and revolutionary' symphonic development,[22] an exploration of its connections with convention can be revealing. When considered in temporal terms, the reorderings and discontinuities that Laufer seems to imply can take on a more subversive character. An embrace of the paradoxes the piece presents has yielded some of its most intriguing and progressive readings. Whittall highlights the interplay between its episodes of volatility and its broader sense of structural balance.[23] Meanwhile, the British composer David Matthews associates the work with a particular kind of symphonic impetus, asserting that it 'is always moving symphonically; evolving, changing direction, sometimes with slow deliberation, sometimes with athletic swiftness'.[24] These characteristics resonate with the influence that Matthews cites Sibelius as having had on his own symphonies, pointing to the seemingly paradoxical 'true stasis' they attain 'through energy and movement': 'I have learnt a lot from his control of pace, his welding together of different kinds of movement, his imperceptible transitions from fast to slow or slow to fast'.[25]

Matthews's concern with energy, motion and pace bears considerable relevance to the conceptual underpinning of *Tevot* that Adès articulates. The work's title carries multiple meanings. In modern-day Hebrew it signifies 'vessels', which is adapted in musical terminology to represent bars of music. For the composer, this more practical concern represents a fundamental need to channel musical energy: 'I liked the idea that the bars of the music were carrying the notes as a sort of family through the piece. And they do, because without bars, you'd have musical chaos.'[26] Meanwhile, in its singular form – *tevah* – the word is utilised specifically in the Bible to represent two particular vessels: Noah's ark and the

[21] Edward Laufer, 'Continuity and Design in the Seventh Symphony', in *Sibelius Studies*, ed. by Timothy L. Jackson and Veijo Murtomäki (Cambridge: Cambridge University Press, 2001), pp. 352–90 (p. 355).

[22] Veijo Murtomäki, *Symphonic Unity: The Development of Formal Thinking in the Symphonies of Sibelius*, trans. by Henry Bacon (Helsinki: Studia Musicologia Universitatis Helsingiensis, 1993), p. 243.

[23] Arnold Whittall, 'The Later Symphonies', in *The Cambridge Companion to Sibelius*, ed. by Daniel M. Grimley (Cambridge: Cambridge University Press, 2004), pp. 49–65 (pp. 62–3).

[24] David Matthews, 'Living Traditions', *Musical Times*, 134/1802 (1993), 189–91 (p. 190).

[25] Richard Duffalo, *Trackings: Composers Speak with Richard Duffalo* (New York: Oxford University Press, 1989), p. 154.

[26] Tom Service, 'Writing Music? It's Like Flying a Plane: Tom Service on Thomas Adès', *Guardian*, 26 February 2007, section G2, p. 23.

Nile-bound reed basket in which the baby Moses is placed by his mother.[27] Adès utilises this imagery to indicate a cosmic narrative for the work, envisioning the planet itself as the vessel in question: 'The earth would be a spaceship, a ship that carries us – and several other species! – through the chaos of space in safety.'[28] This voyage is not simply an escape; where Service suggests connotations of refuge in the title, the composer is quick to emphasise a more teleological narrative: 'A haven sounds as if one is hiding from something, and I don't think that about *Tevot*. In this piece, it's more like a final resolution – a real resolution – rather than that one is escaping from something.'[29] Nevertheless, this trajectory does not translate to musical stability, with the composer introducing 'many quite sudden and instant changes of landscape' not only to render the journey 'truthful' but also 'to give it movement'.[30] This mingling of formal concerns and broader imagery strengthens further Edward Venn's assertion – in light of Adès's own musings on Chopin and Wagner – that the composer's 'understanding of symphonism ... enables conceptual motion from abstract musical procedures via genre and topic to metaphor (and back)'.[31] Venn explores these connections extensively within the context of *Tevot* itself, utilising the work and its accompanying metaphorical framework as a window into the embodied experiences that the composer's music offers more broadly.[32]

Although, as in the Seventh Symphony, these goal-directed concerns are manifested in a careful regulation of tempo, Adès also echoes Sibelius in his careful establishment and manipulation of tonal energy; as with the notions of the symphonic discussed, the apparatus drawn upon throughout this chapter will similarly exploit the implicit conceptual relationships between the musical strategies employed and metaphors of time, narrative, energy and motion. With the opening passages outlined in the introduction to this chapter, both composers are able to set in motion narratives of both tonality and pace in which the continuous, linear experience prized in traditional symphonic thought is allowed to coexist with features that might equally prompt discontinuous, non-linear readings.

[27] Paul Griffiths, 'Thomas Adès: *Tevot*', programme notes, London Symphony Orchestra, conducted by Thomas Adès, Barbican, London, 9 March 2016, p. 8.

[28] Service, 'Writing Music?'   [29] Ibid.   [30] Ibid.

[31] Edward Venn, *Thomas Adès: Asyla* (London: Routledge, 2017), p. 46.

[32] Edward Venn, 'Metaphorical Bodies and Multiple Agencies in Thomas Adès's *Tevot*', in *Music, Analysis, and the Body: Experiments, Explorations, and Embodiments*, ed. by Nicholas W. Reyland and Rebecca Thumpston (Leuven: Peeters, 2018), pp. 133–52.

Tensions and Potential

The long-range structural potential contained within the opening gestures of Sibelius's Seventh Symphony can be articulated principally in terms of an ambiguous but nonetheless palpable harmonic tension. The initial white-note scale in the strings (bars 1–2) has been considered in terms of a variety of harmonic functions, predominantly as being in the C major tonic;[33] in G major as a dominant to that tonic on account of the initial G♮ timpani roll;[34] and in A minor on account of the A♮ cello note that follows.[35] These readings not only underline a degree of tonal uncertainty, but also grant the ensuing A flat minor chord (bar 3) a jarring quality; the searching, *Tristan*-esque chromatic slips in its wake (bars 3–5) underline this lack of cemented tonal centre. Given this initial ambiguity, the subsequent passages assume a crucial role in affirming the central importance of C major.

Although clear allusions to this tonic emerge via both melodies and pedal points from the seventh bar onwards, the sequential repetitions that follow maintain nods towards more dissonant routes. A♭ continues to feature prominently, frequently being normalised within the context of F minor figures. Indeed, it is through this process of harmonic assimilation that G major is reasserted in bar 21, preparing the way for the richly polyphonic string passage that follows, in which C major is increasingly accentuated. The reassertion that begins at bar 50 incites a convergence, the entire ensemble uniting on an unmistakable perfect cadence (bars 59–60), with the arpeggiated trombone theme capping the first significant point of arrival in the work. Tim Howell points to the accumulative process of this introductory passage in support of his broader notion of the 'continuous development technique' that pervades both the thematic and the tonal course of the work; the opening segment acts as a miniaturisation of this principle through its 'initial denial of, but eventual preparation for, the establishment of C major by reinterpretation of the same elements which interrupted that goal in order to confirm it'.[36] In this sense, it comes as no surprise that it is via the re-emergence of A♭s and E♭s that the climax is curtailed, the ensemble jolted into an F minor diversion from bar 71. As the

---

[33] Tim Howell, *Jean Sibelius: Progressive Techniques in the Symphonies and Tone Poems* (New York: Garland Publishing, 1989), p. 87.

[34] Ibid.; and Murtomäki, *Symphonic Unity*, p. 261.

[35] Lionel Pike, *Beethoven, Sibelius and 'the Profound Logic': Studies in Symphonic Analysis* (London: Athlone Press, 1978), p. 204.

[36] Howell, *Jean Sibelius*, p. 87.

ensemble departs from the stability it has so elaborately established, it becomes clear that an audible balancing act has been set in motion.

Although Sibelius's symphony, still rooted in post-Romantic harmonic principles, inevitably exhibits tonal governance in a comparatively cogent manner, it is worth emphasising that *Tevot* displays a similarly considered treatment of both tonality and sonority: both have a profound bearing upon the large-scale structure. Adès sidesteps a more traditional hierarchy in favour of a perpetually shifting sense of tonal magnetism, a notion that he himself articulates as fundamental to his compositional outlook:

The two notes in an interval, or any number of chords, have a magnetic relationship of attraction or repulsion which creates movement in one direction or another. A composer, whether of a symphony or a pop song, is arranging these magnetic objects in a certain disposition. That means that sometimes, in order to understand the weight of one note and the next note to it, you might have to transfer meaning from one to another.[37]

This conception bears particular relevance to the dynamism established at the outset of *Tevot*, not least given the innate tension Adès identifies within the perfect fourth/fifth relationship: 'You must imagine that the fourth is an object, like a single note. It's an atom that is quivering, and it wants to split.'[38] This impulse is initially made explicit through the initial implementation of descending fifths (E♮–A♮–D♮) that in turn gradually shift downwards in semitone steps with distinct rhythmic independence but with a proximity that allows for a broader sense of unified motion: multiplicity within continuity. This semitone slippage of stacked fifths sets a harmonic precedent for the parallel sequences that subsequently emerge, with new falling chains introduced in yet higher registers to enhance an impression of perpetual descent.

This de-emphasis on the beginning or end of these sequences has a harmonic bearing; instead of any hierarchy being established and subsequently uprooted, the 'tonality' of the work moves by allusion: a mercurial point of aural reference that calls to mind the composer's conception of shifting magnetic relationships between notes. This harmonic magnetism, however, arguably creates an aural point of quasi-melodic focus in the shape of the descending semitone shifts that are underlined by the woodwinds. Extending Raymond Monelle's exploration of the semiotic power of

---

[37] Adès and Service, *Full of Noises*, p. 3.   [38] Ibid., p. 33.

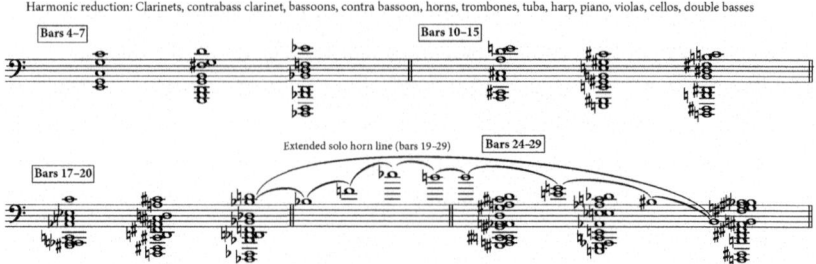

Ex. 6.2 *Tevot*, bars 4–29, harmonic reduction of lower-register homophonic sequences, including solo horn passage

this descending interval – the *pianto* – in musical history,[39] Venn also considers its frequent presence within Adès's output and the interpretive springboard it offers. Beyond the personal expressions of grief that Monelle identifies, Venn discusses the potential for the gesture to convey more cultural concepts of melancholy and nostalgia, not least within the context of *Asyla* and the opera *The Tempest*.[40] Joseph Sowa explores the motivic implications of *pianto* gestures extensively within *Tevot* itself, and though he is justified in acknowledging that these gestures are far from the primary source of its 'affective power', they nevertheless support the implied depart-ure – and accompanying sense of loss – in the journey metaphor that Adès employs.[41] At the outset of the work, however, the most significant contri-bution made by these descending figures is a heightened sense of transience.

The introduction of a contrasting figure in the lower winds and strings in the fourth bar offers an audible foothold, providing a temporal marker beyond the perpetual harmonic descent as it develops through the opening minutes of the work (Ex. 6.2). The block-like homophonic gesture creates a striking juxtaposition, with sporadic successions of three-part chord changes inciting a seemingly independent harmonic course and rate of

[39] Raymond Monelle, *The Sense of Music: Semiotic Essays* (Princeton, NJ: Princeton University Press, 2000), pp. 66–77.

[40] Edward Venn, 'Thomas Adès and the Pianto', in *Proceedings of the International Conference on Music Semiotics in Memory of Raymond Monelle: University of Edinburgh, 26–28 October 2012*, ed. by Nearchos Panos, Vangelis Lympouridis, George Athanasopoulos and Peter Nelson (Edinburgh: International Project on Music and Dance Semiotics, 2013), pp. 309–17; Venn, *Thomas Adès: Asyla*, pp. 31–4.

[41] Joseph Sowa, 'The Art of Transformation: The Heraclitian Form of Thomas Adès's *Tevot* as a Critical Lens for the Symphonic Tradition' (unpublished PhD dissertation, Brandeis University, 2019), p. 8. Sowa examines *Tevot* specifically in terms of a Heraclitean conception of flux, considering its relationship both with Sibelius's Seventh Symphony and with earlier works in the genre.

motion (bars 4–6);[42] in fact, as Venn observes, despite the numerous audible contrasts, the ascending sequence of the upper voice of this initial figure (C♮–D♮–E♭) is in fact cued by elements of the perpetual woodwind and string descent.[43] The corresponding upper-register descent in the consequent iteration of the figure (bars 10–15: E♮–A♯–A♮) contributes to a broader rise and fall that, as Venn also notes, is subsequently underlined by the extended arching horn motive (bars 19–29), which achieves greatest prominence through its upwards leap of a minor seventh (F♮–E♭, bar 21).[44]

The broader generative power of the opening passage of *Tevot* becomes yet clearer when it is considered in light of Sibelius's work. As in the Seventh Symphony, three kinds of tension emerge: between harmonic clarity and ambiguity; between ascending and descending gestures; and, most significantly, between a content-generated need to sustain tonal mobility and a palpable inclination for the material to resolve. Indeed, it is this promise of a potential resolution that underpins the playing out of both structures.

Unfolding Multiplicities

Beyond merely providing contrast, Paul Griffiths suggests that the presence of unstable features within *Tevot* contributes to its apparent resolution, with the ever-shifting melody that dominates the final portion of the piece 'assuring us that continuity and change are two faces of the one phenomenon'.[45] His comment illuminates the broader tension between stasis and flux – or being and becoming – with which both Adès and Sibelius engage in their music. It is a distinction that has long permeated temporal thought; Friedel Weinert traces its formalisation back to pre-Socratic philosophy, contrasting the unchanging 'being' propounded by Parmenides of Elea with the world of changing appearances posited by Heraclitus of Ephesus.[46] However, rather than comprising diametrically opposing conceptions of time (change as either illusory or fundamental; reality as either temporal or atemporal), these two modes can instead be understood as operating within a continuum of varying perspectives. As extended studies

---

[42] Drew Massey draws astute parallels here with the interplay between repeated material played by layered independent instrumental groups in Charles Ives's *The Unanswered Question*. See Drew Massey, *Thomas Adès in Five Essays* (New York: Oxford University Press, 2021), pp. 145–6.

[43] Venn, 'Metaphorical Bodies', pp. 140–2.   [44] Ibid., pp. 144–5.

[45] Griffiths, 'Thomas Adès: *Tevot*', p. 8.

[46] Friedel Weinert, *The March of Time: Evolving Conceptions of Time in the Light of Scientific Discoveries* (London: Springer, 2013), pp. 89–90.

such as those by Jonathan Kramer and David Epstein demonstrate, musical structures can heighten awareness of the potential for such temporal modes to coexist.[47] The handling of rhythmic energy throughout the Seventh Symphony in particular amounts to far more than just a linear ebb and flow; instilled continuities help create more complex perceptual structures, granting listeners the impression of a pluralistic temporal experience. Sibelius's manipulation of pulse – and, in turn, of material – provides a compelling frame within which the tempo relationships and motivic developments utilised in *Tevot* can be considered; in particular, Sibelius's engagement with parallel layers of temporal motion presents a model for blending elements of continuity and change that Adès develops in an engagingly singular manner.

Sibelius's work is managed via a network of speed adjustments (Online Table 6.1).[48] Three slow passages bookend and intersect the structure (bars 1–92, 222–36 and 476–525), while two interceding stretches comprise noticeably more changeable music: fast episodes and moderate, transitory passages. In relation to the musical content they convey, these three broader levels of pace represent parallel temporal threads, each sustaining ongoing strands of interconnected development. The coincidence of both slow and fast music is enhanced by the middleground transitions; in bridging the two extremes, these passages also offer glimpses of the way in which they interlock and overlap, sometimes in paradoxical ways. The carefully staggered metrical shifts of the string chromatic scales in the rallentando (bars 213–22), for example, heighten the continuity of the shift from *Vivacissimo* to *Adagio*, drawing attention to the potential for long ('slow') phrase structures in fast music, and to the presence of rapid, scalic, harmonically unstable gestures within more tonally secure, metrically slower content. These dualities are reinforced by the fact that what is then notated as an acceleration to *Allegro molto moderato* (bars 237–57) might in fact be perceived as a deceleration. In a similar way, the later jump to *Presto* (bar 449) acts as a bridge to the subsequent *Adagio* rather than as an end in itself, the propulsive string sequences providing a palpable real-time demonstration of the way the same material can function within 'slow' and 'fast' contexts. Viewing the work in terms of these contrasting yet cooperating

[47] Jonathan D. Kramer, *The Time of Music: New Meanings, New Temporalities, New Listening Strategies* (New York: Schirmer Books, 1988); David Epstein, *Shaping Time: Music, the Brain, and Performance* (New York: Schirmer Books, 1995).

[48] Timed durations in Online Table 6.1 are taken from Jean Sibelius, Symphony No. 7, London Symphony Orchestra, conducted by Sir Colin Davis (LSO Live LSO0552, 2004).

temporal levels offers a reading of musical energy channelled not in one direction but in three, creating a dynamic multilevel structure. Tempo changes require not so much a linear departure and arrival as an aural readjustment; focus can fall on fast-moving detail or on a slower-moving bigger picture, or it can transition back and forth between the two.

The three passages of 'slow' music that punctuate the Seventh Symphony have been shown not only to frame the architecture of the work, but also to imbue it with stability.[49] For Whittall, it is in the contrast that these episodes provide that the 'strength and originality' of the piece can be found; he writes of them as 'the most explicit thematic and tonal pillars of the unified design', contrasting with the 'imbalance and instability' of the surrounding music.[50] Certainly these sections exhibit a clear degree of consistency, with their recurring trombone theme acting – via a stable arpeggiated shape – as an aural affirmation of both the sonority and the key of C natural: the major mode in the bookending segments, the minor mode in the central, developmental one. Meanwhile, periods of transience are dominated by scalic activity; the linear, seemingly goal-directed nature of such figures directly conveys motion and provides an accumulation – and, at points, a saturation – of harmonic material that contributes to an overriding loss of stability.

However, to characterise these passages simply in terms of stasis and flux does not paint a full picture. Though the three ostensibly static segments perform comparable stabilising functions, they do so in a manner that betrays a particular kind of development that emphasises temporal awareness. The form of the Seventh Symphony evidences a collision of what Howell outlines as a distinction between two attitudes towards temporality: functional, onward-leaning repetition and retrospective, melancholic recollection.[51] The music reveals both a desire to return to the past and a tacit acknowledgement that it can be accessed only as memory. While a desire to return to the affirmation of the opening cadence becomes apparent, the variations that infiltrate the recurrences facilitate an onward,

---

[49] For Pike, the trombone themes that cap the climactic cadences in these passages mark 'high points, or points of reference' (Pike, *Beethoven, Sibelius*, p. 206); meanwhile, for Simon Parmet, the two bookending C major affirmations in particular act as 'corner-stones' for the broader structure. Simon Parmet, *The Symphonies of Sibelius: A Study in Musical Appreciation* (London: Cassell, 1959), pp. 127–29. As evidenced by Online Table 6.1, this 'cornerstone' reading has durational implications, with the relentless changes in pace that characterises the rest of the work held between these two notably longer periods of relative constancy.

[50] Whittall, 'The Later Symphonies', p. 63.

[51] Tim Howell, 'Brahms, Kierkegaard and Repetition: Three Intermezzi', *19th-Century Music Review*, 10/i (2013), 101–17 (pp. 103–4).

developmental function; the audible denial of a full return evokes nostalgia. At such moments, the symphony possesses 'times' that, in spite of the linear narrative, might be heard as 'facing' in opposite directions.

If *Tevot* is considered purely in terms of the metronome markings specified in the score, it might appear to fall into two approximate halves: the first characterised by change, the second by consistency. However, when this is reconciled with an aural impression, along with timed durations, three broader structural segments emerge (Online Table 6.2).[52] The first of these lasts for more than eight minutes but encompasses considerable sequential change, with regular modifications to pulse ensuring a fluctuating, and often fleeting, temporal experience (bars 1–256, 8'19"). This eventually gives way to a shorter section that comprises only forty-six bars of notated material but accounts for a far more substantial portion of musical time – more than four minutes – on account of the significantly lower speed that predominates (bars 257–302, 4'10"). This precipitates the third structural stage – just thirty-six seconds shorter than the first – which effectively maintains a single pulse throughout, with the notated motion doubled from bar 399 (bars 302–444, 7'43"). Though this reading would appear to indicate three radically different passages of music, a pulse of MM 80 – or its doubled expression of MM 160 – recurs frequently through the course of the piece (see bold highlights in the 'pulse' column of Online Table 6.2), providing a point of reference in the midst of change. In this way, it is possible to view *Tevot* as possessing a central pulse, a core 'time' from which departures may be made.[53]

The ambiguously open-ended harmonic sequences that characterise the opening of the work are reinforced rhythmically: the only initial indicators of this core 'time' are the triplet quaver/semiquaver oscillations of the violins, while, on a larger scale, listeners are encouraged to gauge the passing of time by the gradual semitone descents. Wider sensations of pulse and onward motion are imbued but not quantified in terms of an explicitly defined metrical framework. Growing unrest in the opening passage, however, seemingly prompts the first deviations from the central pulse. Divergences emerge from bar 24, as thickening textures begin to

---

[52] Timed durations in Online Table 6.2 are taken from Thomas Adès, *Tevot*, London Symphony Orchestra, conducted by Thomas Adès (LSO Live LSO0798, 2016).

[53] Adès revised the speed markings ahead of the 2014 score publication of *Tevot*, notably including more specific metronome markings – not least with regard to the core pulse – and establishing a more precise network of rhythmic and metrical connections. For details, compare Online Table 6.2 with Venn's Table 1 (based on the original 2007 score) in Venn, 'Metaphorical Bodies', p. 137.

convolute the audible division between different gestures. As the lower chordal gestures gradually lose their rhythmic unity and harmonic coherence, chromatic inflections increasingly infiltrate the stratospheric descending fifths. This ramping up of tonal tension is supported by a gradual crescendo that culminates in a momentary release at bar 53, most of the amassed orchestra suddenly dropping away to reveal a change in metre, content and structure: skittering woodwinds burst into an ongoing dialogue of angular, staccato triplet quavers punctuated by pitched percussion.

This apparently abrupt shift in character sets a precedent for the five minutes of music that follow, in which change and continuity are afforded aural coexistence. Nine further alterations of either tempo or metre ensure a relentless dynamism. Although six iterations of the core pulse appear within the first half of the work, the metrical emphases contained within this framework regularly shift and proliferate by virtue of the material deployed, with each change accompanied by further motivic developments. Drew Massey observes the discontinuity of this 'restless presentation of musical material', noting that it prevents 'the listener from participating in a continuously unfolding and unified musical experience'.[54] An awareness of change is heightened yet further by the increasingly overlapping presentation of these motivic changes, with transformations often occurring in parallel rather than direct succession.

Adès's inclination to employ different temporal levels and layers in his music has been explored elsewhere.[55] *Tevot* certainly exhibits aspects of what Roeder terms 'multiply-paced polyphony', with particular thematic ideas departing from view only to reappear in new guises, often with changing rhythmic properties allowing either a cohesive or pointedly jarring counterpoint with parallel figures.[56] This overlapping technique invites comparison with the parallel temporal streams of Sibelius's Seventh Symphony, the stark juxtaposition of – and interaction between – different materials, metres and tempos engendering an audible plurality; as Howell suggests, 'the illusion of multi-movement symphonic contrasts is actually occurring within the reality of a single-movement entity'.[57]

[54] Massey, *Thomas Adès in Five Essays*, p. 145.

[55] See, for instance, Daniel Fox, 'Multiple Time-Scales in Adès's *Rings*', *Perspectives of New Music*, 52/i (2014), 28–56; Roeder, 'Co-operating Continuities'; and Chapter 5.

[56] Roeder, 'Co-operating Continuities', p. 149.

[57] Tim Howell, 'Jean Sibelius: Progressive or Modernist?', in *Jean Sibelius's Legacy: Research on His 150th Anniversary*, ed. by Daniel Grimley, Tim Howell, Veijo Murtomäki and Timo Virtanen (Newcastle upon Tyne: Cambridge Scholars Publishing, 2017), pp. 241–55 (p. 251).

In spite of all this change, however, an overriding sense of continuity is nevertheless maintained on account of the persisting intervallic character-istics of the material being developed: perfect fifths and semitones – along with audible distortions to augmented fifths (or diminished sixths) and tones – continue to permeate the increasingly canonic and contrapuntal textures. Extrapolations of the perpetual semitone descent in particular (bars 72–91) gradually serve to saturate the tonal and textural palate, precipitating evasive action through striking changes in structural (bar 92), tonal (bar 142) and rhythmic (bar 223) direction. The ubiquity of these intervals strengthens the aural interrelations between motives and gestures; this, in turn, lends the musical discourse an unmistakable linear-ity, disparate rates of motion united in their direction, mobile tonal centres urging all textural components restlessly onwards. Just as with Sibelius's symphony, multiplicity fails to diminish an impulse towards resolution.

Closing the Circle

In Sibelius's Seventh Symphony, as in *Tevot*, it is the tensions inherent in the opening figures that incite structural change. The first tempo shifts are seemingly precipitated by an increase in harmonic activity, with sequential motivic exchanges across the orchestra inciting greater tonal motion with pulse following suit (bars 71–105). As the steadiness engendered by the C major cadence begins to fade through the course of a gradual acceler-ando, tonality becomes more transient, with a variety of new harmonies and pulses explored. Nevertheless, references to the initial tonal friction helps situate this change within the context of pre-existing tensions.[58] Lionel Pike's interpretation of the symphony as comprising two tonal axes – C natural, G natural and D natural on the one hand, A flat, E flat and B flat on the other – seems particularly apt in this light.[59] Sidestepping a more conventional hierarchy, Sibelius uses the harmonic tensions at the outset of the work as a springboard to establish a careful balance between a number of keys. The effect is one of a tonal pendulum that favours a continuum of coexistence over direct conflict; while particular axes predominate formal segments of the work, the aural reality is that both are often present

---

[58] A significant example of this are the A flat chords (bars 117–18), which provide a particularly prominent enharmonic pivot that paves the way for the transience of the forthcoming *Vivacissimo*.

[59] Pike, *Beethoven, Sibelius*, pp. 210–11.

simultaneously to varying extents, continuity of structure being ensured via an integration of contrasting ideas.

Sibelius's implementation of tonal axes helps define further the structural roles that the different levels of speed play. All three levels grant different temporal perspectives upon the tonic, approaching the sonority of C natural by different means and at different speeds. The three *Adagio* segments in essence offer three extended perfect cadences, C♮ – in both its major and minor modes – asserted and reasserted in audible 'slow motion' but rarely without tonal disruptions, principally through figures incorporating A♭. The moderate, transitory formal segments offer less convincing attempts to sustain this tonic, with passing harmonic centres prompted by earlier disruptions (principally A flat, E flat and B flat); beyond simply acting as periods of instability, these sojourns ultimately strengthen the need for tonic recurrence, thus reinforcing the structural security of the symphonic form. Nevertheless, the extent to which this broader balance and stability translates into a sense of catharsis can be questioned. Although the emphatic arrival at the final C major *Adagio* (bar 466) comes notably closer to facilitating resolution, the alternative tonal axis – having helped enable this very return – cannot simply be dismissed. The eventual F minor diversion (from bar 487, a recasting of bar 71) precipitated by E♭ allusions to the minor mode (from bar 484) prompts a failed attempt at structural symmetry; a hoped-for reprise of the introductory string chorale is supplanted by an anguished outburst in the strings (bars 500–3) featuring a held A flat major chord with an added augmented sixth (bar 500), a German sixth construction seemingly devoid, in any direct sense, of its conventional pre-dominant function. A stuttering ascent in the violins then stalls on an A♭ before sinking back to G♮ (bars 504–7), horns and bassoons ushering back in the tonic with a truncated echo of the trombone theme (bars 508–9). Vague allusions to a symmetrical design continue with flute and bassoon exploring slow-motion fragments of the flitting theme they aired in the opening passages (bars 511–17, referencing bars 7–10) atop a tremolo accompaniment.

The closing cadence of the work underlines a resignation to the co-existence of the two tonal axes, the prominent shift from B♮ upwards to C♮ in the strings (bars 524–5) offering a final enharmonic nod to the A flat minor subversion which set the form of the symphony in motion. This last-gasp reminder of enduring tension can provoke a range of broader formal readings regarding the degree to which resolution is achieved. As Adès seems to suggest, in spite of its formal balance, the conclusion of the Seventh Symphony can nevertheless be heard as the perpetuation of a friction that the symphonic structure has 'painfully' failed to fully resolve; the closure of the circle has not necessarily produced catharsis.

Considering *Tevot* in terms of this interpretive paradox proves particularly revealing. The impulse to resolve that pervades the first extended formal segment of the work produces an audible will for the various strands of developed material to converge. The most prominent of these attempts at unification sees the entire ensemble – save for the horns – unite on a disjointed triplet crotchet figure, with descending semitone patterns fragmented by unpredictable leaps in pitch and irregular rhythmic breaks (bars 223–50). When the horns enter, it is only to compound the volatile distortions of this figure, their fanfare-like countermelody characterised by triadic shapes descending by semitone steps. This outburst marks the peak of the palpable accumulation of momentum that began at the outset of the work; the amassed energy dissipates from bar 257 with drifting harmonic sequences now underpinned by ominous fragmentations of the oscillating textures from the opening of the work. A further violent outburst (bar 280), however, precipitates a structural sea change. With a resumption of the initial tempo, Adès calls upon the distinctive sonorities and textures of the opening of the piece – chains of fifths in the upper strings and winds – but implements them in ascending, rather than descending, sequences (bars 286–302); intermittent harmonic sequences in the brass and the upward-leaping horn motive are also reintroduced. The gesture gives the impression not of a direct recapitulation, but of a specifically musical return to a remembered point in the work; this effect of a 'return to' rather than a 'recurrence of' is enhanced by the reversal of pitch direction, a concerted effort to audibly turn back musical time.[60]

Eventually, this ascent plateaus into a stratospheric chorale divided among the violins (from bar 302). Frequent mediant completions provide a newly explicit harmonic rendering of the open fifths that have thus-far dominated, revealing a chain of consonant, major-key sonorities drawn perpetually onwards (Ex. 6.3). The apparent absence of explicit tonal hierarchy in this sequence negates any immediate desire for resolution, imbuing the music with a new kind of stability characterised by clearer parameters of harmonic and rhythmic energy. The pattern established is actually one determined by intervallic change: a recurring pattern of five

---

[60] Venn ('Metaphorical Bodies', pp. 146–51) considers the apparent resolution this passage offers, acknowledging 'an agential strategy recalling traditional symphonic practice'; this, however, is ultimately superseded by a perceived narrative shift enabled through Adès's adapted and extended self-reference to his Violin Concerto ('Paths', figs. 20–4).

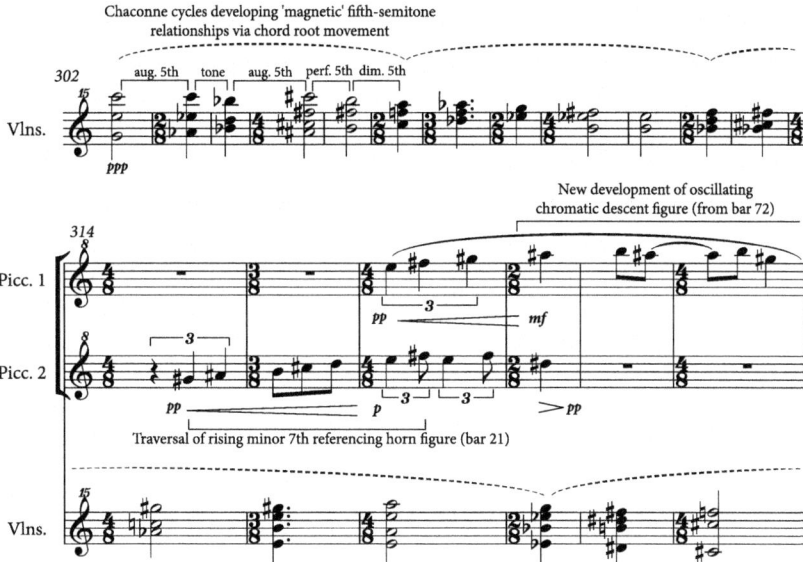

Ex. 6.3 *Tevot*, bars 302–19, reduction

shifts of chord root enables the effect of a fixed sequence moving within an ever-changing context: a marriage of stasis and flux. Sowa aptly describes this figure as a chaconne of transposing cycles, articulating it – in terms of semitones – as a descent of four, an ascent of two, consecutive descents of four and seven and a final ascent of six.[61] This cycle could also be considered as a further development of the magnetic relationships between fifths and semitones that permeate the motivic and tonal character of the work from its very opening, with each pattern accordingly comprising root shifts of an augmented fifth and a tone followed by augmented, perfect and diminished fifths.

This consistency paves the way for a floating melody that emerges in the piccolos (from bar 314), a figure at once novel and familiar: a hybrid of earlier material.[62] A stepwise ascent – a further reversal of the opening descent – in the second piccolo (bars 314–16), allows a spelled-out traversal of the rising minor seventh horn call (bar 21). This is succeeded by a steadier descent: tentative oscillations of tones and semitones are gently

[61] Sowa, 'The Art of Transformation', pp. 22–6.

[62] Massey draws a further parallel with Ives, this time his *Concord Sonata*, in terms of a 'revelatory process' of thematic development, portraying this melody as an 'elemental' expression of material in the wake of rhetorical hunt for material in the first part of *Tevot* (*Thomas Adès in Five Essays*, p. 142).

lowered in pitch in a stabilised rendering of the lower strings figure that first appeared from bar 72. This tranquil new figure aligns with the chaconne and begins to proliferate in counterpoint through the orchestra. The final third of the work's duration proceeds in this manner, its materials united in steady, onward tonal motion. Reconciliation between the conflicting ideas presented in *Tevot* is, in this sense, achieved through a 'revisitation' – and indeed a realignment – of the work's 'origins'.

So powerful does this newly acquired stability prove that it almost seems that the onward tonal path must be deliberately diverted for a conclusion to be reached. At the peak of a gigantic textural and dynamic build, a stalling of tonal motion precipitates a convergence towards an A♮ pedal (from bar 399). Tonal dynamism is now replaced by block-like changes of sonority: two further chordal reassertions, precipitated by solo trumpet figures, combine the continuing upper-register reverberations of the open fifth on an A♮ with bass emphases falling first upon G♮ (bar 415) and then upon D♮ (bar 429), before an emphatic return to the A♮ pedal (from bar 441) is underlined by tuned percussion. The chord fades, oscillations in the violins providing an aural reminder that *Tevot* has returned to the open-fifth resonances with which it began.

How conclusive this closing gesture proves is a matter of perspective. Like the structural symmetry evident in Sibelius's Seventh Symphony, the circularity evident in this return to the opening sonority points to a kind of closure. However, it simultaneously invokes the infinite; circles, by definition, provide closure while inviting continuation. In this sense, however, *Tevot* offers not one circle but perhaps something more akin to a figure of eight. Two evocations of the opening material – one at the centre of the work, the other at its close – suggest both a process of formal re-evaluation and reinvention and a reframing of the three tonal pillars that articulate the form of the Seventh Symphony. Alternative temporal paths are presented: while the work seemingly acknowledges that the past cannot be relived directly, the act of retracing steps can yield new perspectives and approaches.

Symphonic Renewal

To understand the symphony is . . . to understand its capacity for renewal. This is, in part, the product of an inherent flexibility, born of the fact that the aesthetic and technical connotations of the term 'symphonic' have, for much of the genre's history, run considerably ahead of any constraints placed on them by the title 'symphony'. Over time, this has enabled a remarkable generic elasticity, which has allowed composers to shift continuously the symphony's terms of reference.[63]

Though many of its developments have emerged gradually, the history of the symphony has nevertheless frequently been shaped by moments of revolution, specific contributions that – thanks to their radical nature – have opened the floodgates to new aesthetic possibilities. It could be argued, however, that the most significant contributions that both Sibelius's Seventh Symphony and Adès's *Tevot* offer the genre have far more to do with the dialogue they establish with its history. Beyond simply relocating 'the symphony's terms of reference' as Julian Horton suggests, both works expand its formal potential (paradoxically through processes of compression, condensation and layering) while simultaneously affirming older principles of organicism and logic, thus amalgamating what Grimley describes as the 'unity and linear authority' of the nineteenth-century symphony and the 'large-scale expressive and structural counterpoint of different temporalities and musical spaces' that characterised its developments in the twentieth.[64] On the one hand, their forms remain closed on account of their brevity, economy, interconnectedness and symmetry; on the other, they lie invitingly open, their temporal marriages of stasis and flux, continuity and discontinuity, repetition and change inviting reinterpretation. Whether they provide 'resolution' is a question to which each of us can provide our own answers. Perhaps what truly makes these works 'symphonic' is the manner in which they urge us to *ask* that question.

---

[63] Julian Horton, 'Introduction: Understanding the Symphony', in *The Cambridge Companion to the Symphony*, ed. by Julian Horton (Cambridge: Cambridge University Press, 2013), pp. 1–12 (p. 2).

[64] Grimley, 'Symphony/Antiphony', p. 286.

7 | A World in Constant Motion

Adès's In Seven Days

AMY BAUER

The critic Joshua Kosman called Thomas Adès's *In Seven Days: Piano Concerto with Moving Image* (2008) 'both dramatic and reflective, by turns ingratiatingly accessible and dauntingly abstruse. It seems to want to embrace the whole world.'[1] The concerto outlines the biblical creation story in seven connected movements, accompanied by coordinated projections by the video artist Tal Rosner.[2] The narrative begins with Adès's conception of Genesis 1:2, which follows recent scholarship suggesting that the Hebrew *tōhû wābōhû* describes not a chaotic, formless void, but rather an unproductive and empty place, to be shaped, ordered and filled with life.[3] As the composer avers, 'I was simply telling that story – the story of the material and also of "material", all of it, in the world.'[4] The expansive and multifaceted allegory of *In Seven Days* parallels Adès's symphonic works in that it involves the idea of a journey, embracing a modern reading of the Book of Genesis alongside a structural paradigm of musical evolution and growth, with familial links to previous works by Adès and others, as detailed in separate sections below. This capacious model of musical growth and transformation will include the development of a vast tonal edifice from two primary harmonies, reference the birth of the modern orchestra and repurpose traditional compositional techniques from the Renaissance to the present. But *In Seven Days* embraces a meta-musical role as well, through allusions to select works that have broached the subject of creation.

---

[1] Joshua Kosman, 'S.F. Symphony Review: Thomas Adès' Creative Take on Genesis Story', *SF Gate*, 6 March 2015, www.sfgate.com/music/article/S-F-Symphony-review-Thomas-Ad-s-creative-6119376.php.

[2] Given that my focus is on the musical structure and narrative that connects and explains all seven movements, I will not comment on the accompanying video.

[3] David Toshio Tsumura, *The Earth and the Waters in Genesis 1 and 2: A Linguistic Investigation* (Sheffield: Sheffield Academic Press, 1989), pp. 41–3.

[4] Thomas Adès and Tom Service, *Thomas Adès: Full of Noises – Conversations with Tom Service*, paperback ed. (London: Faber and Faber, 2018), p. 31.

In Seven Days and Genesis

In Seven Days merges the figurative and the abstract to parallel modern allegorical readings of biblical creation. A theme and series of seven variations outline each successive 'day', divided into two halves that appear to follow the framework interpretation of the Book of Genesis. The framework interpretation (sometimes called the literary framework view or hypothesis) proposes that Genesis is divided into two 'triads' and three 'kingdoms'; the first triad consists of Days 1–3, while the second consists of Days 3–6.[5] The consecutive days of each triad are paired, as suggested by repeating phrases and images (for instance, Day 1 begins with 'Let there be light', (1:3), while Day 4 begins with 'Let there be lights' (1:14). The first triad establishes the 'creation kingdom', while the second describes the production of two 'creature' kingdoms. Thus an aspect of the creation kingdom is connected to a creature 'king', a connection that Adès establishes musically in the corresponding movements. In addition, the corresponding members of each triad occupy the same register in the overall cosmology: Days 1 and 4 occupy the upper level, in terms of the spiritual (heaven) and location (the sky). Days 2 and 5 transition from upper to lower levels, setting out the sea and sky in the first triad, and the creatures that occupy those realms in the second. Days 3 and 6 are material and deep, marrying the geography of the earth with the creatures that live on it. Table 7.1 matches each of the work's first six movements to its corresponding section of Genesis within the framework narrative.

A consideration of *In Seven Days* as an allegorical representation of Genesis follows not only from the composer's comments on the work, but from his overall aesthetic; as Adès maintains, 'I don't see the distinction between abstract music and programme music. I literally have no idea what that means, because to me all music is metaphorical, always.'[6] Hence *In Seven Days* is both a programmatic illustration of the world's creation and an abstract 'set of double variations'.[7] Adès's embrace of extramusical meaning and connections informs most of his works, from the implications of the original text behind the palimpsest of the early *Darknesse Visible* (1992), for piano, to the ekphrastic basis of moments in *Traced Overhead* (1996), *Arcadiana* (1994) and *Totentanz* (2013), to the programmatic battles of *Living Toys* (1993). The specific allegory implied by *In Seven*

---

[5] Meredith G. Kline, 'Space and Time in the Genesis Cosmogony', *Perspectives on Science and Christian Faith*, 48 (1996), 2–15.

[6] Adès and Service, *Full of Noises*, p. 5.   [7] Ibid., p. 30.

Table 7.1. Comparison between *In Seven Days* and Genesis

First triad			Second triad		
Day 1	Let there be light (1:3).	**Genesis**	Let there be lights (1:14).	**Day 4**
	Movement I: Chaos – Light – Darkness (initial 'chaotic' phrase formed by two chords expressing E/B becomes 'creation theme', followed by variations, moving from high to low)	**In Seven Days**	Movement IV: Stars – Sun – Moon (series of strophic variations in recognisable twentieth-century styles, moving from high to low)	
Day 2	Let there be a firmament in the midst of the waters, and let it divide the waters from the waters (1:6).	**Genesis**	Let the water teem with creatures and let birds fly above the earth (1:20).	**Day 5**
	Movement II: Separation of the Waters into Sea and Sky (piano floats above polymetric, 'granite-like' surface over ascending chaconne in bass)	**In Seven Days**	Movement V: Fugue – Creatures of the Sea and Sky (bass chaconne fragment becomes first subject of double fugue)	
Day 3	Let dry land appear (1:9). Let the land produce vegetation (1:11).	**Genesis**	Let the land produce living creatures (1:24). Let us make man (1:26). I give you every seed-bearing plant ... and every tree that has fruit with seed in it ... for food (1:29).	**Day 6**
	Movement III: Land – Grass – Trees (serial canon moves through 36 iterations, with increasing rhythmic diminution)	**In Seven Days**	Movement VI: Fugue – Creatures of the Land (fugue subject moves a series of overlapping chromatic entries, with increasing rhythmic diminution)	

Days suggests a creation shaped as much by implicit scientific principles as by the theological notion of a supreme being. The piano functions in this context less as a virtuosic soloist than as a guiding force, a 'consciousness' that directs the expansion of the work, drives the generation of harmonic and rhythmic patterns and occasionally arrives, *in medias res*, to comment on the work of creation.[8] Brian Moseley has discussed the link between conscious and unconscious processes that characterises the forms of classic surrealism present in Adès's Mazurkas.[9] He notes a kind of automatism with surrealist effects that occurs when Adès begins with simple conventional objects and allows their elements or traits – for instance, an interval pattern derived from two chords – to passively proliferate in odd and disorienting ways. The novel musical growth that results can be said to manifest subconscious qualities we might never had discovered otherwise. Hence Adès's comments on the piano imply that, as the conscious driver of progress in the concerto, it nudges simple, generative materials towards ever greater heights of expression and technical splendour as befits a scientific and desultory notion of creation, as opposed to one conceived by an omniscient God.

This allegory binds the meta-musical to the programmatic, as the narrative of biblical creation parallels an abstract musical narrative shaped by the refinement of Western musical techniques – such as canon and fugue – which represent in turn a cyclical history of musical development, from early polyphony to twentieth-century modernism and minimalism. But this narrative is hardly straightforward, as suggested by the non-linear bonds between corresponding days of the two-part framework; its twists and turns recall other famous works based explicitly or implicitly on creation stories, as noted below. The tiny circling cells that represent the primordial atoms of Day 1 accrete into a larger cyclic order in the opening phrase (bars 1–3), finally coalescing into what I call the 'creation theme' that forms the basis of thematic paraphrase and allusion in subsequent movements ([F]).[10]

As befits its productive function in the work, this theme has its own 'genesis' earlier in Adès's oeuvre as 'a piece of debris I wanted to rescue from the opera [*The Tempest*]'.[11] The debris in question is a chord progression that outlines the creation theme, first heard as the fully scored orchestral accompaniment to bars 897–903 of Ariel's Act I, Scene 5 aria 'Five Fathoms Deep'. Adès longed to hear the progression scored for four violins,[12] and he accordingly sends the theme through a series of glittering

[8] Zoë Martlew, 'In Conversation: Zoe Martlew', London Sinfonietta, 1 February 2017, https://londonsinfonietta.org.uk/channel/articles/conversation-zoe-martlew.

[9] See Chapter 8.

[10] The score for *In Seven Days* can be viewed at www.fabermusic.com/music/in-seven-days-148/score.

[11] Kirill Gerstein, 'Thomas Adès: "Roots, Seeds & Live Cultures" – "Kirill Gerstein Invites" @ HfM Eisler Berlin', online video interview, 18 June 2020, YouTube, www.youtube.com/watch?v=I0kHP_npxJA.

[12] Adès and Service, *Full of Noises*, p. 30. See also Gerstein, 'Thomas Adès: "Roots, Seeds & Live Cultures"'.

variations as we move through the days of creation before arriving at the four-violin version at the work's close. Register emerges as a structural element in the second movement when the water is separated into sea and sky, while a twelve-note series as both ground bass and canon branches outwards recursively to construct the 'Land – Grass – Trees' of movement III, representing the shift from the upper to the lower level of the first triad. The 'Stars' sparkle high on the piano in the fourth movement as we move back to the upper level of the second triad, while overlapping cycles introduce the 'Sun' and 'Moon' to close, Messiaen-like, with a cycle in the piano. Two fugues birth the 'Creatures of the Sea and Sky' and the 'Creatures of the Land' – again moving from upper to lower – lending movements V and VI a sharper profile, yet sounding an apocalyptic note with the introduction of man. The final 'day' – a hushed 'Contemplation' in strings and piano – ends with a cyclic connection to the first and the promised theme heard in its purest form, in solo strings.

Creation from Chaos

The opening movement 'Chaos – Light – Dark' is the longest in *In Seven Days*, forming a third of the cycle's total duration. As this movement sets out the primary harmonic, rhythmic and metrical complexities of the work, it deserves extended analytical treatment. The allegorical number seven is expressed here on several durational levels. Recursive subdivisions by seven occur at the level of form, metre and rhythmic subdivision. The chaotic swirl of 21/8 – a compound metre in seven – gives way to bars of 3/4 characterised by septuplets in the flutes against regular quavers in the strings (D). The announcement of the creation theme (scored for horns and trumpets) at the outset of the second formal section (F) is in a simple 3/4 metre. Section 3 (beginning G) adopts alternating bars of 2/4 and 3/8 (together lasting seven quavers), against which the solo piano begins with semiquavers in groups of seven. An underlying crotchet pulse at the start of section 4 (H) is clouded by cross rhythms – a pattern developed in sections 5 and 6 (I and J), in which septuplet melodic decorations are accommodated within bars of varying lengths, e.g. the first two bars contain groups of seven notes in the space of eight and six quavers respectively. The final section (beginning at K) is devoted to alternating 3/2 and 2/2 metres; the bar is subdivided by six, then five and finally three as the coda flows without a break into movement II.

Central to harmonic development of the movement (and by extension, the progression of the Genesis narrative) is the structural harmony that anchors

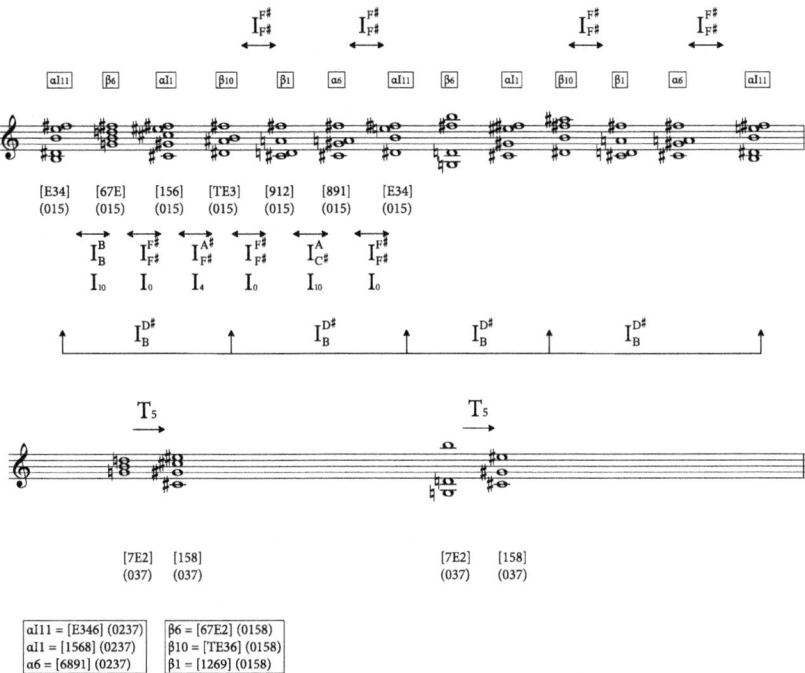

Ex. 7.1 *In Seven Days*, movement I, phrase 1: network of (015) and (037) trichords and accompanying F♯ melody

Adès's 'piece of debris': the diatonic tetrachord (0237), first heard in inversion on B in bar 1 [E346], is shown in Ex. 7.1.[13] (This tetrachord is labelled α_n for convenience, where n stands for the first pitch-class of the chord in transposition, while n in αI_n stands for the first pitch-class of the chord in inversion.) Tetrachord (0158), labelled $\beta_n/\beta I_n$, is the companion of α in the opening phrase and the creation theme. As examples of Adès's conventional objects that 'quiver and spring to life' because of their internal structure,[14] these

---

[13] Pitch-class sets and larger collections follow the conventions set out in Joseph N. Straus, *Introduction to Post-Tonal Theory*, 4th ed. (New York: W. W. Norton, 2016). Pitch-class sets are labelled according to a fixed-do system in which 0 = C, and T and E represent pitch-classes 10 and 11, respectively. Parentheses contain the prime form of a pitch-class set: its reduction to a representative set beginning on 0. Square brackets denote normal form: the actual pitches in the score, presented in the set's most condensed form. The subscript n in T_n/I_n denotes a set's level of transposition or inversion. The axis of inversion may also be indicated by two pitch-classes listed as both superscript and subscript. Distinct pitch-collections are identified by a subscript denoting the first unique semitone in each collection when counting upwards from C (0); e.g. $OCT_{0,1}$ denotes the octatonic collection that contains C and C♯/D♭ (0134679T), and WT_0 denotes the whole-tone collection that contains C. Interval cycles are labelled IC_n, where *n* denotes the interval between successive pitches, and *n,x* identifies the chronologically lowest pitch of each cycle *x* regardless of initial pitch.

[14] Adès and Service, *Full of Noises*, p. 33.

harmonies establish the bright, expansive character of the work from the first stirrings of creation in the opening bar. Here, an upward-reaching motive on B-E to F♯ initiates a periodic structure (antecedent plus consequent) based on alternations of α and β (see Online Ex. 7.1). Such alternations create an extremely homogeneous harmonic language mitigated by the variety of unique transpositions and inversions that occur – all twenty-four forms of the (0237) tetrachord appear at some point in the work –, generating a kind of 'chromatic chaos' in the beginning which gravitates towards regularity as the world takes shape.

Which specific features of (0237) suggest its choice as the central harmony of *In Seven Days*? Most significantly, perhaps, is its genetic link to diatonicism. Any given realisation of (0237) – inverted around its first pitch and combined with the original set – will produce a diatonic collection (with the axis of inversion held invariant). As an example, in movement I, the inversion of F♯-G♯-A-C♯ – (0237), in the normal form [6891] – around F♯ produces B-D♯-E-F♯ (equivalent to inverting the set at I_0), which gives rise to a musical universe anchored in the diatonic collection with four sharps, or E major, which frequently suggests the dominant when B is in the bass. This occurs between chords 6 and 7 of the work's first phrase, which appears in harmonic reduction in Ex. 7.1. Normal forms and their relationship to the prime form are indicated in the box below the example, while the four tetrachords inverted around F♯ are indicated above, with F♯$_5$ the sole common note that links each chord in the phrase. The most prominent autonomous trichords in the work are (015) and the major/minor triad (037), subsets of both primary tetrachords. The annotations directly below the first stave show a series of inverted (015) trichords moving by I_{10}, I_0 and I_4. The non-inverting note is F♯$_5$ in most cases; it is D$_5$ in the second chord and G♯$_4$ in the third, both part of the same whole-tone collection as F♯ (WT$_0$). The chords αI_{11} and β$_{10}$ are further linked by a (015) subset inverted around a D♯-B dyad. The bottom stave indicates the two occasions in which a transpositional relation by perfect fourth (T$_5$) obtains between (037) triads connecting β$_6$ and the new harmony γI_1.[15]

In Seven Days hence relies on two primary tetrachords to both generate its harmonic texture and establish an anthemic theme – centred around F♯ – that will carry through most of the movements to follow. The consistent use of (0237) serves both a sonorous and a semantic function. As a sign of creation, it indexes the diatonic collection as the structure that

---

[15] γ is equivalent to pitch-class set (01368).

arises from the chromatic 'chaos'. Yet the fourth note – appearing a whole tone above the 'root' of the embedded minor triad (037) or below the fifth of the major triad in inversion – defeats any functional pull the triad might inadvertently exert on its surroundings. As a semantic generator of harmonic motion, the asymmetrical division of the fifth and even distribution of intervals found in (0237) promote harmonic motion outward.[16]

The first real theme of movement I, which recurs cyclically throughout the work, appears at $\boxed{\text{F}}$. This 'creation' theme is first heard in the brass, as shown in a reduction in Ex. 7.2, opening on a B_3-$F\sharp_4$ dyad; both pitches serve as common tones throughout most of the passage. They anchor the fluctuating E/B major tonality, while F$\sharp$ serves both as an inversional axis and as a 'fetish note'.[17] The creation theme contains the by now familiar α and β tetrachords, expanding the harmonic palette with pentachords (01368) and (01568), labelled γ and δ respectively. Following the recursive design of the movement, each pentachord includes either tetrachord α or β as a subset. And tetrachord β forms the centre of the two (013568) hexachords that appear in the final progression, labelled ε. In addition to the inversion around C or F$\sharp$, labelled in Ex. 7.2, I have noted significant transpositions by T_8 and T_{11}, which recur later in the work during significant thematic passages. The final appearance of hexachord ε heralds the piano's first entrance; chord ε can also be modelled as the conjunction of a B major and an F sharp major triad (equivalent to chord γ_{10}) with the addition of the all-important note E. The significance of B major at this juncture is no accident; for Adès, keys have allegorical significance, and B major 'has a divine glow'.[18]

As noted above, the piano's entrance at $\boxed{\text{G}}$ emphasises a divided septuple metre through the opening alteration of bars of 2/4 and 3/8 bars. Cyclic rhythmic patterns of varied lengths in percussion and violins establish one layer of the polyrhythmic fabric, as indicated by the rhythmic graphs of $\boxed{\text{G}}^{+5}$ in Online Fig. 7.1. As shown in the graph, regular quaver divisions of the bar occur in the triangle, while the bongos and violin have irregular repeated patterns ten crochets long. The claves have a constantly changing pattern based on the quaver, while the first viola has a diminutional pattern that decreases proportionately. The quasi-regularity of underlying metric

---

[16] The interval class vector of (0237) contains two fifths (ic5) and one of each other interval class save the tritone. (0237) occurs throughout Adès's Violin Concerto as well; see Dominic Wells, 'Plural Styles, Personal Style: The Music of Thomas Adès', *Tempo*, 66/260 (2012), 2–14.

[17] F$\sharp$ serves as a 'fetish note' throughout *In Seven Days* (personal communication from Zoë Martlew). Adès talks more about the function of fetish notes in Adès and Service, *Full of Noises*, p. 48.

[18] Martlew, 'In Conversation'.

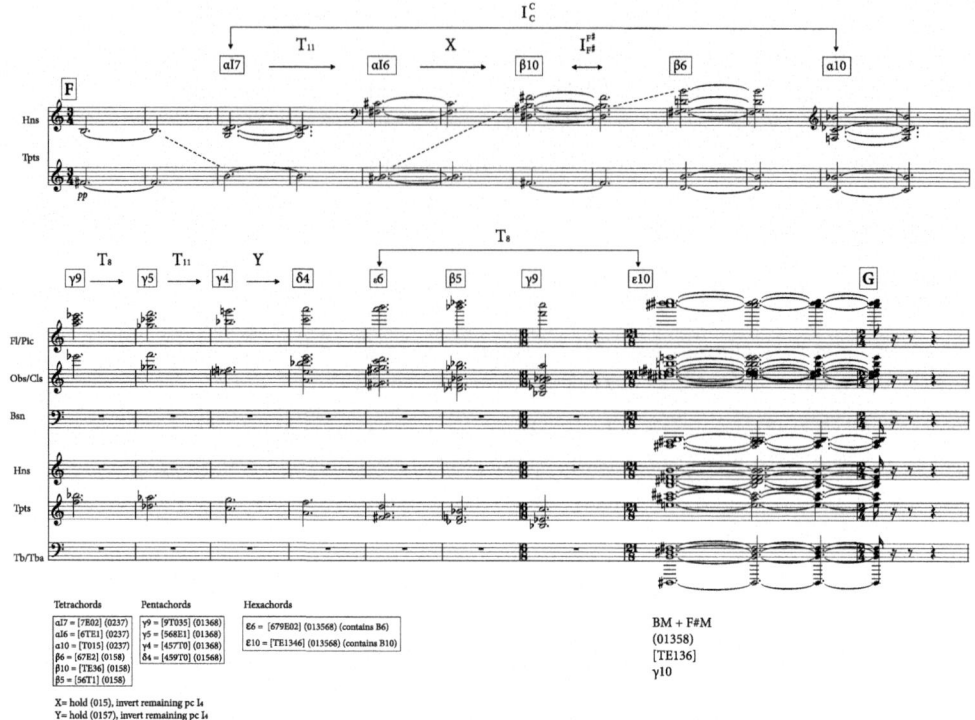

Ex. 7.2 *In Seven Days*, creation theme in brass, progression heralding piano's entrance at [G]

divisions, which articulate divisions of the bar by two (double bass) and both bar and beat by two and three, is accompanied by the desultory attacks of the piano soloist, who floats above and between the additive patterns below. It is tempting to read this passage as an homage to György Ligeti's Piano Concerto (1985–8).

[I] reveals a modern *Teufelsmühle* ('devil's mill') progression, in the mode of a contemporary lament passacaglia.[19] This striking passage is a miniature version of one of Adès's chaconnes, with the familiar 'spiral' shape

---

[19] The 'devil's mill', related to the omnibus progression, appeared in several variants in nineteenth-century harmonic theory. Its most condensed form begins with a root-position dominant seventh chord; the fifth and seventh are held through a chromatic ascent in the bass and chromatic descent in soprano, to culminate in a dominant seventh chord a minor third higher (e.g. C^7 converging on $E\flat^7$). See Marie-Agnes Dittrich, '"Teufelsmühle" und "Omnibus"', *Zeitschrift der Gesellschaft für Musiktheorie*, 4/i–ii (2007), 107–21, www.gmth.de/zeitschrift/artikel/247.aspx. For information on the twentieth-century contemporary lament passacaglia see David Metzer, 'Lament', in *Musical Modernism at the Turn of the Twenty-First Century* (Cambridge: Cambridge University Press, 2009), pp. 144–74; and Amy Bauer, *Ligeti's Laments: Nostalgia, Exoticism, and the Absolute* (Farnham: Ashgate, 2011).

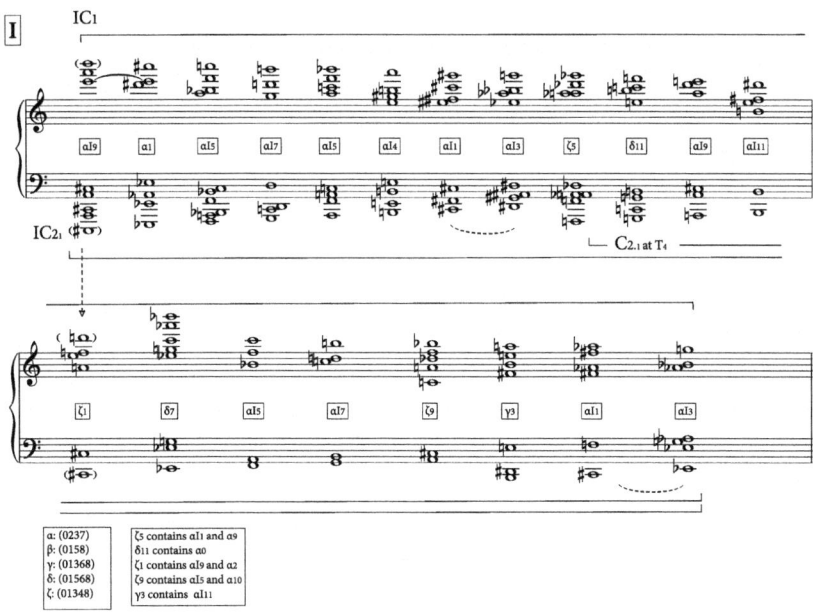

Ex. 7.3 *In Seven Days*, movement I, lament passacaglia at $\boxed{\text{I}}$

transposing material downwards by an 'organic' process.[20] The harmonic reduction of this passage in Ex. 7.3 reveals a chromatic cycle in the uppermost voice (marked IC_1), set contrapuntally against an odd whole-tone cycle in the bass ($IC_{2.1}$), joined by a second whole-tone 1 cycle midway through in the third octave at T_4 of the original cycle. As in the nineteenth-century *Teufelsmühle*, the upper voice descends chromatically over a rising chromatic bassline, beginning on a dominant seventh chord and moving through related harmonies before returning to its original harmony in a new transposition. By pairing the descending chromatic with a rising whole-tone line, Adès preserves the (0237) harmony, alone or as a subset of larger harmonies. As the upper line begins on D, we cannot find a traditional voice-exchange, but we do return to the original harmony in an expanded form; this is indicated by the arrow from top to bottom stave. The descent is completed when chords αI_1 and αI_3 (a whole tone apart) return with the same outer voices, indicated by curved brackets. The harmonic minor collection, chord (0134689) (labelled η), does not appear in this passage, but will become central to the fourth movement of the work; all of the chords in this lament are subsets of both η and the diatonic collection (013568T), with the exception of chord ζ (a subset of η). $\boxed{\text{I}}$ not

---

[20] On Adès's use of chaconnes, see Chapter 5.

only is striking, but also suggests the way in which whole-tone ascending and descending lines will function as both thematic and contrapuntal elements that mediate between the primary harmonies and larger pitch-collections in ensuing Days.

Quartz-Like Logic: Days 2, 4 and 5

The magnificent opening movement of *In Seven Days* serves also as a primer on Adès's 'centrifugal' impulse, beginning from a point – here the E–F$\sharp$ motion and the prominence of (0237) – which then expands outwards. The composer speaks of Sibelius's symphonies having been born of an 'inner desire to go off into an endless horizon of trees or lakes or pure song or whatever it is – the undiscovered country'.[21] The remaining six movements spin this impulse out in a controlled manner: each employs a musical technique, texture and formal design that complement its role in the creation saga. The second movement, 'Separation of the Waters into Sea and Sky', expresses a large ternary ABA form defined primarily by rhythm and metre. We open on the 'divine glow' of B major, with a low B in timpani and a bass pedal B through the first two thirds of the movement. A rhythmic cycle that begins in the orchestra alone expresses the following pattern, repeated three times over a 2/4 metre, as shown in Ex. 7.4a: 1/8 + 7/12 + 7/8 + 7/12 + 7/16. The cue *ossia* stave gives an indication of the manner in which the piano is intended to freely relate to the orchestra's metric articulation. The rhythms of movement II grow more complex until the piano rushes upwards – both hands in triplet semiquavers – to introduce a hocket section at $\boxed{\text{E}}$, with an effect that reminds one of Conlon Nancarrow's irrational rhythms.

Underlying the piano's activity is a chaconne related to the one at $\boxed{\text{I}}$ in the first movement. A slowly rising 'odd' whole-tone scale in the double bass (doubled occasionally by cello) proceeds upwards from B_0 before dropping down an octave to continue rising in WT_0. The chaconne has an algorithmic character whose formula is sketched in Ex. 7.4b. To reconstruct the line one follows the B_0 up the scale until the first 'switch point', whereupon one goes to the new, lower pitch and proceeds upwards again until the next node. A quasi-regularity prevails, in that the chaconne switches seven times at $A\sharp_1$ in WT_0 and seven times at B_1 in WT_1. Yet it

---

[21] Adès and Service, *Full of Noises*, p. 172.

(a)

(b)

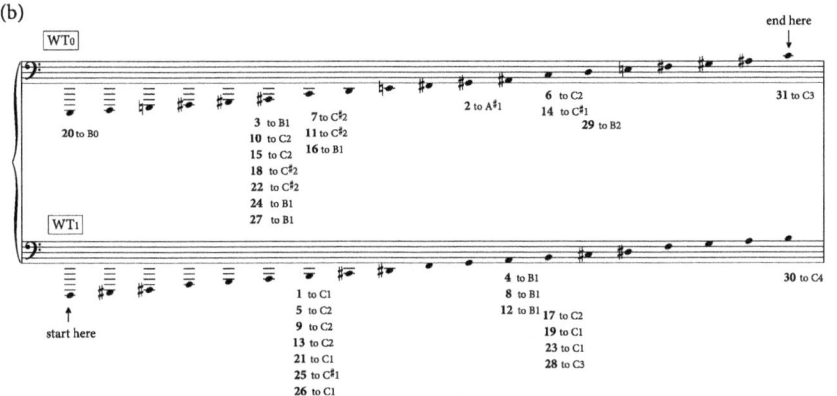

Ex. 7.4 *In Seven Days*, movement II. (a) Bars 1–3, first rhythmic cycle in piano; (b) whole-tone structure of the chaconne

sometimes repeats at the octave before switching scales, climbing anywhere from six to ten pitches before switching collections. We could posit here a kind of 'flicker of the divine' as the low Bs alternate with C and C♯ to begin successive ascents.[22] The pedal B and chaconne cease as the movement reaches G for the final A section.

At this point the piano's rhythmic separation from the orchestra reaches its extreme as the hocket continues, reprising the original rhythmic pattern for nine more cycles. The piano cycle now overlaps with the orchestra's overriding 7/8 metre – expressed as 3 + 2 + 2 – in this final A. Adès explains that the 'terrible' piano part was intended to have its own sense of logic: 'the music is about geology', and the 'ludicrous' time signature gave him a 'quartz-like structure'.[23] The mountains finished, the movement

---

[22] Adès calls C major 'the people's key'. Gerstein, 'Thomas Adès: "Roots, Seeds & Live Cultures"'.
[23] Ibid.

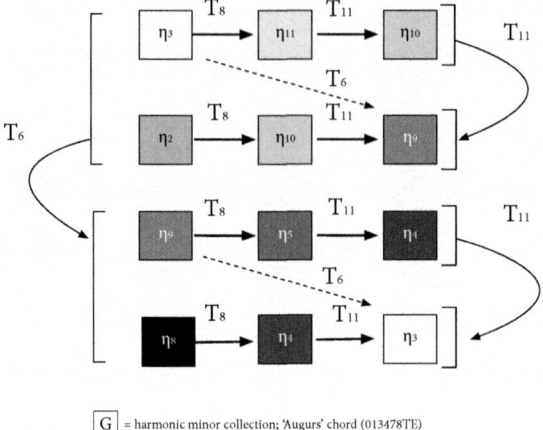

G = harmonic minor collection; 'Augurs' chord (013478TE)

Fig. 7.1 *In Seven Days*, transformational graph of harmonic progression from G to the end of movement IV

closes with a pensive coda that brings back the creation theme from movement I, as indicated by the bracketed section in Online Ex. 7.2.

As noted above, movement II pairs with movement V, while the first forms a pair with the fourth movement, 'Stars – Sun – Moon'. Movement I built up to the creation theme, which then appeared in rhythmic and contrapuntal variations. Movement IV opens immediately with the creation theme in the flutes, moving through the familiar series of α and β tetrachords at a harmonic rhythm of two per bar. Yet unlike the more imposing first movement, 'Stars – Sun – Moon' passes immediately through a cheeky series of much briefer variations, each in a different recognisable early twentieth-century or late twentieth-century minimalist style, with clear allusions to early Philip Glass and mid-period John Adams among others. The chart in Online Table 7.1 gives a sense of the variation time allotted to each successive style and a vague sense of the style represented by each.

At G this cycle halts as the central piano cycle of the movement enters in a stately chorale style, voicing a progression of septads composed entirely of the harmonic minor collection: pitch-class set (0134689), labelled in both Fig. 7.1 and Online Ex. 7.3 as η. This collection famously embodies Stravinsky's augurs chord (see Online Ex. 7.3). A transformational graph in Fig. 7.1 shows the harmonic pattern of phrases from G to the end of the movement. Here we find the same transpositional network from the opening movement mapped onto the η septads.[24]

---

[24] The pianist Vikungur Olafsson named the 'gorgeously organized chaos' of the fourth movement as one of his favourite contemporary works; Olafsson, '5 Minutes That Will Make You Love

Movement V's relation to the second's granitic textures is not immediately apparent. 'Fugue – Creatures of the Sea and Sky' takes the ascending chaconne from the second movement, edits it slightly and flips it to form a descending opening subject, the first of a complex double fugue. Three descending whole tones are followed by two semitones and then by four whole tones, remaining predominantly in WT_1, as shown in the solo trumpet of the reduction in Ex. 7.5. This subject appears three times before a second subject enters in the flute at $\boxed{A}$, with countersubjects drawn from the transitional passage in flutes at $\boxed{D}$ in movement I. The second subject expands into a separate woodwind fugue; the opening descent gradually peeks through the second fugue as fragments of counterpoint, finally emerging in full to announce the entrance of the piano at $\boxed{D}$. These movements display Adès's centrifugal impulse clearly, the desire to spin the creation theme into a wildly varied set of variations. The rhythmic variations over a B pedal in movement II lose touch with that B at the close. Meanwhile, strophic variations that reveal a homophonic impulse in movement IV are followed by a repurposed chaconne as fugue subject in movement V.

Flora, Fauna and the Ascent of Man

Movements III and VI continue variations on the horizontal impulse, drawing on both mid-twentieth-century techniques and an even more committed revival of Baroque fugal practice. Their contrapuntal complexity achieves a kind of sublime surplus of compositional invention, an overload of the senses commensurate with bringing the world to fruition. This excess energy dissipates in a vastly different sense of the sublime in the brief seventh day, the reduction of the linear impulse to a simply descending dyad in crochets over the return of a homophony in service of a hymn-like return of the creation theme.

The third movement 'Land – Grass – Trees' is fully serial, with a twist. Its row is based on a diatonic hexachord (024579) which both appears twice within the diatonic collection and can itself be derived from a (0237) tetrachord inverted around its central semitone.[25] The structure and

21st-Century Composers', *New York Times*, 5 August 2020, www.nytimes.com/2020/08/05/arts/music/five-minutes-classical-music.html.

[25] There are many famous appearances of this hexachord in twentieth-century music, but it is illustrated succinctly by Ligeti's use of complementary (024579) collections in right and left hands in Étude 11, 'En suspens' (1990).

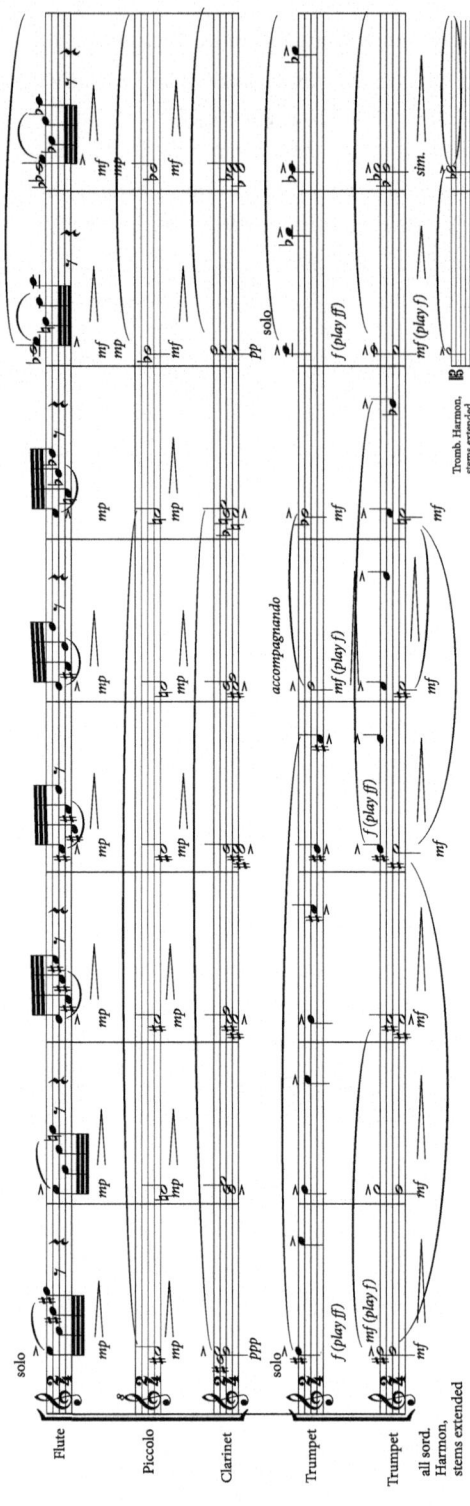

Ex. 7.5 *In Seven Days*, opening fugue in movement V

comportment of the row contain clear historical allusions to the early twelve-note technique of the Second Viennese School. As did Alban Berg, Adès constructs his row to allow the expression of seven major and minor triads, from both discrete and overlapping row segments, as shown in Online Table 7.2.

As did Anton Webern, Adès overlaps each row with the final pitch of the preceding row, as indicated by an annotated reduction of the canonic row's first five appearances in Ex. 7.6. (This is yet another instance of Adès's 'spiral' technique.)[26] In a nod to even earlier canonic technique, row entrances travel around the circle of fourths, each set to a palindromic rhythmic talea based on only two durations: a crotchet and a dotted minim, as shown in the upper right corner of Ex. 7.6. This measured and regal unfolding of the row allows sustained notes to accrue tonal associations as the row unfolds, as indicated by the annotations below the first system.

In an essay on Adès's serial technique, Drew Massey cites *In Seven Days* as an example of the 'serialist sublime'. He situates the use of serialist procedures in the concerto at 'the far end of . . . intelligibility, markedness, and salience . . . The techniques are expanded so far and handled so strictly that they seem to disappear under the weight of their own rigor.'[27] This seems to put Adès's technique on par with Ligeti's micropolyphony – in works such as *Lontano* and the Kyrie of the *Requiem* – through its production of a rigorous compositional structure intended to function below the threshold of perception, as well as suggesting the 'impossible charms' of Messiaen's subterranean isorhythms. Yet the combined color and talea structure of the third movement expresses a uniformly strict and rational expansion that is perceptible up to a point. A rhapsodic treatment of the row follows this exposition in $\boxed{\text{B}}$ and beyond, during which motives are selected from the row and woven into a lyrical theme that travels from woodwinds to strings. The piano's row travels in ever smaller diminutions, becoming more telescoped as it continues, while its dynamics and articulation take on a hysterical tone, resembling Ligeti's 'tempo fugue'.[28] The chart in Online Table 7.3 indicates the speed with which each row cycles through the thirty-six transpositions of the row, expressed in crotchet durations. As the tempo of row entries increases, arpeggiations fill in the

---

[26] See Chapter 5.

[27] Drew Massey, *Thomas Adès in Five Essays* (New York: Oxford University Press, 2021), p. 54.

[28] Ligeti coined the term 'tempo fugue' for a rhythmic procedure in which a progressive rhythmic diminution maintains a proportional relationship among component durations, as occurs in his piano études 'Désordre' (1985) and 'Automne à Varsovie' (1986).

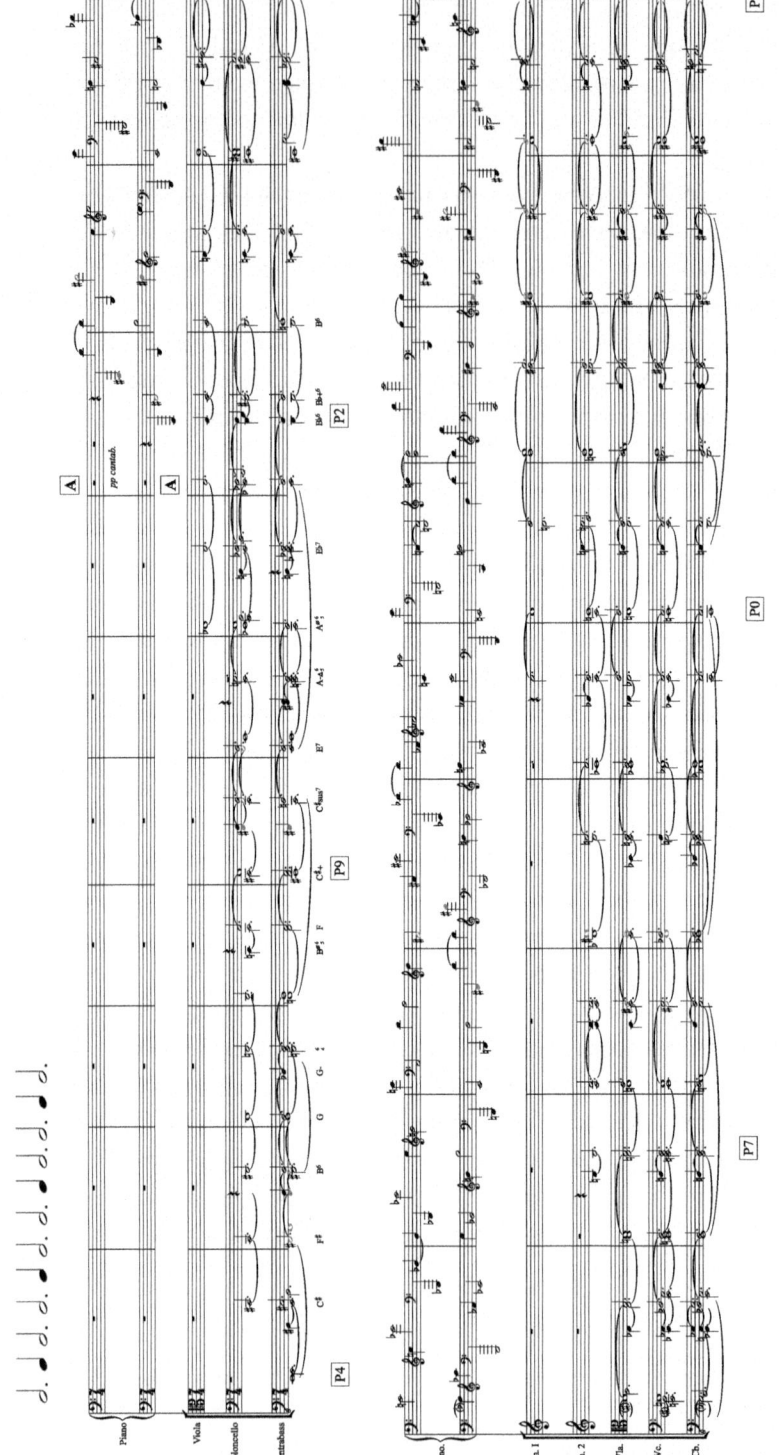

Ex. 7.6 *In Seven Days*, the first five row forms in movement III, with corresponding order numbers, implied tonal harmonies and underlying talea

piano series like the trees and flowers populating the new world. The piano finally drops the row entirely in the coda as the orchestra continues with it unabated. The row dissolves only at the end of the coda after thirty-six statements, with a C major chord sounded quietly in low brass and winds (see Online Ex. 7.4). Any sense of a serial sublime in this movement is disrupted by the programmatic thrust of those movements that succeed it, and by the proliferation of elements that structure Adès's portrait of creation, much like those in Haydn's *Creation* (discussed below).

As we near the end of the Book of Genesis, Adès explores an even more traditional fugue type in movement VI, 'Fugue – Creatures of the Land', one that travels entirely in fifths (if one includes partial and stretto entrances), as shown in Ex. 7.7.[29] The first subject from movement V appears like another lament passacaglia winding its way throughout this movement, beginning in the vibraphone (bar 1). This movement splits the written metre: some instruments are notated in 7/8 and some in 2/4 (for ease of notation), with the minim in 2/4 equated with the double-dotted minim in 7/8. The descending subject has its own diminutional and instrumental journey throughout the movement, beginning in straight crotchets (in 2/4; double-dotted minim in 7/8) and travelling in tandem with other voices until $\boxed{D}$. As it continues woodwinds, glockenspiel and crotales pick up the subject in rhythmically staggered forms, eventually splitting it into smaller, syncopated segments. The piano closes this final, creative movement with a muted transition to the epilogue ($\boxed{H}$ to close).

An exceedingly simple and reverent nineteen-bar epilogue titled 'Contemplation' closes *In Seven Days*, its periodic structure harking back to the progressions that accompanied the themes in the first and fourth movements, as shown by the transformational graph in Fig. 7.2. A three-chord phrase features α chords transformed at T_8 and T_{11} (bars 1–3). This progression is answered by β chords repeated at T_8, connected to the A section through an X transformation holding three tones invariant (bars 4–5). This phrase is completed by the appearance of α in inversion (note the lack of invariant tones with the preceding B harmony, bar 6). As in movement IV, the first phrase repeats at T_6 to form a larger repeated period. The movement closes with a very brief iteration of the very first chord in the entire work, α1, as mentioned above, in four violins.

---

[29] The publisher's website lists the fifth and sixth movements as two halves of a larger fugue: www.fabermusic.com/music/in-seven-days-148.

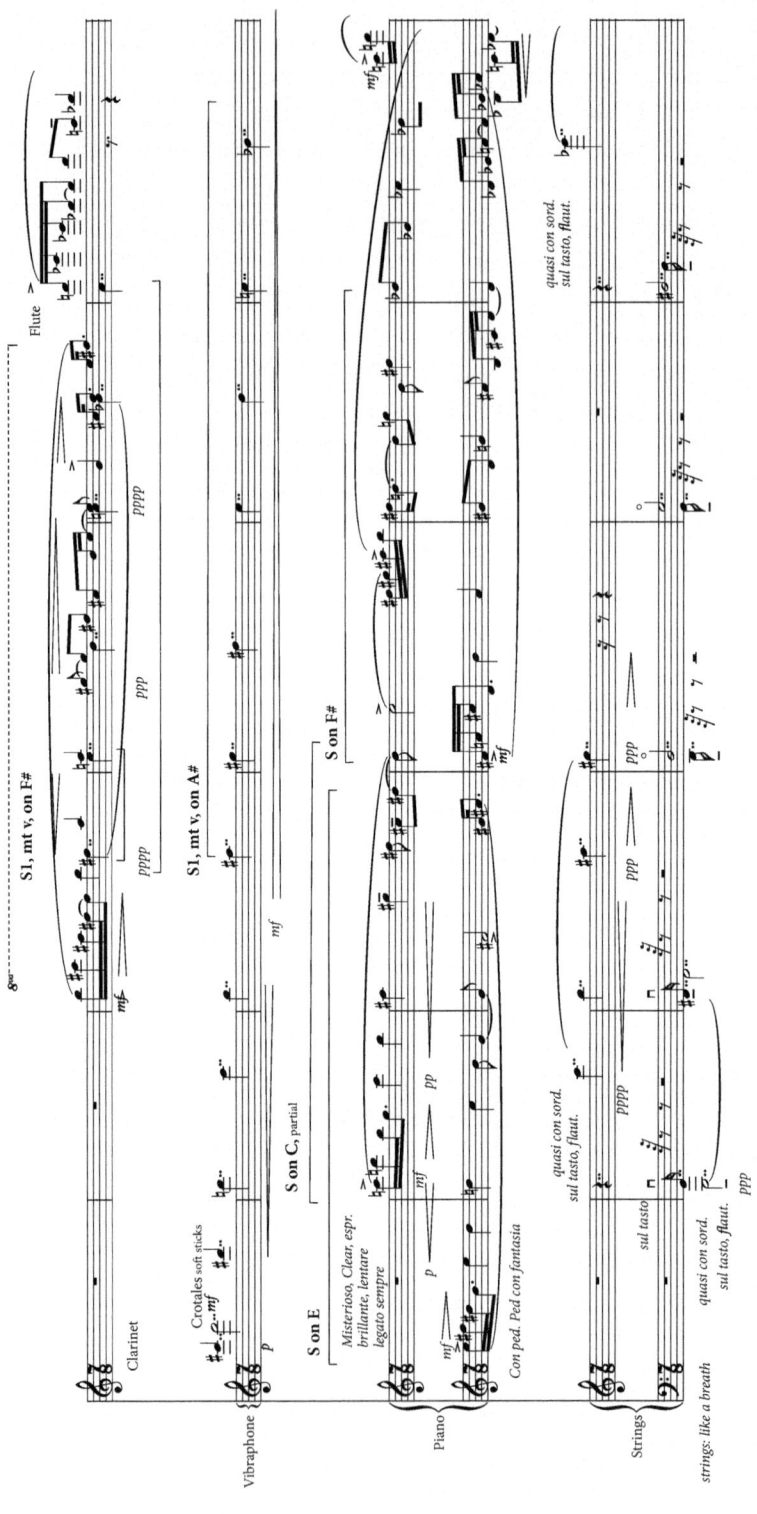

Ex. 7.7 Annotated reduction of the initial fugal entrances in *In Seven Days*, movement VI

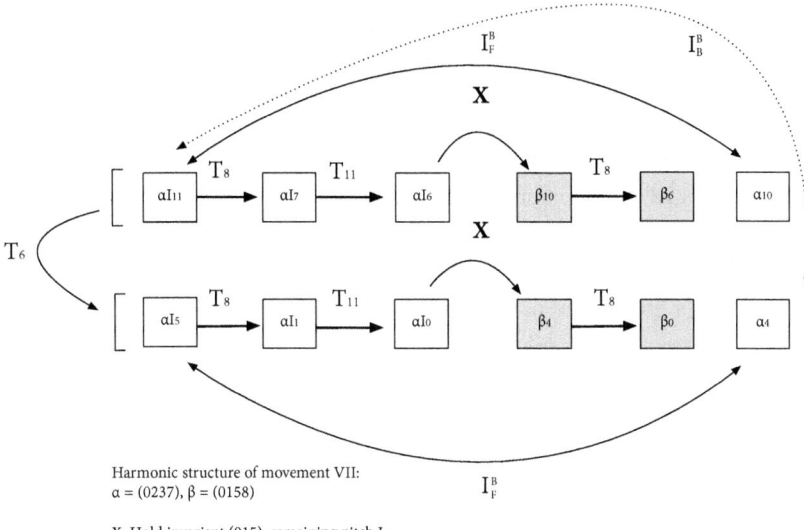

Fig. 7.2 Transformational structure of *In Seven Days*, movement VII

Creation as Virtuosic Re-creation

As he readily admits, Adès draws freely from music of the past, with an unerring sense for the resonance of specific semiotic associations. These range from general connotations of musical techniques such as fugue and twelve-note composition to specific citations, as when a quote from the Sanctus of Beethoven's *Missa solemnis* (1819–24) appears in the horns in movement VI.[30] *Arcadiana* in this respect prefigures *In Seven Days*: its seven parts also pair non-simultaneous movements – even and odd – within a variation form that references Elgar's *Enigma Variations* (1899).[31] Like *In Seven Days*, *Arcadiana* highlights startling changes of gesture, technique and character, and relies on specific topoi within each of the seven movements, whose interrelations house an 'eighth, unheard idea'.[32] Julian Johnson describes a kind of telescope effect that results from *Arcadiana*'s reflection on the past: the earlier musical worlds evoked themselves connoted arcadia, representing 'layer on layer of lateness' in the English music of Elgar which itself reflected on Beethoven.[33] If

[30] Martlew, 'In Conversation'.

[31] See Mark Hutchinson, *Coherence in New Music: Experience, Aesthetics, Analysis* (Abingdon: Routledge, 2016), pp. 24, 30.

[32] Adès and Service, *Full of Noises*, p. 74.

[33] Julian Johnson, *Out of Time: Music and the Making of Modernity* (New York: Oxford University Press, 2015), p. 42.

Arcadiana's citations of Liszt, Mozart, François Couperin and Schubert reflected fragments of a hazy utopian past, *In Seven Days* has a more expansive and formal relation to past works that forged their own creation myths.

I begin with Western music's most iconic work on Genesis, Haydn's *The Creation* (1798), which founded the modern orchestral sound and established a 'veritable encyclopaedia of orchestral techniques that serve to synthesise a wide range of orchestral meanings'.[34] Emily Dolan's argument that Haydn's timbre and orchestration were inextricable from his structural techniques recalls Adès's declaration 'To me there is no distinction between colour and timbre and pitches.'[35] But how do such techniques – timbral or structural – relate to the larger allegorical meaning of a creation narrative? Lawrence Kramer posits a resolutely modern answer to this state of affairs: the oratorio constitutes itself precisely as the withdrawal of the sublime, leaving humanity to contend with its aftermath.[36] Creation as such can occur only with the sublime's withdrawal, which is the condition for essence and subjectivity. This withdrawal takes various forms, from rather mundane, programmatic passages to the striking appearance of light as it distils chaos. Haydn here relies on simple musical devices: an ascending scale – 'a kind of cosmic monochord' – that brings sunrise at No. 12, or the transition to the subdominant as the moon's key.[37] Here we might recall the grand chaconnes and fugue subjects based on whole-tone scales that cycle through the figurative suggestions of emerging light, cracking firmament and evolving life of *In Seven Days*. Kramer reads Haydn's movement from chaos to the image – along with Adamic naming – as feints that secure essence at the cost of sublimity: music as image to a 'music from which the image has been withdrawn' in favour of pure sound. Rather than being a simplistic *ut pictura musica*, Kramer suggests, Haydn's tone-painting both disrupts the sublime and ensures that even the smallest elements of musical structure retain meaning as mimetic forms: 'Such little atoms of mimesis are the reverse of chaotic; they are microcosms of which the more extended form is the analogical portrayal of the world order in motion.'[38] These atoms are similar to the constant transpositions and inversions of (0237) and the elastic metric shifts that simulate growth

[34] Emily Dolan, *The Orchestral Revolution: Haydn and the Technologies of Timbre* (Cambridge: Cambridge University Press, 2013), pp. 147–8.

[35] Adès and Service, *Full of Noises*, p. 156.

[36] Lawrence Kramer, 'Recalling the Sublime: The Logic of Creation in Haydn's *Creation*', *Eighteenth-Century Music*, 6/i (2009), 41–57.

[37] Ibid., p. 48.   [38] Ibid., p. 52.

and change in *In Seven Days*. More telling as a comparison, however, is the 'secular plenitude' that Kramer notes in Haydn's *Creation*; he describes the material heft of the orchestration and its celebration of sensory enjoyment as the oratorio's most significant intervention in the history of creation narratives.[39]

If Haydn's *Creation* seems to prefigure the marriage of timbral and motivic richness that characterises *In Seven Days*, Schoenberg's *Genesis* composition, Prelude for Mixed Chorus and Orchestra Op. 44 (1945), suggests a model for the marriage of historical and modern compositional technique. *Genesis* was the result of the composer and publisher Nathaniel Shilkret's commission for the prelude to a series of seven works on the biblical story, each by a different composer (Stravinsky provided the final movement with *The Tower of Babel*). We might recall that Schoenberg's essay 'Composition with Twelve Tones (1)' opens with a nod to the biblical Genesis, treating the Lord's 'Let there be Light' as an allegory of the composer's role as creator. But the later version of the essay delves into the ethics of dodecaphonic canonic writing; even the writing of fugues 'is a little too easy' given the lack of contrapuntal restrictions, and 'should only be undertaken for some special reason'.[40] Carl Dahlhaus's brief article on *Genesis* recognises the contradictions inherent in Schoenberg's reflections: that a contemporary return to fugue, the highest achievement of contrapuntal composition, signals 'nostalgic longing for the beauty of the past', a demonstration of prodigious technique or a form that specifically demands a section in 'the old style'.[41] Given that a prelude representing chaos should not require a fugue – much less one in which the fugue *precedes* its prelude-like denouement – we must assume some historical criteria, some reason why Schoenberg chose to evoke the spirit of Bach for this project. As Dahlhaus notes, the fugue subject does not correspond to the twelve-note row, but neither is it developed like a theme, although it does preserve one of each canonic form of the row.[42] Dahlhaus traces a possible motive for Schoenberg's odd choice of genre back to Goethe's famous comment that a performance of Bach's fugues summoned up, for the writer, an image of

---

[39] Ibid., p. 57.

[40] Arnold Schoenberg, 'Composition with Twelve Tones (2) (*c.* 1948)', in *Style and Idea: Selected Writings of Arnold Schoenberg*, ed. by Leonard Stein, trans. by Leo Black (Berkeley and Los Angeles: University of California Press, 1984), pp. 245–9 (p. 248).

[41] Carl Dahlhaus, 'The Fugue as Prelude: Schoenberg's *Genesis* Composition, Op. 44', in *Schoenberg and the New Music*, trans. by Derrick Puffett and Alfred Clayton (Cambridge: Cambridge University Press, 1987), pp. 169–73.

[42] Ibid., p. 170.

'eternal harmony ... shortly before the world's creation'.[43] According to Goethe, man cannot and should not create an image of God, but he can suggest Him with the pure abstract beauty of counterpoint (a central theme of Schoenberg's *Moses und Aron*, 1930–2); hence 'Schoenberg's *Prelude* is music about a remark about music.'[44]

If Adès can be said to write music inspired by words on music, it is in the sense, as Alastair Williams notes, that his activity as a composer is inextricable from his discourse.[45] And his composing, we might add, is linked to his activity as a performer and conductor. Adès served as music director and conductor for the San Francisco premiere of *In Seven Days* on 5 March 2015, and it is fruitful to reflect on the works he chose to accompany the concerto. Those included Charles Ives's *The Unanswered Question* (1908; rev. 1935), Darius Milhaud's *La création du monde* (1922–3) and Sibelius's tone poem *Luonnotar* (1913), all works dealing with an aspect of creation outside the conventional biblical account. Ives's *The Unanswered Question* seems the furthest from an explicit creation myth, with its existential question posed against the 'The Silence of the Druids, Who Know, See and Hear Nothing'. What appears to be a slow harmonic cycle thirteen bars long shifts character after the second repetition as a suspended chorale in strings is punctuated by six appearances of 'The Perennial Question of Existence', a five-note segment of the octatonic collection $(_{0,1})$ in solo trumpet. Six responses in winds answer, beginning in $OCT_{0,1}$ but growing slowly more chromatic, to culminate in the full aggregate at the fourth answer as the G major chorale slowly climbs upwards. The answers separate from the chorale/question as their speed increases seven times from the *Largo molto sempre* of the beginning, while the question motive shifts within the bar. The end cycles back to the beginning, in a form that suggests the circularity of existence and the shifting cycles and rhythmic play of Adès's creation story.

Milhaud's *La création du monde* of course follows a quite different, African, creation myth, but one with similar parallels: a full section that

---

[43] Letter to Zelter on 21 June 1827, quoted in Dahlhaus, 'The Fugue as Prelude', p. 172.

[44] Dahlhaus, 'The Fugue as Prelude', p. 173. That works on creation present a daunting task is suggested by the short list of twentieth-century works devoted to Genesis, which include Charles Wuorinen's *Genesis* (1989) for chorus and orchestra; Aaron Copland's *In the Beginning* (1947), a single-movement work for mezzo-soprano and SATB a cappella; and Daniel Pinkham's *In the Beginning of Creation* (1970) for SATB and tape.

[45] Alastair Williams, 'Between Modernism and Postmodernism: Structure and Expression in John Adams, Kaija Saariaho and Thomas Adès', in *The Routledge Research Companion to Modernism in Music*, ed. by Björn Heile and Charles Wilson (New York: Routledge, 2019), pp. 327–52 (p. 344).

embodies the chaotic beginning, followed by a movement dedicated to light and new life. But we move already to man and woman in the third movement, with an entire movement dedicated to their desire. Like that of *In Seven Days*, the tonal framework of Milhaud's *La création du monde* can be identified with two primary tetrachords: a D minor seventh chord (0358) and an F♯ major seventh chord (0158), with E♯/F as the common pivot between them, within a larger, arc-like form that – also as in the concerto – brings back its opening theme in a simple form at the close.[46] Here the oboe functions as the voice of creation, and a fugue that creates the world begins already in the first movement, its tonal order modelling a standard jazz I–ii–V–I progression (D–E–A–D),[47] just as Adès's canon (in movement III) and fugues (in movements V and VI) executed contemporary variations on standard patterns.

Sibelius's *Luonnotar* Op. 70 turns the first runot of the Kalevala into a tone poem for soprano and orchestra where the vocalist incarnates the spirit of nature, who floated alone in the universe before falling into the waves and helping to birth – along with a magical seabird – the world we know. We begin with a floating F♯ minor sonority in the orchestra, which supports a soaring vocal line in F sharp Dorian within a steady pulse that shifts from 2/2 to 3/2 through a variation structure based on rotation.[48] *Luonnotar*'s modal texture supports fleeting octatonic passages, but ends in an eerie glow not dissimilar to that of Adès's epilogue as the stars take their place in the sky; at the close a (0158) tetrachord voiced as F sharp minor with lowered sixth adds the major third without relinquishing the dissonant D and A. In all three works we find minimal thematic and tonal materials set within a cyclic framework. Through rhythmic and contrapuntal development, they chart the evolution of a world, yet that labour ends with a moment of serenity: a simple theme or sonority, carried primarily in

---

[46] Laura Amos, 'An Examination of 1920s Parisian Polytonality: Milhaud's Ballet *La création du monde*' (unpublished PhD dissertation, The University of Texas at Austin, 2007), pp. 106–64. Amos finds outer movements connected by 'simple' tetrachords – polychords composed of those diatonically related triads – while the central movements are connected by polychords composed of triads in a chromatic mediant or double chromatic mediant relationship (p. 111).

[47] The ii⁷–V⁷–I progression is considered the staple progression in jazz and the basis of most chromatic elaborations.

[48] See Tomi Mäkelä, 'The Wings of a Butterfly: Sibelius and the Problems of Musical Modernity', in *Jean Sibelius and His World*, ed. by Daniel M. Grimley (Princeton, NJ: Princeton University Press, 2011), pp. 89–124; and James Hepokoski, 'The Essence of Sibelius: Creation Myths and Rotational Cycles in *Luonnotar*', in *The Sibelius Companion*, ed. by Glenda Dawn Goss (Westport, CT: Greenwood Press, 1996), pp. 135–60. As noted above, F♯ functions as a 'fetish note' for *In Seven Days*.

strings (except in *La création*). As does *In Seven Days*, these works take the listener on a journey, telling 'the story of the material and also of material' and more interested in the questions posed by the effort of creation than in any God lurking behind it.

Given the material and allegorical connections that obtain among these creation narratives, we might expand our search to include a simpler narrative parallel, if one closer to home: Benjamin Britten's theme and variations as an allegory on the creation of the orchestra from a Baroque theme. A *Young Person's Guide to the Orchestra* (1945) also serves us a glittering tutti presentation of the main theme, followed by variations that introduce orchestral groups from high to low. Like Adès in *In Seven Days*, Britten begins with flutes and piccolo and closes the work with a fugue in the creation key of E major – also launched by flute and piccolo – but quickly joined by oboes to close with both themes.[49] Of course unlike *The Young Person's Guide*, *In Seven Days* offers us a contemplative return at the close. The final movement 'pull[s] the camera out at the end', as Adès terms it, to give the listener an aerial view of the entire work.[50] In this sense the epilogue mirrors the work as a whole, as an allegory of the birth and evolution of the orchestra and a variation on the orchestra's own history of creation myths. *In Seven Days* in this sense truly embraces 'the story of the material . . . all of it, in the world' writ large, a musical paradigm of world-building that draws on medieval, Baroque and contemporary compositional techniques to recover the inexhaustible promise of the musical past.

---

[49] I am indebted to Richard Powell for this observation.
[50] Adès and Service, *Full of Noises*, p. 44.

8 | *Musique automatique?* Adèsian Automata and the Logic of Disjuncture

BRIAN MOSELEY

Twenty years after Richard Taruskin fashioned Thomas Adès as a modernist saviour in surrealist garb, to call Adès's music surreal is now a cliché.[1] And while the stereotype's communicative utility remains undeniably evocative, its entrenched position in our discourse easily obscures both surrealism's wonderful elusiveness and the fascinating tangle of associations linking the movement to Adès.[2] In the dialogue that has sprung from Taruskin's influential review, critics have seized primarily on those Adèsian musical effects whose jarring quality emerges from common sounds 'made newly strange'.[3] This observational stance has the benefit of linking Adès to the most recognisable surrealists – and to Salvador Dalí in particular, whose melting clocks and lobster telephones are easily translated into droopy harmonies and disfigured cadences. Taruskin's rendering of the connection frames Adès's surrealism in just this way – suggesting that he transfigures the medium of music into something '"painterly" rather than "narrative"', 'improbable sonic collages and mobiles: outlandish juxtapositions of evocative sound-objects'.[4] By suggesting a visual origin for Adès's incongruous sounds, Taruskin effortlessly situates Adès within the Dalí-dominated strand of object-oriented surrealism.[5] Like Dalí's *Persistence of Memory* and *Lobster Telephone*, Adès's music is in this light brimming with incongruous juxtapositions, recontextualisations, decontextualisations, distortions and disjunctures.

And yes, these are central features of Adès's music that resonate with a particularly rich paradigm of modernist art – both surreal and not surreal.[6]

---

[1] Richard Taruskin, 'A Surrealist Composer Comes to the Rescue of Modernism', *New York Times*, 5 December 1999; reprinted with a postscript in *The Danger of Music and Other Anti-utopian Essays* (Berkeley and Los Angeles: University of California Press, 2009), pp. 144–52.

[2] See Edward Venn, *Thomas Adès: Asyla* (Abingdon: Routledge, 2017); and Drew Massey, 'Thomas Adès and the Dilemmas of Musical Surrealism', *Gli spazi della musica*, 7 (2018), 86–146.

[3] Taruskin, 'A Surrealist Composer', p. 147.   [4] Ibid.

[5] See Salvador Dalí, 'Objets surréalistes', *Le surréalisme au service de la révolution*, 3 (1931), 15–16.

[6] Adès has many familial connections to surrealism as well. His mother, Dawn Adès, is a prominent art historian who specialises in Dada and Surrealism, and, as Drew Massey ('Thomas Adès and the Dilemmas of Musical Surrealism', pp. 93–4) has detailed, his father and brother are also connected to the movement.

But I believe that something central is missing in Taruskin's description of Adès's 'painterly' disjunctions: these purported disjunctions frequently have their basis in a compositional logic that does in fact structure a musical process, or even a narrative. Christopher Fox captured this feature of Adès's works in an article written not long after Taruskin's. Much as surrealist painting derives its 'fantastic nonsense' from 'a logic within the depiction itself', Fox finds in Adès's music a 'wealth of melodic and harmonic detail' that 'can be related to a few intervallic relationships'.[7] Logic of this sort does not make Adès's music any *less* surreal; rather, I will argue below that it makes it *more* so. Locating surrealism *in the music*, Adès engages an aesthetic predating Dalí – one represented in the works of André Breton, André Masson and Max Ernst, who operated under the spell of 'automatism'.

Breton, the chief instigator of early surrealism, viewed automatism and surrealism as synonymous. Automatic thought was a great interest of Sigmund Freud, for whom it represented the spontaneous and non-purposeful behaviours of the unconscious. Dreams are automatic thought par excellence because they are not rationally conceived. Breton, a great admirer of Freud, felt that dreams were grossly neglected, and in his *Surrealist Manifesto* (1924) he argues that we awaken understanding by elevating a dream's marvellous events to a status typically reserved for conscious reality.[8] Automatism as a principle accomplishes this reorientation and becomes the basis of Breton's notion of surrealism:

SURREALISM, n. Pure psychic automatism, by which one proposes to express— verbally, by means of the written word, or in any other manner – the actual functioning of thought. Dictated by thought, in the absence of any control exercised by reason, exempt from any aesthetic concern.[9]

Surrealism, then, exceeds realism by ignoring the active, reasoned coherence of the conscious mind, freeing the seeming incoherence of the passive and unconscious mind and rounding out our understanding of thought itself. In Daniel Albright's telling, this negotiation between the tyranny of consciousness and unconscious freedom occurs most clearly when our senses become disconnected: a 'twittering cow' is 'the primary surrealist act', emerging when 'I . . . walk through a field and watch a distant cow

---

[7] See Christopher Fox, 'Tempestuous Times: The Recent Music of Thomas Adès', *Musical Times*, 145/1888 (2004), 41–56 (p. 45).

[8] André Breton, 'Manifesto of Surrealism (1924)', in *Manifestoes of Surrealism*, trans. by Richard Seaver and Helen R. Lane (Ann Arbor: University of Michigan Press, 1969), pp. 3–47.

[9] Ibid., p. 26.

open its mouth, and hear, at that very instant, the tweet of a bird'.[10] The humour of this image, if we allow it to emerge, comes from a sensory mismatch of eye and ear that refuses to allow our conscious mind to connect our senses. Surrealist automatism encourages us to free these 'suppressed dissonances', which are as much a part of our 'everyday sensory existence' as coherent thought.[11]

Interpreted this way, surrealism's relished incongruities are not fully disjunct but are legitimate, logical manifestations of our unconscious. Surreal automatism therefore asks us to imagine Adès's 'outlandish juxta-positions' as surreal revelations of supressed associations. This chapter's goal is to explore this reorientation by positioning Adès's music in the context of automatism. I believe that this focus enriches our engagement with the music far beyond simply giving us new pictures to imagine as we listen. First, the framework of automatism allows us to incorporate works that have not often been understood as surreal. Much of the literature discussing Adès and surrealism has concentrated on the operas and pro-grammatic pieces.[12] My focus in this chapter is on his four Mazurkas: genre pieces that lack dramatic, textual, pictorial or programmatic content around which we are able to position a surreal reading. Second, the automatic techniques found in literary and visual art link Adèsian surreal-ism to the compositional logic that theorists such as John Roeder and Philip Stoecker have uncovered in the past twenty years.[13] Finally, Adès's automatism suggests a way of composing genuinely surreal music. Breton found music 'confusing', and he does not include it among the modes of surreal artistic creation.[14] By emphasising the 'painterly' nature of Adès's compositions, Taruskin would seem to respond to Breton's critique by suggesting that this music's surreal qualities are found in its visual attri-butes. I, on the other hand, suggest that by attending to the surrealist qualities that are fundamentally musical, we are able to account for those

---

[10] Though he does not discuss Adès, Daniel Albright's formulation of musical surrealism has been, apart from Taruskin's review, perhaps the most influential precursor to our present understanding of Adès and surrealism. See Daniel Albright, *Untwisting the Serpent: Modernism in Music, Literature, and Other Arts* (Chicago: University of Chicago Press, 2000), pp. 291–311.

[11] Ibid., p. 248.

[12] Venn's subject (in *Thomas Adès: Asyla*) is the orchestral *Asyla*. Massey ('Thomas Adès and the Dilemmas of Musical Surrealism') discusses *Powder Her Face*, *Life Story*, *Brahms* and *In Seven Days*.

[13] See, for instance, John Roeder, 'Co-operating Continuities in the Music of Thomas Adès', *Music Analysis*, 25/i–ii (2006), 121–54; and Philip Stoecker, 'Aligned Cycles in Thomas Adès's Piano Quintet', *Music Analysis*, 33/i (2014), 32–64.

[14] See André Breton, *Le surréalisme et la peinture*, rev. ed. (Paris: Gallimard, 1965), p. 1.

marvellous sounds that emerge from logical processes of structured time, thereby adding strength to the notion that music can indeed be surreal.

I return to these themes explicitly in the final part of this chapter, where I examine the three Mazurkas Op. 27 and *Thrift (a Cliff-Flower): Mazurka-Cortège*. But in the meantime, I hope that the specific surrealist connections to Adès's music can remain just at the edge of consciousness as I discuss automatism as a principle and explore automatic techniques found in early surrealist literary and visual art. As I navigate the historical and artistic gaps separating Breton and Adès, Max Ernst, his collage process and the frottage technique in particular will provide a helpful bridge.

Willed Passivity, Conscious Receptivity and the Logic of Surreal Automata

'Automatic' techniques of artistic creation proliferated through literary and visual art in the 1920s. Breton prefigures the definition of surrealism given above by describing his gravitation towards a way of 'automatic writing': in the half-consciousness before sleep one evening, a phrase appeared in Breton's mind – 'There is a man cut in two by a window' – without 'any apparent relationship to the events' of his reality. Excited by its organic, unexpected imagery, he sought out these supressed thoughts by putting himself 'in as passive, or receptive state of mind' as possible ... writing 'quickly, without any preconceived subject'. Automatic writing thus aimed to outrun consciousness and capture an inner 'monologue ... unencumbered by the slightest inhibition'.[15]

Breton's *Les champs magnétiques* (*The Magnetic Fields*), written in 1919 with Philippe Soupalt, was the signal event in the development of early surrealism. Produced with the automatic writing technique, the book puts forth passage after passage of odd images piled on top one another. In its post-war landscape, we are imagined as 'prisoners', not of other humans but 'of drops of water'. The landscape of post-war Europe is anthropomorphised only to reveal that its towns 'are dead' and its walls 'quiet'.[16] It is essential to recognise that while such images present us with an '*extreme degree of immediate absurdity*', surrealists understood them as entirely

---

[15] Breton, 'Manifesto of Surrealism (1924)', pp. 21–4.
[16] André Breton and Philippe Soupault, *The Magnetic Fields*, trans. by David Gascoyne, 3rd ed. (London: Atlas Press, 1985), pp. 25–6.

logical products of thought that '[disclose] a certain number of properties and ... facts no less objective, in the final analysis, than the others'.[17]

Given the imagistic quality of *The Magnetic Fields*, it is unsurprising that Breton positioned visual expression alongside literary expression as one of only two ways to produce surreal art. And visual artists in the 1920s quickly replicated the axioms of automatic writing to produce surreal images. Among the most important are the 'automatic drawings' of Masson and Joan Miró. Each artist's imitations of automatic writing began by their copying Breton's instructions for automatic writing literally. Masson, in drawings such as *Automatic Drawing* (1924), *Furious Suns* (1925) and *Birth of Birds* (1925), began by attempting to free his mind, letting the pen flow freely and spontaneously across the page in hopes of capturing the same unconscious images sought by Breton. Subsequently, these lines were interpreted by Masson into finished drawings.

This added layer of after-the-fact interpretation highlights a significant characteristic of automatic drawing that will be important when we return to Adès. This quality, which I will refer to as 'willed passivity' and 'conscious receptivity', describes how automatic drawing lives in the tension between the *passive state* sought at a drawing's beginning and a conscious mind's *later reflection*. Miró vividly captures these qualities by describing two separate stages of creation: 'I start a canvas without a thought of what it may eventually become. I put it aside after the first fire has abated. I may not look at it again for months. Then I take it out and work at it coldly like an artisan, guided strictly by rules of composition after the first shock of suggestion has cooled.'[18]

As an example of these qualities, consider Masson's *Birth of Birds*.[19] The speed and airiness of the abstract pen strokes produced in the drawing's passive beginning come together into smoothed-over convex angles that point the drawing upwards to the right. The drawing's lines have a purposeful, airy and earthy quality. At its centre, Masson later formed those lines into the vague outlines of a nude female, with breasts made of comets and stars, and two bird-like images with triangular beaks emerging from her lap. Masson's interpretation of the pen strokes seizes on a classic surrealist coupling of humans and beasts, natural and unnatural: the female form merges with the soaring birds, and the natural process of birth

---

[17] Breton, 'Manifesto of Surrealism (1924)', p. 24, original emphasis.

[18] See James Johnson Sweeney, 'Joan Miró: Comment and Interview', *Partisan Review*, 15/ii (1948), 206–12 (pp. 210–11).

[19] At the time of writing, a high-quality reproduction of this drawing is available online at the website of the Museum of Modern Art, New York, www.moma.org.

becomes an analogue for avian flight.[20] *Birth of Birds* foregrounds the *revelatory* aspect of automatic art, linking surrealism to Freud's 'uncanny'. Seeming disjuncture and disorientation are symptoms of both, 'produced when the distinction between imagination and reality is effaced'.[21]

Max Ernst's 1921 exhibition of collage works was, after the publication of *The Magnetic Fields*, the other central event in surrealism's early development. Ernst's collages, as assemblages of pre-existing materials, seem at first to contrast rather sharply with the fluidity and passiveness of automatic writing and drawing. Both Ernst and Breton, however, attempted to ground collage within the overarching principle of automatism.[22] In his *Surrealism and Painting* of 1928, Breton sees the chance encounters in collage elements as the result of an automatic process. By allowing defunct, often discarded items to come into chance association, collage begins from a position of passiveness that is followed, like automatic drawing, by conscious interpretation.

Ernst's related technique of 'frottage' even more clearly highlights the automatic principles of willed passivity and conscious receptivity. In frottage, Ernst places objects below a sheet of paper and then exposes the object's contours by rubbing the paper with a pencil. When a frottage work such as *The Fugitive* (*L'évadé*) is viewed, the breakages in material heterogeneity that are recognisable on the surface foreground the processual quality of collage noted by Elza Adamowicz.[23] The strange creature in the centre of the work is formed from a disparate group of these patterns.[24] The image's unnatural character – is this a creature or a machine? – is brought into relief against the natural materials used to produce it. The leaves that create its trailing fins, the canvas-like material forming its body and the wire-mesh sea below cause one to wonder whether this is a fish floating in mid-air, escaping the water by sprouting wings, or a strange zeppelin whose fish-like form is an adaptation to its marine environment.

---

[20] Julia Kelly draws out many of these observations in *Surrealism: Desire Unbound*, ed. by Jennifer Mundy (London: Tate Publishing, 2001), p. 105.

[21] Sigmund Freud, 'The "Uncanny"', in *An Infantile Neurosis and Other Works (1917–1919)*, vol. 17 of *The Standard Edition of the Complete Psychological Works of Sigmund Freud*, ed. by James Strachey (London: Hogarth, 1955), pp. 217–52 (p. 244). Both Massey ('Thomas Adès and the Dilemmas of Musical Surrealism', pp. 122–30) and Edward Venn, in 'Thomas Adès and the Spectres of *Brahms*', *Journal of the Royal Musical Association*, 140/i (2015), 163–212, discuss Adès in relation to the uncanny.

[22] Breton, *Le surréalisme et la peinture*, p. 27.

[23] Elza Adamowicz, *Surrealist Collage in Text and Image: Dissecting the Exquisite Corpse* (Cambridge: Cambridge University Press, 1998), p. 15. My understanding of collage as 'automatic' is influenced by Adamowicz's work.

[24] Ernst's *The Fugitive* is, at the time of writing, available for viewing online at the website of the Museum of Modern Art, New York, www.moma.org.

To retrieve Adès's music from the periphery of this discussion, frottage represents a critical link between purely automatic writing and drawing and the surreal character of his music. In the work of both Ernst and Adès, seeming disjunctions emerge from the tension of passivity and activity that is inherent in engaging with pre-existing, underlying patterns and processes. Ernst himself felt that the potential for musical automatism could be found in frottage. Musical automatism, he stated, might replace the technique's patterned objects with 'dictations of actual raw resonances, which would place our unconscious in possession of this latent music'.[25] Notably, Ernst's suggestion that 'raw resonances' replace the physical patterns of frottage is centred on a conception of sound as devoid of 'independent aesthetic value'.[26] Patterned floorboards, leaves and breadcrumbs, like common chord successions, scales and generic rhythmic ideas, have no specific meaning.

What, then, are the 'raw resonances' of Adès's automatic musical language? I contend that they are patterns of pitches, intervals and rhythms, occasionally derived from specific pieces by other composers, but also 'natural' or, as Adès might say, 'geometrical', patterns based on numerical sequences and musical properties that are latent in familiar musical objects. These are the patterns, I believe, that Christopher Fox notices when writing of the 'logic' that inheres in the 'fantastic nonsense' of Adès's music, and they include Adès's characteristic interval cycles and rhythmic gestures.[27] That Adès engages them through both the willed passivity and the conscious receptivity common to surrealist automatism is evident not only in his compositional logic but in a great many of Adès's discussions of his music. Adès has described his use of pre-existing materials with recourse to natural imagery whose vividness is reminiscent of the Miró quotation above. Calling them 'live cultures', 'roots' or 'seeds', Adès indicates that he is entranced by old ideas that are 'still not quite set' and that invite 'further experimentation, further unfolding'.[28] Again channelling Miró, he says:

---

[25] See François-Bernard Mâche, 'Surréalisme et musique, remarques et gloses', *La nouvelle revue française*, 264 (1974), 34–49.

[26] Quoted by Anne LeBaron, 'Reflections of Surrealism in Postmodern Musics', in *Postmodern Music/Postmodern Thought*, ed. by Judy Lochhead and Joseph Auner (London: Routledge, 2002), pp. 27–74 (pp. 37–8).

[27] Fox, 'Tempestuous Times', p. 45.

[28] Kirill Gerstein, 'Thomas Adès: "Roots, Seeds & Live Cultures" – "Kirill Gerstein Invites" @ HfM Eisler Berlin', online video interview, 18 June 2020, YouTube, www.youtube.com/watch?v=I0kHP_npxJA.

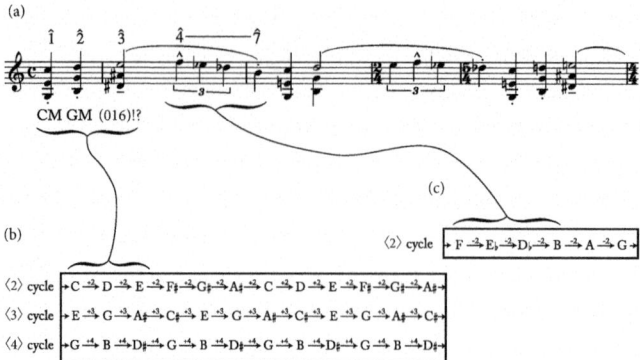

Ex. 8.1 Piano Quintet (2000). (a) Bars 1–4; (b) aligned cycle of intervals for the first three chords; (c) a different interval pattern structure

You can have quite a lot of material that is sort of, if you like, applying for entry to a piece. And in my case, I will scribble something down if it looks promising, tear it off, and stick the piece of paper to the wall physically. And they can sit there, sometimes for years and never make it into anything. And sometimes they suddenly have their moment. And I say 'oh, you'll do' . . . I need time for most things . . . What can happen is I'll do something very quickly and leave it for however long, and then you start to see the things that will never do and then you work on those.[29]

Consider, for example, the opening of Adès's Piano Quintet, shown in Ex. 8.1a. The common chord succession that forms the piece's upbeat – a second-inversion C major chord followed by a first-inversion G major chord – is an ideal musical representation of the conventional object, or 'raw resonance', suggested by Ernst. Adès has described this chord succession in terms redolent of the surprising images that materialise out of frottage:

There was a period where I was fascinated by . . . perfect cadences. And I thought, what happens if I treat it [the first two chords of Ex. 8.1a] not as an inevitable, natural process . . . but I look at those things as a structure . . . If you abstract it a little bit, you see that you have three voices, one moves major second, one moves minor third, one moves major third. And then logically, geometrically the next chord is actually that [the D♯-A♯-E chord in bar 1].[30]

Our sense of surprise at the composite gesture's end is certainly a result of hearing D♯-A♯-E rather than a root-position C major; in Taruskin's terms, it is 'an ordinary event . . . made newly strange'.[31] But imagined within the context of surreal automatism, the patterns of Ex. 8.1b reveal that the

---

[29] Ibid., 00:24:15–00:28:30.   [30] Ibid., 00:29:30.

[31] Taruskin, 'A Surrealist Composer', p. 147.

distortion has a richer meaning. Those intervallic patterns, like Ernst's frottage patterns, are *pre-existing* and inherent in the succession, present for as long as the well-worn chord succession has existed; thus as Breton might say, what we hear at the opening of the Piano Quintet is 'no less objective', no less legitimate than the tonal pattern that would have produced a C major chord.[32] By mining this relic of the musical past for something long ignored, Adès enacts a willed passivity towards it that aligns him with the automatism of Breton, Masson and Ernst. Distortions and disjunctions are revealed in this way to have been present all along and made invisible only by the inherited habits of our conscious mind.

Surrealism on the Inside: Adès's Mazurkas

In a wonderful coincidence, one of the first self-professed pieces of surreal music was itself a mazurka. Written by André Souris and Paul Hooreman in 1925 – a year after Breton's *Surrealist Manifesto* – *Tombeau de Socrate* has generally been read as an attempt to 'out-parody' Erik Satie, who had written his own 'Death of Socrates' and died just weeks earlier.[33] Simple in the extreme, the mazurka is one minute in length and contains a single stave and no bar lines, and its mazurka-like attributes are evident primarily in unadorned metric and rhythmic attributes.[34] Adès – like Souris and Hooreman – had available to him many of the specific qualities that we hear in Chopin's mazurkas along with a set of meaningful, conventional patterns: the mazurka's triple metre, with characteristic accents on the second and third beats; conventional rhythmic patterns, particularly dotted rhythms on the first beat; repeated short, symmetrical phrase structures; bass pedals; an invocation of the Lydian fourth scale degree; and formal plans oriented around thematic and tonal contrast.[35] These mazurka

---

[32] Venn (*Thomas Adès: Asyla*, p. 149) suggests that Adès's compositional logic often 'trigger[s] associations with functional tonality, but which is nevertheless divorced from it', thereby making him 'less a surrealist in the mould of Poulenc *et al.*, and more a *second-order* surrealist, whose semantic innovations arise not from a tilting of the musical logic [of] functional tonality, but rather from a tilting of the musical logic of the surrealists themselves'. I argue, however, that the *logic* of Adès's compositional language, proceeding as it so often does in relationship to the past, is fundamental to the axioms of first-generation surreal thought.

[33] Caroline Potter, *Erik Satie: A Parisian Composer and His World* (Woodbridge, Suffolk: Boydell & Brewer, 2016), p. 236.

[34] Jean-Jacques Nattiez, *The Battle of Chronos and Orpheus: Essays in Applied Musical Semiology*, trans. by Jonathan Dunsby (New York: Oxford University Press, 2004), p. 24.

[35] Jennifer Maxwell has analysed these Mazurkas alongside those of Chopin and composer Karol Szymanowski. Maxwell's sense of connection is confirmed in Adès's interview with Gerstein,

patterns are, to paraphrase Adès, like 'a sort of invisible object', 'chronically volatile', 'like lava'.[36] They are hidden but still living natural materials waiting to exhibit new sides of themselves.

Through his titling of the movements of Op. 27 as First Mazurka, Second Mazurka and Third Mazurka, Adès explicitly indicates a performance order that corresponds, as we will see, to a slow deterioration of those traits that are most topically characteristic of the mazurka. In the First Mazurka the patterns are revealed to the listener in their most characteristic state. Figure 8.1 offers a diagram of its arch form listing a set of mazurka patterns beneath, while Ex. 8.2 shows excerpts from the movement. On its downbeat, Adès immediately invokes the mazurka's characteristic dotted rhythm (here realised in a short–long triplet form), along with a conventional tonic pedal in the bass and emphasis on the Lydian fourth scale degree (D♯, here notated as E♭).[37] As shown in Ex. 8.2a, bars 1–2, that E♭ initiates a series of 'expanding intervals' that generates the melody and, in fuzzy canonic presentation, the piano's middle register. Like the leaves and wire mesh concealed throughout Ernst's *Histoire naturelle*, this expanding interval series (EIS), diagrammed abstractly in Fig. 8.1b, is a staple of Adès's music.[38] Notably, the EIS is a pattern that is automatically self-generating: each interval between successive pitches is one semitone larger than the previous one. The resulting pitch construction produces one of Adès's famously 'irrational' tonal relationships – tritone-related harmonies. This tritone relationship is foregrounded in Ex. 8.2a, in which the D minor seventh above the tonic pedal in bar 1 is followed by a striking G sharp minor seventh in bar 2. (Note that Adès alters the EIS in the second bar, which avoids the A♮ that would have ended it but which has been present in the bass all along.)

where he reveals some specific Chopin mazurkas used as models for the three published as Op. 27. See Jennifer A. Maxwell, 'Tracing a Lineage of the Mazurka Genre: Influences of Chopin and Szymanowski on Thomas Adès's Mazurkas for Piano, Op. 27' (unpublished PhD dissertation, Boston University, 2014); see also Gerstein, 'Thomas Adès: "Roots, Seeds & Live Cultures"', 00:38:30–00:48:00.

[36] Thomas Adès and Tom Service, *Thomas Adès: Full of Noises – Conversations with Tom Service*, paperback ed. (London: Faber and Faber, 2018), p. 4.

[37] Each of these characteristics are found in Chopin's Mazurka in B flat major, which Adès played in his conversation with Gerstein. See Gerstein, 'Thomas Adès: "Roots, Seeds & Live Cultures"', 00:41:00–00:41:15.

[38] The analogy between Adès's EIS and Ernst's various frottage objects is strengthened by the numerous contexts in which Adès uses it. Roeder described the pattern in 'Co-operating Continuities' in connection with the string quartet *Arcadiana*, where it occurs in conjunction with a similar projection in duration (p. 26) and a tango-like passage from *Powder Her Face* (p. 36).

(a)

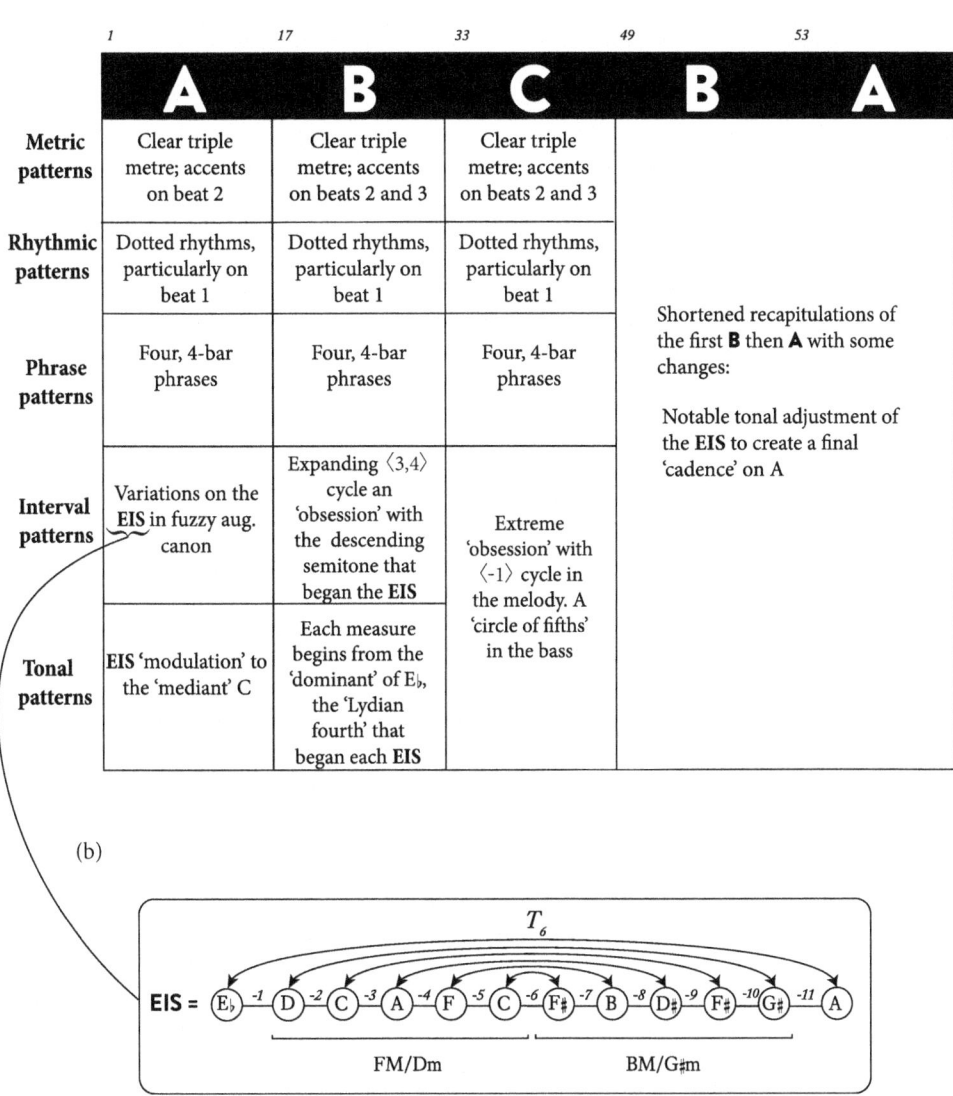

	1	17	33	49	53
	A	**B**	**C**	**B**	**A**
Metric patterns	Clear triple metre; accents on beat 2	Clear triple metre; accents on beats 2 and 3	Clear triple metre; accents on beats 2 and 3	Shortened recapitulations of the first **B** then **A** with some changes: Notable tonal adjustment of the **EIS** to create a final 'cadence' on A	
Rhythmic patterns	Dotted rhythms, particularly on beat 1	Dotted rhythms, particularly on beat 1	Dotted rhythms, particularly on beat 1		
Phrase patterns	Four, 4-bar phrases	Four, 4-bar phrases	Four, 4-bar phrases		
Interval patterns	Variations on the **EIS** in fuzzy aug. canon	Expanding ⟨3,4⟩ cycle an 'obsession' with the descending semitone that began the **EIS**	Extreme 'obsession' with ⟨-1⟩ cycle in the melody. A 'circle of fifths' in the bass		
Tonal patterns	**EIS** 'modulation' to the 'mediant' C	Each measure begins from the 'dominant' of E♭, the 'Lydian fourth' that began each **EIS**			

(b)

$$T_6$$

EIS = E♭ —¹→ D —²→ C —³→ A —⁴→ F —⁵→ C —⁶→ F♯ —⁷→ B —⁸→ D♯ —⁹→ F♯ —¹⁰→ G♯ —¹¹→ A

FM/Dm   BM/G♯m

Fig. 8.1 First Mazurka. (a) Formal diagram and notes; (b) 'expanding interval series'

The Mazurka's first section contains sixteen bars, divided into two-bar variations of this pattern. Not only is this symmetrical division and variation redolent of the mazurka, but so is the patterned 'tonal plan' that Adès binds to the mechanical interval patterns. Example 8.2a interprets the main actions of this plan in three stages. After the initial presentation of the pattern (stage 1), repeated over the course of bars

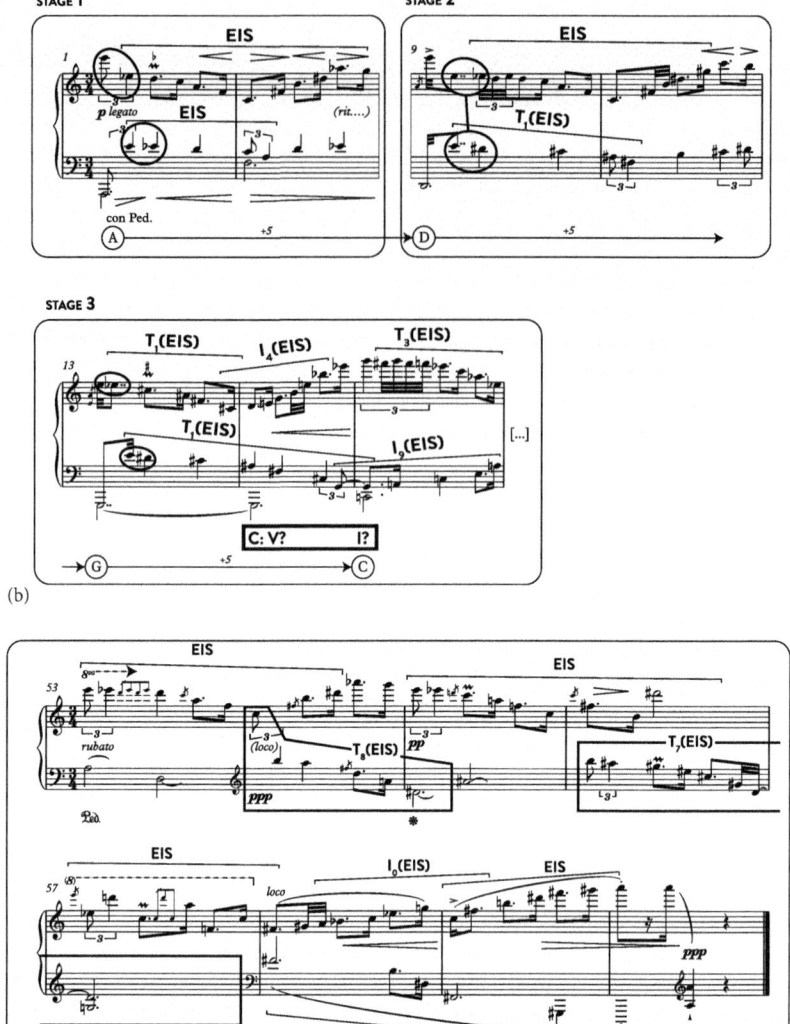

Ex. 8.2 First Mazurka. (a) Bars 1–15, excerpts; (b) bar 53–end

3–8, the right and left hands become unglued in bar 9 (stage 2): the E–E♭ that began each prior iteration of the EIS is reinterpreted, allowing the middle register to play a new version transposed one semitone higher, labelled on the example as 'T_1(EIS)'. Only in the third and final stage do the patterns come back together. In bar 13 the upper melody of this new transposition of the EIS leads to a climactic G_6 on the downbeat of bar 15.

Unfolding in the bass throughout all three stages – and indicated below each stage with a circled pitch name – are characteristic mazurka pedals arranged in an interval pattern of ascending fourths/descending fifths. Perhaps the most conventional of all interval patterns (and replicated in the bass of the Mazurka's central 'C section'), this bass cycle reaches a nadir on the low G_1 of bar 13 just as the upper-voice patterns come together around the transposed EIS. The convergence of these unique patterns gives rise to a melodic inversion of the EIS that joins the bass in a 'perfect cadence' on C in bar 15. C, the mediant of the tonic, A, is a typical destination in the mazurka's tonal form; but here, coupled to the mechanical patterns of melody and bass, the cadence's conventionality is revealed in a new, strange light.

At the passage's recapitulation in bar 53, shown in Ex. 8.2b, varied statements of the EIS enact an opposite procedure to secure a conventional 'tonal adjustment' that ends the piece on the tonic. From bar 54 onwards, simultaneous presentations of the EIS once again become unglued, the piano's middle register melody playing T_8 and then T_7 transpositions while the melody above is fixed on the original. But where in the first A section (Ex. 8.2a, bar 13) those melodies came back together around a transposition leading to the C cadence, here they coalesce in the final bars on the original EIS itself. The pattern here has been reimagined a final time. Three bars from the end, final statements of the EIS begin on F♯, and each unfurls in contrary motion, the statements together sounding all eleven ordered interval classes. Unfolding at different speeds and heading towards the piano's extremes, these final EISs manage to arrive together on the downbeat of the final bar, sounding the tonic A six octaves apart.

In my experience of listening to this passage and playing it for others, the final cadence of the First Mazurka is delightfully funny, and I think its humour is evidence of the surreal possibility of musical process. Most obviously, the final cadence projects a feeling of a 'ludicrous' incongruity of concept and object, to frame it in Schopenhauer's terms.[39] 'Closure', which is referenced so strongly by the final cadence's sudden *pianississimo* and simple octaves, seems incongruous in the context of the mechanistic, patterned music that precedes it. That incongruity is foregrounded by the pattern's musical 'activity', which strongly highlights

---

[39] See John Morreall's discussion of Schopenhauer in *Taking Laughter Seriously* (Albany: State University of New York, 1983), pp. 15–19.

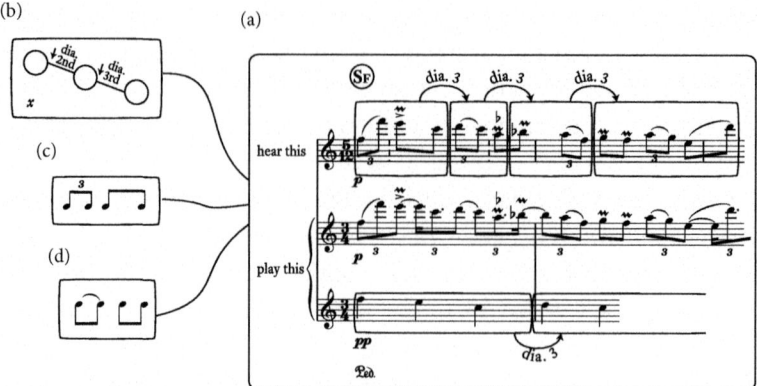

Ex. 8.3 Second Mazurka. (a) Bars 1–2; (b) an intervallic pattern, *x*; (c) a rhythmic pattern; (d) an articulation pattern

our sense of 'passivity' at that moment. Upon its arrival at the simple octave on A, one seems to realise, in retrospect, that the Mazurka's patterns themselves have found a previously concealed association with the conventions of tonal form.

The Second Mazurka more greatly conceals the topical attributes of the mazurka that were explicit in the First. Nonetheless, as the connections between Exs. 8.3 and 8.4 and Fig. 8.2 detail, this Mazurka's extraordinary assemblage of patterned logic comes closest to representing the material heterogeneity of Ernst's frottage works.[40] In Ex. 8.3, I show the three simple patterns that generate the majority of the movement: a pitch pattern labelled *x* in Ex. 8.3b descends a diatonic second and then a third; a rhythmic pattern shown in Ex. 8.3c contrasts two triplet quavers with two straight quavers; and an articulation pattern in Ex. 8.3d alternates two slurred notes with two separated ones.[41] All of these patterns combine to produce the two-voice counterpoint of the Mazurka's opening, which is

---

[40] Adès points to Chopin's Mazurka in C major Op. 24 No. 2 as one model in his interview with Gerstein. Gerstein, 'Thomas Adès: "Roots, Seeds & Live Cultures"', 00:43:15.

[41] The genesis of each pattern is easy to see in Chopin's Op. 24 No. 2, bars 5–6. Adès's explanation of the origins of the rhythmic pattern at Ex. 8.3b is particularly fascinating and relevant in the context of this chapter. Playing bar 5 of Chopin's Op. 24 No. 2, he alters the rhythm of the first two quavers, making them triplet quavers instead. This places the third note, a B♮ which had been located squarely on beat 2, instead just before it, creating the rhythm of his Second Mazurka out of the opening of the Chopin. In his description of this transformation, he describes it botanically as a 'cutting', splitting the Chopin at a particular place from which his piece 'begins to grow'. Gerstein, 'Thomas Adès: "Roots, Seeds & Live Cultures"', 00:44:30–00:45:00.

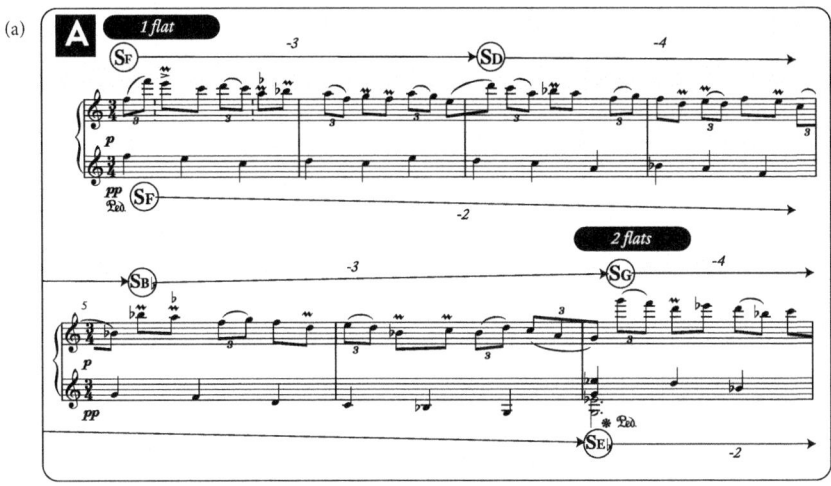

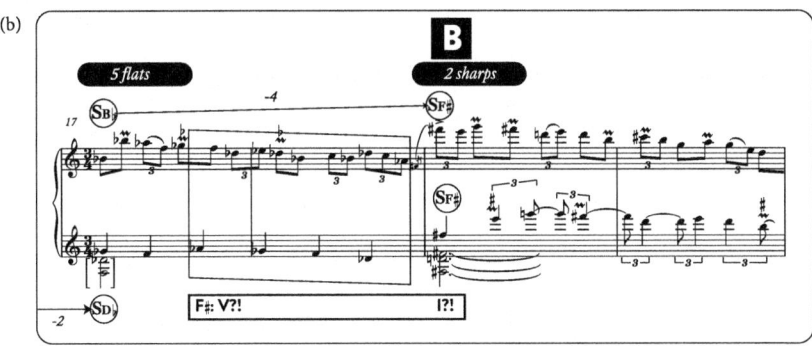

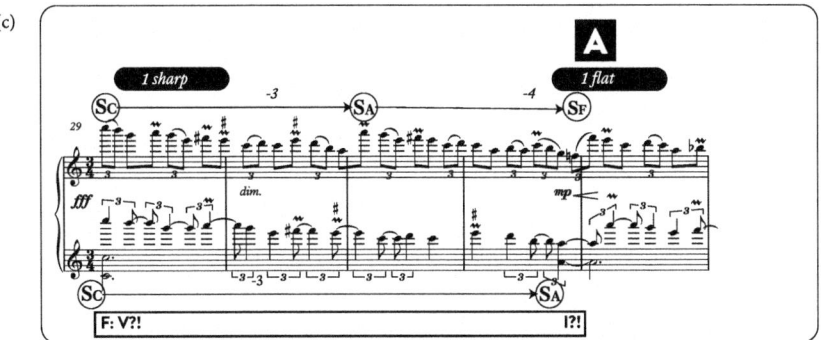

Ex. 8.4 Second Mazurka. (a) Bars 1–7; (b) bars 17–20, 'modulation' to F sharp; (c) bars 29–33, recapitulation on F

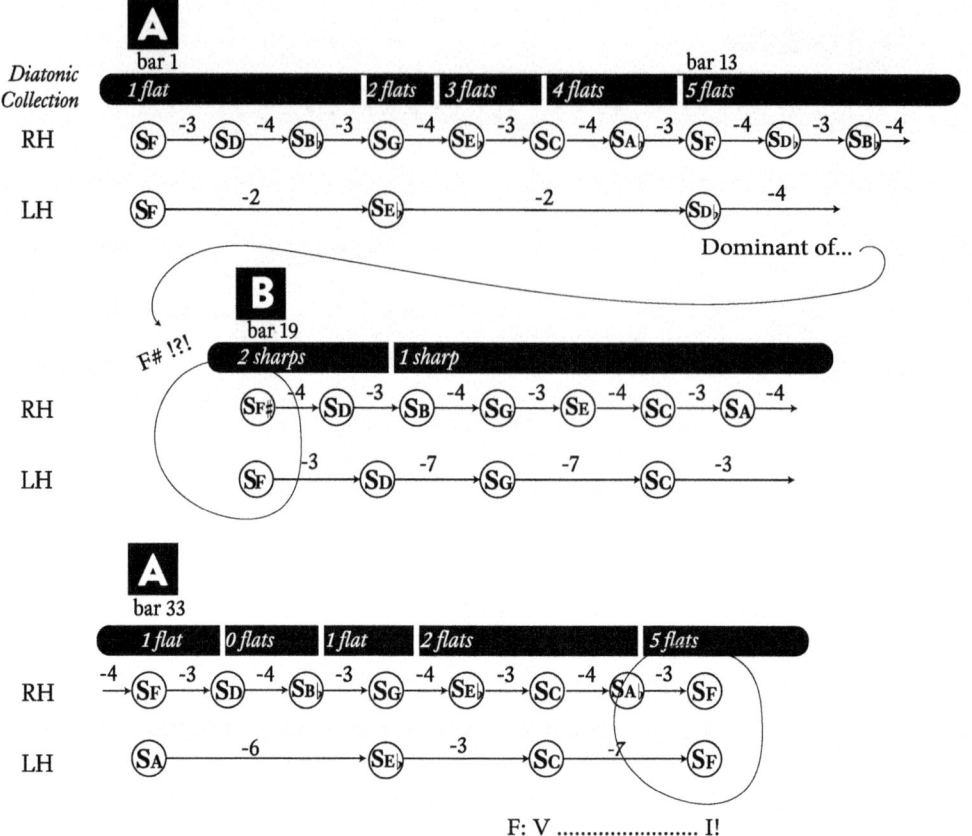

Fig. 8.2 Second Mazurka, formal overview of the first large section

labelled **S** in Ex. 8.3d. While each pattern is applied to the three boxes characterising the right hand, the intervallic pattern in Ex. 8.3a is present in the more slowly unfolded left hand. Those boxes on the top stave of Ex. 8.3d also highlight an overarching pattern: while the rhythm and articulation patterns remain constant, the pitch pattern *x* is sequenced by descending diatonic thirds: F–E–C is followed by D–C–A, Bb–A–F and G–F, ... (A–G–E), ... D.[42] Most striking, both structurally and perceptually, the patterned right hand – further decorated with mordents – implies a 5/12 metre whose attempts to coexist with the simple 3/4 of the left hand have a strong whiff of Breton's absurd. In Ex. 8.3d, the large **S** pattern begins on pitch-class F, and thus I have appended a subscript 'F' to track its presence throughout the Mazurka. Above the stave in the score

---

[42] In Chopin's Op. 24 No. 2, this pattern of descending thirds links bars 5–6 to bars 7–8.

excerpts of Ex. 8.4, I show that the right hand proceeds, for example, through S_F, S_D, $S_{B\flat}$ and S_G; against this, the left hand (diagrammed below the lower stave) plays S_F, then $S_{E\flat}$ and $S_{D\flat}$.

An overview of the Mazurka's large opening passage is shown in Fig. 8.2 with the right and left hands separated to reveal the unique paths that S follows within each. (A comparison of Ex. 8.4 and Fig. 8.2 may aid an understanding of the diagram's layout.) Layered on top of the patterned patterns of S, the right hand moves downwards in a further patterned alternation of three and four semitones while the left hand descends by whole tones. A final pattern is placed on top of it all, as every statement of S is heard within a diatonic context that is subject to its own logic: most clearly, the darkened boxes expose how the diatonic contexts of S generally change chromatically by one accidental in the sharp or flat direction, with some significant exceptions. Thus, while $S_{B\flat}$ in bars 5–6 occur in the context of the one-flat, F major collection of the opening, S_G in bar 7 introduces E♭, thereby creating a two-flat collection.

It is worth pausing to reflect upon the sheer patterned complexity of these examples, particularly in relation to the patterns themselves. In automatic works, we have seen that surrealists felt that a passive mind could reveal new phrases or images hitherto unheard. But these new-found objects were commonly made from old ones. Dismantling Breton's phrase 'There is a man cut in two by a window' into its parts does not reveal anything of interest, nor does separating Ernst's *The Fugitive* into its various patterns. But when subjected to the fantastic logic of automatic thought, these old phrases and materials are given new life. Thus, consider the banal structure of the three patterns in Ex. 8.3, the simple sequences governing S and the bland pattern that organises each diatonic collection. While these are mundane by themselves, Adès illuminates something wonderfully new and complex by allowing them to interact as he does.

Of most consequence are the resulting form and startling tonal structure of the opening passage, some highlights of which are shown in Ex. 8.4. For instance, when S_F returns at bar 13 it is heard just as the left hand's whole-tone pattern has reached $S_{D\flat}$, recasting the opening bars of S_F in a new five-flat diatonic context. An even more striking chromatic motion occurs at the approach to the contrasting B section that begins in bar 19. In the preceding bars (see Ex. 8.4b), the right hand works through $S_{B\flat}$ as the left marks out $S_{D\flat}$. At the end of bar 18, the right and left hand align to produce a quasi-'V–I' cadence in F sharp – 'modulating' up a semitone from the F major opening and inducing a disjointing change in diatonic collection. A similar alignment leads to the A section's recapitulation at bar

33, which is shown in Ex. 8.4c. By bar 29 the independently operating patterns that sequence **S** have come together on **S**$_C$, suggesting the 'dominant' of the F major tonic. As the patterns continue to spin out in bars 29–32, they come together in another 'V–I' cadence, marking the end of the 'B section' and leading to a formal recapitulation. This entire opening sounds to me more like a strange music box with gears whirring around at different speeds than like a mazurka. That surreal image, reminiscent of the natural-cum-unnatural aspects of *The Fugitive*, is nonetheless produced by a *musical process* that structures time.

The progressive deterioration of the mazurka's topical character that began most clearly in the Second Mazurka continues in the Third, which deals with an even more abstract musical pattern, the circle of fifths. Of the many 'raw resonances' suggested by Ernst's analogy, the circle of fifths is one of the most likely. Not only does this famous circle belong to the kind of everlasting 'musical realm' that Adès mentions frequently, but fifths are foundational intervals at many levels of the tonal system and present early in the natural overtone series, and when arranged in a pattern, they produce all twelve pitch-classes. And in both the Third Mazurka and *Thrift*, the circle of fifths plays a foundational role in which Adès situates its raw, resonant power in a new form.

The ostinato that we hear at the opening of the Third Mazurka is shown in Ex. 8.5. Once again, one of the mazurka's most characteristic traits has been obscured. Though in triple metre, this passage occurs at a rather un-mazurka-like tempo of crotchet = MM 44, and while the ostinato's melody preserves the long–short rhythmic characteristic, it is drastically slowed down.[43] The ostinato takes twelve bars to complete and then repeats, and in bar 8 it is accompanied by an odd triad-infused melody. On each downbeat the ostinato's two parts together produce the stark perfect fifths that are boxed in bars 1–3. While the left hand sustains, the right hand plays a single melodic interval that alternates perfect fourths and fifths. The proliferation of these intervals at such a slow tempo produces a strong sense of local diatonicism that is confirmed in the surrounding music: bars 1–2 occur in a diatonic context of seven sharps, suggestive of C sharp

---

[43] When explaining to Gerstein the Mazurka's derivation from Chopin, Adès played Chopin's Waltz in B minor Op. 69 No. 2 and Mazurka in C major Op. 68 No. 2 as models. It is interesting that neither of these pieces are in C sharp, even though Adès says that they demonstrate 'this sort of C sharp minor sound that he [Chopin] has'. And when playing them for Gerstein, he transposes each to C sharp. The referenced Mazurka in C major has a melodic and rhythmic contour that is extremely similar to the melody that begins in bar 8 of the Third Mazurka. Gerstein, 'Thomas Adès: "Roots, Seeds & Live Cultures"', 00:45:00–00:47:00.

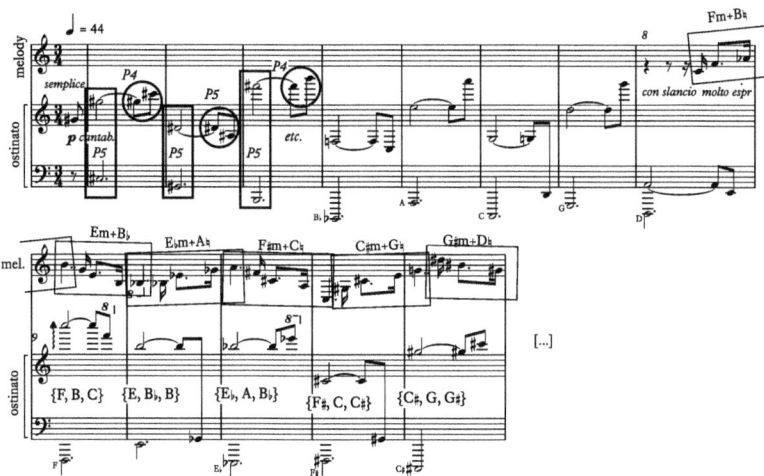

Ex. 8.5 Third Mazurka, bars 1–13

major, and the bass's dip down to G♯ in bar 2 evokes the tonic–dominant progression that begins many ground bass patterns.

Figure 8.3a reproduces the ostinato melody with transpositional arrows added to highlight the relationships described above.[44] The alternating fifths and fourths are shown with arrows along the bottom, while the arrows on the top show a different pattern among the melody's downbeats. This new pattern is a non-retrogradable symmetry, <7,3,11,11,3,7>, that occurs twice in course of the ostinato. Most significantly and surrealistically, we can see through this representation that the 'local diatonicism' noted above occurs in the context of that most chromatic of musical objects, a twelve-note row. Further reinforcing this sense of a diatonicism fantastically reimagined, Adès's twelve-note series is arranged in a complex manner not unlike that which we would find in the music of Alban Berg or George Perle.[45] While the downbeats produce a complete twelve-note series that I have called **S** on the example, the twelve upbeats also create a twelve-note series – this one the retrograde of **S**. Moreover, the downbeats and upbeats are imbricated within **S** in such a way as to create an altogether different twelve-note series that I call **T**; and like **S**, **T** is presented both in prograde and in retrograde.

---

[44] To derive the bass from this example, transpose the bolded circles down a perfect fifth.

[45] This relationship is not far-fetched, as Philip Stoecker implies in 'Aligned-Cycle Spaces', *Journal of Music Theory*, 60/ii (2016), 181–212.

(a)

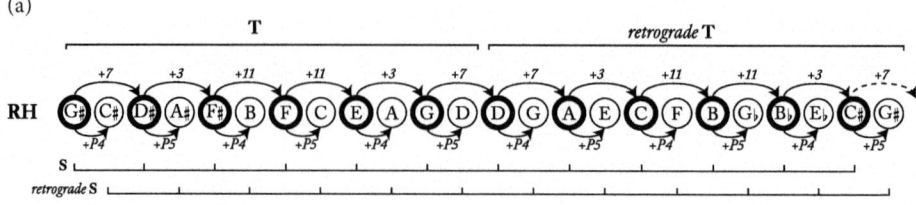

(b)

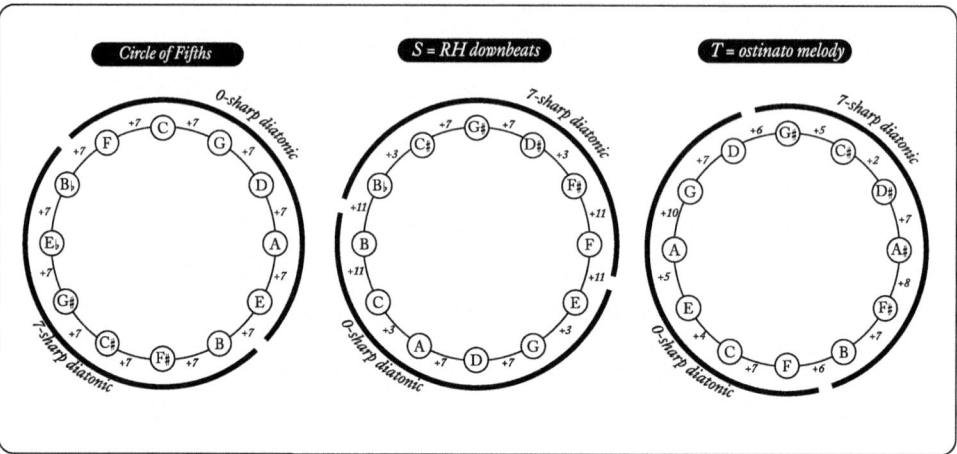

Fig. 8.3 Third Mazurka. (a) Piano ostinato; (b) the circle of fifths compared with Adès's note rows

To foreground how the patterned 'raw resonances' of the circle of fifths structure these twelve-note rows, Fig. 8.3b shows them alongside one another. This figure reveals that some basic components of the circle of fifths are preserved in **S** and **T** while others are altered. For instance, **S** and **T** are patterned productions of all twelve notes, though **S**'s and **T**'s intervallic patterns are complex distortions of the circle of fifth's simple pattern.[46] But their most surreal and perceptually salient commonality is that

---

[46] **S** is a pattern of intervals in non-retrogradable symmetry, while **T** is a pattern of intervals in a different way. **T** contains two interval sequences separated by tritones that are related by retrograde inversion: <5,+2,+7,+8,+5> is the retrograde inversion of <+7,+4,+5,+10,+7>. John Roeder has pointed out to me that **S** embeds two whole-tone collections in alternating order positions. That relationship plays a significant role in the creation of the Mazurka's second section, which begins from the same G♯ that began the first but works through a series of whole-tone canons.

all three project locally diatonic collections whose relationship is maximally chromatic: the 0-sharp and 7-sharp diatonic collections, bracketed on each circle, organise the chromaticism of all three circles in the same way. As a result, when we hear the ostinato at the opening of the Third Mazurka, its local diatonicism occurs within a context of global chromaticism. This diatonic/chromatic arrangement is similarly endemic to the melody we hear at bar 8. Each melodic gesture (the characteristically dotted ideas shown on Ex. 8.5) joins a minor triad and tritone: F minor + B♮, E minor + B♭ and so on. Those tritones interact with the ostinato in such a way that each downbeat colours the ostinato's diatonic perfect fifth with a chromatic tritone, producing a series of accented dissonances that are startling after the pure fifths and fourths of the opening.

Not only is Adès's alteration of the circle of fifths an exploration of Ernst's 'raw resonances', but its diatonicism is also reminiscent of Breton's 'automatic purity'. The plainness of the ostinato's diatonicism – a musical characteristic that nearly everyone has experienced – conceals an underlying chromaticism; that is, Adès's ostinato surrealistically discovers the fundamentally chromatic nature of diatonicism's central structure, the circle of fifths.

Two years after completing the Mazurkas of Op. 27, Adès composed a final mazurka entitled *Thrift (a Cliff-Flower): Mazurka-Cortège*, a portion of which is given in Ex. 8.6. While the three Mazurkas in Op. 27 have a specified order and enact a progressive process of deterioration, *Thrift* exists outside these pieces, and it seems to have been composed in reaction to them. This title uses surrealism's most characteristic language (French) to qualify 'mazurka' with an indication (*cortège*) suggestive of a funeral procession, thereby echoing the mazurka that Souris and Hooreman composed upon the death of Satie. Like the three Mazurkas in Op. 27, *Thrift* uses but obfuscates the patterns typical of the mazurka, though here the obfuscation is so thorough as to seem but a ghost in comparison. (Combined with the funereal implications of *cortège*, the indication 'Liberamente' at the movement's beginning could be interpreted as a double entendre referencing a rhythmic and metaphorical freedom.) Slower than the Third Mazurka, *Thrift* is notated in 3/4 throughout, but this metric structure is primarily a residue of the mazurka's metre. From the very first bar, the right hand plays a patterned alternation of triplet quavers and straight quavers that refuses to confirm the metre's notated bar lines.

The juxtaposition of diatonicism and chromaticism in the Third Mazurka was subtle, but here it is quite stark. While each hand is

Ex. 8.6 *Thrift (a Cliff Flower): Mazurka-Cortège*, bars 1–11

individually diatonic, together the hands are chromatic. Over the first seven bars, the flat-leaning five notes of the left hand, F–D–Bb–G–Eb, are the twelve-note complements of the sharp-leaning notes of the right hand, C#–A–B–F#–E–G#–B#. The structural underpinnings of this fully chromatic collection are, like those in the Third Mazurka, produced by interval patterns that surreally distort the circle of fifths. To demonstrate, Fig. 8.4 shows the individual interval cycles in, respectively, (a) the right hand and (b) the left. The first five bars of the right hand are organised in register around an ascending $\langle 3,2,2 \rangle$ cycle, creating the pitch arrangement F#$_4$–A$_4$–B$_4$–C#$_5$–E$_5$–F#$_5$–G#$_5$–B$_5$. In Fig. 8.4a, that arrangement is in the south-east corner of the circle. At thirty-six notes long, this pitch cycle is three times larger than the circle of fifths, but the two are otherwise somewhat alike: the $\langle 3,2,2 \rangle$ cycle embeds all twelve diatonic and pentatonic collections and mirrors the order of its accidentals.[47] The left hand moves through a different pattern, shown in Fig. 8.4b, that is twice the size of the circle of

---

[47]   To see this most easily, first find at the top of the circle the collection {C, D, E, G, A, B, D} – a collection with no sharps and no flats. Then slide that collection three places to the right, beginning on G, where the collection {G, A, B, D, E, F#} contains only one sharp. Continuing to slide each new collection three places to the right will produce all twelve diatonic collections in the order in which they occur on the circle of fifths.

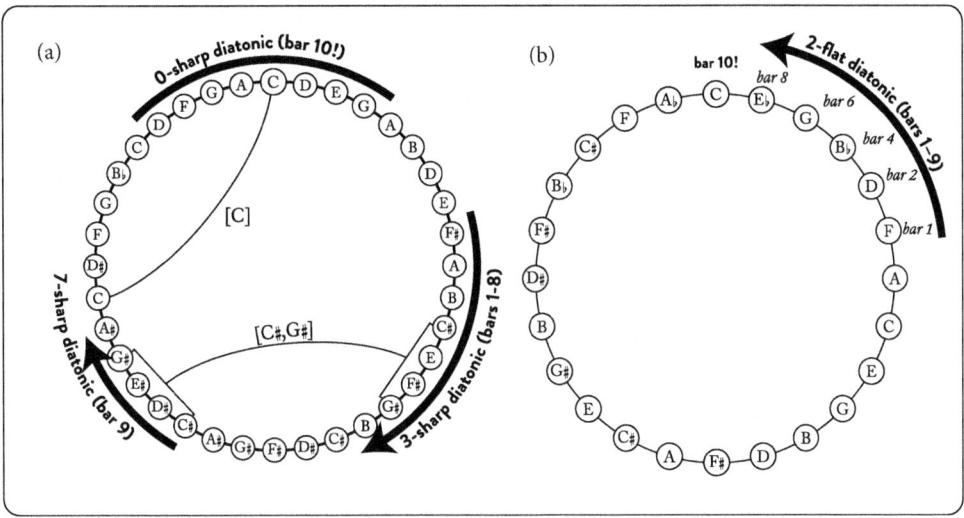

Fig. 8.4 Diatonic characteristics of two large interval cycles used throughout *Thrift*. (a) Piano right hand's ⟨3,2,2⟩ cycle; (b) piano left hand's ⟨3,4⟩ cycle

fifths. Though Fig. 8.4a and Fig. 8.4b are distinct, both are permeated with diatonic collections that mirror the structure of the circle of fifths.[48]

Thrift's opening nine bars combine the metrically disjointed patterns of each hand with similar disjunctions in pitch content. Over the first five bars, the sharp notes from the right hand's ⟨3,2,2⟩ cycle sound as if in a different world from the flat-leaning notes of the left hand's ⟨3,4⟩ cycle. From around bar 6 (see Ex. 8.6), Adès slowly winds the right hand sharpwards, eventually linking the opening three-sharp collection with a seven-sharp collection through the shared fifth shown at the bottom of Fig. 8.4a. At the same time the left hand is moving more slowly and flatwards around the cycle, as shown in Fig. 8.4b. When C_5 is heard in the right hand of bar 10 it is the sharpward continuation of bar 9's interval pattern {C♯, D♯, E♯, G♯, A♯, C}, which Adès links to the C major diatonic at the top of Fig. 8.4a; at just this moment, the left hand also arrives on C, though it has been reached through opposite, flatward motion through the cycle at Fig. 8.4b. Serendipitous as it sounds when we listen, the two pitch

---

[48] Though these two cycles and the circle of fifths have different lengths and present the twelve pitch-classes in different ways, they nonetheless project many similarities. For example, the circle of fifths is embedded in the ⟨3,4⟩ cycle and the ⟨3,2,2⟩ cycle, and the ⟨3,4⟩ cycle is embedded in the ⟨3,2,2⟩ cycle.

patterns have been inching closer to one another since the first bar, and though their coalescence on the luminous C major of bar 10 seems accidental in real time, its arrival has been suggested in the patterned logic all along.

* * *

When I hear this passage at the opening of *Thrift*, the arrival of C major on the downbeat of bar 10 sounds uncommonly beautiful. Accounting for that beauty requires me to appeal to its sense of natural and unnatural, real and imagined – paradoxes that surrealists constantly explored and that we see in works by Breton, Masson and Ernst. To describe the beauty of that stunning C major is as difficult as accounting for the music-box character of the Second Mazurka, the chromatic diatonicism of the Third or the humorous tonal close of the First. In one respect, all of these features are distortions of old objects. But as I have explored throughout this chapter, describing them in only that way misses something crucial: that these distortions realise properties that have always existed in these patterns, but have simply never been heard. The 'raw resonances' of the Third Mazurka and *Thrift* highlight a relationship between chromaticism and diatonicism that has been present all along. Thus in each of these mazurkas, we hear and see some residue of the mazurka as we might find it in Chopin, but these are mazurkas clearly liberated (and often deliriously so) from the mazurka itself. To consider this in an even more radical way, imagine a world in which past and present were swapped, in which Chopin came after Adès. In such a world, we might use the logic underlying those most wild of Adèsian distortions to instead describe their normalcy; and in such a world Chopin becomes the surrealist, his mazurkas showcasing the untapped potential latent in those by Adès.

Breton believed that a proper surrealist should continue to create the universe. 'The God that dwells within us is nowhere near ready to rest on the seventh day. We have yet to read the first pages of Genesis', he says.[49] This quotation says something of how we might understand musical automatism, notwithstanding Breton's disinclinations towards the musical form. By dealing in a musical past whose remnants are not so different from the seemingly fixed contours of Ernst's frottage items, Adès's music reminds us of a musical realm that is never fixed, whose 'first pages' we will never read. Therefore Adès's stated disinclination to respect a 'pre-compositional' phase

---

[49] Albright, *Untwisting the Serpent*, p. 268.

and a 'during-compositional' phase may not be simple composerly posturing.[50] Rather, it suggests precisely the sort of dreamscape that Breton imagined as the goal of surreal art: a dreamscape where new-found associations are understood not as distorted versions of something normal, but as marvellous possibilities whose legitimacy is born of their logic.

---

[50] Adès and Service, *Full of Noises*, p. 4.

9 | Narrating the Dance of Death

Morality and Social Critique in Adès's Totentanz

SCOTT LEE

Originating in the fourteenth century, the Dance of Death is an allegory of the universality of death which has inspired myriad responses across multiple art forms. Thomas Adès's *Totentanz* (2013) sustains this tradition into the twenty-first century, translating into music Bernt Notke's famous fifteenth-century frieze, which depicts wraith-like skeletons taking part in a Dance of Death with members of society in strictly descending order of societal importance (Online Fig. 9.1).[1] Featuring baritone and mezzo-soprano, representing respectively Death and his victims, and scored for a large, percussion-heavy orchestra, *Totentanz* remains Adès's most ambitious work for the concert hall to date. In its quasi-theatrical setting of the anonymously authored text which accompanied the frieze, *Totentanz* serves as an important link between Adès's operatic and concert works.[2]

Beyond this theatricality, I argue that *Totentanz* functions as a musical commentary on the allegory of the Dance of Death and, as an act of narration, is inherently temporal in its conception. This translation from the spatial to the (temporally inflected) narrational is reflected in Adès's suggestion that *Totentanz* is 'not about the painting as a physical object' but instead is about the painting's meaning.[3] Adès's allegorical commentary focuses on issues of morality, continuing an undercurrent in his work from the 'ironic morality tale' of *Powder Her Face* (1995) through to the existential warning to a decadent empire in his apocalyptic *America: A Prophecy* (1999).[4] In public interviews he has often conveyed ambivalence about the relation of his music to society, refusing to ascribe underlying meaning to his works and thereby enabling himself to stay above the fray of cultural arguments.[5] But by engaging with the Dance of Death, a self-evidently allegorical tradition, Adès forfeits any claims of impartiality.

---

[1] Originally on display in Lübeck, Germany, the frieze was destroyed during World War II, though reproductions have survived.

[2] *Totentanz* also continues Adès's lifelong fascination with death. See Edward Venn, *Thomas Adès: Asyla* (Abingdon: Routledge, 2017), p. 11.

[3] Thomas Adès, interview with the author, 1 August 2018.

[4] Thomas May, 'Program Notes: Dances from *Powder Her Face*', Berkeley Symphony, 2 May 2019.

[5] Drew Massey, 'Thomas Adès at 40', *Salmagundi*, 174–5 (2012), 194–202 (p. 201).

In translating into music a frieze with a specific didactic purpose, Adès's narrative choices colour the lessons being communicated, revealing a message of social critique that goes beyond the intent of the original frieze.

Narrating the Dance

A number of cues in the first minute of *Totentanz* suggest to the listener that they are encountering a musical narrative. Trombones open the piece, outlining the traditional musical calling card of death and the devil (a tritone, the *diabolus in musica*). The opening text, sung by the baritone as the Preacher, self-referentially invites audience members to 'come see the play' (bars 13–20), thereby establishing a narrative frame and positioning the Preacher outside it. A ghostly version of the music for the Child appears (bars 17–20), foreshadowing the close of the work, and hints at an external narrative agent – Adès – for it reveals the presence of a persona outside the temporality implied by the text. The baritone, now as Death, then reiterates the introduction, occupying a similar narrative role to the Preacher and inviting all to join the dance (bars 42–7).

Such narrational devices suggest that Adès's *Totentanz* cannot be reduced to a straightforward depiction of the Lübeck frieze in music. Rather, the narrative choices Adès makes in retelling the allegory outlined by the frieze make possible an alternative interpretation. Moreover, the popularity of the Dance of Death has given it myth-like status in the collective imagination, making narrative intervention even more import-ant. Adès sheds light on his priorities as (musical) storyteller in *Totentanz* through a number of narrative strategies, including foreshadowing, inter-textual references, pacing and proportion, and musical characterisation.

Of necessity, narrational strategies differ between different artistic media. Elina Gertsman describes how viewers experience the Reval Dance of Death (a painting almost identical to the Lübeck frieze) by physically moving from left to right, regarding the painting from different visual perspectives at their leisure.[6] She argues that while a literate medieval viewer would have experienced the full effect of the frieze's combined text and visuals, an illiterate or semi-literate viewer could still have appreciated the story through visual signals and oral communication, primed by the

---

[6] Elina Gertsman, 'The Dance of Death in Reval (Tallinn): The Preacher and His Audience', *Gesta*, 42/ii (2003), 143–59 (p. 148).

experiences of encountering other *danse macabre* paintings and hearing homilies on the subject of death given by preachers.[7]

Gertsman's reading of the painting through the lens of embodied perception provides points of departure for a narrative interpretation of Adès's *Totentanz*. Unlike a medieval viewer of the frieze, an audience member listening to Adès's work in a concert hall is confined to a seat for the duration of the performance. The length of the experience is prescribed for them by the composer, and their perspective is limited by the ordering of events in the score. That same audience member may benefit, however, from the immediacy of communication via real-life humans – the singers onstage – rather than painted representations of humans with the written text below. Just as Gertsman's medieval viewers would be able to interpret the frieze by virtue of familiarity with the frame of reference, members of Adès's audience are similarly well positioned to respond to topical allusions – the waltz, pastoral and military allusions and even Lutosławskian techniques – and signifiers of death and the demonic within the music which have been broadly established through canonical classical works. An eclectic network of intertextual references also helps enhance latent meanings for audience members familiar with the cited works.

Although Adès's *Totentanz* is not the first piece inspired specifically by the Lübeck frieze, it bears no obvious connections to the other relatively obscure works based on it.[8] Rather, it is indebted to the broader lineage of pieces depicting the Dance of Death from the nineteenth century onwards, in which Death is made to assume a somewhat demonic character. Adès's strategies for demonic signification were established by a diverse collection of composers, including Berlioz, Saint-Saëns and Mussorgsky, but most pertinently Liszt. In numerous works, these composers established a shared language of demonic representation by chaining together a variety of signifiers, including 'minor key (especially D minor), chromaticism, dissonance ... angular melody (especially tritones), syncopation and tempo fluctuation ... sacred or noble signifiers in the "wrong" context (trombones in Mozart's *Don Giovanni*, the Dies irae in Berlioz's *Symphonie fantastique* and Liszt's *Totentanz*), glissandi, acciacaturas [*sic*], slides, and

---

[7] Ibid., p. 150.

[8] Other works based on the Lübeck frieze include *Totentanz* (1934), a set of fourteen motets by Hugo Distler; *Der Lübecker Totentanz* (1954), an oratorio by the Lübeck church organist Walter Kraft; and *Der Lübecker Totentanz, ein altes Mysterienspiel* (1948), a one-act opera by the Nazi composer Hermann Reutter.

chromatic "slithering".[9] In addition, Liszt often employs quartal and quintal harmonic languages to signify the devil specifically.[10] As I will show, Adès intensifies and expands upon these same demonic signifiers in *Totentanz*, imbuing Death, who is often portrayed as impartial, with a demonic character instead, thereby enabling Death to serve as a surrogate for Adès's expression of social critique.

A comparison between Liszt's and Adès's respective *Totentänze* sets their musical strategies into relief. Liszt takes a different source of the allegory as the basis for his work: Anna Harwell Celenza argues that the set of variations on the *Dies irae* in Liszt's *Totentanz* is based on a set of woodcuts by Hans Holbein the Younger from the 1520s that depict the Dance of Death.[11] Liszt is quite literal in his musical response: the prominent trombones and timpani at the outset of his work correspond to sackbut and kettledrums featured prominently in Holbein's images. Just as skeletons represent Death in Holbein, the *Dies irae* serves as Liszt's theme.[12] Adès similarly translates the flute-wielding skeletons from the Lübeck frieze into a prominent presentation of the *Dies irae* played by piccolos.

But the significant differences between Liszt's and Adès's sources are responsible for structural differences between their musical responses. Holbein's woodcuts often appeared in book format, synthesising the traditions of the Dance of Death and the memento mori.[13] Gertsman argues that viewers would have identified more powerfully with the figures appearing in the frieze than with those in the woodcuts, because of the life-size scale of the painting's figures and the participatory nature of the experience of them that viewers gained by walking alongside the frieze.[14] As I have argued, the introduction of Adès's *Totentanz* embraces this participatory nature, inviting the audience members to join the dance and to see themselves reflected in the story through musical mirrors.

[9] Derek B. Scott, 'Diabolus in Musica: Liszt and the Demonic', in *From the Erotic to the Demonic: On Critical Musicology* (New York: Oxford University Press, 2003), pp. 128–51 (pp. 129–30).

[10] Ibid., pp. 131–2.

[11] Anna Harwell Celenza, 'Death Transfigured: The Origins and Evolution of Franz Liszt's *Totentanz*', in *Nineteenth-Century Music: Selected Proceedings of the Tenth International Conference*, ed. by Jim Samson and Bennett Zon (Abingdon: Routledge, 2016), pp. 125–54 (pp. 125–7).

[12] Ibid., p. 140.

[13] Werner L. Gundersheimer, 'Introduction to the Dover Edition', in *The Dance of Death: A Complete Facsimile of the Original 1538 Edition of* Les simulachres & historiees faces de la mort (Mineola, NY: Dover Publications, 1971), pp. 10–17 (p. 12).

[14] Gertsman, 'The Dance of Death', p. 153.

Liszt's version of *Totentanz* does not include an analogous invitation to participate. This absence denies it the opportunity to communicate an explicitly allegorical function; instead, Liszt prioritises the evocation of macabre imagery.

Adès and the Lübeck Frieze

The Lübeck frieze has a complicated history. Painted on linen wall coverings in the Marienkirche during the plague years around 1463, the original is attributed to Bernt Notke, a prominent painter who lived in Lübeck.[15] The anonymous accompanying text is assumed to be based on a Middle Dutch model, which itself was derived from that included in the Dance of Death mural on display in the Cimetière des Innocents in Paris (widely thought to be the first such portrayal).[16] After centuries of repairs it became necessary in 1701 to replace the Lübeck frieze, so the church painter Anton Wortmann was charged with painting a copy, and the city poet Nathanael Schlott was commissioned to write a new text.[17] During the 1942 bombing of Lübeck, the frieze was destroyed, but detailed photographs taken between the two world wars by Wilhelm Castelli preserve a visual record. A 7.5-metre-long fragment of an almost identical painting in Tallinn, Estonia (previously called Reval), also attributed to Bernt Notke, provides evidence of what the original Lübeck frieze would have looked like.[18]

Commentators have assumed that Adès set solely the original, anonymous fifteenth-century text, but he in fact amalgamated this text with Schlott's 1701 text.[19] The original Low German text features Death and the human dancers speaking in alternating eight-line verses. After an introduction, each of Death's verses takes the same format, consisting of seven lines responding to the previous human dancer's protestations followed by an eighth line calling the next dancer to join. In the 1701 High German text the characters speak in reverse order: Death speaks

---

[15] 'The Lübeck Dance of Death', St Marien zu Lübeck, https://st-marien-luebeck.de/page/172/lübeck-dance-death.

[16] Gertsman, 'The Dance of Death', p. 147.   [17] 'The Lübeck Dance of Death'.

[18] 'The Reval Dance of Death', St Marien zu Lübeck, https://st-marien-luebeck.de/page/173/reval-dance-death.

[19] Adès adapted the text himself, acknowledging advice and assistance from Dr Herbert Grieshop and Dr Thomas Hinzpeter. For discussions of Adès's *Totentanz* as a straightforward setting of the text, see Shapinskaya Ekaterina Nikolaevna, 'Archetypal Plot and Its Interpretations: "Dance Macabre"', *Philharmonica: International Music Journal*, 2 (2016), 45–52; and Edward Venn, 'BBC Proms 2013: David Matthews and Thomas Adès', *Tempo*, 68/267 (2014), 59–61.

four lines first to each dancer, after which the dancer gives a four-line reply. The tones of the texts also differ. The 1701 text conveyed a new, Baroque understanding of death as a long-awaited sleep, supplanting the original text's medieval conception of death as something to be feared.[20] Each culture imposes its own perspective onto the allegory, and Adès is no exception. While some portions of the original text are lost, Adès does not limit his use of the 1701 text only to these sections. Instead he frequently alternates sources, drawing Death's verses from the 1701 text and the victims' responses from the original; he thus demonstrates a preference for the 1701 text's format in which Death's verses appear first and the characters are introduced in each turn of the dance. As I will show below, Adès's textual choices have narrative implications, imparting a sense of disjunction to the dialogue between Death and his victims as if they are talking past each other, unable to fully engage.

Table 9.1 presents Adès's textual compilation and outlines the form of *Totentanz*, describing each section's primary material and extramusical associations. As Venn notes, Adès avoids the potential 'sterility' inherent to the text's mechanically alternating structure by dividing the single-movement work into two large sections separated by a 'raucous' climax, with Death featured prominently in the first half and the victims in the second. This structuring, coupled with the varying lengths of the different episodes, helps provide shape and musical momentum in the work.[21] While providing musical interest, these formal strategies undermine the didactic elements baked into the structures of the text and imagery of the original work. Gertsman describes how the predictability of 'death's repeated return' and the repetition of each character's demise underscore the allegorical message of the inevitability of death.[22] Adès weakens this didactic structure, instead prioritising the maintenance of musical momentum. My analysis of the work, which follows, proceeds chronologically to trace Adès's narrative as it unfolds.

Death and the Preacher

The first four lines of Adès's text are sung not by Death nor by one of his victims, but rather by a Preacher. No such figure appears in the

---

[20] 'The Lübeck Dance of Death'.   [21] Venn, 'BBC Proms 2013', p. 60.

[22] Elina Gertsman, 'Pleyinge and Peyntynge: Performing the Dance of Death', *Studies in Iconography*, 27 (2006), 1–43 (p. 25).

Table 9.1. *Totentanz*, formal overview

Sections	Bars	Textual source	Primary pitch material	Intertexts, topics and text Painting
Introduction and the Preacher	1–41	15th-century (Reval)	Expanding intervals (outlining tritones) (Ex. 9.1), foreshadowing of the Child, *Dies irae* (Ex. 9.2)	Berg's *Lulu*
Death	42–133	15th-century	Expanding intervals/*Dies irae*, descending thirds in bass (Ex. 9.3)	Weeping violin glissandos
Death to the Pope	134–67	15th-century (2 lines) and 1701 (6 lines)	Descending fifths (Online Ex. 9.1a), diminution of *Dies irae* with alternating intervals inverted	Prominent xylophone evokes bones
The Pope	168	15th-century (4 lines omitted)	Stacked fifths, independent melodic strata descending chromatically (Online Ex. 9.1b)	Limited aleatoricism, weeping string glissandos
Death to the Emperor	169–206	1701	Quartal harmony, vocal sequence descending by fourths, *Dies irae* becomes motto with repeated notes	
The Emperor	207–37	15th-century	Vocal line derived from *Dies irae* motto (containing tritone) sequenced down by tone	
Death to the Cardinal	238–57	1701	Rising thirds (Online Ex. 9.2)	
The Cardinal	258–325	15th-century	Descending thirds, return of *Dies irae* (mirrored)	Actual bones used for percussion
Death to the King	326–64	1701	*Dies irae*	
The King	365–420	15th-century (4 lines omitted)	*Dies irae*, builds to local climax recalling introduction of *Dies irae*	
Death to the Monk	421–39	1701 (Death's text to Abbot)	Quintal chords, pitch cell comprising semitone and tone, bassline moves by thirds (Ex. 9.4)	Tolling bells, waltz

Section	Bars	Text source	Musical description	Style/orchestration
The Monk	440–81	1701 (Carthusian's text)	Pitch cell followed by either semitone or tritone, bass and melody always form major third (Ex. 9.4)	Waltz
Death to the Knight	482–513	1701 (4 lines omitted)	*Dies irae* returns, opening quartal chords	Britten's *Ballad of Heroes* 'Scherzo'
The Knight	514–54	1701	Melody derived from *Dies irae* in layered oboe lines	Military allusions: anvils, tenor drums, steel sheet
Death to the Mayor	555–67	15th-century	Expanding intervals (mirrored)	Sighing string glissandos
(The Mayor)		15th-century (combines Chaplain and Nobleman)		
Death to the Doctor	568–77	1701	Expanding intervals over E$\flat$ pedal which later descends chromatically	
(The Doctor)		15th-century (4 lines omitted)		
Death to the Usurer	578–88	1701 (4 lines omitted, last 2 lines added)	Mirrored chromatic expansion out from D	
(The Usurer)		15th-century (4 lines omitted)		
Death to the Merchant	589–611	15th-century (2 lines from Usurer) and 1701 (4 lines omitted)	Rising thirds, Merchant's line uses pitch cell (from Monk), vocal lines form tritones as climax approaches	
(The Merchant)		15th-century		
Climax	612–55		Pitch cells derived from expanding idea, chromatic trichords, ends in quintal chord (Online Ex. 9.3)	Limited aleatoricism
Death to the Parish Clerk	656–7	15th-century	Chromatic trichords	Limited aleatoricism, weeping string glissandos

Table 9.1. (*cont.*)

Sections	Bars	Textual source	Primary pitch material	Intertexts, topics and text Painting
The Parish Clerk	658–86	15th-century	Chains of alternating fifths and semitones	Limited aleatoricism, strings 'following' each other
Death to the Parish Clerk	687–712	15th-century	Quartal harmony descending by semitones	
The Handworker	713–50	15th-century	Repeated downward glissandos contrasted with rising thirds/sixths beneath	Mirror implies self-portrait (Online Ex. 9.4), wailing string glissandos
(Death to the Handworker)		15th-century		
Death to the Peasant	751–821	1701 (4 lines) and 15th-century (4 lines from Hermit)	Whole-tone and Lydian-inflected oscillating motive	Horn riff and rollicking dance evoke pastoral
(The Peasant)		1701		
Death to the Maiden	822–55	1701	Opens with descending scalar vocal line over alternating quintal and F major chords	Schubert's 'Death and the Maiden', tolling bells
The Maiden	856–63	15th-century (2 lines) and 1701 (2 lines)	Alternating fifths/sixths and semitones form chords containing major and augmented triads, descend by tones	
Death to the Child	864–74	1701 (4 lines omitted)	Rising thirds over dominant pedal point in D major	Echoes of Mahler and Strauss
The Child	875–924	15th-century	Rising thirds begin lullaby melody, harmony modulates by descending fifths (Ex. 9.5)	Lullaby

1701 version of the Lübeck frieze, which instead begins with a cautionary prologue.[23] Rather, the opening is derived from the Reval fragment, which scholars believe mirrors the original fifteenth-century Lübeck frieze.[24] Adès's Preacher begins: 'Good folk, come, rich or poor, this way, / come, young and old, to see the play. / And think on this: though every man / would live forever, no-one can.'[25] As noted above, this situates the Preacher outside the main narrative of the Dance, and invites the listener to respond critically to the subsequent allegory of human equality in the face of death.

In a review of the 2013 Proms premiere, Andrew Clements points out the similarity of Adès's opening to the prologue of Berg's *Lulu*.[26] Indeed, both scores begin with two unison trombones outlining a dissonant interval in four accented notes moving in a single direction, followed by showy flourishes which cadence with a thud. The Preacher's entrance parallels that of *Lulu*'s circus animal trainer, whose similar invitation for the audience to see the play serves to equate human interactions to animal savagery.[27] The opera's fundamental question of whether Lulu or society is to blame for her gruesome fate is comparable to the moral question posed by Adès's *Totentanz*. Are humans to blame for their own damnation, or is society at fault?

Such self-reflection is central to the Dance of Death tradition. Adès's use of the German word *Schauspiel* for 'play' comes from a translation of the Low German word *spectel*, meaning 'spectacle', but scholars have argued that the original text actually used the word *spegel*, meaning 'mirror'.[28] Accordingly, Gertsman argues that the frieze was supposed to act not as a 'spectacle of others' suffering' for viewers to take in, but as a reflection of themselves. Visual imagery plays an important role in this identification, drawing the viewer into the dance with the outward gazes of the painted figures and the familiar local scenery in the background.[29]

---

[23] 'Lübeck's Dance of Death: The Preacher in the Pulpit', www.dodedans.com/Etext0.htm.

[24] 'The Reval Dance of Death'.

[25] Though the text is sung in German, quotations in this chapter will be from the English translation.

[26] Andrew Clements, 'Prom 8: BBCSO/Adès – Review', *Guardian*, 18 July 2013, review section, p. 36.

[27] When presented with these similarities, Adès denied a purposeful connection but acknowledged the parallels. Adès, interview with the author, 1 August 2018.

[28] Hartmut Freytag, 'Der Lübeck-Revaler Totentanz von 1463 – *spectel* "geistliches Schauspiel" oder *spegel* "Speculum"?', in *Architectura poetica: Festschrift für Johannes Rathofer zum 65. Geburtstag*, ed. by Ulrich Ernst and Bernhard Sowinski (Cologne: Böhlau Verlag, 1990), pp. 299–306.

[29] Gertsman, 'The Dance of Death', pp. 147–50.

Ex. 9.1 *Totentanz*, bars 1–6

The notion of mirroring, including carnivalesque mirrors which 'distort the other side', is integral to Adès's musical material and hence his narrative approach.[30] The mirroring process can be heard at the outset of the work (Ex. 9.1), in which the trombones outline a tritone through a descending sequence of intervals which expand by one semitone with each iteration, and are answered by trumpets beginning on the same pitch (A_4) but going in the opposite direction.[31] The two lines are then superimposed upon each other simultaneously at the end of bar 3 and extended. The placement of this musical mirror at the beginning of the work supports the allegorical and didactic significance of the idea of (self-)reflection.

Adès omits lines by the Reval Preacher on how to achieve salvation. Instead, as the Preacher intones the text 'come, young and old', we hear a strange premonition of the music which will accompany the Child at the end of the work. This idea eventually becomes a tender Mahlerian lullaby that contrasts with the harsher, antagonistic music accompanying most of the other dancers. On its first appearance, however, the lullaby appears as a ghostly, ephemeral version of its later self (Ex. 9.2, bars 17–20). This moment's unconventional orchestration gives aural hints that this music is out of place. Harmon-muted trumpets, doubled by low flutes, present the lullaby's prominent rising thirds (bar 17). In bar 20, beat 3, stopped horns emphasise the clashing chromatic neighbour note that will become a characteristic feature of the lullaby's melody. Tremolo strings, *ppp*, provide a hesitant harmonically ambiguous accompaniment.

Adès claims a twofold function for this musical foreshadowing. First, it serves a purely musical function, preparing the listener for the surprise of the Child's lullaby. Second, paired with the invitation in the text, the music is designed to indicate that the Child is a stand-in for all of humanity. The invocation of 'young and old', refers not to an actual baby, but to all of us, acknowledging that we all began life as babies.[32] Adès's act of narrative

---

[30] Adès, interview with the author, 1 August 2018.

[31] Numbers above brackets in Ex. 9.1 refer to the number of semitones within each interval.

[32] Adès, interview with the author, 1 August 2018.

Ex. 9.2 *Totentanz*, bars 17–32, foreshadowing of the Child's lullaby

foreshadowing creates a temporal dislocation which has no analogue in the frieze. Music, as a temporal art form, is much better positioned than the visual arts to incorporate such a foreshadowing. Not only does this moment suggest an external narrator, but in doing so it offers hints towards a more nuanced message, suggesting the potential for salvation that every human has as a baby.

The foreshadowing of the Child's lullaby is abruptly interrupted by the introduction of the *Dies irae* in the piccolos, accompanying the Preacher's turn towards the subject of death (Ex. 9.2, bar 21). As if a mirage, the ghostly promise of salvation suddenly disappears, to be replaced by the harsh reality of Death's arrival. The *Dies irae*, a musical symbol for the figure of Death, does not appear in full in *Totentanz*, but despite its modified and curtailed presentation, its power of signification is not lost, for it is immediately recognisable. Modified to emerge naturally from the expanding intervallic idea introduced at the opening of the piece, its second phrase also consists of an inverted version of the first (bars 24–6), forming another musical mirror. Adès claims that its inclusion is mostly the result of a working out of the expanding intervallic idea, and that he took only 'the best five notes'.[33]

---

[33] Ibid.

The halting rhythms of Adès's presentation of the *Dies irae*, along with its centring on the pitch of D, parallels historical methods for signifying the demonic. Adès intensifies the rhythmic irregularity by alternating between traditional time signatures and so-called irrational metres, which function as incomplete triplets, giving the music a limping quality. The orchestration is appropriately severe, emphasising registral extremes – a hallmark of Adès's style – by contrasting multiple versions of the *Dies irae* in the high register with low thuds in the brass and percussion, creating an atmosphere of foreboding.

The *Dies irae* is played first by a single piccolo, serving simultaneously as a musical translation of the pipe-wielding skeleton from the frieze which leads the dance and as a straightforward symbol of Death for the listener unfamiliar with the frieze. Two more piccolos join in with successive iterations of the chant (bars 27 and 32), evoking the ever-increasing numbers of skeletal figures in the frieze. Entering with the piccolos, the Preacher sings Adès's version of the *Dies irae*, which appears at roughly half the tempo of the piccolo version, creating a loose mensuration canon.

Straying from the visual differentiation between the Preacher and Death in the Reval fragment, a number of musical cues suggest that these characters are not fully differentiated from one another in Adès's *Totentanz*, besides both being represented by the baritone. Death is introduced musically by the *Dies irae* while the Preacher is still finishing his speech, creating an overlap between the characters not present in the original frieze. Not only do both characters sing the *Dies irae*, but their vocal lines are almost identical, with no break between their entrances or change in vocal style besides the addition of a doubling trombone, the instrument of death, to Death's line. In flattening the characters into a single principal narrative agential role, Adès subverts the listener's expectation that any two characters be musically differentiated. Adès thus forgoes the original frieze's illusion of multiple didactic perspectives in lieu of communicating his own message through both characters, revealing the Preacher and Death to be surrogates for himself.

In addition to the *Dies irae*, chains of thirds and fifths introduced in Death's opening arias come to play a significant role in the work. Serving as narrative motives, they link together the music for many characters, accumulating allegorical meaning as they are developed. Chains of thirds come to function as symbols for the ideas of damnation or salvation, depending on the direction of their motion. The first such motive is initiated in the bass at Death's introduction, accompanied by rattling percussion that mimics the sound of clacking bones. The bassline is based on descending thirds that underpin the multiple layered iterations of the *Dies irae* above (Ex. 9.3) and is thickened through the addition of a third above. The

Ex. 9.3 *Totentanz*, bars 42–58, descending thirds in bassline at Death's introduction

quality of the thirds (major or minor) varies, both in their melodic motion and in their harmonic stacking, which follow no pattern, thereby creating intervallic chains that act like a spiral which can never repeat, coiling in one direction forever.[34] The orchestration of the bassline obscures changes in register by staggering the points at which instruments jump back up the octave. The result is an orchestrated Shepard tone, giving the illusion of a never-ending descent. Death's text here invites all to join his dance and offers a warning to 'gather good works together, / to be forgiven of your sin'. The downward trajectory of the musical narration suggests a descent after death, implying that for most, the Dance will end in damnation.

From Pope to Child

The intervallic organisation of the music suddenly shifts when Death turns his attention towards the Pope (bar 134). Descending thirds become

[34] Thomas Adès, email to the author, 14 August 2018.

descending fifths, appearing in the vocal line and doubled by the orchestra (Online Ex. 9.1a). Death wastes no time in communicating his lack of regard for social hierarchies, undercutting the Pope's highest rank by sardonically telling him that his 'hat is much too high' and he must 'narrow down' to fit in his coffin. Still, Adès highlights the significance of the first human dancer's entrance with an exclamation of 'Ah, Lord God' by the mezzo-soprano – her first vocal utterance in the work – accompanied by a sweeping *fff* chord in the violins and violas (Online Ex. 9.1b, bar 168). Death's melodic motion by fifth is transformed here into stacked quintal harmony. As the Pope laments the worthlessness of his office in the face of Death, these fifths begin to slide downwards. Each voice forms an independent melodic stratum descending chromatically with weeping glissando gestures that eventually end on the open strings of the violins and violas at the end of the section, representing the Pope's transition to 'naught but earth'. This passage, in which the strings perform independently of the conductor, owes its rhetoric to the limited aleatorism of Lutosławski, to whom *Totentanz* is dedicated. The dissolution of hierarchy within the orchestral personnel mirrors that of society; just as the conductor's rank is made irrelevant, so too is the Pope's. By coupling humanity's weeping entrance with the introduction of quintal harmony, Adès here connects fifths to human suffering (rather than the Lisztian devil).

Death's address to the Cardinal triggers a return of chains of thirds, but here they move in opposing directions, paralleling contradictions in the text. Now in inversion as rising crotchets, the thirds change more rapidly than in Ex. 9.3 and occur in overlapping layers, sometimes generating triads (Online Ex 9.2). Adès characterises this inversion as an 'equal and opposite reaction' to the descending thirds from Death's introduction.[35] When he speaks to the Cardinal, Death's text suggests that the rising thirds correspond to the possibility of salvation: 'My son, I know that here / you undertook much good: I have no inkling, there, / what may be your reward.' The regal character of this section, with majestic rising thirds in the low brass, supports this reading. The direction of the thirds' motion is reversed again from bar 258 for the Cardinal's response to Death, in which he laments the inevitability of death and the worthlessness of his earthly rank, suggesting he is unaware of his possible salvation. Adès's adaptation is responsible for this disconnect in dialogue. While Death's text comes from the 1701 version, the Cardinal's response is taken from the fifteenth-

---

[35] Adès, email to the author, 14 August 2018.

century text, which goes well beyond the 1701 text's expression of regret only for not having achieved the position of Pope before dying. The conflict between these texts is reinforced by the opposing directions of the thirds, conveying humanity's inability to understand death or know what we will face in the afterlife.

Adès amalgamates two characters from the 1701 text to create the Monk: while Death's text is addressed to the Abbot, the response comes from the Carthusian. Textual parallels help explain this choice: both verses reference the number 1,000, and both mention Death calling his victim to follow him in the dance. Outlining oscillating fifths a semitone apart on A-E and B♭-F (bars 421–7), Death calls out: 'Abbot! The tolling bell / has called you to your bed. / Come dance with me, and fill / the crypt that waits prepared.' In a moment of text-painting, the orchestra intones alternating bell-like chords made primarily of stacked fifths, recalling the Pope's quintal harmony. But the tone shifts at the invitation to dance, beginning what Venn calls Death's 'seduction' of the Monk (bar 428).[36] The humorous characterisation of the Monk's musical setting transcends the meaning of the text and suggests a critique of the church. Death entices with images of the afterlife: a cloister with 'a thousand pious brothers'. Adès capitalises on the undertones of homosexuality implied in Death's seduction, conjuring up an accompanying glitzy waltz which lilts and lurches and which is incongruent with the solemn, reluctant expressions on the faces of both the Abbot and the Carthusian in the frieze. In pairing the waltz topic – representing worldly high society – with the supposedly ascetic Monk, Adès pillories the church's hypocritical materialism, going well beyond the commentary offered by the frieze and text.

Chains of thirds reappear in the bass during the waltz, now moving freely in either direction and suggesting that Death is toying impishly with the Monk's salvation (Ex. 9.4). The pitches of the vocal line consistently form a major third above the bass on each downbeat – an orderly process which mirrors the Monk's response to Death: 'My Order bids me strictly / obey a thousand rules.' Other rules are followed as well. The vocal part invariably consists of three-note cells derived from a subset of the expanding intervallic idea which outline a semitone and a tone (e.g. F♯–G–A, bar 429). Each cell begins either a tritone or semitone away from the cell prior to it. The rhythm of the vocal line is also constructed methodically, with each bar restricted to one of only four possibilities consisting of

---

[36] Venn, 'BBC Proms 2013', p. 60.

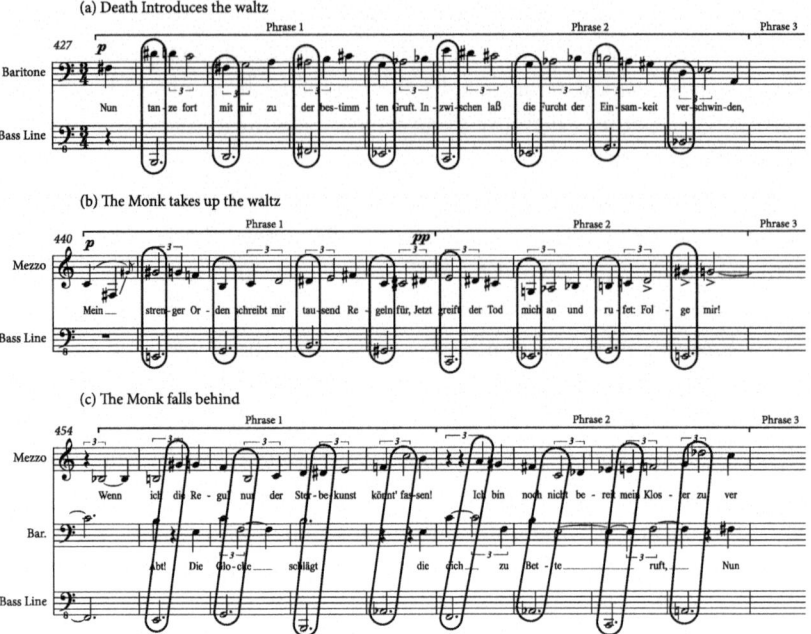

Ex. 9.4 *Totentanz*. (a) Bars 427–35; (b) bars 440–8; (c) bars 452–60

different combinations of a crotchet plus a triplet crotchet divided into a crotchet and a minim.

The waltz is organised into four sections. First, Death initiates the dance by introducing the waltz melody (bars 427–40) in three phrases of four, four and five bars respectively. Second, the monk's response follows (bars 440–52) with the first phrase transposed up a fourth. The next phrase begins in the same transposition as Death's but strays after two bars. Third, they join in a duet (bars 453–67), in which it is clear that the Monk is no equal dance partner for Death. The Monk's text 'If only I could master / The rules of how to die!' is reflected in the music, where the major thirds formed between the vocal line and bassline are now offset by a beat, as if to suggest that the Monk is unable to keep up with Death, always following one step behind. Finally, the orchestra takes up an instrumental version of the waltz (bar 467) made up of simultaneous mirrored versions of the three-note cell, whipping up to a climax which sweeps the Monk away, illustrating his demise.

The Knight's episode interrupts the climax of the Monk's waltz with pounding crotchets from the Taiko drum, accompanied by brassy synco-pated interjections (bar 482). This is followed by the return of the *Dies irae* in piccolos and harp (bar 487). Text-painting and topical allusions combine to suggest an anti-war message, underscored by Death's ridiculing of the Knight. Four clattering anvils evoke the Knight's armour, which Death mentions in his taunting verse: 'From my sharp darts / no iron guards you.' Death's mocking is further enhanced by the doubling of his vocal line by a garishly sliding trombone. Military allusions continue as the Knight boastfully responds to Death, with percussionists playing two military tenor drums and a steel sheet. Adès characterised the image of the Knight in the frieze as 'quite comic' and as posing haughtily with his face completely hidden by an oversized helmet – an image which matches the false heroism of his text: 'You heroes, look at me / armed in might, / manly in bearing, / a lion in fight, / until my enemy / was laid low.'[37]

An intertextual reference helps to convey Adès's social critique, straying significantly from the frieze's allegorical intent. As if prompted by the Knight's mentioning of 'heroes', the beginning of the episode bears some similarity to a moment (beginning at 16) in the Scherzo of Britten's overtly pacifist *Ballad of Heroes*, which is itself labelled a Dance of Death. While at first blush the two passages share only a passing resemblance in their driving, percussive rhythms, the connection is strengthened thanks to Adès's prior allusion to this same moment in the climactic moment (see R) of 'Ecstasio', the third movement of *Asyla*. Indeed, both 'Ecstasio' and the Knight's episode (bar 487) divide the orchestra into two groups, in which one follows the conductor's lead and the other independently performs the pounding rhythms to generate a polyrhythmic texture. Simultaneously, this technique reflects Adès's anti-war critique through a breakdown of the orchestral chain of command. That Adès chose to base his *Totentanz* on a frieze which itself was a casualty of war shows the significance of this pacifist message to the work.[38]

After the Knight, Adès turns to the 'professional classes' made up of the Mayor, Doctor, Usurer and Merchant. While Gertsman argues that the Lübeck and Reval Dances serve as a warning that pride is the 'gravest sin ... the root of all [human] shortcomings and the ultimate source of universal corruption', Adès's narration here suggests a different foundational sin for modern society: materialism.[39] Death deals with the professional classes, who most closely represent contemporary occupations, most harshly and hastily, as if he is '[swatting] them like flies'.[40] Explaining the

---

[37] Adès, interview with the author, 1 August 2018.   [38] See 'The Lübeck Dance of Death'.

[39] Elina Gertsman, *The Dance of Death in the Middle Ages: Image, Text, Performance* (Turnhout: Brepols, 2010), p. 111.

[40] Adès, interviewed in 'Prom 8: Britten, Lutsławski and Thomas Adès', *BBC Proms*, BBC Radio 3, 17 July 2013.

insignificance of these characters, Adès has characterised this central section as a 'huge wave' of musical momentum in which the characters 'get tossed under and disappear'.[41] The Merchant 'is at the very top when they crash', precipitating the chaotic climax of the entire work.[42] In positioning the Merchant as the catalyst for this important structural moment, Adès demonstrates his critical significance in comparison to the other surrounding characters and suggests that materialism is at the root of humanity's suffering. Indeed, Adès refers to him as 'a sort of modern pope' who represents the idea of commerce as the new 'worldwide religion'.[43] The Merchant is given no such priority in the frieze, suggesting significant differences between the works' allegorical emphases. In the approach to the climax, rising chains of thirds return (bar 589), now in minims, bolstering the Merchant's significance and at first appearing to imply the possibility of salvation. But the Merchant's text demonstrates his misconception about how to achieve salvation, mistaking the accumulation of material goods for the gathering of 'good works'.

The Merchant's failure to achieve salvation is conveyed by a sour turn at the climax (bar 612), in which an emphasis on musical mirrors suggests that we should see ourselves reflected in his failure. The climax consists primarily of cells derived from the opening expanding idea, mirrored in simultaneous versions and transpositions. Reaching a wild, sustained frenzy of uncoordinated *ffff* semiquavers on mirrored chromatic trichords in bars 652–3, it culminates in an orchestral tutti on an emphatic chord consisting of all twelve pitches (bar 655), stacked in perfect fifths from the low A of the contrabass trombone up through to a high A in the first violins (Online Ex. 9.3). This conspicuous example of quintal harmony at the moment of greatest musical tension signifies maximum human suffering, the result of failing to achieve salvation. In his review of the premiere, the critic Barry Millington suggested that the incongruity between the Merchant's 'inoffensive contribution' and the apocalyptic nature of the following climax demonstrated that there is often 'no discernible connection between text and music' in the work generally.[44] On the contrary, the virulence of the climax is proportional to the accumulated rage of Death towards all of the human characters from the first half of the work who have failed to be adequately prepared for Death's arrival. But as the impartial arbiter of death, Death is not supposed to have an emotional

---

[41] Adès, interview with the author, 1 August 2018.   [42] Ibid.   [43] Ibid.

[44] Barry Millington, 'Morbid and Yet So Magical', *Evening Standard*, 18 July 2013, Features section, p. 46.

response. Rather, the climax's violence serves to emphasise that Death is a surrogate for Adès's narrating voice, whose critique is actually behind the climax – a significant departure from the frieze's telling.

Adès has described the Handworker as his self-portrait, and it is reflected musically through a huge, exaggerated mirror formed by two opposing sections of the orchestra.[45] Doubled by strings, upper winds, harp and muted trombones, the mezzo-soprano repeatedly wails, leaping up to high registers and sliding back downwards in gross exaggerations of the earlier weeping gesture. Bass clarinets, bassoons and horns snake upwards in thirds and sixths to offer an opposing force, counteracting the chromatic motion above. Adès shows little sympathy for himself in his self-portrait, which contains some of the most grotesque music in the entire piece. The Handworker's text decries his poor work and materialistic nature, and Adès harshly emphasises the word *schlecht* ('poor') through extended *fff* glissandos low in the mezzo-soprano's range. In a hushed moment at the end of the section, the two singers bring the mirror to the fore (Online Ex. 9.4, bars 745–50). While the Handworker exclaims 'Lord, grant me life in heaven!' in a chromatic descent, Death's warning 'your soul shall know much suffering', ascends melodically. Further emphasising the textual disconnect, the singers change words on staggered beats and fail to meet in the middle, instead finishing with a dissonant augmented unison on C♯ and C♮.

Paralleling a generally sympathetic turn in Death's rhetoric (and thereby Adès's critique), the music for the final three dancers initiates a marked shift from the harsh, mocking tone of the music accompanying most of the previous characters, gradually introducing major triads. The third-to-last dancer, the Peasant, is the only character in Adès's *Totentanz* to whom Death promises salvation, which is to be achieved through virtuous manual labour.[46] Death warmly initiates a rollicking dance with the Peasant, propelled by an oscillating horn riff which appropriately evokes the musical topic of the pastoral. Oscillating between B flat and C major sonorities at first (bars 755–68), the harmony is coloured by whole-tone and Lydian touches (i.e. the sharpened fourth degree of the scale) and goes through a number of modulatory transpositions.

---

[45] 'And the handworker, what we call the artisan, is the self-portrait. That's me. That's what I am, in my view. I mean if I fit in anywhere, that's where I fit in.' Adès, interview with the author, 1 August 2018.

[46] The hermit, omitted by Adès, was also promised salvation in the original text of the frieze.

While Death's text is not quite sympathetic to the Maiden, her musical introduction is soft in tone and begins with a subtle nod in the rhythms of the timpani to Schubert's famous 'Death and the Maiden' string quartet (bars 822–5).[47] Oscillating fifth-based sonorities and F major chords evoke the tolling bells of the Monk, and Death again initiates a seductive dance. Unlike the Monk's raucous waltz, however, the music of the Maiden is somewhat reserved in tone, signalling her reluctance. Her plaintive vocal line and its accompanying harmonies instead recall those heard in the Parish Clerk (see Table 9.1); both are derived from the fifth-based structures first introduced by the Pope.

The shift in tone begun with the Peasant is completed in a most remarkable and unexpected fashion in the final scene, in which a dominant pedal introduces a radiant D major key for the Child's unabashedly Romantic lullaby, complementing Death's comforting verse 'You tender babe, behold / the scythe's untimely blow. / Till the last day, sleep now: / sleep on, consoled.' The Child's response emphasises his innocence: 'O Death, how can I understand? / I cannot walk, yet I must dance!' Many have commented on the surprise of this music's emotional directness with its echoes of Mahler and Strauss.[48] Venn offers this critique: 'Whilst undoubtedly being glorious, beautiful music, this sudden identification with a victim, and the suggestion of transcendence, sat awkwardly with the objectivity adopted elsewhere.'[49] The disjunction is undeniable, but serves a narrative purpose. The sudden stylistic change implies the presence of an external agent (Adès), in a similar fashion to the earlier foreshadowing of the Child's music. While Adès's Death has little sympathy for the individual humans, this narrative disjunction reveals Adès's narrative voice and indicates that the Child is meant to represent not a single child but all of humanity. Death therefore does not single out a victim to identify with, but instead shows sympathy towards the universal human condition of suffering. Though this sympathy for the Child may appear contradictory to the more judgemental attitude shown to the rest of humanity, those earlier episodes serve as didactic reflections on the sins that have cost each human their salvation, illustrating unsatisfactory behaviour for the audience.

Musical cues prepare for this final episode's shift in tone and convey its meaning. The introduction of triadic materials in the music of the Peasant

---

[47] Adès, interview with the author, 1 August 2018. This moment also recalls the quotation of 'Death and the Maiden' in *Powder Her Face*.

[48] See, for instance, Millington, 'Morbid and Yet So Magical'; and Venn, 'BBC Proms 2013'.

[49] Venn, 'BBC Proms 2013', p. 60.

Ex. 9.5 *Totentanz*, bars 875–88, modulations by descending fifths in the Child's lullaby

and Maiden, coupled with their more sympathetic texts, softens the suddenness of the transition into the Child's explicitly tonal music. The lullaby's appearance, while surprising, fulfils the promise of the foreshadowing from the beginning of the piece. This final section ties up a number of musical and narrative threads that have been woven throughout the piece (Ex. 9.5). The lullaby's main theme begins with ascending chains of thirds representing the possibility of salvation which is available to all of humankind as innocent children – a possibility also suggested by the contrast of the lullaby's initial D major key with the implied D minor of the *Dies irae*'s first appearance (Ex. 9.2).[50] The theme undergoes a series of modulations by descending fifths, suggesting that despite the change in tone, this Child is heading towards the same fate as everyone else: human suffering is inevitable. Adès has described the elusive nature of the harmony in this ending section: 'I wanted it to feel as though it's in that world where tonic and dominant really mean something. But it's as if I dissolved the rules of it, so they can actually slip into the wrong one. I wanted to have this sense that wherever we are, it's going the same direction.'[51] Indeed, the D major key of the lullaby is never secure for long. Secondary dominant chords coloured by dissonant chromatic neighbour notes tonicise the dominant chord built on A, suggesting a modulation by ascending fifth (bars 878 and 881). But in bar 882 the tonality moves in the opposite direction to G major, a fifth lower than where it started. After a few false modulations back to D (bars 884 and 887), there is a further modulation down by yet another fifth to C major in bar 888. From there a series of tonicisations occur, now descending by thirds – first to A, then to F and finally back to D at the climax of the lullaby in bar 900. These concurrent descending modulations, first by fifths and then by thirds, underscore the significance of these intervallic structures at this important structural moment. The meaning Adès intends with these modulations is clear. While the key of the lullaby shifts, the end result is always the same. A dominant–tonic cadence equals death. Adès strays dramatically from historical techniques, where the demonic is signified by a lack of tonality. Instead, he uses the teleological nature of tonality itself as a symbol for death. The triumphant narrative traditionally conveyed through minor-to-major key transformations is subverted as the piece ends with repeated perfect cadences in D major, which move further and further into the lowest registers of the orchestra, obscuring the cadences' voice leading. The murkiness of the orchestration leaves the listener unable to perceive audibly the cadence as such, making something familiar actually quite strange. While each human's death has been understandable as a didactic stepping stone in the process of familiarising Death, the idea of Death as the inevitable

---

[50] The tonal plan for Liszt's *Totentanz* could be seen as a model, beginning in D minor and ending in D major.

[51] Adès, interview with the author, 1 August 2018.

culmination of human suffering is something beyond the capacity of human understanding, and tonality is but one metaphor we can use to describe it.[52]

* * *

The Romantic turn in the Child's lullaby parallels a turn towards emotional directness in Adès's orchestral works, beginning with *Tevot* (2007), continuing with *In Seven Days* (2008) and *Polaris* (2010) and reaching its most recent representative with the Concerto for Piano and Orchestra (2018). The emotional directness of the final episode of *Totentanz* leads more transparently to conclusions regarding its moral message. The Dance in its original manifestation contained the potential for social critique in illustrating that high rank matters not in death. But Adès takes this message much further, embedding a critique of the hierarchical structure of society in the musical rhetoric of *Totentanz* through prominent use of Lutosławski's 'limited aleatorism'. Metaphors for the orchestra as civil society have been in use since the late seventeenth century, and they apply here.[53] In moments of musical aleatory during the episodes of the Pope, Knight and Parish Clerk, the conductor's role as exclusive leader of the orchestra is diminished, and coordination is determined by individual players, giving a glimpse of a non-hierarchical and collective model of society. While Adès gives the performers agency, he also circumscribes it by prescribing pitches and rhythms, mirroring death's limitation of humans' agency in life. Adès has often paired *Totentanz* with performances of Lutosławski's Cello Concerto, inviting comparisons between the works' climaxes. Problematising our reading of aleatoricism in *Totentanz* as representative of a collective society, Lutosławski's work has often been interpreted – despite his protestations – as a critique of communism, representing the collective's oppression of the individual.[54] But in taking a broad view of the concerto as representing a generalised oppression of the individual, we can interpret *Totentanz*'s aleatoric climax as representing individuality unsuccessfully attempting to break out of societal strictures, which are shown to prevail through the concluding quintal chord.

[52] See also Drew Massey, *Thomas Adès in Five Essays* (New York: Oxford University Press, 2021), p. 148.

[53] John Spitzer, 'Metaphors of the Orchestra – The Orchestra as a Metaphor', *Musical Quarterly*, 80/ii (1996), 234–64 (p. 240).

[54] See, for instance, Clements, 'Prom 8'.

Adès's social critiques – answering the question posed by the opening's reference to *Lulu* – suggest that societal forces like materialism are responsible for the corruption of humans, who come into the world sinless and capable of achieving salvation, as evinced by the Child's lullaby. Just as the setting of the original frieze depicted Lübeck's cathedral – a symbol of the church's supreme power in medieval times as the tallest, most extravagant building in town – one can imagine the modern skyscrapers of consumerist corporations, the dominant power in today's society, lurking in the background of Adès's *Totentanz*. The pacifist message conveyed by the Knight's episode critiques an additional and related hierarchical societal structure, the military. The Peasant, to whom material possessions are of little concern, offers a counter-example to the Merchant and Knight, and through his sympathetic treatment he is suggested as a model for how to achieve salvation.

With plagues common and death a regular feature of medieval life, the Dance was also meant to communicate the urgency of being prepared for death.[55] At the time of writing this chapter, the world is undergoing its worst outbreak of disease in a century. A pandemic cuts across all walks of life, making death a more familiar presence in everyday life than at any other point in recent history. *Totentanz* has unfortunately become remarkably relevant to our current circumstances. Perhaps the work will encourage listeners, jolted by the pandemic's upheaval of day-to-day life, to engage in self-reflection, to question the materialism and other ills of contemporary society that Adès's narration suggests will lead to our damnation. Or perhaps the legacy of *Totentanz* will be its reflection of contemporary society through the lens of the Dance of Death tradition, one that artists will continue to draw on for centuries to come.

---

[55] Gundersheimer, 'Introduction to the Dover Edition', pp. 15–16.

10 | Hearing Voices in Adès's Operas

EMMA GALLON

Much critical attention has been devoted to the singing voice in Thomas Adès's three operas to date.[*] From the soprano Maid's peals of stylised laughter and the baritone Judge's vertiginous leaps in *Powder Her Face* (1995) to the sparkling coloratura of Ariel in *The Tempest* (2003–4) and the acknowledged vocal 'workout' for all fifteen operatic leads in *The Exterminating Angel* (2015–16), the sometimes surprising and frequently stirring sound of the human voice being used in innovative ways in each of Adès's operas has ensured a sustained focus on voice and vocality in reviews.[1]

However, there has been comparatively little academic scholarship on the role of the voice in Adès's works. In fact, rather than simply showcasing the voice to display mere technical brilliance, all three operas are replete with moments in which Adès uses the sound and activity of the resonant singing voice itself as a narrative parameter independently of, in collaboration with and in collision with what these operatic voices have to say – a compositional trait that would benefit from more sustained analytical examination. I start from the premise that recognition of this interpretative complexity and the dynamic expressive potential of the voice is crucial to a deeper understanding of the characteristically multi-layered narratives we encounter in the three pieces. I will discuss a selection of interpretatively salient moments to demonstrate the ways in which interrogating the play between voice as embodied sonority and more metaphorical conceptions of voice as carrier of meaning can help us to access and understand traits in the relationship between surface and structure and the use of musical techniques for semantic ends in Adès's operas.

Michelle Duncan states that 'opera performance calls for a critical engagement that both reads and listens, analyses and experiences' and, in this spirit, the following analyses will bring together elements of two theoretical trends – hermeneutic and material – in voice studies to demonstrate the interpretative potential of examining the variety of voices in

---

[*] The research on *Powder Her Face* in this chapter was made possible with funding from the Arts and Humanities Research Council.
[1] Zachary Woolfe, 'Reaching a New High at the Met Opera', *New York Times*, 8 November 2017, section C, p. 1.

Adès's music.[2] While the discussion will initially centre on the narrative role of phenomenal song, or 'a musical or vocal performance that declares itself openly' in Carolyn Abbate's definition, and an often explicit strategy that links the audibility of voice with its function as conduit for meaning, I will draw on recent work on music and materiality as I foreground the vocal timbres, the mouths, throats and breath, and the noisy non-verbal vocalisations that emanate from the singing bodies in specific performances of Adès's operas.[3] In doing so, I will provide a long-overdue theoretically grounded hearing of the sonorous voices in Adès's music and of the performers that so capture our attention from the operatic stage.

Voice, Materiality and Meaning in *Powder Her Face*'s Popular Song

The second scene in *Powder Her Face* depicts the first in the series of flashbacks that form the operatic narrative.[4] Set in 1934, this flashback centres on the soon-to-be Duchess (the main protagonist of the opera), who gossips languidly with her Confidante and a Lounge Lizard in the drawing room. The Lounge Lizard begins to scat-sing a few notes to himself and puts a record on the gramophone: a Cole Porter-esque popular song dedicated to the Duchess herself (Scene 2, bars 167–304). The song is underpinned by intervallic cycles characteristic of much of the harmony of the whole opera and typical of Adès's musical language more broadly (see Ex. 10.1). Far more aurally prominent, however, are the song's functionally tonal D major, with echoes of topical melodic gestures ('blue notes' and 'sentient decorative notes' in meaningfully strategic locations, for example), and its formal conventions (a verse-refrain-bridge-refrain-coda structure).[5] Drawing on Abbate's terms, this use of pastiche invokes a 'discursive distance' that is the 'sonorous signal for music's voices'.[6] The disruptive effect of this kind of aural separation from the surrounding music, for Abbate, betrays

---

[2] Michelle Duncan, 'The Operatic Scandal of the Singing Body: Voice, Presence, Performativity', *Cambridge Opera Journal*, 16/iii (2004), 283–306 (p. 286).

[3] Carolyn Abbate, *Unsung Voices: Opera and Musical Narrative in the Nineteenth Century* (Princeton, NJ: Princeton University Press, 1991), p. 5.

[4] Scene numbers in *Powder Her Face* are continuous between Acts. Scenes 1–5 are thus in Act I, and Scenes 6–8 in Act II.

[5] Allen Forte, 'Secrets of Melody: Line and Design in the Songs of Cole Porter', *Musical Quarterly*, 77/iv (1993), 607–47 (p. 617).

[6] Abbate, *Unsung Voices*, p. 28.

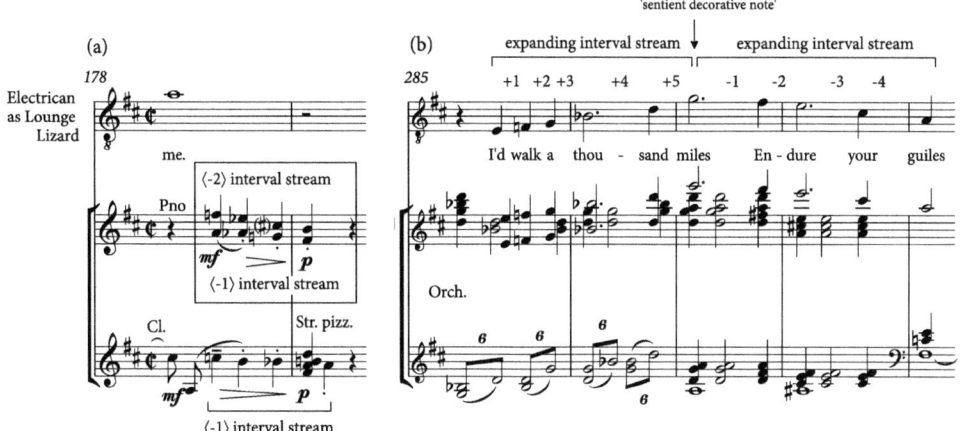

Ex. 10.1 Interval cycles as characteristic harmonic procedures in the popular song in *Powder Her Face*. (a) Act I, Scene 2, bars 178–9, descending whole-tone and semitone streams; (b) Act I, Scene 2, bars 285–9, expanding interval streams

the presence of a narrator, the 'unsung' narrative voice of a detached subject that formulates and orders the discourse in recounting the events.

Abbate's hermeneutics largely sets aside performers in identifying such 'unsung voices', and, indeed, the important role of the tenor's voice specifically has been conspicuously absent in commentary on this scene so far. It is actually the Lounge Lizard's scat-singing that functions as the first musical cue that a phenomenal performance is about to take place, as a signifier of the music of the era. In its improvisatory wordlessness ('ba be dap be doo') it also serves to centre the focus on the voice *as voice*, and in fact the television version of the opera broadcast on Channel Four in the United Kingdom explicitly translates this part of the scene into a choreographed and stylised vocal performance for the tenor Dan Norman, who plays the Lounge Lizard.[7]

Voice, together with its uneasy multifaceted relationship with meaning, has been a subject of intense cross-disciplinary scrutiny.[8] Of particular relevance here are the attempts to re-embody the voice as part of a 'material turn' in opera studies. This materialism consists of:

---

[7] Thomas Adès, *Powder Her Face*, directed for stage by David Alden, directed for television by Margaret Williams (Channel Four Television Corporation, 1999); released on DVD (Digital Classics DC 10002, 2005).

[8] Prominent texts include Jacques Derrida, *Speech and Phenomena and Other Essays on Husserl's Theory of Signs*, trans. by David B. Allison (Evanston, IL: Northwestern University Press, 1973); Roland Barthes, 'The Grain of the Voice', in *Image Music Text*, essays selected and trans. by Stephen Heath (London: Fontana Press, 1977), pp. 179–89; Adriana Cavarero, *For More than One Voice: Toward a Philosophy of Vocal Expression* (Stanford, CA: Stanford University Press, 2005); and Mladen Dolar, *A Voice and Nothing More* (Cambridge, MA: MIT Press, 2006).

The timbre or 'grain' of the sounding voice. The flesh, membrane, mucus, and cartilage of the mechanism that produces it. The masks, veils and scrims that hide, throw, conceal, disguise, or displace it. The vocoders, phonographs, synthesisers, and microphones that enhance, distort, or play with it. The sheer sonic pleasure voice produces but also the fears, anxieties and tensions that set it in motion.[9]

In this light, Norman's stylised use of exaggerated rubato, portamento and phrasing and his manner of clipping note durations with early consonants to emphasise a certain wittiness in the words are significant. Tellingly, while most critics have focused on the song's resemblance to the style of the composers Cole Porter and Noel Coward, Adès in fact refers to the dapper film and theatre *singer* Jack Buchanan as a source of inspiration for the song, leading Nicholas David Stevens to suggest that 'Adès went into his own songwriting process with the Buchanan *sound* in mind.'[10] Norman certainly appropriates the kind of nasal timbre and 'friendly drawling voice' for which Buchanan was famous.[11] In responding to the need to convey difference musically between the phenomenal song and the non-phenomenal body of the opera, Adès opens up a space for performers' agency and the exploitation of vocal timbres for signifying purposes.

'I can hear them': Ariel's Voice as Sonorous Force

Taking the cue from the distinctly musical portrayal of Ariel in Shakespeare's *The Tempest*, the dramatic scenario in Adès's operatic adaptation of the play sets up much of the music of Ariel, re-gendered as a coloratura soprano, as phenomenal.[12] In two key places in Act III, Scene 2 the stage directions state, 'Ariel plays soft music' (249) and 'Ariel makes a musical sound' (261), overtly linking the character's music to the magical occurrences we witness, such that we understand that Ariel's magic takes the form of sound. Elsewhere I have discussed this connection between music and magic and the aural marking of many of these passages with functionally tonal C major harmonies.[13] Here I focus on one passage in

---

[9] Martha Feldman and Judith T. Zeitlin, 'The Clamor of Voices', in *The Voice as Something More: Essays toward Materiality*, ed. by Martha Feldman and Judith T. Zeitlin (Chicago: University of Chicago Press, 2019), pp. 3–33 (p. 4).

[10] Nicholas David Stevens, 'Lulu's Daughters: Portraying the Anti-Heroine in Contemporary Opera 1993–2013' (unpublished PhD dissertation, Case Western Reserve University, 2017), p. 79 (emphasis added).

[11] 'Last of the "Knuts"', *Times*, 21 October 1957, p. 12.

[12] In this chapter, I will follow the score and refer to Ariel the character with male pronouns, but will use female pronouns when referring to the soprano performer.

[13] Emma Gallon, 'Narrativities in the Music of Thomas Adès' (unpublished PhD dissertation, Lancaster University, 2011), pp. 287–90.

Ex. 10.2 The 'tempest' dyads underpinning the harmonic language of *The Tempest*. (a) Two eighteen-dyad cycles in full; (b) Act I, Scene 5, 92–93, inner strings and voice only, superimposition of pairs of adjacent dyads in 'Five Fathoms Deep'

particular: the 'Five Fathoms Deep' aria (Act I, Scene 5, 90–93[+4]), in which Ariel sings a song of the drowned King of Naples to (magically) transport Prince Ferdinand to the island's shore.[14] Like much of Ariel's music in the first act, the aria is breathtakingly high, reaching E_6 on several occasions. The phenomenal nature of the performance – an example of Ariel's magic made through sound that is audible to the characters within the fictional story – is established through the textual cues that frame the aria; it is introduced by Prospero, who commands, '[b]ring me Ferdinand. Sing!', and Ferdinand's line that immediately follows the aria is '[a]s I sat weeping I heard singing'. Nevertheless, I contend that the scored music itself does not signal 'discursive distance' in the same way as some of Ariel's other magical sounds. Harmonically, it is weaved into the same musical fabric as the rest of the opera, and the extremity of the pitch and occasional angularity of the melodic line are characteristic of the coloratura role's virtuosic part, which establishes a complex set of relationships between voice, sound, language and body.

Example 10.2 shows the connection between the harmonic language that underpins the entire opera and that of Ariel's aria. The opera's harmony is derived from two eighteen-dyad cycles, each containing every chromatic pitch twice in combination with either a minor third or perfect fifth and

---

[14] See also Michael Halliwell, '"Voices within the Voice": Conceiving Voice in Contemporary Opera', *Musicology Australia*, 36/ii (2014), 254–72, who reflects on many similar themes in his reading of Ariel's music and the 'problematization' of voice in opera in Adès's *The Tempest*.

patterned as a series of transposed 'retrograde-inversion chains' in such a way that the perfect fifths appear twice in each cycle (Ex. 10.2a).[15] The two cycles provide the kernel for the majority of the musical ideas in the opera and are set out in their most mechanical or 'geometrical' form in the opening overture depicting Prospero's revenge storm.[16] Ariel's aria is constructed entirely from these 'tempest' harmonies; each chord is formed relatively rigidly through the superimposition of two adjacent dyads within a cycle, regularly switching between the two cycles (Ex. 10.2b).

The dramatic connections between the overture and the aria, and the associated musical symbolism, are clear: on Prospero's command Ariel has first caused, and now calms, the storm. In general, and especially in the first act, Ariel's music is bound to Prospero's in this way, through the use of the 'tempest' harmonies and melodically constricting semitones with their dysphoric topical resonances.[17] It is the music of Prospero's revenge: his books and magic, his rules and language. It is these features that have encouraged commentators to interpret Ariel's enslavement by Prospero as one of 'silencing' Ariel's voice through language, and it is significant that when Ariel is finally liberated at the end of the opera the spirit's lines consist entirely of *wordless* vocalisations.[18] The release from Prospero is equated with a release from the (colonialising) restrictions of language. While not altogether disagreeing with this reading, from a vocal and material perspective I would, however, question the extent to which we actually hear Ariel as trapped by language throughout the opera. The exceptionally high pitch and technical demands of the lines have a tendency to annihilate the audibility of the words.[19] In addition, in 'Five Fathoms Deep' in particular, the extremely slow tempo further divorces sound from linguistic sense. Ariel's power therefore comes to be associated with the sheer force of the voice itself, separate from language.

---

[15] See Chapter 11 and Scott Lee, 'Musical Signification in Thomas Adès's *The Tempest*' (unpublished PhD dissertation, Duke University, 2018), p. 160.

[16] 'Geometrical' is Adès's term, referring to the unnatural origin of the storm (as Prospero's creation) with clear implications for its musical realisation: Thomas Adès and Tom Service, *Thomas Adès: Full of Noises – Conversations with Tom Service*, paperback ed. (London: Faber and Faber, 2018), p. 163.

[17] See Edward Venn, *Thomas Adès: Asyla* (Abingdon: Routledge, 2017), p. 158.

[18] See Chapter 4. See also Michael Halliwell, 'The Sound of Silence: A Tale of Two Operatic Tempests', in *Silence and Absence in Literature and Music*, ed. by Werner Wolf and Walter Bernhart (Leiden: Brill, 2016), pp. 196–219.

[19] Michel Poizat discusses the anatomical causes and psychoanalytic implications of the operatic soprano's 'cry' as 'voice-object' detached from language in *The Angel's Cry: Beyond the Pleasure Principle in Opera*, trans. by Arthur Denner (Ithaca, NY: Cornell University Press, 1992).

Duncan fittingly states that '[a]s anyone who has ever heard opera knows, the singing voice has moments where it tears language apart, or tears itself apart from language. Certainly the voice as well as and in addition to the body, says more, or says differently, than it means to say.'[20] These characteristic tensions between words, music and body in opera are exploited for signifying purposes in this aria, as an examination of two performances by Cyndia Sieden (The Royal Opera, London, February 2004) and Audrey Luna (Metropolitan Opera, New York, November 2012) will show.[21]

The set of Tom Cairns's Royal Opera production – the dark-lit stage with its unnatural green spotlighting and angular 'impossible' objects, such as the giant book around which much of the first act is staged – exposes the artifice in *The Tempest*'s drama. The mechanical nature of the events that befall the stranded courtiers, entirely premeditated and bound through magic to Prospero's rule of law, is highlighted by the equally mechanical appearance of the movements made by Sieden's Ariel throughout the 'Five Fathoms Deep' aria; her arms in the first part of this aria are usually straight, either in parallel with or at a right angle to her body, and on one occasion she makes a rapid cyclical motion with her left arm. Her expression is neutral, and her movements infrequent and like clockwork; she resembles a wound-up puppet, an automaton carrying out Prospero's wishes. The geometric straps and shackles that adorn Sieden's costume at once point to Ariel's enslavement and echo the angular shapes that make up Cairns's island. Moreover, the predominantly green and black colours of her costume and painted skin, along with her positioning in front of a green spotlit rock throughout the aria, again cause Ariel to blend visually into the island environment.

The result is a renewed focus on voice. Through the minimising of bodily presence and expression, the vocal sound alone becomes the source of the magical power: phenomenal, and 'performative' in J. L. Austin's sense, as an utterance that does not simply report an action or event but brings about the action itself.[22] Sieden's voice itself is ethereal, an effect she achieves through creating a certain vocal thinness with relatively minimal

---

[20] Duncan, 'The Operatic Scandal of the Singing Body', p. 294.

[21] The 2012 Met Opera production has been released on DVD: Thomas Adès, *The Tempest*, produced by Robert Lepage and directed by Gary Halvorson (Deutsche Grammophon DVD 0040 073 4932, 2013). There is no commercially available recording of the 2004 Royal Opera production, but the production's 2007 revival was released on CD: *Thomas Adès: The Tempest*, Royal Opera, conducted by Thomas Adès (EMI CD 6952342, 2009).

[22] J. L. Austin, *How to Do Things with Words* (Cambridge, MA: Harvard University Press, 1962), p. 6.

vibrato starting late in the note. It is almost impossible to make out any words; sound is split apart from language in Michel Poizat's 'pure cry'.[23] The overriding ethereality of the quality of the voice links topically to the supernatural, supporting the interpretation that, in this production, the magic lies in vocal resonance.

Towards the end of the aria, Sieden's Ariel climbs up to sit on top of the rock, moving away from the action onstage to look down on Ferdinand as he appears on the shore – almost in the manner of a detached observer, a narrative storyteller who relates the action happening below. This moment of detachment corresponds with a stylised quotation of a traditional bell pattern in descending fifths in the music on 'I can hear them' (referring to the bells) at $\boxed{93}$, breaking the established harmonic pattern and the music's otherwise 'hermetically sealed' frame (see Ex. 10.2b). Here is Abbate's 'discursive distance' in the score, pointing musically from another place towards this aria as phenomenal performance and mirrored by Ariel's momentary shift to onlooking narrator in a passage that is otherwise entirely fixated on the singing voice as all-powerful sonorous force.

This interpretation comes close to that of Halliwell, who, rather than focusing on the 're-gendering' of Shakespeare's male Ariel in the part for female coloratura soprano, states that Adès 'de-genders' the character, as the part's technical demands produce an 'inhuman' force.[24] However, paradoxically, I argue that the humanity of the performer is never more apparent than when the voice is pushed to such extremes – in Sieden's and Luna's cases, in tackling this stratospheric part, and in the precarity of each attack and the demands on the vocal apparatus that produces it. Sieden makes use of actively voicing the consonants at the beginnings of words as a springboard up to this aria's higher pitches, and Luna's voice cracks on the penultimate note – an E_6 – at the end of this punishing aria. As Martha Feldman states, 'most of us sense that some kinds of vocal failure – constituted here as deliberate vulnerability and fragility – when emitted by a virtuoso, can be as necessary to the arsenal of the extraordinary singing voice as lyricism, pyrotechnics, or eloquence, and at least as apt to affect its auditors'.[25]

Indeed, 'Five Fathoms Deep' calls to attention the physicality of performance, something that is brought to the fore in particular in Robert

---

[23] Poizat, *The Angel's Cry*, p. 40.   [24] Halliwell, 'The Sound of Silence', p. 207.

[25] Martha Feldman, 'Voice Gap Crack Break', in *The Voice as Something More: Essays toward Materiality*, ed. by Martha Feldman and Judith T. Zeitlin (Chicago: University of Chicago Press, 2019), pp. 188–208 (p. 188).

Lepage's 2012 production for the Metropolitan Opera, New York. Lepage's scenario, with set by Jasmine Catudal, locates the action in a reconstruction of the La Scala opera house in eighteenth-century Milan. At the beginning of this aria, Luna's Ariel is placed centre-stage and stands on a prompter's box with the auditorium (both that of the set and the Metropolitan Opera House) surrounding her: an explicit performance. She is brightly spotlit and faces the audience directly with open palms, inviting us to concentrate our attention on her body. Luna displays more bodily movement than Sieden in several ways. She incorporates shoulder rolls, fluttering hands and jerks of the head into her performance, giving the impression of some kind of winged creature; this is emphasised by the costume design, which is partly feathered and features embellishments resembling bones, a skull cap and bird-like blue face paint accentuating the eye sockets. Luna's Ariel is more of an active participant in the scene, in contrast with the shifts between disembodied sonority and detached narration of Sieden's Ariel. She uses overt hand gestures to mirror (i.e. 'magically' manipulate) the movement of Ferdinand upstage. Throughout the aria she moves downwards into a crouching position, closer to the action and in direct interaction with Ferdinand; again this is unlike Sieden's motion upwards and away from central focus, eventually blending into the set.

Vocally, there is a greater richness to Luna's performance than to Sieden's, with more of the body in her voice; ethereality is less the aim here. There is slightly more attack on each syllable, and the more extensive, wider vibrato begins immediately after each attack. We hear more of the teeth and the lips in the formation of each word and see the mouth and throat movement producing the vibrato, particularly at the line '[t]hose are pearls that were his eyes' ($\boxed{90}^{+6}$–$\boxed{90}^{+9}$). Luna's rather menacing facial expression, as compared with Sieden's expressive neutrality, suggests a sense of greater agency and intent on the part of Ariel; this Ariel is not a disinterested automaton that simply enacts Prospero's plans.[26] The whole effect is rather sinister as a result of the visceral, more explicit embodiment of this creature's vocal exhortations and the self-conscious nature of this sung performance.

What the two productions have in common is the focus on the sound of voice as power. Prospero's real victory as captor is that he has managed to harness this voice for his own purposes. However, Luna's performance also

---

[26] This observation was made by Edward Venn in '"Mysterious Things": Interpreting Adès's Opera', presentation at 'Be Not Afeard: Language, Music and Cultural Memory in the Operas of Thomas Adès', Senate House: London, 25 April 2017.

leads to the realisation that Ariel's entrapment is *bodily* rather than (or perhaps as well as) through language. In this reading, it becomes important that in the final moments of the opera, Ariel's liberated wordless vocalisations happen offstage, as instructed in the score's stage directions. Now unseen, the focus is entirely on Ariel's vocalise as pure incorporeal sound, an unleashed power that is too unbearable for Caliban in Lepage's production, and he clamps his hands over his ears in terror as the opera ends.

Leticia Sings

In the above discussion I touched on Austin's notion of performativity. However, Duncan notes that 'Austin was lamentably silent on the role of voice' and contends that '[if] it is possible to do something by saying something, then it must be possible to do something by singing something'.[27] This notion of the singing voice that effects change through its very resonance – a performative voice – will be instructive in the following discussion of Leticia's final phenomenal song in *The Exterminating Angel* based on the 1962 surrealist film by Luis Buñuel, which provides the release for the story's characters who inexplicably find themselves trapped in a house after attending a dinner party (Act III, Scene 6, bars 912–75). The moment in which the guests leave the house is the only true plot event in the opera, which otherwise explores what happens when all will to act is lost. In a convincing reworking of Buñuel's ending, Leticia's voice becomes – as the other guests implore her to sing, realising that this alone will allow them to escape – an explicit driver for plot.[28]

The aria is based on a twelfth-century text, *Zionide*, by the Hebrew poet Yehuda Halevi, with its apt depiction of homesickness and longing.[29] Much as in the writing for Ariel, the vocal tessitura is consistently high, with a large proportion of the melody lying between D_5 and F_6 – another virtuosic accomplishment for Luna, for whom the part of Leticia was originally written. As I will argue, it is an example of Adès's tendency to place as much structural and signifying importance on sonority as on so-called primary musical parameters, a consistent feature of his works in general.

---

[27] Duncan, 'The Operatic Scandal of the Singing Body', p. 289.

[28] See also Laura Tunbridge's discussion of this phenomenal song in 'Exterminating the Recording Angel', *Opera Quarterly*, 35/i–ii (2019), 63–76 (p. 72).

[29] Christian Arseni, '"Why do we ever do anything?" Thomas Adès and Tom Cairns Talk about *The Exterminating Angel*', in *The Exterminating Angel* programme booklet, Salzburger Festspiele, 22 July–31 August 2016, pp. 46–57 (p. 55).

Extended solo passages are actually relatively uncommon in *The Exterminating Angel*, and this is perhaps a musical inevitability given the dramatic need to have all fifteen operatic leads onstage almost all of the time. Nevertheless, the moments in which the vocal texture thins out for sustained passages such as solo arias often occur at key junctures structurally or in the story. This is arguably true of the operatic function of the aria in general (where linear time seems to pause when something of significance is explored) but is even more marked in this opera, as such moments stand in such stark contrast with the predominant thickness and complexity of the vocal sonorities.

In addition to this saturation with human voices there is one more important voice to mention: that of the Exterminating Angel. In an interview for the Royal Opera, Adès spoke of the 'element of the supernatural' in Buñuel's film and what he perceives as almost an 'unspoken sound' that seems to occur whenever someone tries and fails to leave the room.[30] In his opera, Adès makes that sound tangible through the use of the timbrally distinctive ondes Martenot. Its theremin-like monophonic sound, notoriously difficult to describe in purely musical terms, has an eerie and supernatural character. Adès employs the ondes Martenot whenever one of the characters fails to leave the room, and thus for him, its distinctive sound becomes 'the voice of this exterminating angel', representing its 'destructive force – an absence'.[31] I do not want to over-read or labour this superficial symbolism; however, it invites a particular mode of thinking about sound, timbre and voice in the opera with compelling interpretative implications for Leticia's final aria.

Isabella van Elferen conceptualises timbre as 'an aesthetic of present absence' owing to its three inherent paradoxes: while timbre often requires highly specific means of production, a 'multitude of factors' can influence its actual sonic appearance; timbre sometimes acts as a sign, but does not point to anything knowable; and timbre, especially vocal timbre, has a clear bodily origin but it does not necessarily have an identity.[32] For van Elferen, 'while timbre is audibly and tangibly present, the experience of this presence indicates the absence of anything concrete, anybody in particular'.[33] In selecting such a distinctive sonority in the ondes Martenot, Adès

---

[30] Royal Opera House, 'Insights into Thomas Adès' *The Exterminating Angel* (the Royal Opera)', 27 March 2017, YouTube, www.youtube.com/watch?v=kMsHvvEi-G8.

[31] Arseni, '"Why do we ever do anything?"', p. 54.

[32] Isabella van Elferen, 'Dark Timbre: The Aesthetics of Tone Colour in Goth Music', *Popular Music*, 37/i (2017), 22–39 (p. 37).

[33] Ibid.

foregrounds this characterising element of timbre to give sound to the absence that becomes a 'destructive force' in this story.

A brief example illustrates this. One of the more extended passages for the ondes Martenot is Blanca's 'Over the Sea' aria in Act II, Scene 1 (bars 1375–425), a phenomenal performance in which Blanca passes the time at the piano. In fact, the passage could properly be thought of as a duet between Blanca's mezzo-soprano and the ondes Martenot, as we (the audience in the opera house, though *not* the characters in the story) hear the ondes Martenot's melodic line closely intertwining with that of Blanca. It is strongly reminiscent of Lucia's 'Il dolce suono' from the 'mad scene' in Gaetano Donizetti's *Lucia di Lammermoor*, in which the soprano duets with the glass harmonica, an instrument with a strikingly similar ethereal sound to that of the ondes Martenot.[34] The symmetry that characterises the lines' harmonic basis in a six-dyad cycle in four rotations (again constructed from 'retrograde-inversion chains') is matched by extensive echoing, inversions and mirroring within and between the lines' melodic patterns.[35] The effect is claustrophobic, and the sense that Blanca's melody is being somewhat stifled is heightened towards the end of the passage as Blanca sings '[b]irds tell me!' for the final time (bars 1416–17), the pitches of which are repeated exactly by the ondes Martenot. This instance of exact repetition triggers a further eight full bars in which Blanca sings 'tell me' ten times on a repeating B♭–A cell, at first echoed by the ondes Martenot and then in unison: it is as if the song has been put on pause, a needle stuck on a record player (a hiatus tellingly broken by Leticia's interjection, perhaps foreshadowing the circumstances of the guests' eventual release). In the complete reduction of Blanca's song to musical repetition and semantic and linguistic redundancy, a manifestation of the loss of will, alongside the foregrounding of the ondes Martenot's pure timbre in its prominent part – its 'aesthetic of present absence' – we hear the voice of the Exterminating Angel that silences Blanca's own.

If the ondes Martenot makes audible the absence of the will to act through timbre's 'present absence', then the inverse is true of the sheer force of Leticia's voice in her final aria: the virtuosity and power of the highest notes affirm her live presence. Feldman's discussion of virtuosity as a human performer 'toying with failure' is again relevant here and, in fact, comes very close to Adès's own view: for Adès, '[v]irtuosity pits the

---

[34] Serendipitously, the guests in *The Exterminating Angel* attended a performance of *Lucia di Lammermoor* immediately before convening at the house for the dinner party.

[35] See Chapter 11.

individual against failure'.[36] The performance of this song is high-stakes both for the character Leticia, who knows that escape from the room is dependent on her voice – the stage directions describe her as looking 'anxious. ... This time she knows she must sing' – and for the soprano who must tackle the song right at the end of this demanding work. In her performance at the Salzburg Festival on 28 July 2016, Luna opted out of some of the higher notes, instead choosing to sing a number of the scored optional pitches at the octave below, for example in the line 'I am the wail of jackals' (bars 942–4). It was also possible to hear audible breaks in her voice on some of the highest notes. Like the character, this soprano 'toys with failure'. None of this, however, detracts from the bodily power and success of the performance; indeed it is emphasised as, along with a lyricism as yet unheard in her part, Feldman's 'vulnerability and fragility' become part of Luna's 'arsenal'. In foregrounding the embodied and powerful, yet vulnerable, voice of Luna-Leticia, the work elevates her sonorous *human presence* and claims victory over the Angel's force of *absence*, the extinction of the will to act, and the guests are free to leave. Adès may have been thinking of *The Exterminating Angel* when he stated that 'virtuosity is our victory over time, over extinction'.[37]

Phenomenal song is used at strategic junctures in Adès's operatic narratives. The heightened attention given to the sounding voice at these pivotal moments has allowed examination of the important signifying role that the material voices of the performers contribute alongside identification of the 'unsung' musical narrators as recounters and drivers of plot. However, as phenomenal song occurs relatively infrequently in Adès's operas, a more extended discussion is required to claim that the key traits identified are representative more broadly of his compositional thinking. I will finish by offering an expanded hearing of the voices – physical, musical and metaphorical – across a larger narrative scale in the non-phenomenal body of *Powder Her Face* with particular reference to Margaret Williams's Channel Four production.

'Won't they be silenced?' Drowning Out the Duchess's Voice

Philip Hensher, the librettist for *Powder Her Face*, has described the piece as structured around two 'silencings', citing Wayne Koestenbaum's

---

[36] Feldman, 'Voice Gap Crack Break', p. 188; Adès and Service, *Full of Noises*, p. 108.
[37] Adès and Service, *Full of Noises*, p. 109.

argument that opera gives voice and sexuality to women ultimately only in order to silence them.[38] The Duchess, whose indiscreet infidelities and high-profile divorce lead to her public humiliation and downfall, is first silenced by sex and then by (metaphorical) death. When the two silencings are recognised as pivotal to the opera's construction and to the plot that traces the Duchess's social downfall, it is clear that the notion of the voice and its metonymical relationship to identity, selfhood and subjectivity is crucial to an understanding of the piece. Indeed, the very first sung lines are bound up entirely with the Duchess's voice and identity. Scene 1 opens in the Duchess's expensive hotel room and immediately introduces us to her 'voice' in the libretto and musically, in a melody that becomes representative of the Duchess, both through the text 'I was beautiful. I was famous. I was young. I was rich, girl' (bars 171–9) and through the music's derivation from the tango overture, with its apt associations with women's seduction, erotic scandal and social mobility.[39] This can be seen in Ex. 10.3a, and I refer to it as the 'Duchess theme'. However, it is not actually the Duchess's character that sings these lines. Her voice is stolen and re-embodied by the hotel Electrician, dressed in the Duchess's fur and heels in a carnivalesque burlesque and mimicking her for the laughing Maid's amusement. This initial encounter with the Duchess's voice and her identifying music in parody is an important way of signalling the significance of voice in the opera, its relationship to identity and, crucially, the threat of its loss. It supplements the non-chronological presentation of events in opening up the gap between the Duchess's self-regard and the perception of her by others, which the rest of the opera proceeds to fill: the scene begins in the operatic present, 1990, before going back and tracing through the Duchess's memories the episodes that led her here.

The many guises in which silence appears in the piece help to condemn Adès and Hensher's Duchess to a somewhat ambiguous place among the tradition of operatic heroines who sing their own tragic undoing. Silence is most fundamentally understood in an aural context as the absence of sound. Nevertheless, Hensher's emphasis on silence as pivotal to the operatic action, and the agency invoked by his term 'silencing', indicate its dramatic function alongside the audible media of text and music.

---

[38] Philip Hensher, 'Sex, Powder and Polaroids', *Guardian*, 29 May 2008, G2 section, p. 23; Wayne Koestenbaum, *The Queen's Throat: Opera, Homosexuality, and the Mystery of Desire* (New York: Poseidon Press, 1993).

[39] Marta E. Savigliano, 'Whiny Ruffians and Rebellious Broads: Tango as a Spectacle of Eroticized Social Tension', *Theatre Journal*, 47/i (1995), 83–104.

Ex. 10.3 The 'Duchess theme' in *Powder Her Face*. (a) Act I, Scene 1, bars 171–9, voice, first instance of the theme as sung by the Electrician; (b) Act II, Scene 8, bars 304–11, voice, final, altered 'Duchess theme'

Moments of performative silence (silencing) play a key narrative role even at times of intense musical and verbal activity: as we have already seen in Scene 1, the suppression of the Duchess's voice – her selfhood – by noisy gossip, dissent, ridicule and judgement is a recurrent dramatic theme. Silence is therefore conceived here as a cross-domain narrative strategy, as aspects of the music, text and drama assume dynamic and shifting roles and responsibilities in conveying the overall narrative trajectory of the social downfall of the Duchess within a dominant patriarchy.

The first of Hensher's structural silencings occurs in Scene 4 (bars 212–328), which is set in 1953 and depicts the Duchess's adulterous seduction of a Waiter who provides room service in her hotel room. The main motivic material centres on a falling B♭–A semitone motive first heard in an altered form in Scene 1, immediately recalling the image of the parodied, ridiculed Duchess that initially invited laughter. To begin with, the vocal activity primarily consists of the Duchess's recitative-like material; its rhythmic inconsistency, frequent repeated pitches and sudden large intervallic leaps, far from the usual tight musical logic, stately rhythms and often sequential patterning of her music thus far, highlight the frenzied demands she makes of the initially submissive Waiter. The entirely hummed aria that follows at bar 262, derived wholly from the falling semitone motive – the so-called fellatio aria – therefore stands in stark contrast with the Duchess's preceding torrent of words in the silencing it effects. It depicts a crucial shift in power that has occurred between bars 212 and 262.

The power relationship between the Duchess and the Waiter is at first conventional according to their respective statuses: she commands and he obeys, despite voicing fears for his job. The shift begins at bar 224, where the stage directions instruct that the 'Waiter stands up, not nervously, but – quite suddenly – sexily'. This is underscored in Williams's production, as it is the first instance in which Dan Norman as the Waiter looks fully at Mary Plazas's Duchess without averting his eyes or blinking in embarrassment. Of the male gaze, Laura Mulvey states that 'in a world ordered by sexual imbalance, pleasure in looking has been split between active/male and passive/female'.[40] In Scene 1, bars 364–9, we heard the Duchess ask, '[w]hen they see me, won't they be silenced? Won't they be struck dumb?' The gap between this mistaken belief of the Duchess and reality is reinforced at this moment in Scene 4. Instead Mulvey's power relationships are now in play: rather than achieving her desired control and admiration when the Duchess secures the male gaze, what she gains is on the newly powerful Waiter's terms as soon as he gazes upon her, transcending the social hierarchy between them.

However, Abbate argues that power relations in opera are conveyed in aural as well as visual terms. The 'overwhelming sound of female operatic voices' therefore poses a contradiction for the operagoer in that '[v]isually, the character singing is the passive object of our gaze. But aurally, she is resonant: her musical speech drowns out everything in range, and we sit as passive objects, battered by that voice. As a voice she slips into the male/ active/subject position.'[41] Here, Abbate outlines Catherine Clément's para-dox of the operatic woman who sings so powerfully and triumphantly of her own demise.[42] Yet Plazas as the Duchess is not permitted this power at this moment. The very nature of the hummed aria denies Plazas's voice of

---

[40] Laura Mulvey, *Visual and Other Pleasures* (Basingstoke: Palgrave Macmillan, 1989), p. 19.

[41] Carolyn Abbate, 'Opera; or, the Envoicing of Women', in *Musicology and Difference: Gender and Sexuality in Music Scholarship*, ed. by Ruth A. Solie (Berkeley and Los Angeles: University of California Press, 1993), pp. 225–58 (p. 254).

[42] Catherine Clément, *Opera, or the Undoing of Women*, trans. by Betsy Wing (Minneapolis: University of Minnesota Press, 1988).

resonance and the ability to form words; the vocal acrobatics she displayed previously are forcefully restricted. Aptly, Steven Connor describes the function of the 'mm' sound in English as 'a kind of silence made audible – the sound of not speaking ... By a logic of approximation, the sound ... also comes to signify the holding back of speech altogether, or *the imposition of silence*.'[43] Thus by failing to overwhelm the audience with the characteristic vocal power of the operatic heroine, and the domination of the aria by the falling semitone motive as a submissive echo of the Waiter's repeated order for her to 'be quiet!', the music works in tandem with the text and the drama to narrate the performative silencing of the Duchess.

Hensher's second silencing, the silencing by metaphorical death in Scene 8, is constructed quite differently, with greater interpretative ambiguity in its structural and signifying layers. The scene returns to the operatic present in 1990. It depicts the eviction of the Duchess from the hotel room she can no longer afford, thus bringing about her ultimate social demise. Extended quotations from Schubert's 'Death and the Maiden' quartet and 'Lullaby', the first of Mussorgsky's *Songs and Dances of Death*, make clear the association between her social downfall and death. Much of the scene is dominated by the Duchess's final aria (bars 87–318), which is, by turns, a nostalgic account of the past and an expression of desperate dread of the future. She eventually begins to slip in and out of reality as she calls to her absent nursemaid and realises that she has nothing and no one left, pleading with the Hotel Manager (who enters at bar 273) for his pity. There is a surprising tenderness in the libretto of this aria, perhaps prompting feelings of sympathy towards the Duchess in a way that the earlier scenes avoid.

The potentially redemptive quality of the aria text is heightened by the musical surface: the Duchess's melody reaches its registral and dynamic climax at bar 287 as she sings '[h]old me', arriving at a sustained B_5. At this point, Plazas is *finally* allowed to project the 'overtly female and musical force' of her voice, to quote Abbate, that was denied in Scene 4; this coincides with the libretto, which rather conventionally reveals aspects of the Duchess's humanity before the end.[44] Plazas's vocal performance is warmly husky in its lower registers, with breathy, sobbing interjections and a richness even in the highest notes, a surfeit of emotional 'sound-signifiers' that clearly contrast with the cold cynicism of the opera's coloratura role.

[43] Steven Connor, *Beyond Words: Sobs, Hums, Stutter and Other Vocalizations* (London: Reaktion, 2014), p. 73 (emphasis added).
[44] Abbate, 'Opera; or the Envoicing of Women', p. 232.

In this way, the Duchess begins to join the tradition of operatic women who, though marginalised, scandalised and punished by the system, retain their expressive power through their singing voice. But even at this moment, the Duchess has already been silenced. The musical surface leading to this point is repeatedly undercut thematically and harmonically, revealing that the Duchess's voice as identity has already been subdued. This occurs primarily through the recollection of earlier musical material and its associations, as will be outlined below.

Throughout the opera, the key of B flat minor is used at pivotal moments relating to the suppression or judgement of the Duchess by a male authority: for example, at the end of Scene 2 as the Duke arrives to meet the Duchess while they are courting, leading seamlessly into a flash-forward of their ill-fated marriage, and at the end of Scene 5 when the Duke gleefully finds an explicit photograph of the Duchess committing adultery. The entrance of the highly misogynistic Judge who performs the court trial in Scene 6 is also accompanied by a sustained B♭ pedal. Through cumulative association, B flat minor can be interpreted as representing not only the Duchess's downfall, but also the role of patriarchy and male judgement in the acceleration of her downfall. Eventually, B flat minor appears in the Duchess's own lines in the final aria as she calls for her long-gone nurse and realises that the only people who were ever good to her were paid for it. Perhaps most significantly, at bar 55 the Duchess attempts to regain control and status with the words '[y]ou'll have to come back. I haven't – I – I – I need – I need to have my things packed'. However, her defiant statements are undercut, and her inevitable undoing betrayed, not only by the stammer in the soprano's physical voice, but also by the B flat minor of the persecuting male voices that silence her own.

In bars 98–103 the Duchess reflects that she has probably had too many servants in her life to count. A re-use of motivic material, here from the Waitress's Scene 3 'Fancy' aria, highlights the theme of servitude in the Duchess's words and recalls the contrast in the lifestyles of the rich upper classes and the servants, of which the Waitress sings bitterly. However, the Waitress's material in the earlier scene is strikingly characterised by the laughter that punctuates it in a repeated three-note pattern. This is not the natural laugh of the Maid in Scene 1, but is ironic and bitter in its high stylisation – an expression of felt injustice. In the Duchess's assimilation of the Waitress's melody into her own in Scene 8 this stylised laughter motive is omitted, revealing that servants such as the Waitress no longer have the need to laugh ironically. The social downfall of the Duchess causes the hierarchy to overturn within this opera's frame, and the Waitress is permitted to speak of a small triumph over aristocracy, even with the Duchess's own physical voice.

At the same time, the Duchess's own musical signifiers begin to disappear. Her rendition of her signature popular song from Scene 2 is cut short at bar 181 at the line '[t]here's nothing in all the world', which she aptly repeats. In addition, the final time we hear the 'Duchess theme' realised in full, in bar 304 (see Ex. 10.3b), it seems to have turned a full circle to unconscious self-parody, which links it with the Electrician's original parodic statement in Scene 1: the Duchess becomes a caricature of herself in her attempt to assault the Hotel Manager, which is underscored by sniggering trombone slurs, now perhaps provoking a mixture of pity, laughter and distaste. In this dramatic context, it is hard to reconcile this theme with the beautiful, rich Duchess of her heyday for whom we are supposed to understand it once stood. Despite the emotional power of the physical voice of Plazas's Duchess throughout much of this scene, the voice that metaphorically stands for her subjectivity has become all but unrecognisable. The redemptive text, which encourages us to feel sympathy for the Duchess even at this late stage, is set against her almost farcical assault on the Hotel Manager; her melody, while resonant and powerful, is 'drowned out' by the musical material of those who ridicule and judge her.

As a result, the long tradition of the operatic heroine who sings of her own undoing is playfully invoked and, at the same time, cruelly subverted in the character of the Duchess and the operatic presentation of the narrative of her demise. The unlikeability of the Duchess and the aligning of our loyalties with her mistreated servants make it difficult for us to pity the Duchess completely for her downfall. Moreover, the vocal power with which operatic sopranos overwhelm us and capture our emotions is denied to the Duchess in the music, text and drama in a variety of ways. The opera exposes the misogynistic tradition of killing off operatic women for the perceived threat of their sexuality, through forcibly silencing the Duchess at these two pivotal moments. Despite the silence, the opera leaves us with a richer picture of what Adès's compositional voice has to say.

* * *

At the beginning of this chapter I stated that by examining vocality it would be possible to access and understand compositional traits in the surfaces and structures of Adès's operas. Some of the predominant techniques identified in the above analyses include opening up spaces for performers' agency; exploiting tensions between words, music and body for semantic purposes; and placing equal structural and signifying importance on sonority as primary musical parameters. From this list we can infer the consistency with which Adès thinks of his music in material terms. His own words support this view: '[t]o me there's no distinction between colour and timbre and pitches. You can't just analyse something based on the pitches alone ... You must say, :"This E flat at this pitch on the horn", you must understand through the colour as well, or else it's meaningless.'[45] But more than this, it has been possible to discern the integral role that the sonorous material voice plays in the discursive presentation of the operatic narratives, alongside musical and linguistic acts of narration. By taking a multifaceted theoretical approach to hearing voices in Adès's operas I hope to have provided a deeper understanding of those works, as well as highlighting the interpretative potential of recognising voice's complex narrative roles in opera more broadly.

[45] Adès and Service, *Full of Noises*, p. 156.

11 | The RICH Logic of Adès's *The Exterminating Angel* and *The Tempest*

JOHN ROEDER

Thomas Adès's highly crafted operas can be appreciated from many different perspectives. I enjoy their theatrical virtuosity, and I am curious about how scholars and audiences will assess their place in opera history. As a theorist of contemporary composition, however, I feel drawn to investigate how their musical materials are organised to direct time. For my enquiries I take licence from a tweet which the composer posted around the time he completed *The Exterminating Angel*:

> On all my scores from now on
> [a photograph of a sign showing a phone number for requesting building maintenance]
> WE ALL WANT *this structure to be* PERFECT!
> *'Please let us know about anything that isn't right.'*[1]

What should we understand him to mean by 'structure', what makes a structure 'perfect', and what does it have to do with the temporal flow of his music? In an interview with Christian Arseni for the Salzburg premiere of *The Exterminating Angel*, the composer invokes scientific metaphors:

At first one is dealing with individual notes, or two notes. It's rather like watching an embryo develop, the difference being that you might understand the DNA of this tiny cell later on and see how it relates to everything else. Rather the larger structure eventually develops from trying to link these cells together. My image of music as a natural process, as a living, growing organism, is a fairly precise analogy of an opera and the way in which it is created.[2]

In an earlier conversation with Tom Service, he attributes agency to these 'tiny cells':

You must imagine that the fourth is an object, like a single note. It's an atom that is quivering, and it wants to split. And depending on the way that is done, something

---

[1] @Thomas_ades, 1 February 2015.

[2] Christian Arseni, "'Why do we ever do anything?' Thomas Adès and Tom Cairns Talk about *The Exterminating Angel*', in *The Exterminating Angel* programme booklet, Salzburger Festspiele, 22 July–31 August 2016, pp. 46–57 (p. 46).

is generated. It can become a melody ... if somebody sings it, as Prospero does in *The Tempest*. There are infinite ways it can go ...

[I]f you ... stack fourth upon fourth, you wind up with total entropy, with all twelve notes of the chromatic scale as a sort of block. So to make the thing quiver and spring to life, I would want to move the upper [note of the fourth] upwards by a semitone ... I start with the interval of a fourth in a lot of pieces, I've been drawn to that a lot. *Asyla*, *Living Toys*, *The Tempest*, *Powder Her Face* all start with a fourth of some kind.[3]

He draws a sharp distinction between these generative processes and operatic music which proceeds by the accretion of leitmotivs, stating that '[S]o much of *Parsifal* is dramatically absurd ... I don't find Wagner's an organic, necessary art. Wagner's music is fungal ... His material doesn't grow symphonically – it doesn't grow through a musical logic – it grows parasitically.'[4]

In Adès's second opera, *The Tempest*, I perceive the kind of logical, generative, organic process he describes. Example 11.1 represents it in a series of steps. It begins in Ex. 11.1a with a dyad, two simultaneous pitches, a perfect fifth apart. Imagine, in the composer's terms, that this dyad is an 'atom' which is 'quivering', ready to 'split'. According to what principle shall it change? If all of the 'infinite ways' were equally possible, no structure could emerge. Instead, let us admit only minimal displacement, using the two intervals Adès mentions: one of the atom's pitches takes one step down the chromatic scale, and the other pitch takes one step down the circle of perfect fourths. The resulting dyad forms a new interval, a minor third. I will refer to this particular voice leading of a perfect fifth to a minor third as α. It is represented by the vector diagram below the stave, in which the integer labels on the arrows denote pitch-class intervals measured in semitones.[5] To clarify the structure visually,

---

[3] Thomas Adès and Tom Service, *Thomas Adès: Full of Noises – Conversations with Tom Service*, paperback ed. (London: Faber and Faber, 2018), p. 33.

[4] Ibid., p. 15. For a fuller consideration of the composer's attitudes about leitmotivs, see Scott Lee, 'Musical Signification in Thomas Adès's *The Tempest*' (unpublished PhD dissertation, Duke University, 2018), pp. 1–10.

[5] In the text, when referring informally to intervals, I will follow the composer in using familiar names such as 'perfect fourth' and 'minor third'. In the examples, however, intervals are specified with integers that denote the number of chromatic steps they span. So a perfect fourth is represented with a '5' on the examples, meaning five semitones, and a minor third with a '3'. In the chromatic pitch-class world, the interval from one note to another can be expressed as either a positive or negative integer (for example, C to G could be either 7 or −5); I use negative integers when I want to associate the interval with descending pitch. Also, the same integer may represent two different but 'enharmonically equivalent' diatonic intervals. For example, in Ex. 11.1a the intervals from B to F♯ and from D♯ to B♭ are both labelled as '−5', and accordingly I will refer to both as a 'perfect fourth' despite notating the latter as an augmented third.

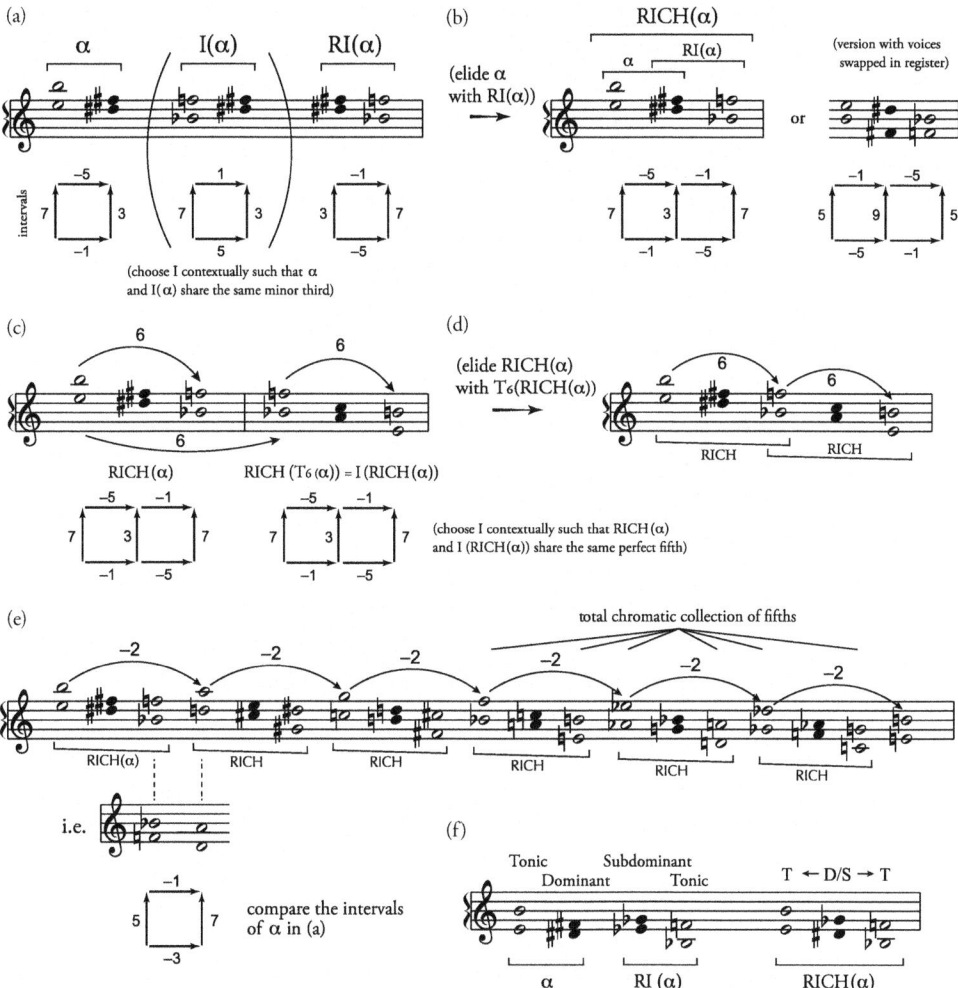

Ex. 11.1 *The Tempest*, retrograde-inversion (RI) chains of dyads, option 1. (a) α: voice leading and transformations; (b) RICH(α); (c) RI-chains of RICH(α)s; (d) repeated RI-chaining produces a four-dyad cycle; (e) RICH(α) transposed repeatedly by a whole tone forms an eighteen-dyad cycle; (f) tonal-functional allusions

perfect fifths are represented on the stave with open noteheads and minor thirds with solid noteheads.

Now the pitches of the minor third 'quiver', as it were. A 'logical' way for them to change, shown on the right side of the stave in Ex 11.1a, would be by the same minimal paths which the pitches of the initial perfect fifth followed, but with the intervals exchanged: the pitch that was changed to by a semitone changes downwards by a fourth, and the pitch that was changed to by a fourth changes downwards by a semitone. The resulting pitches form a perfect fifth. This succession from minor third to perfect fifth is a retrograde inversion (RI) of α, as demonstrated by the chord pairs labelled I(α) and RI(α).

Now, since RI(α) begins with the minor third which ends α, we may elide the dyad pairs as shown in Ex. 11.1b. The resulting series of three dyads (perfect fifth–minor third–perfect fifth) is called the retrograde inversion chain of α, or RICH(α) for short. This RICH is a contextual operation, meaning that we have chosen an inversional centre which will preserve the minor third for these specific pitches.[6] The rightmost portion of Ex. 11.1b shows that a related succession can be derived from α by exchanging its two voices in register, making the dyad succession perfect fourth–major sixth–perfect fourth. For the sake of analytical comparisons, though, I will consistently represent α as the version with perfect fifths, recognising that equivalent perfect-fourth versions exist.[7]

Example 11.1c shows that the two fifths which begin and end RICH(α) are a tritone apart. It would be 'logical' to extend this succession by using the same principle of motion, starting from the second fifth, Bb-F: change each voice alternately downwards by a semitone and a perfect fourth, resulting in another RI-chain which is a tritone transposition (and also an inversion) of the first. We can then elide the two chains to yield the dyad succession shown in Ex. 11.1d. The concluding perfect fifth, E-B, is the same as the first fifth in α; we have achieved closure by circling back to the beginning. As elegant as this procedure may be, however, it does not offer much harmonic variety: its four dyads hardly suffice to make a phrase, much less an opera.

So instead of eliding RI-chains, let us transpose the entire RICH(α) succession minimally by one step down the whole-tone scale, as shown in Ex. 11.1e. The immediate succession of perfect fifths in this progression can be rationalised as a voice-leading process which involves the same intervals as α. Repeating the whole-tone transposition five more times returns the succession to the first fifth of the sequence, achieving closure.

---

[6] RICH was first explored systematically by David Lewin in *Generalized Music Intervals and Transformations* (New Haven, CT: Yale University Press, 1987), pp. 180–8. See also Jonathan Kochavi, 'Some Structural Features of Contextually-Defined Inversional Operators', *Journal of Music Theory*, 42/ii (1998), 307–20. Ironically, considering Adès's low opinion of Wagner, some of Lewin's most striking examples are from *Parsifal* and the *Ring* cycle.

[7] Adès has said, 'I hear a fourth as an inverted fifth; the top note is the bass.' Adès and Service, *Full of Noises*, p. 33.

I will refer to this succession of eighteen dyads as the 'α cycle'.[8] It is much better suited to extended composition but still elegant. Its six minor thirds together comprise all twelve notes of the chromatic scale, and the total chromatic is also created twice by the six perfect fifths in each half of the cycle.

To a listener primed by Western tonality these dyads and their voice leading may seem at once familiar and disorienting, as suggested by the annotations on Ex. 11.1f. If one takes the perfect fifths to define tonal centres, the α succession sounds like a tonic–dominant opening progression, and its RI alludes to a plagal cadence. When linked enharmonically into RICH(α), though, their succession precipitously traverses two keys a tritone apart, a separation traditionally conceived as quite distant.[9]

This process generates the dyad successions that assert themselves immediately in *The Tempest*. The first scene's depiction of a shipwreck begins, as shown in Ex. 11.2a, with the perfect fifth E-B. Following the transformations of Ex. 11.1b, a minor third, D♯-F♯, follows that fifth (bar 2), which is then replaced by another, B♭-F (bar 5), completing an RI-chain. Then another perfect fifth, D-A (bar 6), appears, with a different orchestral colour, and when that changes to the minor third C♯-E we realise that the initial RICH (α) is being transposed downwards by a whole tone. But first the low brasses begin to roil. Rapidly they blare pairs of quavers in two streams which replay the opening dyad chain in reverse order, then transpose that retrograde repeatedly upwards by whole tone. The high, slowly descending chain moves through its minor third C♯-E (bar 7) to meet this low, quickly ascending sequence on an A♭-E♭ fifth, then dissolves.

Now differently paced waves of RI-chains arise simultaneously. In the first set, shown on the lower two staves of Ex. 11.2b, a rapid sequence of them ascends by whole tone isorhythmically in alternating quavers and crotchets, while another version of the same sequence ascends by whole tone in minims. Their concurrence creates a mensuration canon. When the two streams eventually coincide on D-A, the faster one reverses the

---

[8] The pervasive recurring dyads in *The Tempest* have been observed by Hélène Cao, *Thomas Adès le voyageur: devenir compositeur, être musicien* (Paris: MF Éditions, 2007) and Emma Gallon, 'Narrativities in the Music of Thomas Adès' (unpublished PhD dissertation, Lancaster University, 2011). Lee, 'Musical Signification', p. 11, arranges all eighteen dyads into a cycle without focusing on the underlying generative process of RI-chaining that I explore here.

[9] Adès, in Adès and Service, *Full of Noises*, p. 163, characterises such progressions as 'geometric' (referring to their origin in voice-leading patterns) yet still exerting a harmonic logic. See Felix Wörner, 'Tonality as "Irrationally Functional Harmony": Thomas Adès's Piano Quintet', in *Tonality since 1950*, ed. by Felix Wörner, Ullrich Scheideler and Philip Rupprecht (Stuttgart: Franz Steiner Verlag, 2017), pp. 295–311.

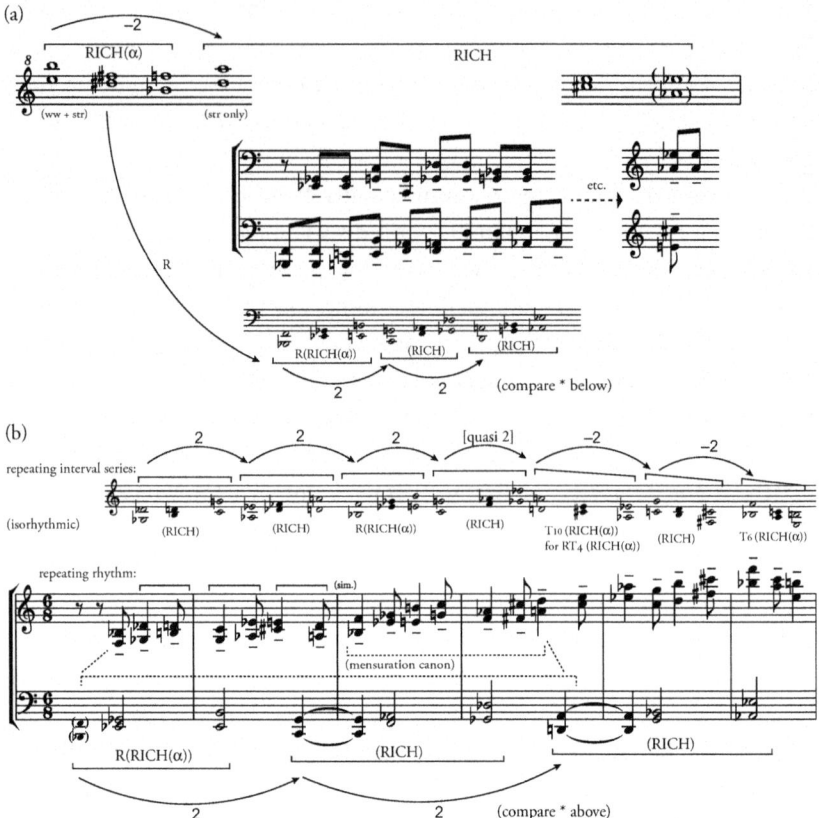

Ex. 11.2 *The Tempest*, RI-chaining directs the dyads at the opening. (a) Summary of Act I, Scene 1, bars 1–8; (b) concurrent polyrhythmic streams of RI-chains in Act I, Scene 1, bars 11–16

direction of its pattern but not its contour, mimicking the way in which two swells meeting in the ocean appear to bounce off each other. Much of the remainder of the prologue proceeds similarly, culminating in the castaways singing the opening progression.

Throughout the first act the dyads frequently recur in their α-cycle patterns. But they also appear in different arrangements. These can best be understood by focussing not on the entities themselves, but on the processes by which they change. Such processes operate in Adès's other music, and the 'transformational attitude' needed to appreciate them comports well with the composer's dynamic conception of how his 'cells' and 'atoms' develop.[10]

---

[10] John Roeder, 'Co-operating Continuities in the Music of Thomas Adès', *Music Analysis*, 25/i–ii (2006), 121–54; John Roeder, 'A Transformational Space Structuring the Counterpoint in

For instance, RICH(α) progressions structure the scene which follows. Miranda, harrowed by the castaways' moans, beseeches her father to explain the cause of the storm. Her melody derives, as shown on the left half of Online Ex. 11.1, from the flickering of a three-voice 'aligned-cycle' counterpoint which also appears in Adès's near-contemporaneous compositions.[11] The lower voice ascends by four semitones, the middle voice by three and the upper voice by two. The resulting chords change from C major through G major to a more dissonant chord which will soon become the catch-sound of Ariel.[12] After dwelling on this initial progression, Miranda's music transforms into a similar counterpoint, shown on the right side of the example, with the same intervals 2, 3 and 4 redistributed to middle, bottom and top voices respectively.[13] With the tempest's RI-chains still resounding in memory, the listener may notice that both chord progressions embed α dyad successions. Miranda's words associate these successions with Prospero and with the powers that capsized his usurping brother's ship.

Prospero avoids answering her pleas directly, but nevertheless makes it quite clear whose powers they are. Doubled by emphatic *sforzandi* in the orchestra, he declaims the entire α cycle, as shown in Ex. 11.3. Its dyads, which are abstracted harmonically below the score, rarely sound as simultaneities; rather, they interlock melodically as shown by the beamed pitches above the score. Such obsession manifests Prospero's narcissistically vengeful 'logic': we now understand that he commands the forces that drove the storm dyads. (Not one to miss driving a point home, he repeats the whole cycle again.) In retrospect, the unchained α dyads in Miranda's music

---

Adès's "Auf dem Wasser zu singen'", *Music Theory Online*, 15/i (2008), https://mtosmt.org/ issues/mto.09.15.1/mto.09.15.1.roeder_space.php; and John Roeder, 'Transformation in Posttonal Music', *Oxford Handbooks Online*, 4 August 2014, www.oxfordhandbooks.com/view/10 .1093/oxfordhb/9780199935321.001.0001/oxfordhb-9780199935321-e-4; Daniel Fox, 'Multiple Time Scales in Adès's *Rings*', *Perspectives of New Music*, 52/i (2014), 28–56. On the aesthetics of adopting a 'transformational attitude', see Lewin, *Generalized Musical Intervals*, pp. 158–9.

[11] Philip Stoecker, 'Aligned-Cycle Spaces', *Journal of Music Theory*, 60/ii (2016), 181–212. Adès mentions the progression in Adès and Service, *Full of Noises*, p. 28.

[12] Ariel's chord, containing a semitone, a tritone and a perfect fourth, belongs to the same type (016) as the musical notes spelled by the composer's name – A, D and Es (= E♭) – which Raúl sings in *The Exterminating Angel* when he implores Blanca to play something 'by Adès' (Act I, bars 655–8). This recurring sonority in Adès's music might therefore be regarded as his signature, like Bach's musical cryptogram B♭–A–C–H (= B♮).

[13] Philip Stoecker, 'Voice-Leading Waves in *The Tempest*', presentation at 'Be Not Afeard: Language, Music and Cultural Memory in the Operas of Thomas Adès', Senate House, London, 24 April 2017.

Ex. 11.3 *The Tempest*, Act I, Scene 2, 20, Prospero lays out the complete α cycle

might be understood to suggest that she shares some of her father's attributes but not his controlling character.

As Prospero recounts his betrayal, the α cycles yield to seemingly different music, yet his transformational logic remains in force. For instance, one of his couplets, shown in Online Ex. 11.2, sequences a four-interval motive which alternates descending semitones and descending fifths. Such dual-interval cycles appear elsewhere in Adès's oeuvre, as for instance in the second movement of *Asyla* and in the Piano Quintet, but four features of this passage make it appropriate specifically for the opening of *The Tempest*. Its intervals are the same as those in α. Their alternation constitutes an RI-chain of trichords, as demonstrated below the main stave. The motive is sequenced in the same way as RICH(α) was, by whole tone. And the passage is isorhythmic, with its repeating interval series set to a repeating rhythm of a different length, as were the faster-moving waves during the opening storm (Ex. 11.2b). Thus even without a clear α cycle, Prospero's music proceeds according to his established modus operandi.

After a scene with Ariel, the RICH(α)s reappear and resume sequencing down by whole tone, as shown at the beginning of Ex. 11.4a. At this point

Ex. 11.4 *The Tempest*, Act I, other RI-chains. (a) Caliban RI-chains a different pair of dyads, β, 60; (b) concurrent canonic RICH(β) streams, 62

the listener may have learned the α cycle well enough to anticipate how it will continue once begun, and the composer plays with this expectation. Specifically, a B-F♯ fifth, boxed in the example, is attained via the cycle, so one would expect either an E♭-B♭ fifth or an A♯-C♯ minor third to follow. Instead, a D-F minor third appears, coinciding with the abrupt entrance of Caliban. This warping of the established pattern not only provides a corresponding aural surprise, but may also be heard to depict his recalcitrance. The example labels this new dyad succession as β and shows how it is composed from one of the 'infinite' other voice-leading paths available from the perfect fifth: one of the pitches changes by an ascending minor third rather than by a descending perfect fourth. Nevertheless, like α, β undergoes RI-chaining, moving through the D-F to Db-Ab. A transposition of the new chain downward by a major third establishes it as a new pattern. Then the chain sequences in a special way which was not available for α: because its fifths are a whole tone apart (rather than a tritone; compare Ex. 11.1d), several successive whole-tone transpositions of itself can be elided together, and so that transposition seems more consistent with the material than it does in the α chain. In a passage a little later in the scene, shown in Ex. 11.4b, as Caliban demands to know how Prospero wrecked the ship, he sings to a series of chords which can be analysed as a canon of RICH(β) sequences, like the RICH(α) canons during the Scene 1 tempest (Ex. 11.2b). The allusion is clinched not by a literal reprise of the storm music, as might occur in a leitmotivic opera, but by a recurring manifestation of the same generative principles.

These are a few examples of how the transformational process of RI-chaining, consistent with the composer's conceptions, directs music in the first act of *The Tempest*. It manifests plainly as the α cycle of dyads, but it also drives different textures – canons, single lines with interlocking dyads and isorhythm – and animates different cycles as well: in Miranda's petition and Prospero's cursing of Naples we hear motives which are not RI-chains of α or β, but which allude to them by embedding α or by chaining trichords which contain the voice-leading intervals of α. I do not claim that RICH generates the entire work; this is only Act I, when we are being introduced to the characters. But its prominence suggests that we should listen for similarly 'logical structures' in Adès's third opera, *The Exterminating Angel*. In the spirit of its storyline, in which guests enter the same house twice, let us revisit the theory of RICH dyad cycles with one small change which makes a big difference.

In the passage shown in Ex. 11.5a, we begin afresh with a perfect fifth. Its notes 'quiver', ready to 'split'. Let us choose a slightly different change from that in *The Tempest*, but still minimal: as before, one pitch in the atom takes one step down the chromatic scale, but the other pitch takes one step down the whole-tone scale (instead of the circle of fourths) such that the resulting dyad forms a tritone (instead of a minor third). (Fifths are represented with open noteheads and tritones with solid noteheads.) I will refer to this voice leading as χ. As with α, I will consistently represent χ with perfect fifths, recognising that equivalent perfect-fourth versions can be obtained by exchanging the voices' registral positions.

Now the pitches of the tritone 'quiver', as it were. A 'logical' way for them to change, shown on the right side of Ex. 11.5a, would be by the same minimal paths which the pitches of the initial perfect fifth followed, but

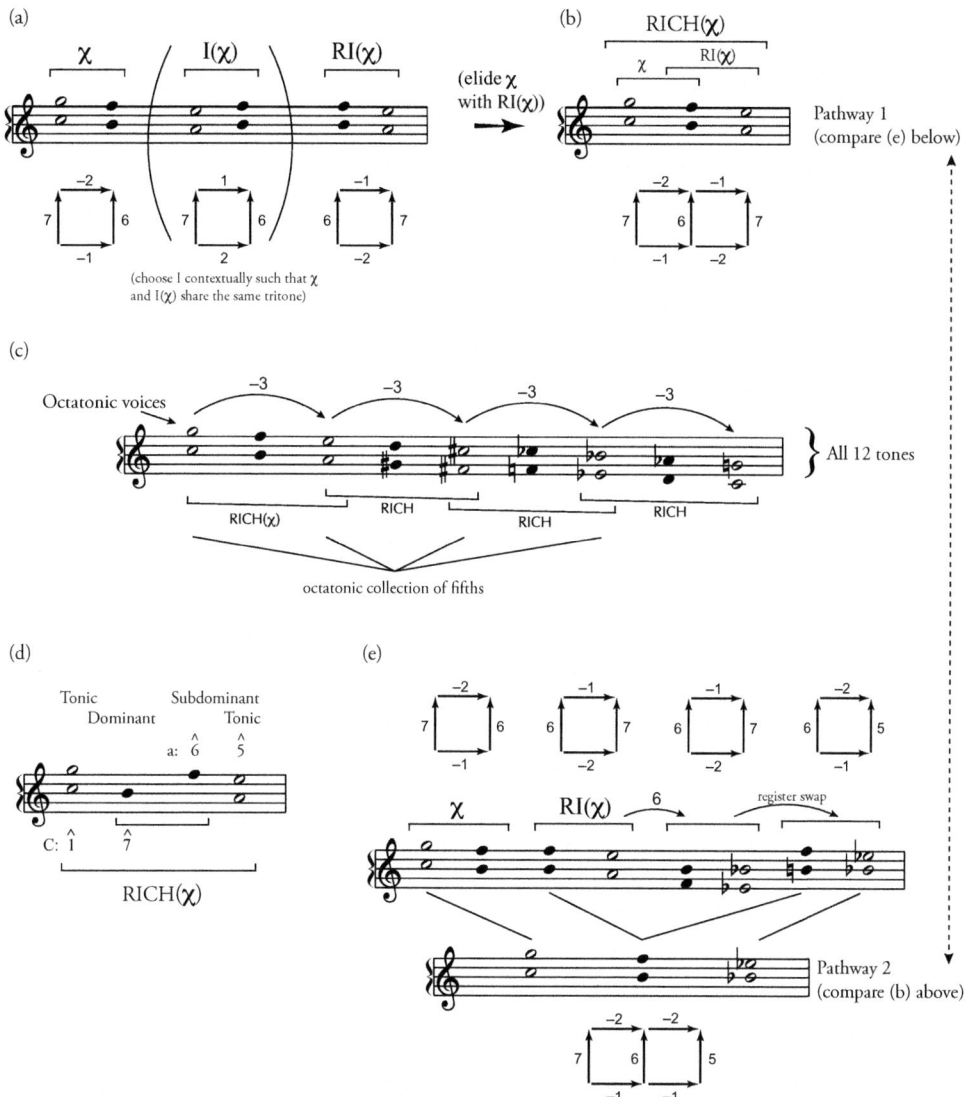

Ex. 11.5 RI-chains of dyads, option 2, as in *The Exterminating Angel*. (a) χ: voice leading and transformations; (b) RICH(χ); (c) repeated RI-chaining produces an eight-dyad cycle; (d) tonal-functional allusions; (e) a special feature of χ opens up multiple pathways

with intervals exchanged: the pitch that was changed to by a semitone changes downwards by a whole tone, and the pitch that was changed to by a whole tone changes downwards by a semitone. The resulting pitches form a perfect fifth. This succession from tritone to perfect fifth is an RI of χ, and by eliding it with the original χ, as shown in Ex. 11.5b, we obtain an RI-chain of χ, or RICH(χ) for short.

Example 11.5c shows that the perfect fifths that begin and end RICH(χ) are a minor third apart. It would be 'logical' to extend this succession, starting from the second fifth, by changing each voice alternately by descending semitone and whole tone, producing another RI-chain. Repeating the same procedure twice more leads to closure on the same fifth that began the sequence, after a variegated succession of eight dyads that I will call the χ cycle. It is shorter than the α cycle of *The Tempest* but more elegant: each voice is an octatonic scale (alternating whole tones and semitones); the perfect fifths taken together form an octatonic scale; and the tritones together form the diminished seventh chord which is the complement of that scale. The atonal symmetry of this structure is enlivened by a harmonic-functional hearing it affords, which is sketched in Ex. 11.5d. The B may be taken as part of the dominant to the C tonic implied by the C-G fifth. When the B-F tritone changes to A-E, though, the F evokes plagal root motion in A minor. So, in concert with the motivic voice-leading process I have described, RICH(χ) links keys a minor third apart by eliding dominant and subdominant functions.

Because the second interval in χ is a tritone, it is possible to vary this dyad succession in an 'organic' way. As we first contemplated it, RICH(χ) moves C-G to A-E through the tritone B-F. Example 11.5e shows that the tritone transposition of RI(χ) begins on the same tritone, B-F, with the voices exchanged in register, and that the χ progression moves this tritone to the fifth Eb-Bb. Eliding the tritone in this latter progression with the tritone in χ opens up a second pathway from C-G, to Eb-Bb, in addition to the original pathway to A-E. This gives more flexibility to the χ cycle in comparison to the α chain, which offered only one route that could be travelled backwards or forwards. The voice leading in this alternative pathway pits repeated whole tones in one voice against repeated semitones in another, a process which Edward Venn has found in passages of *The Exterminating Angel* that do not explicitly state the χ cycle, such as the church-bell prelude and the guests' entrance music.[14]

Unlike in *The Tempest*, the χ cycle does not manifest itself immediately at the beginning of *The Exterminating Angel*. Rather, it emerges gradually along with dramatic manifestations of a mysterious power that saps the protagonists' will. This association first becomes explicit at two moments

[14] Edward Venn, 'Thomas Adès's *The Exterminating Angel*', *Tempo*, 71/280 (2017), 21–46 (pp. 42–4).

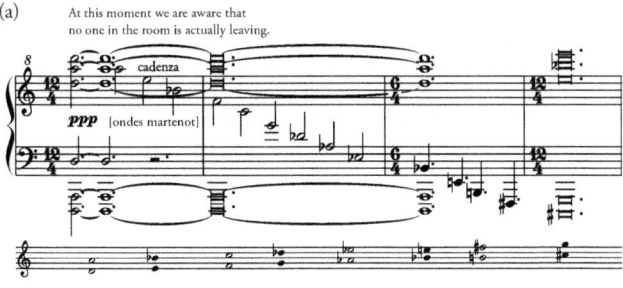

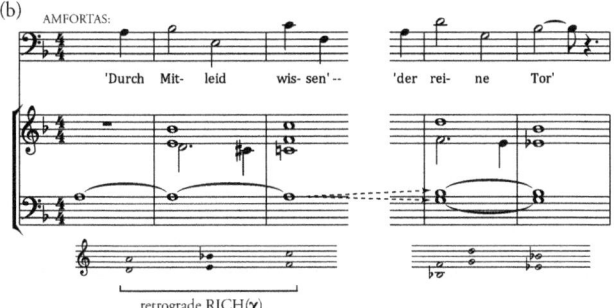

Ex. 11.6 *The Exterminating Angel*, early manifestations of the complete χ cycle. (a) Act I, Scene 6, bars 726–9; (b) RICH(χ) in a principal leitmotiv of Wagner's *Parsifal*, Act I, bars 319–26

during a crucial juncture in Act I, Scene 6. Just before the first passage, shown in Online Ex. 11.3, the operatic soprano Leticia has ignored the guests' demands for her to sing, a decision she will eventually need to reverse in order for them to escape the house. The characters have begun to shed the decorum appropriate to their social stations. During one especially awkward exchange of dialogue, the string section engages in a restless flowing texture which comes into focus at bar 704. The reduction below the score shows that its music plainly presents an ascending version of the complete eight-dyad cycle built from the RI-chains of χ. The stage directions at that moment give the first indication of the 'spell' that is beginning to tighten the guests in its grip. In a subsequent passage, shown in Ex. 11.6a, the first guest seeks to leave but is delayed. The orchestral instruments wedge out to registral extremes and then freeze on a quiet D-A fifth. Into this registral and temporal void enters the eerie ondes Martenot playing a 'cadenza' which runs through the entire ascending χ cycle as a melodic line of descending fourths and tritones. The stage directions specify that 'at this moment we are aware that no one in the room is actually leaving'.

In light of the composer's disparagement of Wagner's music and *Parsifal* in particular, it is striking how closely RICH(χ) resembles one of the principal leitmotivs of that opera. Ex 11.6b shows how the beginning of the '*reine Tor*' motive can be heard as an RI-chain connecting the fifths D-A and F-C by way of the tritone E-B♭. The musical allusion invites appreciation of a similarity between the operas' scenarios: like the angel's guests, the despairing knights of the Grail yearn for deliverance, be it even death, from their magical incapacitation. But even if one dismisses these references as unintentional or ironic, they offer insight into Adès's compositional attitude cited above. Like a leitmotiv, the χ cycle pervades *The Exterminating Angel*; Alex Ross and Edward Venn have noted several instances of its dyads.[15] What seems to interest the composer, though, is the underlying 'logic' by which they develop and change, not simply the entities themselves. Merely to catalogue their instances would be like gathering mushrooms which pop up 'parasitically' whenever the weather turns gloomy. Rather, I will show that RI-chaining provides an 'organic' principle for the unfolding of the dyads, as well as other materials, by considering passages which manifest its structuring force.[16] Our survey of the various ways in which RICH was deployed in *The Tempest* will help us to recognise it in *Angel*.

We saw in Exs. 11.5c and e that the RICH(χ) cycle has a special flexibility related to its serial structure: from a single tritone, B-F, we can move by χ or the retrograde of χ to every one of the four perfect fifths in the cycle. Example 11.5d also showed abstractly how χ affords sensations of harmonic-tonal progression. The first extended passage based on the χ cycle, excerpted in Ex. 11.7, exploits both of these structuring tendencies. It is a duet, labelled 'Berceuse' in the score, between the young lovers Eduardo and Beatriz. Already the audience may have intuited that they are prime targets for angelic extermination: they were not introduced during the guests' entrance (bars 112–13), and when they joined in the chorus importuning Leticia to perform, they proclaimed, 'we will not leave this house', without adding 'until she sings' as the other guests did (bars 672–5). Having already been introduced to the complete χ cycle (by the passages

---

[15] Alex Ross, 'An Explosive Opera of "The Exterminating Angel"', *New Yorker*, 22 August 2016, www.newyorker.com/magazine/2016/08/22/thomas-ades-the-exterminating-angel (para. 6 of 11). Venn, 'Thomas Adès's *The Exterminating Angel*', pp. 43–4, calls the perfect fifth–tritone alternation 'motif *x*'.

[16] On musical transformations as 'forces' that impel changes of musical objects, see David Lewin, 'Transformational Techniques in Atonal and Other Music Theories', *Perspectives of New Music*, 21/i–ii (1982–3), 312–71.

Ex. 11.7 *The Exterminating Angel*, Act I, Scene 8, Berceuse, χ-generated tonality. (a) Bars 858–73; (b) bars 890–7

quoted in Ex. 11.6), we can easily perceive it here. The analysis noted under Ex. 11.7a highlights the serial structure of the beginning of the number: it shows how the tritone B-F repeatedly initiates two-bar groups and changes in turn to each of the χ-cycle fifths built on E♭, C, A and F♯, using the alternative pathways afforded by the special property of χ. The lovers' melodies are mostly octatonic, tracing the voice leading of χ, and they often compose out the other tritone A♭-D in the χ cycle.

However, these descriptions are incomplete unless we consider the tonal affordances of the progression that are activated by the melody and rhythm. Eduardo's first pitches make a stepwise appoggiatura to the mediant of the E flat minor key suggested by the E♭ over bass B♭ in the accompaniment. There follow two more progressions from that tritone to the same fifth, suggesting plagal harmonic progression and rhythmically prolonging the tonality. At the beginning of a third repetition, Beatriz answers by transposing Eduardo's tune up a major sixth, and the tritone changes unexpectedly as a dominant to the C-G fifth, thus stabilising C minor, but more briefly. The key of A minor is then attained plagally and prolonged through the same melodic and rhythmic techniques. The minor-third sequencing creates a strong expectation that the music will continue similarly to F sharp minor. What happens instead is somewhat surprising and expressive. Beatriz does move from the B-F tritone to F♯-C♯, as if from dominant to tonic, but without the appoggiatura to the mediant, and the accompaniment revives the low B♭, which unexpectedly toggles the mode to major. Why this striking emphasis on her word 'home' and on this pitch? The B♭ together with the F and the F♯-C♯ fifth form a major seventh chord characteristic of the symmetrical hexatonic scale, which alternates semitones and minor thirds. It is used throughout the opera, along with the χ cycle, to symbolise the 'abulia' that afflicts the characters. B♭ also appears strongly tonicised in a bell-like motive which rings at the two moments in the opera when characters die (Act II, Scene 1, bar 1724, and Act III, Scene 3, bar 418). Accordingly, I hear the change of mode and the intrusion of B♭ here to portend the oblivion that will be the lovers' future 'home'.

A few bars later (Ex. 11.7b), as the couple succumb to sleep, the violins spin out a delicate high progression which alternates a diminished seventh chord with fifths and with added-sixth and minor seventh chords. As the analysis below the score shows, these chords derive serially from the interaction of two concurrent streams of RI-chains, often in canon, like Caliban's music in Ex. 11.4b. But, again, rhythm and melody promote a tonal interpretation. Emphasis accrues to the longer chords in the lilting

5/8 rhythm and to the chords at the contour peaks of the melody, and the plain fifths have clearer roots than the seventh chords. Accordingly, I hear an overall modulation from C to E flat touching only lightly on A and F sharp. These tonal processes endow the χ cycle with an ominous affect. It appears as the beguiling call of a siren, whose varying pacing and directedness, produced by the changing weights of the sonorities and their voice leading, disguise the implacable serial symmetry that will soon claim the lovers' lives.

In contrast to all these plain χ cycles at the end of Act I, Act II introduces new sorts of pitch symmetry and chord progressions, densely chromatic polychords and whirling waltz rhythms. Nevertheless, the χ cycle reasserts itself whenever anyone tries to leave, in passages whose dyads have been cited by Ross and Venn. The potentially comic situation becomes grim when Señor Russell sickens to the point of death and the guests prove incapable of taking him to the hospital. The ensuring hysteria mobilises the structural features of the χ cycle into a parody of a familiar contrapuntal form.

Example 11.8 analyses two expositions of this so-called 'Fugue of Panic'. As in traditional fugues, the texture gradually accumulates with successive imitative entries of a subject-countersubject pair. The subject can be heard as derived from an interlocking of the dyads of the first half of the complete χ cycle, just as Prospero interlocked his α-cycle dyads in *The Tempest* (Ex. 11.3). The example identifies its forms by their first long note, disregarding the variable anacrusis. Since the second half of the cycle is a tritone transposition of the first half, the motion from C to F♯ across the first statement of the subject is reciprocated in the answer by motion from F♯ back to C, giving pitch closure to the subject-answer pair.

RI-chains also structure the accompanying voices, as analysed on the lower stave of the first system. Starting from the first note of the answer, F♯, the countersubject interlocks the dyads of an RI-chain, which then repeats a semitone higher. Its last note, A♭, becomes the incipit of the next statement of the subject, shown in Online Ex. 11.4. Then another complete χ cycle generates this subject on A♭ and its answer a tritone away on D. Their countersubjects are structured as previously. After one more entrance on A♭, the subject re-enters on B♭ and completes another χ cycle, as shown on the bottom system of Ex. 11.8. On its second perfect fifth, G-D, Leticia begins her own version of the complete cycle starting with the same notes, in the manner of a fugal stretto. Thus the structure of the cycle determines the pacing of thematic material and focal pitches in the fugue.

Ex. 11.8 *The Exterminating Angel*, Act II, Scene 1, bars 1456–65 and 1476–85, RICH(χ) structure and fugal design

RI-chaining exerts a more abstract but still distinctive influence in the surreal Act III. As the company teeter on the brink of starvation, two facets of their predicament manifest in the duet between Blanca, who bewails her hunger, and the Doctor, who exhorts the guests to cease fighting. The lower stave in Online Ex. 11.5a analyses how their material derives from multiple concurrent streams of RI-chains in the orchestra, which are signalled by χ's familiar alternating fifths and tritones in one of the lines.

Out of nowhere, in a miracle worthy of the Old Testament, sheep materialise and pour into the drawing room. Ushering them in, a series of seventh chords, shown in Online Ex. 11.5b, ascends inexorably from the lowest register of the orchestra. This common harmonic signifier of

Ex. 11.9 *The Exterminating Angel*, Act III, interlude, bars 537–41, repetitions of a diminished seventh chord progression embed χ-cycle fifths and transpose along RI-chains of hexatonic and diatonic tetrachords

operatic sorcery would be right at home in *Parsifal* (specifically, its Act II and III preludes). However, the preceding duet affords hearing the progression more organically as another way of connecting chords which result from the superposition of two RI-chains, as detailed by the diagram on the right of the example.

As the guests prepare to slaughter the lambs, the processional morphs into a series of diminished seventh chords, shown in Ex. 11.9, harmonising a melody and rhythm which ironically parody Bach's 'Sheep May Safely Graze' (an additional bassline is not shown). This too may be heard to manifest the content of the χ cycle. Since any two different diminished seventh chords form an octatonic scale, each pair can be heard to embed all four of the cycle's perfect fifths, as diagrammed below the score. But more organically the passage also manifests the pervading logic of RICH. The melody of the chord progression moves down and then up, each move being harmonised by the same succession of octatonic scales, bracketed below the score. On the way down, the melody alternates minor thirds and semitones, forming a hexatonic RI-chain which resembles Prospero's RI-chains of alternating intervals in Online Ex. 11.2. On the way up, over the same succession of harmonies, the melody alternates minor thirds and whole tones to spin the Bach melody into a diatonic RI-chain.

Even when the χ chains themselves seem absent, the intervallic processes and note collections often recall their intervals and the RICH generative principle. For instance, in Act II (Scene 1, bars 1375–425) Blanca sings an

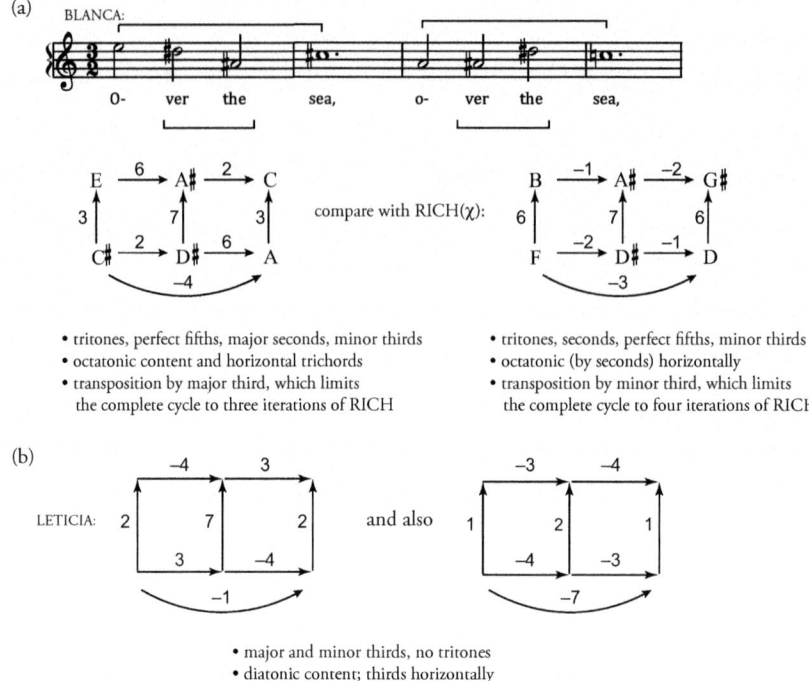

Ex. 11.10 *The Exterminating Angel,* Blanca's and Leticia's RI-chains compared. (a) Blanca: Act II, Scene 1, bars 1375–8; (b) Leticia: Act III, Scene 6, bars 912–31

obsessive aria seeking a way 'over the sea' to 'islands of gold'. As analysed in Ex. 11.10a, her first two phrases, which are strict pitch inversions of each other, share the dyad D♯-A♯ and can be conceived as a realisation of the RI-chain of dyads diagrammed below the score. Like Caliban's chains to Prospero's in Ex. 11.4a, this structure bears a strong resemblance to RICH (χ): tritones and seconds dominate the horizontal dimension; the only thirds in the structure are minor; and since the beginning and ending dyads are a third apart in each case, they can be rechained only a few times, as we saw in Ex. 11.5c. Moreover, the note content of Blanca's chain is octatonic like the horizontal dimensions of the χ cycle. Thus, while she avoids alternating the fifths and tritones that are characteristic of the χ cycle, she seems unable to escape its influence. The futility of her wish is symbolised by the ondes Martenot 'angel' shadowing her closely in canon.

This aria and other similar scenes pose fundamental questions about the characters' agency and destiny. To the extent to which RICH(χ) exerts control, the changes of pitch within melodies and voice leading seem inevitable, constrained and predictable. In the interview about this opera, Adès explicitly addresses these questions:

Music has a tendency to arrange itself either in terms of patterns or cycles. On a tiny scale, in a single bar, as well as on the huge scale of an entire opera there is always the possibility to decide *not* to be part of a pattern ... [I]n *The Exterminating Angel* ... [w]e have figures trapped within cycles of thought and others who, like Leticia, fight against the cycles and patterns. To arrive at a real musical resolution, the patterns and cycles have to be subdued, recombined by the composer's hand to produce a new doorway, if you like. And that's exactly what Leticia does at the end.[17]

The analysis above suggests that comparing the music of Blanca and Leticia – both of them musicians whose arias allude to Jewish exile – might clarify how the latter 'subdues' the χ-cycle patterns.

The turning point in the plot comes in Act III, Scene 6 when Leticia realises that the guests have wandered back to the same positions in the room which they were at before they became trapped. In effect, she perceives that they are caught in a gigantic cycle which they are about to re-enter, and she intuits the opportunity to break out of it by changing her mind and accepting the guests' invitation to perform. Clearly, she should not sing any of the music which currently entraps them, especially chains derived from the χ cycle. Blanca had no success with them.

Her solution, which she repeats in a soaring aria, is analysed in Ex. 11.11. Arseni noticed and the composer confirmed that this melody does not contain tritones or semitones, which we have seen are distinctive of χ.[18] These absences take on greater significance when we attend to the way in which Leticia orders her intervals in the context of the expectations that RICH(χ) has established across the opera up to this moment. Every time she sings a perfect fifth, ascending or descending, she creates the potential to construct χ or an inversion of χ by singing a particular tritone between the next two notes. The two possibilities are diagrammed at the top left of the example: each requires her to sing a minor second in the same direction as the perfect fifth she sang first. She already demonstrated her command of this χ process in the 'Fugue of Panic' (Ex. 11.8).

---

[17] Thomas Adès, quoted in Arseni, '"Why do we ever do anything?"', pp. 55–6 (emphasis original).

[18] In 'Why do we ever do anything?' (p. 55), Arseni observes, 'Leticia's aria comes as a release, also in musical terms. It's striking that it contains not a single half-tone or tritone, intervals that have occurred very frequently up to this point', to which Adès responds, 'Actually, there are no dissonances in Leticia's aria at all.'

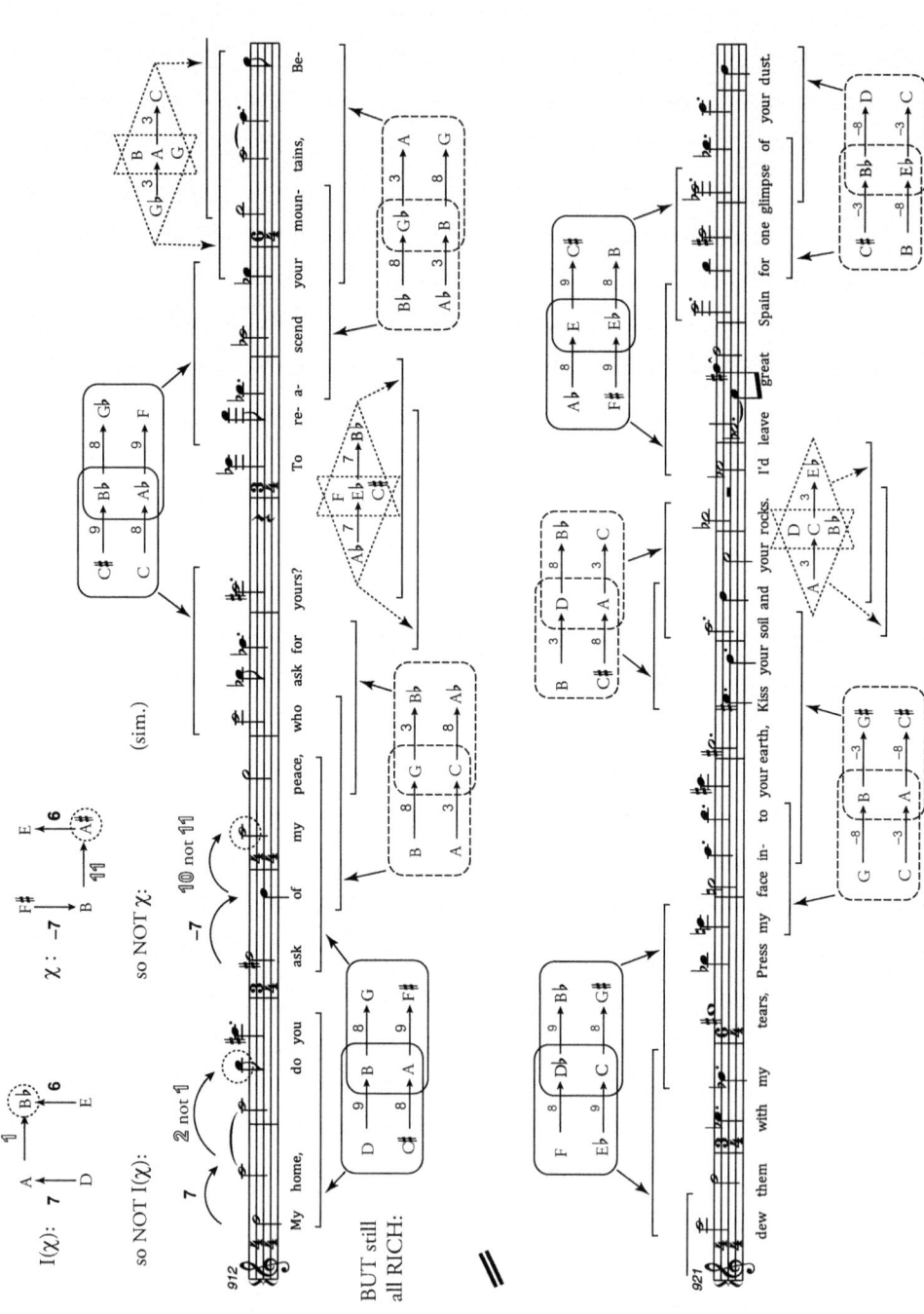

Ex. 11.11 *The Exterminating Angel*, Act III, Scene 6, bars 912–31, non-χ RI-chains in Leticia's aria

She opens her aria with an ascending fifth, D to A, as if initiating some form of χ. She then sings a step in the same direction, but it is a major second, from A to B, instead of a minor second. That makes it impossible to construct χ or its inversion, so she follows with another whole tone instead of a χ tritone. Next, she presents another fifth, descending from F♯ to B, but then moves a minor seventh up, from B to A (that is, a major second down, with the second note transposed up an octave), again preventing the formation of χ. She continues similarly, singing fifths which could initiate χs, but then the wrong-sized seconds in the wrong direction. In this vivid way her process renounces χ.

Nevertheless, her melody employs the same processes as Blanca's did, just as her words similarly express longing for another land. Both singers begin with a pair of inversionally related tetrachords which share two notes, as in an RI-chain of dyads. Indeed, Leticia goes on to exploit her mastery of RICH by freely alternating two related structures, which are shown respectively in Ex. 11.11 by solid and dashed rectangles. Their intervallic contents are analysed in Ex. 11.10b. Like Blanca's structures and RICH(χ) shown in Ex. 11.10a, they are RI-chains involving perfect fifths and major seconds, but otherwise they are substantially different. They are completely diatonic, in contrast with the other characters' χ-derived octatonicism. Each of the two dimensions involves different types of intervals from Blanca's and those of the χ cycle, and since the beginning and ending dyads are a semitone or perfect fourth apart, Leticia's structures can be rechained the maximum number of times, running through all vertical fifths and whole tones. In actuality her chaining is not so mechanical: by alternating different types of RICH, she generates a less predictable and longer – if still repeated – line. (Dashed triangles show a third type of chaining that she uses, involving two tetrachords linked by a shared trichord, which appears only across the pauses between her phrases.) Thus her aria projects an aura of creative exuberance, subverting χ while still operating within the governing RICH logic of the opera. With the tight octatonic circularity of χ broken, the guests are finally freed to leave the drawing room (although they still will soon be trapped again onstage by the hexatonic cycle of the 'Solemn High Requiem' at the end of Scene 6, bars 1052–72).

This liberating aria invites comparison with the finale of *The Tempest*, Ariel's offstage vocalise, a likewise stratospheric, extended, cycling melody. Online Ex. 11.6 displays the score schematically, omitting bar lines in order to clarify the repeated rhythms. It shows a closed rigid design. Each voice, such as the one analysed in Ex. 11.12a, isorhythmically combines a

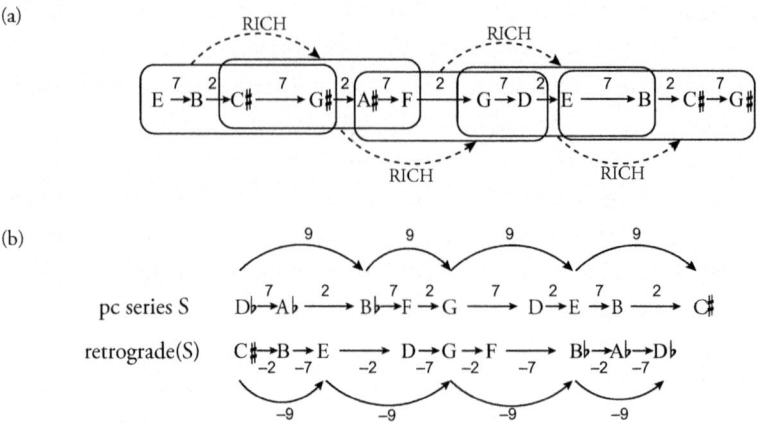

Ex. 11.12 *The Tempest*, Act III, Scene 5, ⟨332⟩, chaining and cycling in Ariel's concluding vocalise. (a) RI-chain in Ariel's vocalise; (b) retrograde canon accompanying Ariel's vocalise

repeated three-duration rhythm with an RI-chain of two intervals. Nine times the orchestra iterates a retrograde canon of these voices, as diagrammed in Ex. 11.12b. Meanwhile Ariel vocalises the same isorhythmic pattern as the upper orchestral line, but it is at half speed, transposed successively by tritone and timed to align (at the dashed boxes in Online Ex. 11.6) with simultaneous C♯s or Gs in the orchestral canon. The process begins and ends with the E-B dyad that began the opera (Ex. 11.2a), including the specific pitch E_6 unique to Ariel. The airy spirit literally disappears into a pure self-sufficient sound-structure. In contrast, Leticia will not conform to such a perfect but annihilating process. Rather than ring up the composer's 'maintenance hotline', however, she throws a spanner into the χ works and retools the RI-machinery for her own purposes.

With these examples I hope to have coordinated and expanded other scholars' observations about the presence of dyads in both of Adès's recent operas. Rather than focus on the dyads' recurrence, however, I have shown how they participate in an overarching constructive procedure, RI-chaining. Both works extend RICH progressions into cycles of dyads with special structural properties. As distinctively temporal processes, these cycles establish patterns that can be realised, twisted or broken in various dramatic situations. Their strong implicative charge and the variety of experiences they afford distinguish the dyad cycles from the comparatively static and consistently signifying Wagnerian leitmotivs as those are facilely conceived. As we attend not only to these musical atoms but also to the processes by which they quiver, split, chain together and mutate into stricter or looser cycles, we can better appreciate the thematic interplay of free will and collective abulia in *The Exterminating Angel*.

Such attention to process may also provide insight into Adès's other works, especially as one considers the differences among passages of varied scope and formal function. In the drama-driven operas, where at any given moment many 'layers of desire' interact, RI-chaining seems to manifest itself on relatively local scales and with varying degrees of presence, ranging from brief foreground χ-cycle chaining in the more orchestral-focused transitional passages (such as that shown in Online Ex. 11.3) to more variegated and deeply structural chaining processes in the set pieces, such as the Berceuse, the 'Fugue of Panic', Blanca's song and Leticia's final aria.[19] In his more abstract instrumental compositions, however, RICH seems to interoperate across much more extended time-spans with fewer but similarly extended temporalities, all tugged by the 'magnetic' poles of underlying 'geometric' tonalities.[20] A more robust understanding of this complex of processes and their interaction could not only lead to a better appreciation of how Adès controls musical flow on the very largest scale, but also help place his serial and tonal techniques in the historical context of those of Liszt, Berg, Stravinsky, Janáček, Ligeti, Kurtág and many other composers for whom he professes admiration.

---

[19] Adès and Service, *Full of Noises*, p. 11.   [20] Ibid., p. 10.

12 | Sonic Allegory in Adès's *The Exterminating Angel*

YAYOI UNO EVERETT

In Walter Benjamin's late writing on Charles Baudelaire, the experience of allegory is characterised by a sudden change of referentiality and abrupt discontinuity, transforming the poet's observations of the physical world into an aggregation of signs that reveals his profound state of alienation. Benjamin claims that allegory arises in perpetual response to the human condition of being exiled from the truth. Taking cues from Benjamin's theory and Luis Buñuel's aesthetic strategies, this chapter offers a hermeneutic reading of *The Exterminating Angel* (2015–16) as sonic allegory on the basis of Adès's manipulation of topics, motives, cycles and musical time.

Exiled from Spain during the height of the Franco regime, Buñuel spent a few years in the United States before moving to Mexico in 1942. Starting with *Un chien andalou* (1929, made in collaboration with Salvador Dalí), Buñuel criticised bourgeois social cohesion based on conformity to established institutions for stifling creativity and, in turn, used surrealist elements to shock people out of their complacency; during its Paris premiere, Buñuel famously watched the film behind the screen and played audio excerpts from Wagner's 'Liebestod' and Argentine tango as live accompaniment.[1] In *L'âge d'or* (1930), which came to be known for its blatant and scathing critiques of bourgeois culture and the Roman Catholic Church, Buñuel defined his surrealist aesthetics through a macabre and asynchronous montage of visual images and soundtracks.[2]

The plot of *El ángel exterminador*, filmed some thirty years later, concerns a group of aristocratic and bourgeois guests who find themselves unable to leave the room in which they have enjoyed an after-opera dinner. The music of the film is limited to the diegetic sounds of tolling church bells, one of the characters, Blanca, playing the piano and the congregational singing of *Te Deum* in a church. Surreal effects in the film include hallucinatory images (e.g. a hand floating in the air) and, more importantly,

---

[1] Hanna Lewis, *French Musical Culture and the Coming of Sound Cinema* (New York: Oxford University Press, 2019), p. 41.

[2] Ibid., p. 48.

the disruption of time through uncanny 'double takes' early on in the film; as the host ushers in the guests into the foyer of the mansion, the maids try to leave without being noticed, and the film circles back in time to replay the same scene, albeit from a different viewpoint. A similar 'double take' occurs in the next scene, where the guests give a toast to Leticia. While Buñuel did not comment on the explicit meaning of the film, it is possible that the title refers to the Society of the Exterminating Angel, a Catholic group in Spain (started in 1821) that was created to kill liberals.[3]

So what did Adès take away from Buñuel's film? The plot remains nearly the same as in the film, with some of the characters of the film combined in the opera to reduce the number of singers required.[4] Adès and his librettist Tom Cairns preserve the temporal ruptures caused by the aforementioned 'double takes' and the surreal elements in the opera's *mise en scène*. The obvious departure from the film is the ondes Martenot, which, as Adès claims, gives voice to the Exterminating Angel 'in the sense that this instrument is heard whenever a figure says something that contributes to the situation of immobility'.[5] The crisis (of entrapment) brings out the worst in people: some throw tantrums, another hallucinates, and others simply give up and expire on stage, as with the suicide of the young lovers. All the while, the ondes Martenot hovers over the singing voices, mirroring or 'ghosting' them, and at other times sounding out its own cyclical motive at the musical foreground. Cyclical processes unfold like cogs in the wheels of a gigantic machine, often superimposing vocal utterances in ascent over descending cycles in the orchestra.

In my reading, I argue that the opera departs from the eponymous film by ushering in a spatio-temporal 'collapse' of diegetic time and slippage into 'allegorical' time. At the onset, the protagonists are at first situated within the diegetic time and place circa the 1960s and in Mexico City (as in Buñuel's film), yet by the end they are catapulted into some other existential realm marked by a suspension of time.[6] By distorting sonic elements,

---

[3] Under the presidency of Juan Cavia González, then Bishop of Osma, anticlerical and revolutionary activists were persecuted without fair trial in the 1820s. See Gerald Brenan, *The Spanish Labyrinth: An Account of the Social and Political Background of the Spanish Civil War*, 2nd ed. (Cambridge: Cambridge University Press, 2014), p. 69.

[4] Edward Venn, 'Thomas Adès's *The Exterminating Angel*', *Tempo*, 71/280 (2017), 21–46 (p. 32).

[5] Christian Arseni, '"Why do we ever do anything?" Thomas Adès and Tom Cairns talk about *The Exterminating Angel*', in *The Exterminating Angel* programme booklet, Salzburger Festspiele, 22 July–31 August 2016, pp. 46–57 (p. 54).

[6] Venn turns to Deleuze's philosophy of time, specifically the principle of eternal return, in underscoring 'the rites and rituals of the bourgeoisie' and their struggle to defeat the force that entraps them. See Venn, 'Thomas Adès's *The Exterminating Angel*', p. 36.

Adès establishes a musico-dramatic opposition in the course of the opera between false optimism and the eventuality of doom. This opposition translates into a battle between the socialites' wilful interventions and the force that strips them of their will. In what I refer to as 'allegorical' time, the distinction between past, present and future dissolves; the protagonists as well as the sonic elements are stripped of their identities and, by the end of the opera, disappear into an existential void. Drew Massey emphatically points out the suspension of telos as the source of dramatic tension in the opera, noting that 'the beginning and ending of the opera, in particular, provide musical images that imply a seemingly never-ending story'.[7]

My allegorical reading intersects with Adès's description of the Exterminating Angel as 'an absence – an absence of will, of purpose, of action ... You could say that extermination is what we're fleeing from when we leave a room, when we do anything at all. In a way, the opera throws me back on how miraculous it is that we *can* and *must* act, indeed that we are alive at all.'[8] How does this notion – an absence or stripping away of will – manifest itself in Adès's music, and more broadly, in my allegorical reading of the opera's *mise en scène*?[9] How does Adès's manipulation of topical conventions, cycles and disruption of temporality generate a shift in trajectory from diegetic to 'allegorical' time? To answer such questions, I turn to Benjamin's modernist theory of allegory in constructing a reading of the opera as *sonic* allegory that resists closure.

On Benjamin's Theory of Allegory and *The Exterminating Angel*

Contemporary operas, more often than not, *defy* conventional narrative forms by privileging non-linear modes of storytelling, which blur the distinction between realism and myth, and by reducing operatic characters to archetypal representations.[10] In John Adams's *Doctor Atomic* (2005), for example, what begins as a re-enactment of the Manhattan Project and the test explosion of the atomic bomb segues to an ending that blurs the

---

[7] Drew Massey, *Thomas Adès in Five Essays* (New York: Oxford University Press, 2021), p. 154.

[8] Thomas Adès, quoted in Arseni, 'Why do we ever do anything?', pp. 51–3 (emphasis original).

[9] Thomas Adès, *The Exterminating Angel*, produced by Tom Cairns and directed by Gary Halvorson, DVD (Erato 9029552550, 2019).

[10] Yayoi Uno Everett, *Reconfiguring Myth and Narrative in Contemporary Opera: Osvaldo Golijov, Kaija Saariaho, John Adams, and Tan Dun* (Bloomington: Indiana University Press, 2015), p. 39.

spatio-temporal boundary of the opera's diegesis and the actual explosions that took place in Hiroshima and Nagasaki. The dramaturgical structure of Adams's earlier opera *The Death of Klinghoffer* (1991) oscillates between 'mythical' and historical temporalities in polarising the conflicts between Jews and Palestinians and, in turn, setting broader allegorical themes (e.g. the biblical notion of good versus evil) into relief.[11] In *The Exterminating Angel*, the temporal and referential discontinuities serve a different dramaturgical purpose from documentary-based contemporary operas: not only are topics and other stylistic conventions distorted syntactically, but their meaning and associations become unmoored. While the narrative trajectory follows the arc of dramatic irony, the conclusion of the opera defies resolution through the suspension of telos.

So what can be gained from turning to Benjamin's theory of allegory? Allegories are commonly understood as stories with a hidden universal message, such as the Orpheus myth, which in the Middle Ages was transformed in the Christian tradition into a moral allegory against excessive passion. Drawing on Benjamin's writings on Baudelaire, Bainard Cowan spells out the central tenets of *modern* allegory as follows:

- Whereas Baroque allegory brought out the esoteric-contemplative aspect, Baudelaire's modernist allegory emphasises the suddenness of discontinuity and change in referentiality;[12]
- In reference to Baudelaire's poetry, allegory came to be seen as mere convention, not grounded in experience, cut off from being and concerned only with manipulating its repertoire of signs;
- And, unlike the Romantic symbol, which Benjamin saw as 'an artificial isolation of the nostalgic impulse within allegory', modern allegory deals with the self-combating tension (*Zweideutigkeit*) that characterises human life;
- Existence-in-absence-of-truth: as a mode of expression, modern allegory arises in perpetual response to the human condition of being exiled from the truth that it would embrace: simply put, allegory could not exist if truth were accessible.[13]

---

[11] See Yayoi Uno Everett, 'John Adams's *The Death of Klinghoffer*: Straddling the Fence between Myth and Realism', in *Singing in Signs: New Semiotic Expressions of Opera*, ed. by Gregory Decker and Matthew Shaftel (New York: Oxford University Press 2020), pp. 339–66.
[12] See Bainard Cowan, 'Walter Benjamin's Theory of Allegory', *New German Critique*, 22 (1981), 109–22 (p. 121).
[13] Cowan, 'Walter Benjamin's Theory of Allegory'.

In Baudelaire's poem 'Le cygne' from *Les fleurs du mal* ('The Flowers of Evil', 1857), the poet draws on an image of a distressed swan to allegorise his search for the vanished Paris of his youth. Through the juxtaposition of disparate images (including Andromache from the *Iliad*, a swan in the gutter and an African immigrant) and the breaking of continuity of thought, Baudelaire compels the reader to wrestle with images and meanings of words beyond their literal contexts. The disconnected images of the poem communicate to the reader an inner experience of the narrator, filled with melancholy and indissoluble tension. Critical of the bourgeoisie's attachment to commodity, Benjamin claims that Baudelaire's poetry 'bears traces of the rage needed to break into this world, to lay waste its harmonious structures'.[14] In their shared expression of modern malaise, Baudelaire's strategies for juxtaposing disparate images in a poem parallel Buñuel's asynchronous audiovisual strategies that violate social norms.

I transcode the tenets of Benjamin's allegory into my reading of *The Exterminating Angel* as follows. First, I argue that the temporal discontinuity and change in referentiality in Adès's music induce temporal ruptures in the unfolding of the opera that presage the eventual turn towards 'allegorical' time. The use of descending intervallic cycles in the music accompanying the two entrances of the guests and the slowing-down of tempo accompanied by a widening of orchestral register generate a perception of being submerged into another temporal realm (Act I, Scene 3, bars 217–44). Similarly, the distant tolling of bells, which initially marks the passing of time in Act I (Scene 8, bars 844–53) and Act II (Scene 1, bars 1724–33), dissolves into a blurry orchestral backdrop that symbolises death in Act III (Scene 3, bars 419–24), further removed from diegetic place and time.

Second, stylistic references are destabilised through subversion or inversion of meaning. Borrowed styles and references, which initially allude to the characters' habits and norms, recur with an ironic twist: distorted quotations of *Die Fledermaus* waltz satirise the idiotic behaviour of the character Raúl (Act II, Scene 1, bar 1539); Leonora's hallucinatory aria alludes to Wagner's 'Liebestod' from *Tristan und Isolde* (Act III, interlude, bar 240); J. S. Bach's 'Sheep May Safely Graze' is subverted into an interlude that precedes the slaughter of sheep that wander into the room with the guests (Act III, interlude, bar 537); and the hostess Lucía Nobile's dinnertime aria to ragoût (Act I, Scene 4, bars 327–84), set to a decadent

---

[14] Walter Benjamin, *The Writer of Modern Life: Essays on Charles Baudelaire*, ed. by Michael W. Jennings (Cambridge, MA: Harvard University Press, 2006), p. 149.

waltz reminiscent of Ravel's *La valse*, finds its ironic (and quasi-musical) inversion in a later aria to cooked lamb.[15] Benjamin's second tenet of allegory, 'the manipulation of the repertory of signs' that is no longer grounded in experience, finds its corollary in the semantic dissolution of topics and motives that ushers in 'allegorical' time. In the conclusion of this chapter, I will discuss more fully how the dissolution of meaning corresponds with the allegorical condition of 'existence-in-absence-of-truth'.

The third tenet of Benjamin's allegory has to do with the manifestation of the self-combating tension (*Zweideutigkeit*). From the onset, Adès's shifting musical references establish an ongoing tension between the wilful behaviour of the socialites (manifested in their vocal utterances) and the orchestral undercurrent that works against it. The entry of the guests into the host's mansion (Act I, Scene 3, bar 65 and the 'double take' at bar 163) is accompanied by a rhythmically lopsided passacaglia over which a cheerful exchange of greetings ('Enchanted!') is sung as a recurring three-note motive with an ascending sixth. This melodic ascent is countered by the instrumental passacaglia cycle as it spirals downwards. When the opera singer Leticia is asked by the other guests to sing at the end of the first evening, pressure is placed upon her by the guests, who urge her on with simultaneously ascending and descending lines, set to the words 'We will not leave this house until she sings' (Act I, Scene 6, bar 674). These opposing tendencies are manifested simultaneously in musical passages, pitting the characters' assertion of will against the negation or stripping-away of will. When the socialites and their loved ones gather together to sing the concluding 'Solemn High Requiem' (Act III, Scene 6, bar 1052–end), the musical opposition erupts into a state of self-combating tension, in which the vocal utterances from 'Lux aeterna' repeat endlessly against the ondes Martenot's menacing triplet figurations.

With these considerations in mind, Table 12.1 presents a synoptic overview of the motivic and topical figures that shape the musico-dramatic opposition in *The Exterminating Angel*. In spite of the temporal disruption and distortion of references, recurring motives, topics and cyclical processes generate a tightly knit nexus of associations and connections, corroborating Adès's remark that the opera 'delves into an underground river of meaning'.[16] While the selections are by no means exhaustive, the recurring motives include church bells (CB), a dactylic rhythm of short–short–long (D), a 'savage' leitmotiv (S – see below) and the cadenza in

---

[15] Venn, 'Thomas Adès's *The Exterminating Angel*', p. 39.
[16] Adès, cited in Arseni, '"Why do we ever do anything?"', p. 47.

Table 12.1. *The Exterminating Angel*, synoptic overview of motivic and topical figures

Act I

Category									
Motives (starting bar)	CB: (bar 1) AIC ⟨-2, 1⟩	D: servants try to escape (bar 37) [musical notation]	D: ditto (bar 137)	S: 'We call her a savage' (bar 308) AIC ⟨1,2⟩, ⟨2,1⟩	D: bear appears (bar 427)	D: 'brava, Blanca' (bar 642)	S: 'Not leave until she sings!' (bars 674 and 702)	OM: cadenza (bar 726) ⟨2,1⟩, ⟨1,2⟩	CB: clock strikes five (bar 844)
Topics/ others (starting bar)	P: Guests' Entry I (bar 65) AIC ⟨-2,1⟩	P: Guests' Entry II (bar 163)	W: at the dinner table (bar 246)	W: Ragoût aria (Ravel's *La valse*) (bar 327)	Blanca's solo & variations (bar 524)	W: 'Stalled' waltz (bar 731)	W: lop-sided waltz (bar 756)	B: Eduardo/Beatriz (bar 854)	M: Interlude: (bar 907) [offstage drums]

Act II

Category						
Motives (starting bar)			S: Interlude: Julio serves coffee (bar 1282)	OM: duet with Blanca, 'Over the sea' (bar 1375) [3/2 metre]	F: Fugue of panic (bar 1457)	S: 'not like this!' (bar 1660) C.B: clock strikes two (bar 1724)
Topics (starting bar)	W: L asks for breakfast (bar 1031)	W: 'Stalled' waltz: 'I told you!' (bar 1091)	W: waltz tempo; go to boudoir (bar 1207)	L: 'Spoons' lament aria (bar 1304)	P: Doctor's fit (bar 1540) 'Abulia' W: Distorted Quotation (*Die Fledermaus*) (bar 1539)	B: love-death aria (bar 1778)

Category	Act III											
Motives (starting bar)	References 'Solemn High Requiem' (bar 223)	**S**: Francisco's tantrum (bar 298)	**CB**: clock strikes noon (bar 341)	**CB**: Distorted bells (bar 419)	**S**: Nobile settles a fight (bar 481)	**D**: Sheep and Bear Interlude (bar 537) [notation]	**S**: 'Try again!' (bar 631)	**OM**: (bar 690) 'We need blood'		Blanca plays Paradisi (bar 875)	**OM/CB**: clamouring bells (bar 1028)	
Topics/ others (starting bar)	Chorus: 'What can we do?' (bar 1); 'Mariachi' interlude / **F**: Hunger fugue (bar 93) [3/2 metre]	Leonora's aria; quotes Wagner's 'Liebestod' (bar 240)	Guitar interlude: (bar 310) [Leonora hallucinates]	**B**: Eduardo/ Beatriz lullaby (bar 381)	**W**: Distorted Ravel *La valse* (bar 449)		Chorus: Onstage/ offstage (bar 576)	**W**: Lambs aria (bar 661)	**B**: Silvia sings (bar 760)	**R**: Lux aeterna (bar 791)	Leticia sings (bar 912)	**R**: 'Solemn High Requiem' (bar 1052) [offstage drums]

Motives: CB = church bells; D = dactylic rhythm ('Sheep May Safely graze'); S = 'savage' leitmotiv; OM = ondes Martenot.

Topics: W = waltz; P = passacaglia; F = fugue; L = lament; B = berceuse ('Lux aeterna'); R = Requiem ('Lux aeterna').

AIC = aligned interval cycle (see below).

descending fourths articulated by the ondes Martenot (OM). Topics include waltz (W), passacaglia (P), fugue (F), lament (L), berceuse (B) and Requiem (R).[17] Furthermore, under 'others', I include singular occurrences of significant arias and interludes.

The overall shift in dramatic trajectory towards 'allegorical' time is induced by the ebb and flow of topics and motives, which brings about the eventual dissolution of diegetic time. Temporal discontinuities can be observed at several registers. At the local level, the oscillation between the dactylic motive (D) and the passacaglia topic (P) at the beginning of Act I (see the downward arrows in Table 12.1), corresponding with the double entrance of the guests, can be interpreted as an early indication of temporal ruptures that resist the teleological progression of time. So are repetitions of topics that appear out of nowhere, such as the fragmented return of the passacaglia cycle following the 'Fugue of Panic' (Act II, bar 1457). The waltz topic (W), which conveys opulence and false optimism (Act I, bar 327), becomes increasingly fragmented (Act II, bar 1091) and distorted (Act III, bar 449) as the characters' habitual ways of life fall apart. Act III heightens the sense of discontinuity through the accelerated change of pace in topics and stylistic references, as people (chorus) outside the mansion try to intervene and communicate with those who are trapped inside the mansion. The choral lament that opens Act III is quickly followed by a festive 'Mariachi' interlude, the obsessive-compulsive ballet and the hunger fugue (F).

Amid the seeming chaos, there are musical numbers that establish stability in the temporal unfolding of the opera. Blanca's solo aria 'Over the Sea' brings stability and continuity through her dialogue with the ondes Martenot in Act II, and Leticia's aria 'My Home, Do You Ask of My Peace' enables the guests to break the spell and leave the mansion, at least momentarily, in Act III. Blanca sings her nostalgic tune from her childhood in a soft and lingering 3/2 metre while the ondes Martenot steadily inverts her four-note rising motive in canon (Act II, Scene 1, bars 1375–408). The sense of expansiveness in Leticia's aria can be attributed to the steady tempo and figurations in the orchestra and to the deployment of 6/4 metre at the height of the aria on the words 'I am the jackals' (Act III, Scene 6, bars 942–3). It does not seem at all coincidental that the temporally stable

---

[17] Topics are designated as such based on the evocation of pre-existing conventions, although Adès's modes of topical deployment range from allusion (e.g. lament) to stylistic or literal quotation (e.g. waltz) and are distorted or fragmented. The entries of motives and topics in Table 12.1 overlap due to space limitation, but they occur strictly in succession as indicated by the beginning bar number.

arias are associated with the two women, who appear to possess an affinity
with the mysterious force.

Continuity is afforded by the recurrence of particular interval cycles.
Adès refers to repeating pitch patterns as a metaphor for 'cycles' that trap
people in their behaviour and habits of thought; some are trapped within
cycles, while others fight against them, and then they are recombined to
produce new 'doorways'.[18] For the purpose of analysing cyclical processes
in *The Exterminating Angel*, I use a simplified notation for Philip Stoecker's
aligned interval cycles (AICs).[19] This system is combined with others for
labelling cycles, which range from simple to compound, in order to illustrate specific recurrences of interval cycles that form a wedge.[20]

It is no coincidence that two seemingly unrelated musical motives,
notably the 'savage' leitmotiv (S) and the ondes Martenot (OM) cadenza,
can be found to share an identical AIC. The leitmotiv (S) recurs periodic-
ally within each act, chronicling the socialites' futile attempts at taking hold
of the situation. The enigmatic motive recurs in whole or in part in the
opera as a bridge or gateway that opens or closes a 'doorway', so to speak.
As shown in Ex. 12.1a, the motive is characterised by a zig-zagging melody
that first appears when Francisco calls Leticia a 'savage' for possessing
special abilities (bars 308–9). It is derived from two interlocking AICs
consisting of alternating semitones and tones. This is notated in Ex. 12.1a
as an AIC of $\langle 1,2 \rangle$ and $\langle 2,1 \rangle$ embedded within $< >$; for clarity, the pitch-
classes of the two voices and the number of semitones between them
appear to the right. Note how the vocal melody draws partially from the
underlying cycles (while the orchestra presents them in full), omitting
certain notes and 'flipping' from one voice to another as indicated by the
pattern formed by circled pitches.[21] When the character of Francisco sings

---

[18] Adès, quoted in Arseni, '"Why do we ever do anything?"', p. 56.

[19] In Stoecker's AIC, the main integers refer to the generating interval cycles and the subscripted
ones to the starting pitch-classes. For example, $\langle 2_0,10_{11} \rangle$ refers to an ascending interval cycle
2 that begins on pitch-class 0 in the lower voice, counterpointed by a descending interval cycle
2 beginning on pitch-class 11 in the upper voice. Using this system, Stoecker uncovers the
myriad ways in which Adès generates materials for *The Tempest*, *Lieux retrouvés* and the Piano
Quintet through the construction of three-part AICs. See Philip Stoecker, 'Aligned-Cycle
Spaces', *Journal of Music Theory*, 60/ii (2016), 181–212 (p. 196).

[20] Specifically, $\langle -2,1 \rangle$ refers to a two-part AIC in which a descending interval cycle 2 (whole tone)
in the lower voice is accompanied by an ascending interval cycle 1 in the upper voice. $\langle 1,2 \rangle$
refers to a combination cycle, alternating between interval class 1 and 2, which unfolds in a
single vocal or instrumental line.

[21] The pattern of 'flipping' from one voice to another is demonstrated in Stoecker's analysis of *The
Tempest*. See Philip Stoecker, 'Voice-Leading Waves in Thomas Adès's *The Tempest*',
presentation at 'Be Not Afeard: Language, Music and Cultural Memory in the Operas of
Thomas Adès', Senate House, University of London, 24 April 2017.

(a)

AIC <⟨1,2⟩, ⟨2,1⟩>

○ = D 2 E 1 (F) 2 G 1 G♯ 2 A♯ 1 (B) 2 C♯
○ = A♭ 1 A 2 B 1 C 2 D 1 (D♯) 2 (F) 1 F♯

(b)

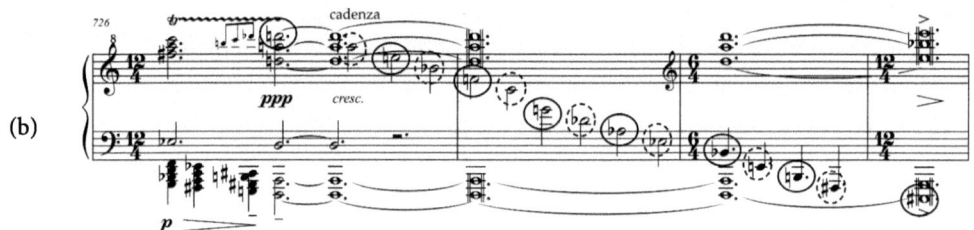

AIC <⟨2,1⟩, ⟨1,2⟩>

○ = D 2 E 1 F 2 G 1 A♭ 2 B♭ 1 B 2 C♯
○ = A 1 B♭ 2 C 1 D♭ 2 E♭ 1 E 2 F♯ 2* G♯

* ⟨1,2⟩ pattern
broken

Ex. 12.1 *The Exterminating Angel*, aligned interval cycle (AIC) in (a) the 'savage' leitmotiv (Act I, Scene 4, bars 307–9); and (b) the ondes Martenot cadenza (Act I, Scene 6, bars 726–9)

this material, the ondes Martenot can be heard 'ghosting' his melody an octave above. Whenever the 'savage' motive recurs in the opera, it is associated with the socialites' erratic behaviour, for example, to express frustration (e.g. Act II, Scene 1, bar 1660) or to break out of the spell (e.g. Act III, Scene 6, bar 661).[22]

When the ondes Martenot's cadenza appears towards the end of Act I (Scene 6, bar 726), the same AIC is realised differently to form a line that descends in fourths (perfect or augmented). Although the surface contour and rhythmic configuration differ from those of the 'savage' leitmotiv, the cadenza shares the same AIC in reverse, as shown under Ex. 12.1b. The solid circle refers to the upper voice, while the dashed circle refers to the

---

[22] I think there is something 'campy' about this motive, as the expanding wedge signals to the audience that something eerie and labyrinthian is about to take place, which is similar to the theme of the television show *The Twilight Zone* in its affective register.

lower. The fourths in ascent or descent become associated with the ondes Martenot. For example, the fourths in ascent are thematised in Blanca's duet with the voice of the Exterminating Angel (Act II, Scene 1, bar 1375), while their form in descent recur when Leonora sings about having a premonition about a key that 'opens the door to the unknown' (Act III, Scene 6, bar 690).

In summary, the synoptic overview of Table 12.1 demonstrates the intensifying discontinuities of the opera. Motives and topics undergo distortion and fragmentation and contribute to the suspension of telos, while interval cycles and motivic connections provide underlying continuity. I will now turn to a more in-depth analysis of a selection of musical numbers, focussing on passages where topics and motives signify opulence and false optimism on the one hand, and on those where the recurring cyclical procedures signify doom and entrapment on the other. These opposing processes embody the battle between the protagonists and the mysterious force while inducing the eventual shift in narrative trajectory from diegetic to 'allegorical' time.

Musical Signifiers of Opulence and False Optimism

How does the Viennese waltz emerge as an expressive signifier of opulence and false optimism in *The Exterminating Angel*? Among the numerous stylistic conventions that Adès alludes to in the course of this opera, the waltz topic plays a prominent role in underscoring the disconnect between false optimism and doom and in undermining the socialites' control over the crisis of entrapment. The Viennese waltz does not simply cue us into the opulence of the socialites' lifestyle, but also tells us that their world is built on appearance and deception – one that falls apart faster than they realise. As Venn remarks, 'the repeated failure of the waltz topic to ever coalesce into a genuine waltz ... serves to blur and critique the stability of its topical identity'.[23]

From a Marxist perspective, a musical topic that signifies opulence and false optimism translates into *commodity*, definable as a material condition by which any relationship could be expressed in objectified (monetary) terms. Commodification is the condition that Benjamin saw as the source of Baudelaire's malaise in his time, whose alienating effects elicited an allegorical response. When Lucía sings her 'ragoût' aria to a Viennese

---

[23] Venn, 'Thomas Adès's *The Exterminating Angel*', p. 39.

waltz, she does so with the adoration of a privileged class of people who fetishise the finer things in life. Similarly, Francisco's 'spoons' aria speaks not only of a habitual attachment to using proper utensils, but of fetishisation of the spoon as an object that symbolises his wealth and privilege.

The Viennese waltz, as can be heard for instance in Richard Strauss's *Der Rosenkavalier* (1911), is freighted with meanings that arise from the effects of commodification, ranging from nostalgia for a bygone era to aristocratic decadence or sheer debauchery. In Act I (bars 48–50), as the Marschallin sings to Octavian 'Jedes Ding hat seine Zeit' ('Everything has its time'), the accompanying waltz embodies such nostalgia; just as the waltz has become obsolete by the turn of the twentieth century, she fears that her 'shelf life' as Octavian's lover has passed. In a slightly later scene when Baron Ochs of Lerchenau flirts with Octavian (bars 143–7), now disguised as a chambermaid, the accompanying waltz suggests aristocratic debauchery. When the Baron shamelessly flirts with Octavian, the descending arabesque figuration with a mordent mimics his flirtatious gesture as a melodic anacrusis to the waltz. The vocal line consistently ends with an ascending leap, usually by the interval of a sixth, as an expressive signifier of Baron's act of impropriety.

The recurring waltz topic in *The Exterminating Angel* draws on such characteristics from *Der Rosenkavalier* but undergoes further distortion through hyperbole, fragmentation and decontextualisation. As it undergoes progressive distortion in the later acts, it emerges as a symbol of the socialites' bourgeois status, which is decimated by the mysterious force that strips them of their will and privilege.

In Act I of *The Exterminating Angel*, we find a hyperbolised waltz, characterised by decadence and false optimism. Lucía, the hostess and arguably the most pretentious character in the opera, introduces the ragoût as an appetiser. Example 12.2a shows an excerpt from this aria; note how the major sixth anacrusis is repeated three times with an exaggerated leap of a thirteenth when Lucía sings 'appetite!'. Lucía's boastful attitude is reinforced by the five-beat extension in the rising arpeggiation in the orchestra, rendered comical and lopsided by the replacement of a standard V–I cadence with the bass motion from E to A♭.

When Lucía sings 'Liver, honey and almonds' (Act I, Scene 4, bars 360–3), the phrase structure normalises to a unit of four plus four (see square brackets) as the hostess and her guests participate in a call-and-response. Although one might expect the bassline to unfold in an ascending-fifth sequence, Adès violates one's musical expectation with a

Ex. 12.2 *The Exterminating Angel*, Viennese waltz topics in Acts I, II and III. (a) Act I, Scene 4, bars 352–64, 'ragoût' aria; (b) Act II, Scene 1, bars 1091–5, 'stalled' waltz; (c) Act III, Scene 4, bars 448–52, fragmented waltz

progression that moves swiftly from D to A flat to C, and the composite harmony often includes added dissonances, augmented triads and whole-tone extensions. In spite of the 'wrong' notes and the disruption of the normative phrase structure associated with the waltz topic, the affective quality of the Viennese waltz in the 'ragoût' aria remains grandiose, ecstatic and celebratory. The outwardly expanding texture of the um-pah-pah followed by an arabesque figuration appears to be modelled on the third waltz from Ravel's *La valse* – a twentieth-century symphonic work which Ravel characterised as 'a dancing, whirling, almost hallucinatory ecstasy'.[24]

Somewhat later, Raúl throws a tantrum by blaming the hosts for inviting him and the other guests to the dinner party in the first place (Act II, Scene 1, bars 1596–605). As Raúl and Edmondo argue, fragmented quotations of another prominent Viennese waltz are heard. Two short excerpts from this passage are reproduced in Online Ex. 12.1. In Online Ex. 12.1a, the instrumental line takes the dactylic rhythm of the vocal melody ('You led us') and inverts it, then develops it sequentially into two-bar units. Initially there is a grouping dissonance that results from the unfolding of the vocal line's three-bar hypermetric units (see dotted parentheses) against the accompaniment's two-bar ones (see square brackets). As shown in Online Ex. 12.1c, the vocal melody turns out to be a literal quotation from the second waltz theme in Johann Strauss Jr's *Die Fledermaus*, comprising phrases A and B. In Adès's manipulation, as shown in Online Ex. 12.1a, phrase A appears in the key of D major, while the consequent phrase B is transposed to G flat major. In a passage slightly later, Leticia quarrels with Raúl over his idiotic behaviour. As shown in Online Ex. 12.1b, Leticia chimes in with an augmentation of phrases A and B in the key of A flat major, albeit with rhythmic distortion and omission of some notes. Raúl's response 'if you weren't a woman' significantly distorts phrase B, which is immediately followed by Leticia slapping Raúl. While the waltz topic recurs in many guises as signifiers of false optimism and debauchery, it is in this slapstick moment that Adès showcases a literal (albeit distorted) quotation of a well-known waltz.

In its subsequent appearances, the waltz topic becomes progressively distorted through fragmentation and other types of deformation. As a case in point, I call attention to a passage I identify as a 'stalled' waltz. It occurs when the Colonel wants people to leave so that he can get on with his affair with Lucía, but notices that no one is leaving (Act I, Scene 7, bar 731). After he pulls Lucía close and kisses her passionately, a sequence of quintuplet figuration followed by an accented quaver is heard, while the bassline ascends chromatically from E♭ to F♯. The same 'failed' fragment recurs at the beginning of Act II, Scene 1 (bar 1091), when the Colonel observes that the women are unable to leave the drawing room. As shown in Ex. 12.2b, the musical gesture fails to materialise into a fully fledged waltz with an um-pah-pah accompaniment. Later, in Act III, when Roc tries to molest

---

[24] Sevin H. Yaraman, *Revolving Embrace: The Waltz as Sex, Steps, and Sound* (Hillsdale, NY: Pendragon Press, 2002), p. 108.

Leticia in her sleep, the same fragment re-emerges as a recognisable waltz topic, complete with an um-pah-pah accompaniment and a V–I cadence in D (bars 448–54), as shown in Ex. 12.2c. By this point, the fragmented waltz no longer connotes opulence, but rather the states of chaos and desperation from which there is no escape. Because it seems to come out of nowhere, decontextualised, its collage-like recurrence in the middle of Act III sounds jarring and hallucinatory.

Another prominent signifier of opulence is found in Francisco's 'spoons' aria (Act II, Scene 1, bar 1304). Here, the hexatonic cycle in the accompaniment, typically associated with the magical and uncanny,[25] works against Francisco's wilful intervention to obtain a proper spoon to stir his coffee. When the butler Julio serves coffee and cold meats for breakfast the morning after the dinner party, Francisco whines that he cannot possibly stir coffee with a teaspoon, which he finds to be too large. Online Ex. 12.2 shows the score of the opening passage, whose texture, mode and tempo allude to a pastoral lament. Note the breath marks in the vocal melody (Act II, Scene 1, bars 1304–5), which accentuate Francisco's state of exasperation, and the vocal leaps that repeatedly emphasise an ascending sixth as he sings in protest of an egregious breach of etiquette.

The notes circled in the accompaniment in Online Ex 12.2 highlight the bassline and the accompanying chords; these correspond with the three-part AIC, which alternates between $\langle -5,-5,-2 \rangle$ and $\langle 1,1,-2 \rangle$. The bass and middle voices move down by a fourth and up by one semitone, while the top voice moves down consistently by two semitones. These harmonic progressions can be described more simply as a sequence of interrupted cadences in F sharp major, D major and B flat major, where the framing chords form a hexatonic cycle by virtue of the T_{-4} cycle.[26] What complicates the composite musical framework is Francisco's vocal melody, which consistently clashes with the underlying major triads; for example, note how A in the vocal melody clashes with A♯ in the accompanying F sharp major triad, and G♮ clashes with G♯ in the implied dominant seventh chord (see the dotted circled notes with arrows in Online Ex. 12.2).

---

[25] A hexatonic cycle comprises a set of six major and minor triads related by parallel (P) and leading-note exchange (L) functions. See Richard Cohn, 'Uncanny Resemblances: Tonal Signification in a Freudian Age', *Journal of the American Musicological Society*, 57/ii (2004), 284–325.

[26] T_n refers to the interval of transposition by *n* semitones formed between non-contiguous segments at the level of a phrase or longer stretches of music; e.g. the motion from C♯$_1$ to E$_1$ will be designated as T_3, while the motion in reverse will be indicated as T_{-3}. As shown in Online Ex. 12.2, PL functions are synonymous with transposing triads at T_{-4}.

Francisco's pathetic plea is echoed by an octatonic countermelody (see bracketed passages in Online Ex. 12.2) played by woodwind instruments, which works against the grain of the hexatonic cycle in the accompaniment. While this first cycle breaks apart, the second phrase (bars 1308–11) completes the second hexatonic cycle starting and ending on E♭. The clash between the vocal line and harmony still persists; note how D♯ works against the D♮ in the instrumental line at bar 1309 and the B♭ rubs up against B♮, the major third of G major, at bar 1310. A third hexatonic cycle begins on E (E–B–C–G–G♯–D♯), although the first two notes are replaced by others at bar 1314. When Lucía responds by imitating Francisco's melody starting on G♯ in the bar that follows, she blames her butler, Julio, for the obvious mishap. To my ears, this aria embodies a conflict between the character's tenacious clinging to a standard of living that can no longer be supported and the underlying progression, which subtly mocks and negates it. The ascending sixth motive in the vocal melody is no longer associated with the false optimism of the previous waltz topic, but rather with Francisco's – and by extension, all of the guests' – state of desperation.

Musical Signifiers of Doom and Entrapment

From the clamour of the church bells in the prologue to the concluding 'Solemn High Requiem' (see Table 12.1), Adès repeatedly puts into place a wedge-based cyclical process that reveals itself in the unfolding of the opera as a signifier of doom and entrapment. The wedge-like expansion of the church bells from G_4 can be codified as AIC $\langle -2,1 \rangle$ in the present system (see Table 12.1, Act I, Scene 1, bar 1).[27] In the discussion below, I focus on how this cyclical process relates to three subsequent scenes that establish and solidify the sense of doom and entrapment that usher in 'allegorical' time in the concluding scene.

The first is the initial entrance of the guests, in which the characters are introduced to one another by the hosts, Eduardo and Lucía Nobile. The exchange of greetings seems perfectly innocuous and fit for a comic opera. The accompanying music, however, undermines the sense of frivolity at several registers. Adès establishes a sinister mood by adopting a passacaglia bass anchored to a contracting rhythmic cycle. The latter consists of an

---

[27] See also Venn, 'Thomas Adès's *The Exterminating Angel*', p. 42.

irregular succession of 4/4 and 5/4 metres made lopsided by the insertion of incomplete triplets in 1/6 and 2/6 metres. With respect to the pitch organisation, the pattern alternates between high and low registers to create a wedge, outlining a chromatic descent that spans an octave, combined with an inner voice that ascends by whole tones. To my ears, this compound melody alludes to a familiar habanera: a slower and more graceful version of the contradanse which gained popularity in nineteenth-century Cuba. The distorted allusion to a popular Cuban dance suggests that this number is intended as a dance of courtship not just among the guests, but with the Exterminating Angel – and by implication with death. As each guest is introduced, this cycle is transposed successively downwards through the circle of fifth (T_{-5}), so that the next cycles begin on F (bar 73), B♭ (bar 83), E♭ (bar 93), A♭ (bar 101) and D♭ (bar 112) respectively. From this point onward, the process dissipates and returns to C (bar 126), coinciding with Leticia's introduction to the crowd where she sings 'Enchanted!' at the top of her register.

Example 12.3a shows the continuation of the passacaglia wedge cycle beginning on E♭ at bar 93. It can be formalised into a sequence of three-note segments related by AIC $\langle 2,-1 \rangle$, transposed sequentially by a minor third (T_{-3}). Starting at bar 98, the downward progression is overlaid by vocal entries of the 'Enchanted' motive, a greeting exchanged between guests, characterised by an ascending sixth followed by a descending whole tone or semitone. When the succession of 'Enchanted' motives is combined into one line (e.g. C♯–B–A♯–G♯), a descending line based on alternating whole tones and semitones emerges. Leticia's vocal melody, in contrast, snakes its way up to the high A♭$_5$ in ascending chromatic steps ($\langle 1 \rangle$). When this entrance music repeats for the second time (as in the film's 'double take'), the registral span widens to six octaves and a third (bar 217) and the tempo slows down to create a sensation of being submerged into a realm where there is no point of return. Massey comments that the progression 'signals the situational eeriness that the guests inhabit, even if they are not yet aware of it'.[28] At the end when Leticia hits the highest note on F$_6$, Adès marks in the score, 'the guests disappear within the orchestra' (bar 217), as if to punctuate the point at which the submersion takes place.

A second major milestone on the path towards doom and entrapment is the march interlude at the end of Act I. After the socialites notice that

---

[28] Massey, *Thomas Adès in Five Essays*, p. 155.

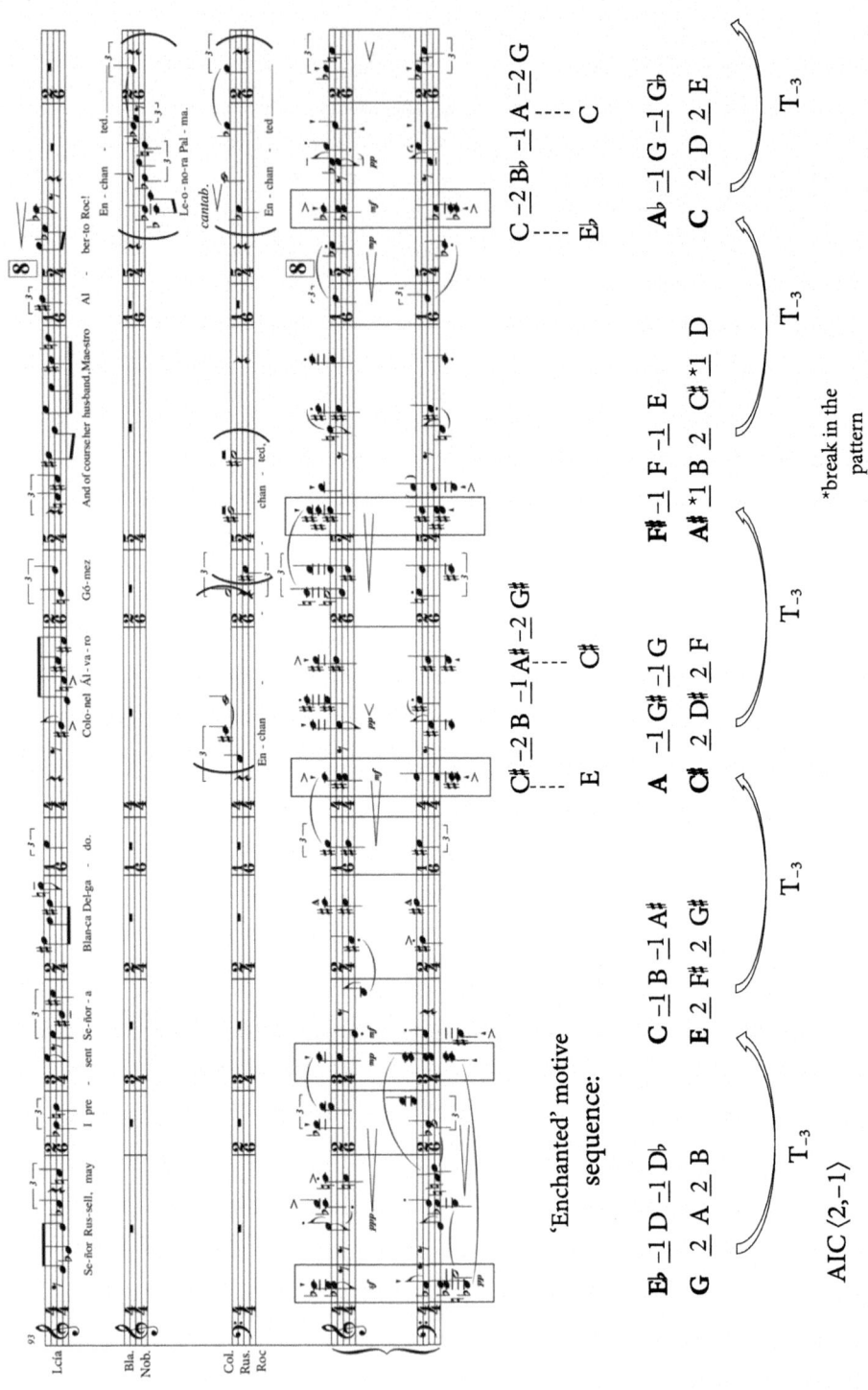

Ex. 12.3 *The Exterminating Angel*. (a) Act I, Scene 3, bars 93–103, passacaglia wedge cycle; (b) Act I, interlude, bars 907–15

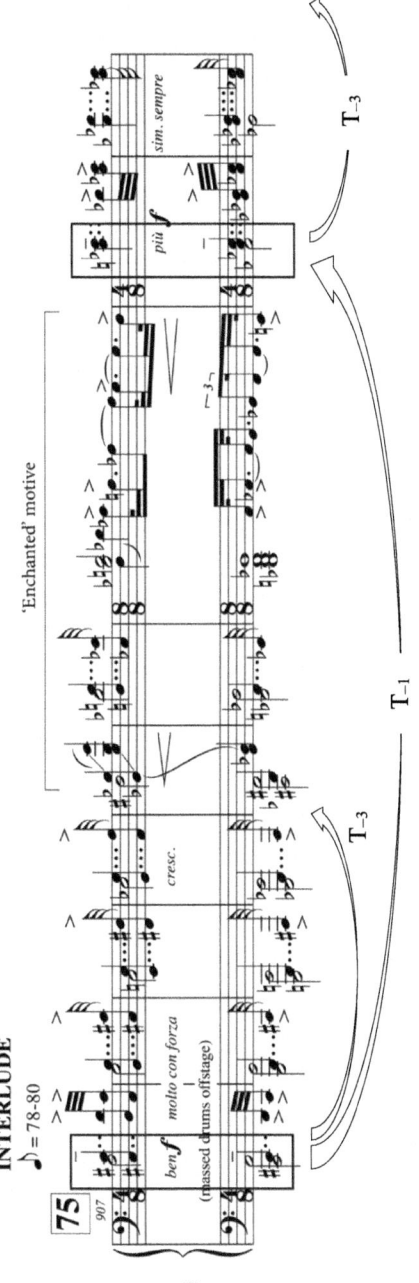

Ex. 12.3 (*cont.*)

something is preventing them from leaving, they give up in frustration and go to sleep in their hosts' drawing room. As the stage turns dark, the slow nocturnal music gives way to a feverishly loud march; the dynamic intensity reaches its apex and then recedes, creating a quasi-doppler effect of a troop of soldiers marching towards us and then departing.

As shown in Ex. 12.3b, the march interlude relates to the entrance music by sharing chord progressions that spiral downwards. The antecedent phrase (bars 907–10) is related to the consequent (bars 911–13) by a descending minor third (T_{-3}), and this theme is related to its next transposition by a semitonal descent (T_{-1}); that is to say, the accompanying harmony descends from A major to F sharp major when the 'Enchanted' motive appears, and then the same progression repeats starting on A flat major and moves downwards to F major by T_{-3}. There is something uncanny in the way the rhythm 'collapses' as it were (the rhythmic subdivision is rendered fluid) at the end of the phrase in 8/8 metre. This interlude signals the key moment that corresponds with *anagnorisis* in dramatic irony: the audience's recognition of what is at stake, that the characters are doomed. By co-opting the 'Enchanted' motive, which it repeats itself over and over again, the ondes Martenot announces its arrival to the sleeping guests.

And from here onwards, the pacing of temporal and referential discontinuities accelerates towards the breakdown of diegetic time. The march interlude does not recur in the course of the opera, but the passacaglia wedge cycle makes its appearance in the middle of the 'Panic' fugue (Act II, Scene 1, bar 1457) as the doctor tells everyone to stay calm so that he can engage in 'a clinical analysis of abulia'. This is quickly followed by a vocal ensemble in which they sing 'abulia' in ascending chromatic lines, corresponding with the three-part AIC $\langle 1,1,1 \rangle$ (bars 1558–65). By the third act, the guests have been deprived of food and water and are willing to take desperate measures to survive. Here is a macabre scene involving three sheep and a bear, which make their virtual appearance onstage. As the hungry guests gather around the sheep with the intent to kill, this interlude is heard over the descending octatonic harmonies, and the dactylic rhythm that accompanies the servants' quarrel (Act I) is repurposed into an interlude that misquotes J. S. Bach's 'Sheep May Safely Graze'. Referential discontinuity can be observed when Adès inverts the bucolic image of sheep grazing in the meadow as the socialites prepare to kill them for food. The interlude is followed soon afterwards by the 'lamb' aria (Act III, Scene 6, bar 661). Here, the music retreats to the three-part AIC $\langle 1,1,1 \rangle$ to showcase the attitudes of the deranged socialites. Their vocal utterances on how the lamb tastes – 'lamb is perfectly cooked', 'delicious' and 'a little too pink for me' – are set to descending sixths, which inverts the 'ragoût' aria's anacrusis of an ascending sixth.

Soon afterwards, the socialites put their heads together and repeat the sequence of events during the first night; Bianca plays a piece at the piano (which the characters identify as being by Paradisi), and Leticia sings a majestic aria based on a text from a twelfth-century Hebrew poem, which expresses a longing for one's homeland.[29] Suddenly, without any resistance, they are all able to walk out of the mansion and be reunited with their loved ones.

In the final scene, however, we find out that the reversal of fortune (*peripeteia*) turns out to be false. As the characters and their loved ones gather together and sing onstage, the church bells ring continuously as the music transforms itself in the concluding 'Solemn High Requiem'. Adès subverts the redemptive meaning of 'eternal rest' associated with 'Lux aeterna' by having the choir repeat the three-note motive on 'ae-ter-na', accompanied by the ondes Martenot's menacing triplet figurations, clamouring church bells and pounding chords played by the orchestra. As the music grows louder, the characters on stage continue to talk, embrace each other and move around restlessly, and some lose the impulse to do anything. People are, once again, unable to leave. The three-chord progression on 'ae-ter-na' shown in Ex. 12.4 repeats eight times as the opera comes to a halt *in medias res*. In addition, the offstage percussion returns at the conclusion of the opera, effectively linking the 'Solemn High Requiem' with the march interlude heard at the conclusion of Act I. For me, the music signifies the point of no return and also the moment when the self-combating tension locks. The characters continue to assert their will *as if* they are trapped in singing 'aeterna' in an endless loop.

Example 12.4 provides a reduction of the three-chord progression in the chorus and orchestra. The bassline (D–G♯–G) emphasises fourths and tritones, the intervallic building-block of the ondes Martenot motive and the trichord featured in Blanca's aria, while the soprano line inverts the contour of the 'Enchanted' motive. The English translation of the text, 'free us from death and bring eternal light', is now reduced to the Latin word for 'eternal'. Below the score excerpt in Ex. 12.4, the ondes Martenot's triplet figurations present a variation of the wedge cycle from the passacaglia. Note how the upper and lower cycles flip-flop as the initial AIC ⟨-1,2⟩

---

[29] See Chapter 11 for an in-depth analysis of interval cycles in this number.

Ex. 12.4 *The Exterminating Angel*, Act III, Scene 6, bars 1067–8, 'Solemn High Requiem'

changes to ⟨-2,1⟩. Taking the AIC of the passacaglia wedge cycle ⟨2,-1⟩, the first presents it in inversion, the second in retrograde.

The entrance music, the march interlude and the 'Solemn High Requiem' are by no means the only music that signify doom and entrapment in the opera. Yet the connections forged between them are particularly significant. These numbers underscore the importance of the cyclical wedge idea (AIC ⟨-2,1⟩) and the 'Enchanted' motive in providing musical continuity throughout the opera in spite of the acceleration in the rate at which topics and motives oscillate throughout Act III.

In summary, *The Exterminating Angel* plays with the suspension of telos through temporal and referential discontinuities and unmooring of meaning. There are several interlinking factors that usher in 'allegorical' time: the cyclical repetition that brings about the cessation of telos, the amalgamation of sounds into a collective void and, with it, the dissolution of meaning attributable to individual sounds. What begins as an undertow of eeriness created by the hidden cycles in the 'entrance' music becomes enacted into a fully fledged suspension of time in the 'Solemn High Requiem', whose soundscape *unsettles* because the ritual of drumming, church bells and the frenzied ondes Martenot come together to signify oppression in an endlessly repeating loop. Caught in an endless loop, the choral outcry ceases to reference 'Lux aeterna' as it merges with the incessant sounds of the accompanying instruments.[30] The 'Solemn High Requiem' is the key moment that signals a 'crisis of representation', harking back to another facet of Benjamin's allegory pertaining to the *destabilisation* of representation mediated by commodity.[31] The protagonists and the sonic referents (e.g. the ondes Martenot as the Exterminating Angel, the singing of 'Lux aeterna') are emptied of their referential meanings as the material world of the storyline breaks down and gives way to the 'existential' collapse. The story world defined by wealth, privilege and class ceases to exist.

Related to the dissolution of meaning and diegetic time in the opera is Benjamin's claim that truth exists but it is ultimately not accessible (the 'existence-in-absence-of-truth'). The actions, process and forms of representation in the opera constitute what we may interpret as truth, yet there is no certainty. We can make various conjectures as to what the Exterminating Angel signifies in the opera, but it cannot be pinned down to any one thing. In my experience, the acousmatic march interlude at the end of Act I took a sharp turn towards allegory; while anchored to the surreal impetus that drives the narrative, this sonic moment signalled a firm departure from the film's diegesis.

One may circle back to Buñuel's surrealist aesthetics and see how my allegorical reading of the opera compares with the concluding scene from *El ángel exterminador*: the congregation and the priests are trapped inside the church, while sheep roam freely outside. The authority of human agents is subverted and undermined, and the previously subjugated animals are set free. However, there is nothing in the film that indicates a

---

[30] The effect is not unlike Buñuel's audiovisual strategy at the end of *L'âge d'or*, in which incessant drumming drowns out the diegetic sounds. Lewis claims that the incessant repetition of the drumming acts as 'an auditory equivalent' to the lack of resolution or consummation of love in *L'âge d'or*. See Lewis, *French Musical Culture*, p. 50.

[31] 'The claim that Baudelaire's allegory made, visible to us today if not to his contemporaries, was that the rule of the commodity as interpretant contained within itself a lack or contradiction that would eventually render it untenable as the guarantor of meaning.' Matthew Wilkens, 'Toward a Benjaminian Theory of Dialectical Allegory', *New Literary History*, 37/ii (2006), 285–98 (p. 294).

departure from the diegetic time and place. The opera's *mise en scène* for the 'Solemn High Requiem' moves beyond Buñuel's critique of authoritarianism. Perhaps it is the absence of meaning, the unmooring of signifiers from their signifieds, that renders the final scene of the opera much more compelling than the film. Anthony Tommasini, in his review of the Salzburg Festival's 2016 production, mentions that the huge wooden door frame 'evokes both a proscenium and the threshold that the guests are unable to cross' and 'allows for the suggestions of the scope the opera is seeking: beyond the domestic to the societal and existential'.[32] Returning to Adès's broader conjecture regarding the 'absence of will', it may not be far-fetched to say that the conclusion of the opera challenges us to grapple with the acousmatic expression of an existential void, whatever this may entail.

[32] Anthony Tommasini, 'Review: In This Opera, You Can Depart, but You Can Never Leave', *New York Times*, 29 July 2016, www.nytimes.com/2016/07/30/arts/music/review-thomas-ades-the-exterminating-angel-opera-salzburg-festival.html.

Bibliography

A list of performances and recordings of Adès's music is maintained at www.thomasades.com. Scores of many of Adès's works can be accessed through his publisher, Faber Music, at www.fabermusic.com/we-represent/thomas-adès.

***

Abbate, Carolyn, 'Opera; or, the Envoicing of Women', in *Musicology and Difference: Gender and Sexuality in Music Scholarship*, ed. by Ruth A. Solie (Berkeley and Los Angeles: University of California Press, 1993), pp. 225–58.

    Unsung Voices: Opera and Musical Narrative in the Nineteenth Century (Princeton, NJ: Princeton University Press, 1991).

Adamowicz, Elza, *Surrealist Collage in Text and Image: Dissecting the Exquisite Corpse* (Cambridge: Cambridge University Press, 1998).

Adès, Thomas, '"Nothing but Pranks and Puns": Janáček's Solo Piano Music', in *Janáček Studies*, ed. by Paul Wingfield (Cambridge: Cambridge University Press, 1999), pp. 18–35.

    programme notes on *Arcadiana*, 1994, www.fabermusic.com/music/arcadiana-2365.

    programme notes on *Chamber Symphony*, 1990, www.fabermusic.com/music/chamber-symphony-2009.

    programme notes on *Concerto Conciso*, 1997, www.fabermusic.com/repertoire/concerto-conciso-2822.

    programme notes on *Concert Paraphrase on* Powder Her Face, 2009, www.fabermusic.com/music/concert-paraphrase-on-powder-her-face-5420.

    programme notes on *Living Toys*, 1993, www.fabermusic.com/music/living-toys-2373.

    programme notes on *Violin Concerto – Concentric Paths*, 2005, www.fabermusic.com/repertoire/violin-concerto-4.

Adès, Thomas and Tom Service, *Thomas Adès: Full of Noises – Conversations with Tom Service*, paperback ed. (London: Faber and Faber, 2018).

Ahmed, Sara, *Strange Encounters: Embodied Others in Post-Coloniality* (London: Routledge, 2000).

Akala, *Natives: Race, Class, and the Ruins of Empire* (London: Two Roads, 2018).

Albright, Daniel, *Untwisting the Serpent: Modernism in Music, Literature, and Other Arts* (Chicago: University of Chicago Press, 2000).

Almquist, Steve, 'Not Quite the Gabbling of "A Thing Most Brutish": Caliban's Kiswahili in Aimé Césaire's *A Tempest*', *Callaloo*, 29/ii (2006), 587–607.

Amos, Laura, 'An Examination of 1920s Parisian Polytonality: Milhaud's Ballet *La création du monde*' (unpublished PhD dissertation, The University of Texas at Austin, 2007).

Archbold, Paul, 'Philip Hensher and Meredith Oakes in Conversation with Paul Archbold', presentation at 'Be Not Afeard: Language, Music and Cultural Memory in the Operas of Thomas Adès', Senate House, London, 25 April 2017.

Arnold, A. James, 'Césaire and Shakespeare: Two Tempests', *Comparative Literature*, 30/iii (1978), 236–48.

Arseni, Christian, '"Why do we ever do anything?" Thomas Adès and Tom Cairns Talk about *The Exterminating Angel*', in *The Exterminating Angel*, programme booklet, Salzburger Festspiele, 22 July–31 August 2016, pp. 46–57.

Ashcroft, Bill and Pal Ahluwalia, *Edward Said*, 2nd ed. (London: Routledge, 2009).

Ashcroft, Bill, Gareth Griffiths and Helen Tiffin, *The Empire Writes Back: Theory and Practice in Post-colonial Literatures*, 2nd ed. (London: Routledge, 2002).

Aum, Shin Young, 'Analysis of *America: A Prophecy* by Thomas Adès' (unpublished DMA disssertation, University of Illinois at Urbana-Champaign, 2012).

Austin, J. L., *How to Do Things with Words* (Cambridge, MA: Harvard University Press, 1962).

Baker, Paul, *Fantabulosa: Dictionary of Polari and Gay Slang* (London: Continuum, 2002).

Bal, Mieke, Jonathan Crewe and Leo Spitzer, eds., *Acts of Memory: Cultural Recall in the Present* (Hanover, NJ: University Press of New England, 1999).

Barthes, Roland, 'The Grain of the Voice', in *Image Music Text*, essays selected and trans. by Stephen Heath (London: Fontana Press, 1977), pp. 179–89.

    'Myth Today', in *Mythologies*, trans. by Annette Lavers (New York: Hill and Wang, 1972), pp. 109–59.

Bauer, Amy, *Ligeti's Laments: Nostalgia, Exoticism, and the Absolute* (Farnham: Ashgate, 2011).

Benjamin, Walter, *The Writer of Modern Life: Essays on Charles Baudelaire*, ed. by Michael W. Jennings (Cambridge, MA: Harvard University Press, 2006).

Bonds, Mark Evan, 'Symphony: II. 19th Century', *Grove Music Online*, www .oxfordmusiconline.com/grovemusic.

Bostridge, Ian, 'Me and My Monster', *Guardian*, 6 February 2004, Friday pages section, p. 8.

Boulukos, George, *The Grateful Slave: The Emergence of Race in Eighteenth-Century British and American Culture* (Cambridge: Cambridge University Press, 2007).

Braithwaite, Edward Kamau, *Islands* (London: Oxford University Press, 1969).

Brenan, Gerald, *The Spanish Labyrinth: An Account of the Social and Political Background of the Spanish Civil War*, 2nd ed. (Cambridge: Cambridge University Press, 2014).

Breton, André, *Le surréalisme et la peinture*, rev. ed. (Paris: Gallimard, 1965).

'Manifesto of Surrealism (1924)', in *Manifestoes of Surrealism*, trans. by Richard Seaver and Helen R. Lane (Ann Arbor: University of Michigan Press, 1969), pp. 3–47.

Breton, André and Philippe Soupault, *The Magnetic Fields*, trans. by David Gascoyne, 3rd ed. (London: Atlas Press, 1985).

Campbell, Margaret, Duchess of Argyll, *Forget Not: The Autobiography of Margaret, Duchess of Argyll* (London: W. H. Allen, 1975).

Cao, Hélène, *Thomas Adès le voyageur: devenir compositeur, être musicien* (Paris: MF Éditions, 2007).

Caplin, William, 'Topics and Formal Functions: The Case of the Lament', in *The Oxford Handbook of Topic Theory*, ed. by Danuta Mirka (New York: Oxford University Press, 2014), pp. 415–52.

Castle, Charles, *The Duchess Who Dared: The Life of Margaret, Duchess of Argyll* (London: Sidgwick & Jackson, 1994).

Cavarero, Adriana, *For More than One Voice: Toward a Philosophy of Vocal Expression* (Stanford, CA: Stanford University Press, 2005).

Celenza, Anna Harwell, 'Death Transfigured: The Origins and Evolution of Franz Liszt's *Totentanz*', in *Nineteenth-Century Music: Selected Proceedings of the Tenth International Conference*, ed. by Jim Samson and Bennett Zon (Abingdon: Routledge, 2016), pp. 125–54.

Césaire, Aimé, *Une tempête: adaptation pour un théâtre nègre d'après 'La tempête' de Shakespeare* (Paris: Éditions du Seuil, 1969).

Clément, Catherine, *Opera, or the Undoing of Women*, trans. by Betsy Wing (Minneapolis: University of Minnesota Press, 1988).

Clements, Andrew, 'Prom 8: BBCSO/Adès – Review', *Guardian*, 18 July 2013, review section, p. 36.

Clendinnen, Inga, *Ambivalent Conquests: Maya and Spaniard in Yucatan, 1517–1570* (Cambridge: Cambridge University Press, 1987).

Cohn, Richard, 'Uncanny Resemblances: Tonal Signification in a Freudian Age', *Journal of the American Musicological Society*, 57/ii (2004), 284–325.

Connor, Steven, *Beyond Words: Sobs, Hums, Stutter and Other Vocalizations* (London: Reaktion, 2014).

Cook, Nicholas, *Beyond the Score* (New York: Oxford University Press, 2013).

'Inventing Tradition: Webern's Piano Variations in Early Recordings', *Music Analysis*, 36/ii (2017), 163–215.

Cowan, Bainard, 'Walter Benjamin's Theory of Allegory', *New German Critique*, 22 (1981), 109–22.

Culshaw, Peter, 'Don't Call Me a Messiah', *Daily Telegraph*, 1 March 2007, features section, p. 33.

Dahlhaus, Carl, 'The Fugue as Prelude: Schoenberg's *Genesis* Composition, Op. 44', in *Schoenberg and the New Music*, trans. by Derrick Puffett and Alfred Clayton (Cambridge: Cambridge University Press, 1987), pp. 169–73.

Dalí, Salvador, 'Objets surréalistes', *Le surréalisme au service de la révolution*, 3 (1931), 15–16.

Derrida, Jacques, *Speech and Phenomena and Other Essays on Husserl's Theory of Signs*, trans. by David B. Allison (Evanston, IL: Northwestern University Press, 1973).

Díaz, Gisele and Alan Rodgers, *The Codex Borgia: A Full-Color Restoration of the Ancient Mexican Manuscript*, ed. by Bruce E. Byland (Mineola, NY: Dover, 1993).

Dibble, Jeremy, 'Venice and Opera: Tradition, Propaganda and Transformation', in *Venice and the Cultural Imagination: 'This Strange Dream upon the Water'*, ed. by Michael O'Neill, Mark Sandy and Sarah Wootton (Abingdon: Routledge, 2016), pp. 59–78.

Dittrich, Marie-Agnes, '"Teufelsmühle" und "Omnibus"', *Zeitschrift der Gesellschaft für Musiktheorie*, 4/i–ii (2007), 107–21, www.gmth.de/zeitschrift/artikel/247.aspx.

Doğantan-Dack, Mine, 'In the Beginning Was Gesture: Piano Touch and the Phenomenology of the Performing Body', in *New Perspectives on Music and Gesture*, ed. by Anthony Gritten and Elaine King (Farnham: Ashgate, 2011), pp. 243–65.

Dolan, Emily, *The Orchestral Revolution: Haydn and the Technologies of Timbre* (Cambridge: Cambridge University Press, 2013).

Dolar, Mladen, *A Voice and Nothing More* (Cambridge, MA: MIT Press, 2006).

Donaldson, James, 'Living Toys in Adès's *Living Toys*', presentation at the Annual Meeting of the Society for Music Theory, Columbus, OH, 8 November 2019.

Doumerc, Eric, 'Caliban Playing Pan: A Note on the Metamorphoses of Caliban in Edward Kamau Brathwaite's "Caliban"', *Caliban: French Journal of English Studies*, 52 (2014), 239–50.

Dubiel, Joseph, Marion A. Guck and Bryan Parkhurst, 'Hearing as Hearing-as', *Music Theory and Analysis*, 4/ii (2017), 229–70.

Duffalo, Richard, *Trackings: Composers Speak with Richard Duffalo* (New York: Oxford University Press, 1989).

Dumas, Paula E., *Proslavery Britain: Fighting for Slavery in an Era of Abolition* (Cham: Springer, 2016).

Duncan, Michelle, 'The Operatic Scandal of the Singing Body: Voice, Presence, Performativity', *Cambridge Opera Journal*, 16/iii (2004), 283–306.

Dyer, Richard, 'It's Being So Camp As Keeps Us Going', in *Camp: Queer Aesthetics and the Performing Subject: A Reader*, ed. by Fabio Cleto (Ann Arbor: University of Michigan Press, 1999), pp. 110–14.

Edwards, Adrian, 'Adès: *Colette* (Original Motion Picture Soundtrack)', *Gramophone*, 96/1173 (2019), 58.

El-Enany, Nadine, *(B)ordering Britain: Law, Race and Empire* (Manchester: Manchester University Press, 2020).

Ellis, Jim, 'Conjuring *The Tempest*: Derek Jarman and the Spectacle of Redemption', *GLQ: A Journal of Lesbian and Gay Studies*, 7/ii (2001), 265–84.

Epstein, David, *Shaping Time: Music, the Brain, and Performance* (New York: Schirmer Books, 1995).

Everett, Yayoi Uno, 'John Adams's *The Death of Klinghoffer*: Straddling the Fence between Myth and Realism', in *Singing in Signs: New Semiotic Expressions of Opera*, ed. by Gregory Decker and Matthew Shaftel (New York: Oxford University Press 2020), pp. 339–66.

Reconfiguring Myth and Narrative in Contemporary Opera: Osvaldo Golijov, Kaija Saariaho, John Adams, and Tan Dun (Bloomington: Indiana University Press, 2015).

Fanon, Frantz, *Peau noire, masques blancs* (Paris: Éditions du Seuil, 1952).

Feldman, Martha, 'Voice Gap Crack Break', in *The Voice as Something More: Essays toward Materiality*, ed. by Martha Feldman and Judith T. Zeitlin (Chicago: University of Chicago Press, 2019), pp. 188–208.

Feldman, Martha and Judith T. Zeitlin, 'The Clamor of Voices', in *The Voice as Something More: Essays toward Materiality*, ed. by Martha Feldman and Judith T. Zeitlin (Chicago: University of Chicago Press, 2019), pp. 3–33.

Felski, Rita, *The Gender of Modernity* (Cambridge, MA: Harvard University Press, 1995).

The Limits of Critique (Chicago: University of Chicago Press, 2015).

Finlay, Joseph, 'A Jewish Quarterly Interview with Thomas Adès', *Jewish Quarterly*, 60/iii–iv (2013), 126–7.

Forte, Allen, 'Secrets of Melody: Line and Design in the Songs of Cole Porter', *Musical Quarterly*, 77/iv (1993), 607–47.

Fox, Christopher, 'Tempestuous Times: The Recent Music of Thomas Adès', *Musical Times*, 145/1888 (2004), 41–56.

Fox, Daniel, 'Multiple Time-Scales in Adès's *Rings*', *Perspectives of New Music*, 52/i (2014), 28–56.

Freud, Sigmund, 'The "Uncanny"', in *An Infantile Neurosis and Other Works (1917–1919)*, vol. 17 of The Standard Edition of the Complete Psychological Works of Sigmund Freud, ed. by James Strachey (London: Hogarth, 1955), pp. 217–52.

Freytag, Hartmut, 'Der Lübeck-Revaler Totentanz von 1463 – *spectel* "geistliches Schauspiel" oder *spegel* "Speculum"?', in *Architectura poetica: Festschrift für Johannes Rathofer zum 65. Geburtstag*, ed. by Ulrich Ernst and Bernhard Sowinski (Cologne: Böhlau Verlag, 1990), pp. 299–306.

Gallon, Emma, 'Narrativities in the Music of Thomas Adès' (unpublished PhD dissertation, Lancaster University, 2011).

Gapud, Alex J., 'Displacing Empire: Aphasia, "Trade", and Histories of Empire in an English City', *History and Anthropology*, 31/iii (2020), 331–51.

Garavito, César A. Rodriguez, 'Prólogo' to Roberto Fernández Retamar, *Todo Caliban* (Bogotá: ILSA, 2005), pp. 13–24.

Gertsman, Elina, 'The Dance of Death in Reval (Tallinn): The Preacher and His Audience', *Gesta*, 42/ii (2003), 143–59.

   The Dance of Death in the Middle Ages: Image, Text, Performance (Turnhout: Brepols, 2010).

   'Pleyinge and Peyntynge: Performing the Dance of Death', *Studies in Iconography*, 27 (2006), 1–43.

Giffney, Noreen and Myra J. Hird, eds., *Queering the Non/human* (Farnham: Ashgate, 2008).

Gopal, Priyamvada, *Insurgent Empire: Anticolonial Resistance and British Dissent* (London: Verso, 2019).

Graham, Michael, 'Shakespeare and Modern British Opera: Into *The Knot Garden*' (unpublished PhD dissertation, Royal Holloway, University of London, 2017).

Gray, Cecil, *Sibelius: The Symphonies* (London: Oxford University Press, 1935).

Greenwood, Jacqueline Susan, 'Selected Vocal and Chamber Works of Thomas Adès: Stylistic and Contextual Issues' (unpublished PhD dissertation, Kingston University, 2013).

Griffiths, Paul, programme notes on Thomas Adès, Mazurkas Op. 27, 2009, www .fabermusic.com/repertoire/mazurkas-5475.

   'Thomas Adès: *America: A Prophecy*', note to recording (EMI 5 57610-2, 2004).

   'Thomas Adès: *Tevot*', programme notes, London Symphony Orchestra, conducted by Thomas Adès, Barbican, London, 9 March 2016, p. 8.

Griffiths, Trevor, '"This Island's Mine": Caliban and Colonialism', *Yearbook of English Studies*, 13 (1983), 159–80.

Grimley, Daniel, 'Symphony/Antiphony: Formal Strategies in the Twentieth-Century Symphony', in *The Cambridge Companion to the Symphony*, ed. by Julian Horton (Cambridge: Cambridge University Press, 2013), pp. 285–310.

Gundersheimer, Werner L., 'Introduction to the Dover Edition', in *The Dance of Death: A Complete Facsimile of the Original 1538 Edition of* Les simulachres & historiees faces de la mort (Mineola, NY: Dover Publications, 1971), pp. 10–17.

Halliwell, Michael, 'The Sound of Silence: A Tale of Two Operatic *Tempests*', in *Silence and Absence in Literature and Music*, ed. by Werner Wolf and Walter Bernhart (Leiden: Brill, 2016), pp. 196–219.

   '"Voices within the Voice": Conceiving Voice in Contemporary Opera', *Musicology Australia*, 36/ii (2014), 254–72.

Hatten, Robert S., *Interpreting Musical Gestures, Topics, and Tropes: Mozart, Beethoven, Schubert* (Bloomington: Indiana University Press, 2004).

   A Theory of Virtual Agency for Western Art Music (Bloomington: Indiana University Press, 2018).

Henry, Paget, *Caliban's Reason: Introducing Afro-Caribbean Philosophy* (New York: Routledge, 2000).

Hensher, Philip, 'Sex, Powder and Polaroids', *Guardian*, 29 May 2008, G2 section, p. 23.

Hepokoski, James, 'The Essence of Sibelius: Creation Myths and Rotational Cycles in *Luonnotar*', in *The Sibelius Companion*, ed. by Glenda Dawn Goss (Westport, CT: Greenwood Press, 1996), pp. 135–60.

Hook, Julian, 'Rhythm in the Music of Messiaen: An Algebraic Study and an Application in the *Turangalîla Symphony*', *Music Theory Spectrum*, 20/i (1998), 97–120.

Horton, Julian, 'Introduction: Understanding the Symphony', in *The Cambridge Companion to the Symphony*, ed. by Julian Horton (Cambridge: Cambridge University Press, 2013), pp. 1–12.

Howell, Tim, 'Brahms, Kierkegaard and Repetition: Three Intermezzi', *19th-Century Music Review*, 10/i (2013), 101–17.

　'Jean Sibelius: Progressive or Modernist?', in *Jean Sibelius's Legacy: Research on His 150th Anniversary*, ed. by Daniel Grimley, Tim Howell, Veijo Murtomäki and Timo Virtanen (Newcastle upon Tyne: Cambridge Scholars Publishing, 2017), pp. 241–55.

　Jean Sibelius: Progressive Techniques in the Symphonies and Tone Poems (New York: Garland Publishing, 1989).

Hutchinson, Mark, *Coherence in New Music: Experience, Aesthetics, Analysis* (Abingdon: Routledge, 2016).

Indiana Loiterer III, 'rrreviews: Powder Her Face at BAM', *Parterre Box*, 35 (December 1998), https://parterre.com/review35.html.

Johnson, Julian, *Out of Time: Music and the Making of Modernity* (New York: Oxford University Press, 2015).

Kaufmann, Miranda, *Black Tudors: The Untold Story* (New York: Simon and Schuster, 2017).

Keller, Hans, 'The State of the Symphony: Not Only Maxwell Davies's', *Tempo*, 125 (1978), 6–11.

Kelly, Julia, *Surrealism: Desire Unbound*, ed. by Jennifer Mundy (London: Tate Publishing, 2001).

Kermode, Frank, *The Sense of an Ending: Studies in the Theory of Fiction* (New York: Oxford University Press, 1967).

Kleinhans, Chuck, 'Taking Out the Trash: Camp and the Politics of Parody', in *The Politics and Poetics of Camp*, ed. by Moe Meyer (Abingdon: Routledge, 1994), pp. 182–201.

Kline, Meredith G., 'Space and Time in the Genesis Cosmogony', *Perspectives on Science and Christian Faith*, 48 (1996), 2–15.

Kochavi, Jonathan, 'Some Structural Features of Contextually-Defined Inversional Operators', *Journal of Music Theory*, 42/ii (1998), 307–20.

Koestenbaum, Wayne, *The Queen's Throat: Opera, Homosexuality, and the Mystery of Desire* (New York: Poseidon Press, 1993).

Kosman, Joshua, 'S.F. Symphony Review: Thomas Adès' Creative Take on Genesis Story', *SF Gate*, 6 March 2015, www.sfgate.com/music/article/S-F-Symphony-review-Thomas-Ad-s-creative-6119376.php.

Kramer, Jonathan D., *The Time of Music: New Meanings, New Temporalities, New Listening Strategies* (New York: Schirmer Books, 1988).

Kramer, Lawrence, 'Recalling the Sublime: The Logic of Creation in Haydn's *Creation*', *Eighteenth-Century Music*, 6/i (2009), 41–57.

Kumar, Rebecca, '"Do You Love Me, Master?": The Erotic Politics of Servitude in *The Tempest* and Its Postcolonial Afterlife', in *Early Modern Black Diaspora Studies: A Critical Anthology*, ed. by Cassander L. Smith, Nicholas R. Jones and Miles P. Grier (Cham: Springer, 2018), pp. 175–96.

Lamming, George, *The Pleasures of Exile* (London: Michael Joseph, 1960).

Lane, Peter Van Zandt, 'Narrative and Cyclicity in Thomas Adès's Violin Concerto' (unpublished PhD dissertation, Brandeis University, 2013).

Lara, Irene, 'Beyond Caliban's Curses: The Decolonial Feminist Literacy of Sycorax', *Journal of International Women's Studies*, 9/i (2007), 80–100.

LaRosa, Christopher, 'Formal Synthesis in Post-tonal Music' (unpublished MM dissertation, Boston University, 2015).

Lasch, Pedro, *Black Mirror/Espejo negro* (Durham, NC: Duke University Press, 2010).

'Last of the "Knuts"', *Times*, 21 October 1957, p. 12.

Laufer, Edward, 'Continuity and Design in the Seventh Symphony', in *Sibelius Studies*, ed. by Timothy L. Jackson and Veijo Murtomäki (Cambridge: Cambridge University Press, 2001), pp. 352–90.

LeBaron, Anne, 'Reflections of Surrealism in Postmodern Musics', in *Postmodern Music/Postmodern Thought*, ed. by Judy Lochhead and Joseph Auner (London: Routledge, 2002), pp. 27–74.

Lee, Scott, 'Musical Signification in Thomas Adès's *The Tempest*' (unpublished PhD dissertation, Duke University, 2018).

Leech-Wilkinson, Daniel, 'Compositions, Scores, Performances, Meanings', *Music Theory Online*, 18/i (2012), https://mtosmt.org/issues/mto.12.18.1/mto.12.18.1.leech-wilkinson.html.

Leech-Wilkinson, Daniel and Helen M. Prior, eds., *Music and Shape* (New York: Oxford University Press, 2017).

Leong, Daphne, *Performing Knowledge: Twentieth-Century Music in Analysis and Performance* (New York: Oxford University Press, 2019).

Lewin, David, *Generalized Music Intervals and Transformations* (New Haven, CT: Yale University Press, 1987).

'Transformational Techniques in Atonal and Other Music Theories', *Perspectives of New Music*, 21/i–ii (1982–1983), 312–71.

Lewis, Hanna, *French Musical Culture and the Coming of Sound Cinema* (New York: Oxford University Press, 2019).

Lie, Nadia and Theo d'Haen, 'Preface', in *Constellation Caliban: Figurations of a Character*, ed. by Nadia Lie and Theo d'Haen (Amsterdam: Rodopi, 1997), pp. i–iii.

Lockhart, James, 'Introduction', in *We People Here: Nahuatl Accounts of the Spanish Conquest of Mexico*, ed. by James Lockhart (Berkeley and Los Angeles: University of California Press, 1993), pp. 1–46.

Lockhart, James, ed., *We People Here: Nahuatl Accounts of the Spanish Conquest of Mexico* (Berkeley and Los Angeles: University of California Press, 1993).

Luciano, Dana and Mel Y. Chen, 'Has the Queer Ever Been Human?' *GLQ: A Journal of Lesbian and Gay Studies*, 21/ii–iii (2015), 183–207.

Mâche, François-Bernard, 'Surreálisme et musique, remarques et gloses', *La nouvelle revue française*, 264 (1974), 34–49.

Mäkelä, Tomi, 'The Wings of a Butterfly: Sibelius and the Problems of Musical Modernity', in *Jean Sibelius and His World*, ed. by Daniel M. Grimley (Princeton, NJ: Princeton University Press, 2011), pp. 89–124.

Mannoni, Octave, *Psychologie de la colonisation* (Paris: Éditions du Seuil, 1950).

Martlew, Zoë, 'In Conversation: Zoe Martlew', London Sinfonietta, 1 February 2017, https://londonsinfonietta.org.uk/channel/articles/conversation-zoe-martlew.

Massey, Drew, 'Thomas Adès and the Dilemmas of Musical Surrealism', *Gli spazi della musica*, 7 (2018), 86–146.

'Thomas Adès at 40', *Salmagundi*, 174–175 (2012), 194–202.

Thomas Adès in Five Essays (New York: Oxford University Press, 2021).

Matthews, David, 'Living Traditions', *Musical Times*, 134/1802 (1993), 189–91.

Maxwell, Jennifer A., 'Tracing a Lineage of the Mazurka Genre: Influences of Chopin and Szymanowski on Thomas Adès' *Mazurkas* for Piano, Op. 27' (unpublished DMA dissertation, University of Boston, 2014).

May, Thomas, 'Program Notes: Dances from *Powder Her Face*', Berkeley Symphony, 2019.

McNeir, Waldo, 'Shakespeare's Epilogues', *CEA Critic*, 47/i–ii (1984), 7–16.

Mellor, Andrew, 'Adès: Piano Concerto; *Totentanz*', *Gramophone*, 97/1187 (2020), 36.

Metzer, David, *Musical Modernism at the Turn of the Twenty-First Century* (Cambridge: Cambridge University Press, 2009).

Meyer, Moe, 'Introduction: Reclaiming the Discourse of Camp', in *The Politics and Poetics of Camp*, ed. by Moe Meyer (Abingdon: Routledge, 1994), pp. 1–22.

'Under the Sign of Wilde: An Archaeology of Posing', in *The Politics and Poetics of Camp*, ed. by Moe Meyer (Abingdon: Routledge, 1994), pp. 75–109.

Millington, Barry, 'Morbid and Yet So Magical', *Evening Standard*, 18 July 2013, features section, p. 46.

Mirka, Danuta, 'Introduction', in *The Oxford Handbook of Topic Theory*, ed. by Danuta Mirka (New York: Oxford University Press, 2014), pp. 1–57.

Monahan, Seth, 'Action and Agency Revisited', *Journal of Music Theory*, 57/ii (2013), 321–71.

Monelle, Raymond, *The Sense of Music: Semiotic Essays* (Princeton, NJ: Princeton University Press, 2000).

Moore, Christopher and Philip Purvis, 'Introduction', in *Music & Camp*, ed. by Christopher Moore and Philip Purvis (Middletown, CT: Wesleyan University Press, 2018), pp. ix–xvi.

Morreall, John, *Taking Laughter Seriously* (Albany: State University of New York, 1983).

Mulvey, Laura, *Visual and Other Pleasures* (Basingstoke: Palgrave Macmillan, 1989).

Murtomäki, Veijo, *Symphonic Unity: The Development of Formal Thinking in the Symphonies of Sibelius*, trans. by Henry Bacon (Helsinki: Studia Musicologia Universitatis Helsingiensis, 1993).

Nattiez, Jean-Jacques, *The Battle of Chronos and Orpheus: Essays in Applied Musical Semiology*, trans. by Jonathan Dunsby (New York: Oxford University Press, 2004).

Ng, Samuel, 'The Hemiolic Cycle and Metric Dissonance in the First Movement of Brahms's Cello Sonata in F major, Op. 99', *Theory and Practice*, 31 (2006), 65–95.

Nikolaevna, Shapinskaya Ekaterina, 'Archetypal Plot and Its Interpretations: "Dance Macabre"', *Philharmonica: International Music Journal*, 2 (2016), 45–52.

Nixon, Rob, 'Caribbean and African Appropriations of *The Tempest*', *Critical Inquiry*, 13/iii (1987), 557–78.

Oakes, Meredith, *The Tempest* (London: Faber, 2004).

Ohriner, Mitch, 'Grouping Hierarchy and Trajectories of Pacing in Performances of Chopin's Mazurkas', *Music Theory Online*, 18/i (2012), https://mtosmt.org/issues/mto.12.18.1/mto.12.18.1.ohriner.php.

Olafsson, Vikungur, '5 Minutes That Will Make You Love 21st-Century Composers', *New York Times*, 5 August 2020, www.nytimes.com/2020/08/05/arts/music/five-minutes-classical-music.html.

Olusoga, David, *Black and British: A Forgotten History* (London: Pan Macmillan, 2016).

Parmet, Simon, *The Symphonies of Sibelius: A Study in Musical Appreciation* (London: Cassell, 1959).

Pellegrini, Ann, 'After Sontag: Future Notes on Camp', in *A Companion to Lesbian, Gay, Bisexual, Transgender, and Queer Studies*, ed. by George E. Haggerty and Molly McGarry (Malden, MA: Blackwell, 2007), pp. 168–93.

Pike, Lionel, *Beethoven, Sibelius and 'the Profound Logic': Studies in Symphonic Analysis* (London: Athlone Press, 1978).

Poizat, Michel, *The Angel's Cry: Beyond the Pleasure Principle in Opera*, trans. by Arthur Denner (Ithaca, NY: Cornell University Press, 1992).

Porter, Andrew, 'Pianistically Young, Gifted, and Blu-Tack'd', *Observer*, 17 January 1993, arts section, p. 46.

Potter, Caroline, *Erik Satie: A Parisian Composer and His World* (Woodbridge, Suffolk: Boydell & Brewer, 2016).

Raykoff, Ivan, 'Transcription, Transgression, and the (Pro)creative Urge', in *Queer Episodes in Music and Modern Identity*, ed. by Sophie Fuller and Lloyd Whitesell (Urbana: University of Illinois Press, 2008), pp. 150–76.

Restall, Matthew, *Seven Myths of the Spanish Conquest* (New York: Oxford University Press, 2003).

Retamar, Roberto Fernández, 'Sobre cultura y revolución en la América Latina', *Casa de las Américas*, 12/lxviii (1971), 124–51.

Rickards, Guy, *Jean Sibelius* (London: Phaidon Press, 1997).

Rink, John, 'The State of Play in Performance Studies', in *The Music Practitioner: Research for the Music Performer, Teacher and Listener*, ed. by Jane W. Davidson (Aldershot: Ashgate, 2004), pp. 37–51.

Rink, John, Neta Spiro and Nicholas Gold, 'Motive, Gesture and the Analysis of Performance', in *New Perspectives on Music and Gesture*, ed. by Anthony Gritten and Elaine King (Farnham: Ashgate, 2011), pp. 267–92.

Roeder, John, 'Co-operating Continuities in the Music of Thomas Adès', *Music Analysis*, 25/i–ii (2006), 121–54.

'A Transformational Space Structuring the Counterpoint in Adès's "Auf dem Wasser zu singen"', *Music Theory Online*, 15/i (2008), https://mtosmt.org/issues/mto.09.15.1/mto.09.15.1.roeder_space.php.

'Transformation in Post-Tonal Music', *Oxford Handbooks Online*, 4 August 2014, www.oxfordhandbooks.com/view/10.1093/oxfordhb/9780199935321.001.0001/oxfordhb-9780199935321-e-4.

Rogers, Lynne, 'Dissociation in Stravinsky's Russian and Neoclassical Music', *International Journal of Musicology*, 1 (1992), 201–28.

'Stravinsky's Break with Contrapuntal Tradition: A Sketch Study', *The Journal of Musicology*, 31/iv (1995), 476–507.

Ross, Alex, 'An Explosive Opera of "The Exterminating Angel"', *New Yorker*, 22 August 2016, www.newyorker.com/magazine/2016/08/22/thomas-ades-the-exterminating-angel.

'Roll Over, Beethoven: Thomas Adès', *New Yorker*, 26 October 1998, pp. 111–41.

Roys, Ralph L., *The Chilam Balam of Chumayel* (Washington, DC: Carnegie Institution, 1933).

Rupprecht, Philip, 'Images in Sound: Movement, Harmony and Colour in the Early Music', in *The Music of Simon Holt*, ed. by David Charlton (Woodbridge, Suffolk: Boydell & Brewer, 2017), pp. 56–79.

Said, Edward, *Culture and Imperialism* (New York: Vintage Books, 1994).

Saldívar, José David, *The Dialectics of Our America: Genealogy, Cultural Critique, and Literary History* (Durham, NC: Duke University Press, 1991).

Savigliano, Marta E., 'Whiny Ruffians and Rebellious Broads: Tango as a Spectacle of Eroticized Social Tension', *Theatre Journal*, 47/i (1995), 83–104.

Sawyer-Lauçanno, Christopher (trans.), *The Destruction of the Jaguar: Poems from the Books of Chilam Balam* (San Francisco: City Lights Publisher, 1987).

Schoenberg, Arnold, 'Composition with Twelve Tones (2) (c. 1948)', in *Style and Idea: Selected Writings of Arnold Schoenberg*, ed. by Leonard Stein, trans. by Leo Black (Berkeley and Los Angeles: University of California Press, 1984), pp. 245–9.

    'Folkloristic Symphonies', in *Style and Idea: Selected Writings of Arnold Schoenberg*, ed. by Leonard Stein, trans. by Leo Black (Berkeley and Los Angeles: University of California Press, 2010), pp. 162–84.

Scott, Derek B., 'Diabolus in Musica: Liszt and the Demonic', in *From the Erotic to the Demonic: On Critical Musicology* (New York: Oxford University Press, 2003), pp. 128–51.

Service, Tom, 'Altered States', *Guardian*, 29 August 2002, G2 section, p. 17.

    'Writing Music? It's Like Flying a Plane: Tom Service on Thomas Adès', *Guardian*, 26 February 2007, p. 23.

Seymour, Claire, '*Powder Her Face*, ENO', *Opera Today*, 8 April 2014, www.operatoday.com/content/2014/04/powder_her_face.php.

Shakespeare, William, *The Tempest*, Folio I (1623), ed. by Paul Yachnin, Internet Shakespeare Editions, University of Victoria, https://internetshakespeare.uvic.ca/Library/facsimile/overview/book/F1.html.

Shaw, Kyle, 'Promiscuity, Fetishes, and Irrational Functionality in Thomas Adès's *Powder Her Face*' (unpublished PhD dissertation, University of Illinois at Urbana-Champaign, 2018).

Simpson, Robert, 'Introduction', in *The Symphony*, vol. 2: *Elgar to the Present Day*, ed. by Robert Simpson (Aylesbury: Penguin Books, 1966), pp. 9–14.

Singh, Jyotsna G., *Shakespeare and Postcolonial Theory* (London: Bloomsbury, 2019).

Sontag, Susan, 'Notes on "Camp"', in *Against Interpretation: And Other Essays* (New York: Farrar, Straus and Giroux, 1966), pp. 275–92.

Sowa, Joseph, 'The Art of Transformation: The Heraclitian Form of Thomas Adès's *Tevot* as a Critical Lens for the Symphonic Tradition' (unpublished PhD dissertation, Brandeis University, 2019).

Spiro, Neta, Nicholas Gold and John Rink, 'The Form of Performance: Analyzing Pattern Distribution in Select Recordings of Chopin's Mazurka Op. 24 No. 2', *Musicae Scientiae*, 14/ii (2010), 23–55.

Spitzer, John, 'Metaphors of the Orchestra – The Orchestra as a Metaphor', *Musical Quarterly*, 80/ii (1996), 234–64.

Spitzer, Michael, *Metaphor and Musical Thought* (Chicago: University of Chicago Press, 2004).

Spivak, Gayatri Chakravorty, 'Can the Subaltern Speak?', in *Marxism and the Interpretation of Culture*, ed. by Cary Nelson and Lawrence Grossberg (Chicago: University of Illinois Press, 1988), pp. 212–314.

Stevens, Nicholas David, 'Lulu's Daughters: Portraying the Anti-heroine in Contemporary Opera 1993–2013' (unpublished PhD dissertation, Case Western Reserve University, 2017).

Stoecker, Philip, 'Aligned Cycles in Thomas Adès's Piano Quintet', *Music Analysis*, 33/i (2014), 32–64.

'Aligned-Cycle Spaces', *Journal of Music Theory*, 60/ii (2016), 181–212.

'Harmony, Voice Leading, and Cyclic Structures in "Chori"', *Music Theory and Analysis*, 2/ii (2015), 204–18.

'Voice-Leading Waves in The Tempest', presentation at 'Be Not Afeard: Language, Music and Cultural Memory in the Operas of Thomas Adès', Senate House, London, 24 April 2017.

Straus, Joseph N., *Introduction to Post-Tonal Theory*, 4th ed. (New York: W. W. Norton, 2016).

Sweeney, James Johnson, 'Joan Miró: Comment and Interview', *Partisan Review*, 15/ii (1948), 206–12.

Taruskin, Richard, 'A Surrealist Composer Comes to the Rescue of Modernism', *New York Times*, 5 December 1999; reprinted with a postscript in *The Danger of Music and Other Anti-utopian Essays* (Berkeley and Los Angeles: University of California Press, 2009), pp. 144–52.

Thiong'o, Ngũgĩ wa, *Decolonising the Mind: The Politics of Language in African Literature* (Nairobi: East African Educational Publishers, 1981, reprinted 1986).

Tommasini, Anthony, 'Review: In This Opera, You Can Depart, but You Can Never Leave', *New York Times*, 29 July 2016, www.nytimes.com/2016/07/30/arts/music/review-thomas-ades-the-exterminating-angel-opera-salzburg-festival.html.

Travers, Aaron, 'Interval Cycles, Their Permutations and Generative Properties in Thomas Adès's *Asyla*' (unpublished PhD dissertation, University of Rochester, 2004).

Tsumura, David Toshio, *The Earth and the Waters in Genesis 1 and 2: A Linguistic Investigation* (Sheffield: Sheffield Academic Press, 1989).

Tunbridge, Laura, 'Exterminating the Recording Angel', *Opera Quarterly*, 35/i–ii (2019), 63–76.

Van Elferen, Isabella, 'Dark Timbre: The Aesthetics of Tone Colour in Goth Music', *Popular Music*, 37/i (2017), 22–39.

Vaughan, Alden T. and Virginia Mason Vaughan, eds., The Tempest: *A Critical Reader* (London: Bloomsbury, 2014).

Vellianitis, Alexi, 'Kuusisto's Joke: Reconstructing the Rubble of Tonality in Thomas Adès' Violin Concerto' (unpublished MA thesis, University of Oxford, 2012).

Venn, Edward, 'Asylum Gained? Aspects of Meaning in Thomas Adès's *Asyla*', *Music Analysis*, 25/i–ii (2006), 89–120.

'BBC Proms 2013: David Matthews and Thomas Adès', *Tempo*, 68/267 (2014), 59–61.

'Metaphorical Bodies and Multiple Agencies in Thomas Adès's *Tevot*', in *Music, Analysis, and the Body: Experiments, Explorations, and Embodiments*, ed. by Nicholas W. Reyland and Rebecca Thumpston (Leuven: Peeters, 2018), pp. 133–52.

'"Mysterious Things": Interpreting Adès's Opera', presentation at 'Be Not Afeard: Language, Music and Cultural Memory in the Operas of Thomas Adès', Senate House, London, 25 April 2017.

'Thomas Adès and the Pianto', in *Proceedings of the International Conference on Music Semiotics in Memory of Raymond Monelle: University of Edinburgh, 26–28 October 2012*, ed. by Nearchos Panos, Vangelis Lympouridis, George Athanasopoulos and Peter Nelson (Edinburgh: International Project on Music and Dance Semiotics, 2013), pp. 309–17.

'Thomas Adès and the Spectres of *Brahms*', *Journal of the Royal Musical Association*, 140/i (2015), 163–212.

Thomas Adès: Asyla (Abingdon: Routledge, 2017).

'Thomas Adès's Freaky Funky Rave', *Music Analysis*, 33/i (2014), 65–98.

'Thomas Adès's *The Exterminating Angel*', *Tempo*, 71/280 (2017), 21–46.

Wagner, Richard, 'Über die Benennung "Musikdrama"', in *Gesammelte Schriften und Dichtungen*, vol. 9 (Leipzig: E. W. Fritzsch, 1872), pp. 359–65.

Watkins, Holly, *Metaphors of Depth in German Musical Thought: From E. T. A. Hoffman to Arnold Schoenberg* (Cambridge: Cambridge University Press, 2011).

Webster, John, *The Duchess of Malfi*, ed. by Brian Gibbons, 5th ed. (London: Methuen Drama, 2014).

Weinert, Friedel, *The March of Time: Evolving Conceptions of Time in the Light of Scientific Discoveries* (London: Springer, 2013).

Wells, Dominic, 'Plural Styles, Personal Styles: The Music of Thomas Adès', *Tempo*, 66/260 (2012), 2–14.

White, Michael, 'Stars of Tomorrow Shine Today', *Independent*, 17 January 1993, arts section, p. 18.

Whittall, Arnold, 'The Adès Effect', in *British Music after Britten* (Woodbridge: Boydell, 2020), pp. 255–69.

'Form', *Grove Music Online*, www.oxfordmusiconline.com/grovemusic.

'James Dillon, Thomas Adès, and the Pleasures of Allusion', in *Aspects of British Music of the 1990s*, ed. by Peter O' Hagan (Aldershot: Ashgate, 2003), pp. 3–27.

'The Later Symphonies', in *The Cambridge Companion to Sibelius*, ed. by Daniel M. Grimley (Cambridge: Cambridge University Press, 2004), pp. 49–65.

Wiebe, Heather, 'Prospero's Ossified Isle: Thomas Adès's *The Tempest*', *Opera Quarterly*, 30/i, (2014), 166–68.

Wilkens, Matthew, 'Toward a Benjaminian Theory of Dialectical Allegory', *New Literary History*, 37/ii (2006), 285–98.

Williams, Alastair, 'Between Modernism and Postmodernism: Structure and Expression in John Adams, Kaija Saariaho and Thomas Adès', in

The Routledge Research Companion to Modernism in Music, ed. by Björn Heile and Charles Wilson (New York: Routledge, 2019), pp. 327–52.

Wilson, Samuel, 'An Aesthetics of Past–Present Relations in the Experience of Late 20th- and Early 21st-Century Art Music' (unpublished PhD dissertation, Royal Holloway, 2013).

Woolfe, Zachary, 'Reaching a New High at the Met Opera', *New York Times*, 8 November 2017, section C, p. 1.

Wörner, Felix, 'Tonality as "Irrationally Functional Harmony": Thomas Adès's Piano Quintet', in *Tonality since 1950*, ed. by Felix Wörner, Ullrich Scheideler and Philip Rupprecht (Stuttgart: Franz Steiner Verlag, 2017), pp. 295–311.

Yaraman, Sevin H., *Revolving Embrace: The Waltz as Sex, Steps, and Sound* (Hillsdale, NY: Pendragon Press, 2002), p. 108.

Zabus, Chantal, 'Against the Straightgeist: Queer Artists, "Shakespeare's England", and "Today's London"', *Études anglaises*, 61/iii (2008), 279–89.

Other Multimedia Resources

Adès, Thomas, *The Exterminating Angel*, produced by Tom Cairns and directed by Gary Halvorson, DVD (Erato 9029552550, 2019).

    Powder Her Face, directed for stage by David Alden, directed for television by Margaret Williams (Channel Four Television Corporation, 1999); DVD (Digital Classics DC 10002, 2005).

    The Tempest, produced by Robert Lepage and directed by Gary Halvorson, Metropolitan Opera, DVD (Deutsche Grammophon DVD 0040 073 4932, 2013).

BISrecordsVIDEO, 'A Chat in the Park, Part I: Thomas Adès Discusses His Music with Violinist Peter Herresthal, Conductor Andrew Manze and Music Journalist Tom Service', 12 February 2014, YouTube, www.youtube.com/watch?v=OAhcZwi3f0Q.

Gerstein, Kirill, 'Thomas Adès: "Roots, Seeds & Live Cultures" – "Kirill Gerstein Invites" @ HfM Eisler Berlin', online video interview, 18 June 2020, YouTube, www.youtube.com/watch?v=I0kHP_npxJA.

Goehr, Alexander, 'The Reith Lectures – The Survival of the Symphony: The Old Warhorse', BBC Radio 4, 18 November 1987, www.bbc.co.uk/programmes/p00h196j.

London Symphony Orchestra, 'Thomas Adès: *Asyla, Tevot, Polaris*', online video interview, 28 February 2017, YouTube, www.youtube.com/watch?v=xEZe4-y720I.

'The Lübeck Dance of Death', St Marien zu Lübeck, https://st-marien-luebeck.de/page/172/lübeck-dance-death.

'Lübeck's Dance of Death: The Preacher in the Pulpit', www.dodedans.com/Etext0.htm.

Massey, Drew, 'Thomas Adès in Conversation with Drew Massey', presentation at 'Be Not Afeard: Language, Music and Cultural Memory in the Operas of Thomas Adès', Senate House, University of London, 25 April 2017, video available at YouTube, www.youtube.com/watch?v=Ng5jIUtiLZk.

'$_{Mz}$Attack' plugin, CHARM Mazurka Project, www.mazurka.org.uk/software/sv/plugin/.

'The Reval Dance of Death', St Marien zu Lübeck, https://st-marien-luebeck.de/page/173/reval-dance-death.

Royal Opera House, 'Insights into Thomas Adès's *The Exterminating Angel* (the Royal Opera)', 27 March 2017, YouTube, www.youtube.com/watch?v=kMsHvvEi-G8.

Sonic Visualiser, www.sonicvisualiser.org.

Index